French Autobiography

French Autobiography
Devices and Desires

ROUSSEAU TO PEREC

MICHAEL SHERINGHAM

CLARENDON PRESS · OXFORD

This book has been printed digitally and produced in a standard design
in order to ensure its continuing availability

OXFORD
UNIVERSITY PRESS

Great Clarendon Street, Oxford OX2 6DP

Oxford University Press is a department of the University of Oxford.
It furthers the University's objective of excellence in research, scholarship,
and education by publishing worldwide in

Oxford New York

Athens Auckland Bangkok Bogotá Buenos Aires Cape Town
Chennai Dar es Salaam Delhi Florence Hong Kong Istanbul Karachi
Kolkata Kuala Lumpur Madrid Melbourne Mexico City Mumbai Nairobi
Paris São Paulo Shanghai Singapore Taipei Tokyo Toronto Warsaw

with associated companies in Berlin Ibadan

Oxford is a registered trade mark of Oxford University Press
in the UK and in certain other countries

Published in the United States
by Oxford University Press Inc., New York

ISBN 0-19-815843-2

For
Priscilla, Sam, and Olivia

Preface

This book is concerned with the process of autobiography, the interplay between autobiographers, their circumstances, their materials, and their readers. The main focus is on Rousseau and his successors in France but the approach is not primarily historical. By comparison with the novel or poetry (at least since the Romantics) autobiography has progressed in fits and starts. The gap dividing a handful of indisputably major practitioners from a bevy of lesser ones, together with the complex relationships between autobiography and other varieties of self-oriented work—memoirs, the *journal intime*, the *roman personnel*, the *récit poétique*—tend to deny a sense of continuous development. This means that any attempt to 'join up the dots' and create a historical line across tracts of uninhabited country will be a hazardous and tendentious business. Moreover, the multitude of social, political, cultural, ideological, philosophical, and literary developments which may account for the *differences* between, say, Rousseau's *Confessions*, Stendhal's *Vie de Henry Brulard*, and Sartre's *Les Mots* are too diffuse to provide the basis for a history of French autobiography except in the most general terms. On the other hand, the filiations between the books I have mentioned are probably best understood with reference to the ways in which their authors dealt with enduring problems and challenges. To start from these is not to lose sight of history, but rather to construe historical changes—an evolving canon of texts, fluctuating concepts of the self, altered socio-cultural configurations, new literary forms—as aspects of the situation each autobiographer confronts. History, in other words, may be seen as a facet of that *otherness* which, as I shall argue throughout this study, pervades the autobiographer's enterprise.

Autobiography is a self-centred business. Although I shall emphasize the diversity of autobiographical desires, the wish to fathom the self—to trace its trajectory, to elucidate its idiosyncrasies, to pin down its elusiveness—is always present in some degree. But the realization of this wish is beset by vicissitudes which, in broad terms, may be linked to the engagement with what is other. Desiring the self, we might say, the autobiographer must first encounter alterity: other texts, other ideas, other people. In the first place, and perhaps primordially, there is the inevitable 'doubling' which arises when we turn our attention inwards. The moment we attend to the self, the gap between past and present is aggravated by a gulf between perceiver and perceived. 'Quel œil peut se voir soi-même?' asks Stendhal: perhaps we have a 'self' only from the point of view of others. Self-scrutiny, at any rate, seems to engender self-estrangement: to focus on the self may be to fossilize or transmute so that it becomes something other. This leads on to another form of otherness—that of the self as a 'textual' construct. First, to embody oneself in a book is to deal with extremely heterogeneous materials: public and private, subjective and objective, ancient and modern, trivial and momentous; incidents, memories, encounters, turning points, anecdotes, personal legends and apocrypha, documents (correspondence, publications, diaries) widely discrepant in vintage and relevance. To sift, order, and classify, as the autobiographer must, is in some measure to appropriate and to harmonize, but there is always the danger that uniformity will be achieved at the expense of authenticity. In reducing the otherness of their materials, autobiographers may be inclined to augment that of their product. Second, the autobiographical self is constructed in language: as a linguistic performance autobiography relies on various kinds of discourse, style, and literary convention; as a genre closely associated with narrative, it obliges its adherents to come to some accommodation with the commitments—to sequence and concatenation for example—which narrative has tended to imply. Third, the product of the autobiographical enterprise is a textual artefact: the book itself is other, an external object whose own history begins as the autobiographer's ink begins to dry. To speak from beyond the grave—Chateaubriand's characterization of his own desire as autobiographer—may not be to speak in a voice we would recognize as our own. The wish to monumentalize the self, to take advantage of art's shaping powers in the effort to transmute the incoherences of a life into the regularities of a story, is often perceptible in autobiography; but it may conflict with a desire to tune in to the self's elusive channel, to catch the strains of its particular tune amidst the cacophony of experience. The sense of a disparity between the self as a historical phenomenon, perceptible in a life history, and the self as something outside and perhaps at odds with history is a recurrent theme. To perceive this does not, however, empower us to think of autobiography as a literary act which tends, by its reliance on language, literary form, and public discourse, to disfigure a pristine self inherently independent of these agencies. It points rather to a picture of autobiography as a passage through and a constant negotiation with different forms of otherness.

To Rousseau, the least clubbable of men, we owe the creation of a club. On the foundations he laid in the *Confessions* an autobiographical tradition quickly sprang up, with the result that writing an autobiography came to involve, willy-nilly, an encounter with other practitioners, an intertextual engagement with other texts. But, as Rousseau amply demonstrated, the autobiographer also deals with a pre-existent body of ideas about the nature of human lives: explicitly or implicitly an autobiography has a theoretical dimension. Even when autobiographers become ideologues in their own right, creating 'customized' systems of beliefs and values as the framework for the account of their lives, they write in the margins of major conceptual systems, existing narratives, or paradigms of selfhood at large in philosophy and psychology. The ideological aspect of autobiography reflects the fact that it is a private activity conducted in the public eye. To write is to presuppose a subsequent act of reading, and the imagined reader is another manifestation of the otherness with which the autobiographer must reckon. How should the reader be framed: as friend, ally, pupil, accomplice, *semblable, alter ego*; or as butt, whipping-boy, ignoramus, tyrant? In adopting a stance towards the reader autobiographers choose their tone and decide where they stand; but they do so in the dark: the reader is the Other, and remains so to the end.

Accents of disquiet and unease are often perceptible, if we listen carefully, in the autobiographer's voice: far from being unequivocally triumphal, the apotheosis of the sovereign ego, autobiography is an anxious genre. Yet the transactions between desire and otherness—between autobiographers and memories, self-images, concepts, readers, intentions—translate themselves into those devices by means of which autobiographers, from Rousseau onwards, have made their impression on the genre. This is where we often find what is most valuable and productive (from both a literary and a personal point of view) in autobiography. A 'device' can mean both a stratagem, a plan devised to fulfil a certain aim, and an emblematic figure. Both senses apply to the kinds of device I have in mind: the urge to make connections and the figure of the chain in Rousseau; the scribbled plans and diagrams in Stendhal's *Vie de Henry Brulard*; the superimposition of disparate temporal frameworks in Chateaubriand; the figure of the Devil in Gide; the piling up of incidents in Green; collage, self-quotation, and enumeration in Leiris; Sartre's *accelerando* style; fantasy and hallucination in Leduc; the switching of pronouns in Gorz; fragmentation in Barthes; the juxtaposition of two narratives in Perec; the use of two narrating voices in Sarraute. Such features, which give these autobiographies their particular flavour, reflect the vicissitudes of autobiographical desire. They betray the writer's awareness of the problems and contradictions which beset his or her undertaking, manifesting the critical insight and self-conscious lucidity which has been a hallmark of French autobiography. Discontinuous as it may be, the line which runs from Rousseau to Sarraute features works whose enduring power is closely linked to the ways in which they are riven—creatively—by the manifold difficulties and anxieties autobiography may involve.

Too much talk of anxieties would, however, be unduly sombre. The devices I have pointed to, and the pressures from which they spring, also account for the vitality of these works and the fascination they exert. The autobiographies discussed in this book feature some of the liveliest, most inventive writing to have emerged from France in the last two centuries. By focusing exclusively on works whose status as autobiographies is unlikely to be disputed I have not only sought to avoid wearisome questions of demarcation but to celebrate the vigour and variety of the species in its own right. Here are real men and women confronting (and evading), in a host of different ways, the intractable realities of their lives. To attend closely to what they make of this task, to observe the transformation of real occasions into textual moments and the effect this process may have on the writer's current sense of identity, is to be party to an activity in which the textual and the existential are indissolubly fused.

In the chapters which follow I look at how sixteen French writers from Rousseau to Sarraute dealt with challenges of the sort I have outlined. Chapter 1 focuses on issues raised by the ways autobiographers declare their intentions; this provides the opportunity to survey a number of critical approaches to autobiography, from Dilthey to Gusdorf, Lejeune, and Ricœur. Chapter 2, on Rousseau's *Confessions*, considers the tribulations prompted by the allure of narrative causality. This is complemented by the next chapter which by studying closely the remarkable diagrams in *Vie de Henry Brulard* emphasizes forms of resistance to narrative order in Stendhal. Thereafter the polarity between Rousseau and Stendhal, their contrasting approaches to the self, becomes a recurrent theme of this book (similarly, many of the writers discussed feature in more than one chapter as they are examined from different angles). Chapters 4, 5, and 6 deal with three vital areas: the treatment of incidents, the relation to the reader, and the challenge of ideology. In each case general discussion, involving the attempt to classify different types of strategy, is followed by sections on specific writers: Chateaubriand, Green, and Leiris in the case of incidents; Genet, Leduc, and Sarraute where the reader is concerned; Renan, Gide, and Barthes in relation to ideology. Chapter 7 extends the discussion of autobiography and ideology by examining a 'family' of texts written under the aegis of a particular body of ideas—those of Sartrean existentialism: works by Genet, Leduc, Beauvoir, Gorz, and Sartre himself feature here.

The next chapter is devoted to *La Règle du jeu*, the four-volume work by Michel Leiris which is one of the cornerstones of twentieth-century autobiography. The last chapter is concerned with the status of memory in autobiography. Concepts of memory from Saint Augustine to Freud to Paul de Man provide a context for the discussion of Rousseau and Stendhal, Sarraute, Barthes, and Duras, as well as Nabokov, James, and Benjamin; the chapter ends with Georges Perec's *W ou le souvenir d'enfance*. A brief postscript, which raises the issue of an autobiographical canon in conjunction with the question of innovation, brings the book to a close.

Contents

Acknowledgements

The Faculty of Humanities in the University of Kent, and the British Academy, are to be warmly thanked for grants in support of research for this book. I would also like to thank the staff of the Bibliothèque municipale in Grenoble for help with illustrations. I have greatly profited from the opportunity to outline some of my ideas to audiences in the universities of Cambridge, Kent, London, Nottingham, Oxford, and Reading, and would like to thank the organizers of those occasions. Parts of Chapters 3, 4, and 5 have previously appeared in *Romance Studies, Paragraph, Dalhousie French Studies,* and Robert Gibson (ed.), *Studies in Fiction in Honour of Vivienne Mylne* (Grant and Cutler, 1988). I am grateful to the editors and publishers for granting me permission to incorporate this material in modified form. Throughout the gestation and composition of the book I received invaluable help and stimulation from many friends and colleagues. Reluctantly, I must confine my expression of warm gratitude to a list of some of their names: Caroline Bailey, Sheila Bell, Michael Bishop, Yves Bonnefoy, Malcolm Bowie, Celia Britton, Keith Carabine, Mary Ann Caws, George Craig, John Eakin, David Ellis, Johnnie Gratton, Peter Hainsworth, Ann Jefferson, Diana Knight, David Kynaston, Philippe Lejeune, Laura Marcus, Bernard McGuirk, Valerie Minogue, Madeleine Renouard, Philip Robinson, Richard Stamelman, Philip Thody, Christopher Thompson, Bill Watson, Emma Wilson. At Oxford University Press I have greatly benefited from the advice and support of Virginia Llewellyn Smith, Catherine Clarke, and Andrew Lockett. For practical help of various kinds I am indebted to Chrissy Emms, Sheila Holness, Jane Meenehan, and Janine Warren. Lastly, the dedication of this book to my wife and children expresses my pleasure in recalling their cheerful patience and encouragement.

I

Intentions and Transactions

I

Je forme une entreprise qui n'eut jamais d'exemple, et dont l'exécution
n'aura point d'imitateur.

(Rousseau, *Les Confessions*)

    For with my best conjectures I would trace
    The progress of our being . . .

        (Wordsworth, *The Prelude*)

    Faire un livre qui soit un acte . . .

        (Leiris, *L'Age d'homme*)[1]

Autobiographers frequently bombard us with claims about their motives
and intentions, sometimes once and for all at the outset, sometimes
recurrently; some autobiographers (Stendhal and Michel Leiris for
example) offer a running commentary on their performances, revealing
fluctuations, transformations, crises of intention. Critical reaction to this
phenomenon may take a number of forms. One response is to see it as of
relatively minor importance since, the argument would go, motives
advanced by autobiographers are secondary by comparison with the primal
impulse from which autobiography allegedly springs, that of bringing form,
meaning, and coherence to past and present experience. A second approach
might be to deny the existence of any primal motive and to suggest that
autobiography should be seen as involving, characteristically, a cluster of
motives—and hence of sub-genres such as the confession, the apologia, the
memoir—which combine in different dosages in given texts. The often
contradictory discourse about intentions would reflect, on this view, the
generic instability of autobiography and the hybrid nature of any given
sample. A third approach would construe talk about intentions as a sign of
the 'contractual' nature of autobiography, and emphasize the form and
function, rather than the content, of such discourse. In averting to his or her

---

[1] *Les Confessions*, 5; *The Prelude* [1805], Book ii, 78; *L'Age d'homme*, 14.

intentions, the autobiographer directs the reader's attention to the generic specificity of the text, and principally its referential status: this is an autobiography, such interjections say, written by a real person, and you must read it as such. Finally, perhaps as an extension of the last view, it is possible to see statements of intent as part of the discourse of autobiography. Whatever the overall guiding impulse (if any), or the uncertainty about genre, writing autobiography tends, of itself, to produce fluctuations of intent. When autobiographers comment on their motives, and particularly when they seem to revise and update them as they go along, they are usually responding to problems and pressures which have arisen in the process of writing about themselves. The last view is closest to the intentions and motives of this book, where autobiography will be seen primarily as act and narrative process. But, by way of introduction, it is useful to pursue further the various ways of looking at autobiographical intention we have sketched thus far.

The first can be traced back to Wilhelm Dilthey, the great nineteenth-century pioneer of the 'Human Sciences', who asserted that 'In autobiography we encounter the highest and most instructive form of the understanding of life.'[2] In actively reflecting on their lives autobiographers, according to Dilthey, carry a stage further a process already characteristic of the individual's relationship to his or her own past: 'The person who seeks the connecting threads in the history of his life has already, from different points of view, created connections which he is now putting into words. . . . Constantly changing connections have been formed from different standpoints within life itself, so that the task of historical presentation is already half-performed by life.'[3] Autobiography—the search for connections—brings no substantial increment; rather it articulates and manifests a structural cohesiveness (*Zusammenhang des Lebens*) to which every past experience has contributed. The meaning of events resides in their participation in a whole, but 'lived experience' (*Erlebnis*) already involves the spontaneous integration of fragments into an evolving totality.[4] Autobiography is important not because it creates anything new but because it reveals the 'closely-woven' meanings of past moments, externalizing the

---

[2] W. Dilthey (1831–1911), *The Construction of the Historical World in the Human Studies*, in *Selected Writings*, ed. by H. P. Rickman, 214.

[3] *Selected Writings*, 215.

[4] *Erlebnis* is not the product of rationality applied to raw data but a synthesis of perception and understanding, 'a silent thought which is our original grasping of the world'. In view of this ongoing process, which 'builds' my life, the meaning I confer on a past experience is already conditioned, in circular fashion (the 'hermeneutic' circle), by the impact the experience has had on my life (see *Selected Writings*, 185).

'constituents, regularities and relationships which constitute awareness of the course of a life; knowledge of the passage of one's life is as real as experience itself'.[5] Since he conceives it as an activity based on an innate faculty or competence, Dilthey's view of autobiography hardly admits of a disparity between the autobiographer's goal—to manifest the structural cohesiveness of a life—and the end-product of his or her labours. If, however, autobiographical understanding does range beyond *Erlebnis* it is, as Dilthey's discussions of specific autobiographies show, by virtue of notions such as those of purpose and value.[6] To understand the meaning of one's life may involve a supplementary act of comprehension (*Verstehen*) through which we relate our own experience to the wider context of the historical world, and evaluate its significance. However, this extension of scope does not alter the relatively restricted and normative view of the autobiographer's aims to be found in Dilthey. Despite this, it can be argued that his account of the 'connectedness of life' provides a more subtle picture of the relation between past and present experiences, memories and meanings, fragment and totality, than is to be found in many later theories of autobiography. This is primarily because Dilthey conceived the potential meaning of a life not as a fixed structure but as a dynamic process, a constantly self-revising totalization, involving a mobile network of relational meanings rather than a chain of causes and effects, a particular role, or self-image.[7] Diltheyan 'connectedness', moreover, has an enduring value in the context of autobiography because its dynamic, relational character encompasses an exceptionally wide range of human experiences.[8]

Later theorists have often followed Dilthey in seeing the goal of autobiography in terms of the individual's quest for the purpose and value of

---

[5] *Selected Writings*, 186.

[6] On this point, and for an interesting general account of Dilthey and autobiography, see L. Marcus, 'How Shall We Live? A Metacritique of Autobiographical Criticism'.

[7] 'Because remembering involves recognition everything past is a reproduction, structurally related to a former experience. . . . in this process there arises a view of the continuity of mental life in time which constitutes the course of a life. In it every single experience is related to the whole. This continuity of life is not a sum or quintessence of successive moments but a unity constituted by relationships which link all the parts.' *Selected Writings*, 185.

[8] The capacity to establish connections between past events and the totality of our life depends on a more general ability to discover a 'living system in the given'. Defining understanding as 'a rediscovery of the I in the Thou' (p. 208), Dilthey often identifies 'mind-created structures' which express human reality: 'Everything in which the mind has objectified itself contains something held in common by the I and the Thou. Every square planted with trees, every room in which seats are arranged . . .' (p. 221). In the spheres of biography and autobiography this means that gestures, facial expressions, and minor incidents deserve as much attention as obvious turning points.

his or her life, but have attenuated or jettisoned the notion of a pre-existent structure of meaning. If the idea of cohesiveness is retained, it tends to be seen as a construct, a personal myth or, in John Cowper Powys's phrase, a 'life-illusion'.[9] Georges Gusdorf, for example, in a seminal essay, suggested that autobiographers may think they are involved in a process such as the one described by Dilthey, whilst in fact they create the meanings they claim to find: 'Il y a donc un écart considérable entre le projet avoué de l'autobiographie, qui est de retracer simplement l'histoire d'une vie, et ses intentions profondes, orientées vers une sorte d'apologétique ou de théodicée de l'être personnel.'[10] Similarly, Roy Pascal's theory of autobiography is Diltheyan in its stress on the 'mutual reflection of all elements in their evolution, the intimate and dynamic identity of experiences and events with the writer', and on the identification of a 'homogeneous entity'; but it departs from Dilthey in its depiction of the autobiographer's struggle to create 'an order of values that is his own', 'an ideal image of himself', a satisfactory *Gestalt*.[11] In Gusdorf and Pascal the vital link between the autobiographer's aim and his achievement is considerably weakened. The 'life' constructed in autobiography is not, as in Dilthey, sanctioned by a pre-existing cohesiveness, but is the product of a 'will-to-form' reflecting, in Gusdorf's case, the evolution of the Western concept of selfhood,[12] and in Pascal's case, a need which expresses itself primarily in aesthetic terms. However, for these theorists no less than for Dilthey, autobiography manifests (or should manifest) a single aim, or 'metaphysical urge' as Pascal puts it,[13] whose criterion is unity. 'Mon unité personnelle', writes Gusdorf, 'l'essence mystérieuse de mon être, c'est la loi d'assemblage et d'intelligibilité de toutes les conduites qui furent miennes, de tous les visages où j'ai reconnu des signes et attestations de mon destin.'[14] The search for a satisfactory *Gestalt* (Pascal) or 'loi d'assemblage' (Gusdorf) is regarded as a universal motivational force behind the diversity of autobiographical texts and pretexts. The will-to-form diagnosed in

---

[9] J. C. Powys, *Autobiography*, 6.

[10] G. Gusdorf, 'Conditions et limites de l'autobiographie', 229.

[11] R. Pascal, *Design and Truth in Autobiography*, 188, 193–4. For a searching overview and critique of autobiography criticism see J. Loesberg, 'Autobiography as Genre, Act of Consciousness, Text'.

[12] In 'De l'autobiographie initiatique à l'autobiographie genre littéraire', Gusdorf relates the rise of autobiography to an inward turn brought about by a transformation of religious belief in the post-Renaissance period which led to a 'désacralisation de l'espace du dedans' (p. 988).

[13] *Design and Truth*, 182: 'The purpose of true autobiography must be "Selbstbesinnung", a search for one's inner standing'.

[14] 'Conditions et limites', 227.

autobiography (determined by what Gusdorf calls 'le postulat du sens')[15] is interpreted as a desire for unity and homogeneity, the quest for a cohesiveness which, while it no longer has the assurance of an empirical basis in the psychological processes of the individual, and may thus be based on delusion, is considered essential to the genre. The advantage of this perspective is that it avoids the confusion of autobiographical truth with strict factual veracity or correspondence; the disadvantage is that it erodes excessively the distinction between autobiography and fiction. For Gusdorf the 'anthropological' significance of an autobiographical narrative lies in the way it may be said to offer 'le symbole, en quelque sorte, ou la parabole, d'une conscience en quête de sa propre vérité'.[16] If the notion of a quest is important here, as it is in Pascal, the emphasis falls on its affirmative rather than its interrogative aspect: the overall aims and orientation of the quest are taken for granted. In being tethered to a restricted view of autobiographical intentions the will-to-form in autobiography is regarded as a factor which transcends the process of textual construction.

A different picture emerges, however, when we consider the will-to-form not as a primordial intention but in the context of autobiography as activity and process. Consider, for example, the following: Montaigne's postulation of 'une forme sienne, une forme maistresse', marking the particular way each individual has of bodying forth 'l'humaine condition';[17] Rousseau's claim to establish, in *Les Confessions*, an 'enchaînement d'affections secrètes'[18] linking inner dispositions with outer occasions; Julien Green's declared ambition, '[de] retrouver le fil plus fin qu'un cheveu qui passe à travers ma vie, de ma naissance à ma mort, qui guide, qui lie et qui explique'; Michel Leiris's desire that *L'Age d'homme* should gather his life into 'un seul bloc solide (objet que je pourrais toucher comme pour m'assurer contre la

[15] 'Ce postulat du sens dicte le choix des faits à retenir, des détails à relever ou à écarter, selon l'exigence de l'intelligibilité préconçue', 'Conditions et limites', 232. The passage reveals the gap between Gusdorf and Dilthey. For Dilthey 'the category of meaning' manifests the inherent connectedness of past and present in a human life (*Selected Writings*, 216), while for Gusdorf 'le postulat du sens' is inevitably an illusion: 'l'illusion commence d'ailleurs dès le moment où le récit *donne un sens* à l'événement...', 'Conditions et limites', 232. D. Foster, *Confession and Complicity in Narrative*, 4, points to a different kind of conflict, in confessional narratives, 'between intention (to reveal the truth) and effect. Intention is not the origin of truth; as Nietzsche declared . . . , "intention is merely a sign and symptom that still requires interpretation". Specifically, it is a symptom of the narrator's desire to master his story.'

[16] 'Conditions et limites', 234.

[17] *Essais*, iii, 2, 26.

[18] *Œuvres complètes*, i. 1149. Whenever possible quotations from Rousseau in the present work will be to the Pléiade volumes. Following the practice of other critics I have modernized spellings.

mort)'; the 'certain intricate watermark', discerned by Vladimir Nabokov, 'whose unique design becomes visible when the lamp of art is made to shine through life's foolscap'.[19] Important as they are, these images—'forme', 'enchaînement', 'fil', 'bloc'—by no means monopolize the texts in which they occur; indeed they are rivalled, and in some cases outdone, by other images, and often belied in practice. If they possess a generic character it is as moments in a process where the lure of form, closure, and definition asserts itself over, but is often in turn countered by, the appeal of open-endedness and indefinition.[20] As much as to a transcendent goal, they refer us to a dynamic process, a quest for form which acts as a structuring force in the elaboration of the autobiographical text (in autobiography self-construction is inseparable from textual construction, a *milieu* which accentuates questions of form and formlessness); these images express a particular kind of desire stemming, as desires do, from lack and absence. One way of looking at this is in terms of what might be called the fetishistic dimension of autobiography. The fetishist fixes on and overvalues something small and graspable which can be dominated and possessed, as a substitute for the elusive and intangible object of desire.[21] By analogy, the autobiographer, in redressing a sense of amorphousness, and in response to a desire for shape and definition, may fix on particular manifestations of selfhood and, by a kind of synecdoche, make them stand for an abeyant totality. Autobiographers often convey the impression that their textual effigies have the attraction of miniatures or scale models, an appeal which may be associated with the mind's disposition to classify and order.[22] The

---

[19] In, respectively, *Jeunes années*, i. 76; *L'Age d'homme*, 20; *Speak Memory*, 22.

[20] In a striking passage from *La Statue intérieure*, 28, François Jacob contrasts the plural repertoire of roles and images which spring to mind as he reviews his past with what he calls his inner statue: 'Je porte ainsi en moi, sculptée depuis l'enfance, une sorte de statue intérieure qui donne une continuité à ma vie, qui est la part la plus intime, le noyau le plus dur de mon caractère. Cette statue, je l'ai modelée toute ma vie. Je lui ai sans cesse apporté des retouches. Je l'ai affinée. Je l'ai polie. La gouge et le ciseau, ici, ce sont des rencontres et des combinaisons. Des rythmes qui se bousculent'.

[21] In Freud's writings see esp. *Three Essays on the Theory of Sexuality* (1905), and the later essay, 'Fetishism' (1927). It is interesting to note that Rousseau's *Confessions* (as well as the autobiographical work of Restif de la Bretonne) provided earlier theorists, notably A. Binet in his 'Le Fétichisme dans l'amour' (1887), with what they saw as vital source-material. On this see Emily Apter, *Feminizing the Fetish*, 18 ff.

[22] See Lévi-Strauss, *La Pensée sauvage*, 34–5. In *Metaphors of Self: The Meaning of Autobiography*, 28–9, J. Olney discusses, and quotes in full, a remarkable document consisting of a single sheet of paper on which Cardinal Newman, over a period of 72 years, recorded successive transformations in his life. This extraordinary miniature autobiography, with its scraps of selfhood marshalled within the strict compass of a single rectangular surface, is the supreme exemplification of the aspect of autobiographical writing which concerns us here. Its best counterpart might be the pair of trousers in Beckett's *Endgame*,

autobiographical manikin or homunculus (which may be linked with an image 'in the mind's eye') is amenable, portable, available to scrutiny, a 'transitional object' to be cherished in the context of an otherwise unpromising environment.[23] One of its avatars is the autobiographer's own name, pseudonym, or sobriquet: 'Nous, Michel de Montaigne', 'Pauvre Jean-Jacques', 'cet Henry', 'Poulou', 'Tachok', 'la petite blanche'.[24] Yet if it seems legitimate to cite such usages, and other forms of self-designation, as illustrations of the way autobiography often involves the 'fetishizing' of the self, the construction of an ego, some qualification is necessary. The author's name, and indeed any other feature of the text which serves as the token of a delineated self-image, may just as easily be invested with quite different affective connotations; self-distance may be involved, or the repudiation of settled images and identities. What this means is that the fetishizing of the self, as an aspect of the will-to-form in autobiography, has no more than the status of a moment in a dialectical process, a negotiation with oneself and others carried out in the medium of the written word.

The point can be made in another way with regard to the motif of the *self as book* in autobiography. 'Livre consubstantiel à son autheur', wrote Montaigne of the *Essais*.[25] Yet when he observed that his book was coming to seem more real, more knowledgeable, more concrete than he felt himself to be,[26] Montaigne indicated the precarious, paradoxical basis of the equation between self and book; for there is more than one way in which the text can be regarded as a model of the self. On the one hand, the book is solid, portable, voluminous, legible, authoritative, permanent: a monument, a mausoleum. The imagery of the self as *volume* could be pursued from Montaigne, to Rousseau (who placed a copy of his *Dialogues* on the

lovingly cherished—as finite, circumscribed, comprehensible, by contrast with the messy, chaotic, infinite world—by Nagg in his telling of the joke about tailor and customer: 'But my dear Sir, my dear Sir, look—*(disdainful gesture, disgustedly)*—at the world—and look—*(loving gesture, proudly)*—at my trousers!'

[23] On the 'transitional object', see D. W. Winnicott, *Playing and Reality*. Clearly, to recall and reconstruct childhood scenes is literally to engage with a 'smaller' self. On this see R. N. Coe, *When the Grass was Taller*. The development of photography gave most people access to miniature representations of themselves in the past.

[24] Respectively: Montaigne, Rousseau, Stendhal (*Vie de Henry Brulard*), Sartre (*Les Mots*), Sarraute (*Enfance*), Duras (*L'Amant*). I discuss self-designation in Sartre, albeit in another perspective, in Ch. 7.

[25] *Essais*, ii. 18, 326.

[26] Ibid. 8, 73. Comparing his book to a child, Montaigne observes: 'ce peu de bien que je luy ai faict, il n'est plus en ma disposition; il peut sçavoir assez de choses que je ne scay plus, et tenir de moy ce que je n'ay point retenu et qu'il faudroit que, tout ainsi qu'un estranger, j'empruntasse de luy, si besoin m'en venoit. Il est plus riche que moy, si je suis plus sage que luy.'

altar of Notre-Dame), to Chateaubriand, Leiris, and Laporte. But, on the other hand, the book is also voluminous in an earlier sense: 'full of turnings or windings, containing or consisting of many coils or convolutions' (*OED*): in the same writers, from Montaigne to Laporte, one could pursue identifications where the twists and turns of writing are felt to mirror the self's plurality, its resistance to capture.[27] In this case what is fetishized is not a stable mirror-image of the self, which can be exported from text to life, but the profusion of signs, tokens, and traces of selfhood which are generated as the autobiographer 'processes' memories, conjectures, and documents. The autobiographical text is valorized not as product but as process, not as the reflection of existing images (notably the labels which come from the Other) but for its capacity to dispel fixity as it engenders a suite of provisional recognitions, an ever-extensible sequence of provisional fetishes.

The ambiguities we have located in the identification between self and book bear out our earlier observation that the will-to-form in autobiography, with its fetishistic dimension, should be given its due not as a single, primal impulse, but as a desire among others at large in the process of autobiographical construction. As Philippe Lejeune has trenchantly observed, 'écrire son histoire, c'est essayer de se construire, bien plus qu'essayer de se connaître'.[28] Similar issues can be pursued in connection with the motif of the autobiographical turning point, whose role in the disclosure of unity and coherence in human lives was stressed by Dilthey. An obvious paradigm was provided by Augustine's interpretation of his conversion as an event which made sense of the apparently formless flux of happenings which preceded it. However, for Dilthey the identification of turning points is part of the continuous process through which we confer shape on our life as we live it by relating parts—individual experiences and phases—to a (changing) whole. The totality is ever-changing: 'the whole is only there for us when it becomes comprehensible through its parts . . . Our view of the meaning of life changes constantly.'[29] For Dilthey, then, notwithstanding the Augustinian paradigm, the turning point is not

---

[27] The whole of Roger Laporte's 'biographical' (his term) enterprise could be considered in terms of the interplay between these two versions of the Book: between writing as endless *dérive* and the written as potential *Grand-Œuvre*—a totality which is both desired and resisted. Laporte's most enduring aim is that writing should be process without product, a biography only of the self in the act of writing, yet *Une Vie* (1986) gathers the scattered parts or *séquences* of his work together in one—monumental—volume.

[28] *L'Autobiographie en France*, 84.

[29] *Selected Writings*, 236.

necessarily a fixed *point de repère* but a flexible heuristic device rooted in a dynamic process of understanding. Since Dilthey, however, there has been a marked tendency to tether the autobiographical turning point to a framework close to the 'once and for all' model of Christian conversion and revelation. Karl Weintraub, for example, talks of the 'necessary point of view' in autobiography which can only occur 'somewhere beyond a moment of crisis or beyond an experience, or a cumulative set of experiences which can play the same function as a crisis'.[30] Crisis and conversion provide the standpoints from which a life can be represented as possessing architectonic form. The idea has undeniable appeal, yet when taken to be prescriptive it severely limits the canon of autobiography, and it also underestimates the sense of doubt, the explicit element of conjecture, which often accompanies the postulation of turning points in secular autobiography. Henry James's fragment, 'The Turning Point of My Life', will provide a vivid illustration.

A friend, James reports, put it to him that 'every man's life has had its turning point'. The novelist could not at first see how this might apply in his own case, but the friend persisted: surely James's year at the Harvard Law School, where he spurned legal studies but began writing creatively, 'must have' constituted a turning point? 'Let me say at once', James observes,

that I welcomed the suggestion—for the kindly grace of it, the element of antique charm and bedimmed romance that it placed, straight away, at the disposal of my memory; by which I mean that I wondered whether I mightn't find, on ingenious reflection, that my youth *had* in fact enjoyed that amount of drama. I couldn't, I felt, be sure . . .[31]

James's scepticism could scarcely be more patent: 'ingenious reflection' sounds like a euphemism for arbitrary fabrication; 'romance' and 'drama' seem to place the turning point squarely in the domain of fiction. James, we may surmise, is politely holding his friend's idea at arm's length, savouring it in purely aesthetic terms. Consider, however, the novelist's fine evocation of the 'momentous junctures in question': 'Occasions of the taking of the ply that is never again to be lost, occasions of the true vocation or the right opportunity recognized more or less in a flash, determinations in short of

---

[30] 'Autobiography and Historical Consciousness', 824. In his introduction to an edition of Goethe's *Dichtung und Wahrheit* Weintraub writes: 'As an interpretative act autobiography is possible only because a turn of time, prior to the writer's vantage point, has opened inner lines of sight upon a life which could not be seen prior to such a turn', p. xxi. See also, by the same author, *The Value of the Individual*. Cf. G. Gusdorf, 'Toute autobiographie procède d'une conversion': 'De l'autobiographie initiatique à l'autobiographie genre littéraire', 975.

[31] 'The Turning Point of My Life' (1900), 438.

character and purpose and above all of a sharper and finer consciousness.'[32] The element of melodrama is undeniable, but so is the powerful appeal of the idea. James's fragment highlights the ambiguity of turning points; while his friend thinks they have an objective or official status, James sees them as the products of ratiocination and semi-fictive construction. To look for a turning point is to examine one's life in a certain way, responding to the appeal of 'the question itself', using it to distinguish the things one has 'kept in', from those which have 'ceased to be part of oneself'. For James, the turning point, we could say, is a cognitive device which fosters a certain kind of attention to the self.

James's stance epitomizes the epistemological caution of many twentieth-century autobiographers. More generally, however, his attitude illuminates the essentially hypothetical status of the turning point in secular autobiography. Rousseau's celebrated illumination on the road to Vincennes, when he spied the announcement of the Dijon essay prize, may justly be interpreted as a descendant of the Augustinian conversion scene: this moment is viewed retrospectively as a watershed after which his existence as a whole took on a new shape, albeit for the worse since the event marked the origin of his career as writer and public figure.[33] Yet Rousseau's turning point does not really function in the same way as Augustine's. The absence of an anagogic framework not only secularizes the experience but denies its authority, placing a heavy burden on the author's rhetoric, laying bare his dependence on laws of cause and effect, canons of *vraisemblance*, and so forth. In fact the vulnerability of the secular turning point has several aspects, some of which will emerge more fully in later chapters of this book. The moment their identification depends on explanatory systems, specified or implied by the text, turning points become the epiphenomena of particular discursive strategies, and specific ideological presuppositions. Any developmental account of human identity, indeed any attempt to historicize a life, requires turning points as an engine requires fuel. But, without the sanction of a single overarching masterplot, turning points tend to proliferate as they serve the ends of particular strategies of understanding. Rousseau's *Confessions*, as we shall see, present us with a succession of turning points, thus at once celebrating and devaluing the very notion, the profusion becoming a symptom of anxiety rather than certainty. In the case of a later writer, John Stuart Mill, turning points have become part of the autobiographer's stock-in-trade. At one level, Mill's autobiography

---

[32] 'The Turning Point of My Life' (1900), 437.
[33] *Œuvres complètes*, i. 351.

conforms to Weintraub's specifications since it centres on a 'crisis in [his] mental history' which involved a conversion from a mechanistic view of the individual to the acknowledgement of feeling.[34] But within this overall structure specific turning points—a reading of Bentham, the impact of a passage from Marmontel's autobiography, the discovery of Wordsworth, a walk near Pangbourne[35]—have become no more nor less than grammatical tools in the reconstruction of a life's syntax, aids to the retrospective dramatization of gradual processes.[36] As sites of meaning, turning points pertain less to prior experience than to narrative understanding.

The pre-eminence of 'scenes of reading' in Rousseau and Mill points to a further aspect of autobiographical turning points—their strongly intertextual character. It would be hard to exaggerate the remarkable paradigmatic power of the Augustinian scenario in which conversion is preceded by a revelation involving written authority. 'Tolle, lege!': take and read—a voice is heard, an instruction followed, a text read, a life transformed.[37] Each segment of this sequence is subject to wide variation, but the basic structure figures repeatedly in autobiographical narratives, from Petrarch's letter recounting his ascent of Mont Ventoux (where the text is from Augustine himself), through Saint Teresa, Rousseau, George Sand, Newman, Edmund Gosse, and onwards.[38] This may be interpreted as the perpetuation of a religious prototype (comparable to the secularized meanings acquired by such notions as the vocation or calling) which, in a secular context, confers the authority of an established pattern on the autobiographical narrative.[39] But as links in an intertextual chain such turning points function

---

[34] J. S. Mill, *Autobiography*, ch. 5.

[35] 'When I laid down the last volume of the Traité I had become a different being', 42. The Marmontel passage is on p. 85; the Wordsworth on p. 88; the walk on p. 89.

[36] As Mill acknowledges: 'But these few selected [turning points] give a very insufficient idea of the quantity of thinking which I carried on respecting a host of subjects during these years of transition', *Autobiography*, 101. It is interesting to observe that Mill's reservations about the status of turning points are matched by reservations with regard to the 'doctrine of the formation of character by circumstances' (p. 101) which lead him to discriminate carefully between different varieties of broadly associationist doctrine from Condillac to Harvey. This current of thought, so pervasive in the late 18th and early 19th centuries, might be said to devalue turning points precisely to the degree that it overvalues them.

[37] Augustine, *Confessions*, viii. 177.

[38] Petrarch, *Rerum Familiarum Libri I- VIII*, trans. Aldo S. Bernardo, iv. 1, 172–80 (178) (see the excellent discussion of the passage in T. Green, *The Light from Troy*); Teresa of Avila, *Confessions*, 58 (see the discussion of this text in B. Mandell, 'Full of Life Now'), 69; G. Sand, *Histoire de ma vie*, 953–6; J. H. Newman, *Apologia pro vita sua*, 87; E. Gosse: *Father and Son*, 171.

[39] On this tendency in British autobiography from Bunyan to Gosse, and its links to the act of reading, see L. H. Peterson, *Victorian Autobiography*. See also A. Fleishman, *Figures of Autobiography*.

in a different way from their religious models. The authority they invoke is now that of convention rather than revelation: the turning point is a figure as much as a real event. And this confirms our general hypothesis that, in secular form, turning points occupy an intermediate zone between past and present, experience and writing. As much as anything else, an autobiographical turning point is an event in the textual reconstruction of the past, an event in writing. When later writers—Michel Leiris, for example— explicitly make the context and temporality of writing predominate over those of the recorded past, they accentuate and radicalize what is implicit in many of their predecessors. As was suggested by James's response to his friend, turning points, like the will-to-form of which they are one expression, may most usefully be regarded not as primary intentions, determining autobiography from within, but as elements in the process of autobiographical construction, symptoms of a specific kind of awareness characteristic of what might, using the word in its phenomenological sense, be called autobiographical intentionality.[40]

II

Increasingly, the danger of prescriptiveness inherent in identifying a primal impulse behind autobiography (usually that of determining the unity and cohesiveness of one's life) has found critical recognition. Often, however, this has simply led to the insistence that there are many kinds of autobiography, and to the creation of classes such as 'intellectual', 'poetic', or 'spiritual' autobiography, and sub-genres such as the 'childhood' or 'récit d'enfance'.[41] This may lead to valuable insights, but it tends to blur the question of how motives operate in autobiographical writing. On the face of it, Francis Hart's influential essay, 'Notes for an Anatomy of Modern Autobiography', does not warrant this objection since, in opposing the shibboleths of unity and coherence, the author repeatedly contends that 'refocusing' of intention should be seen as a distinctive feature of autobiographical texts. 'Every autobiography', he writes, 'can appropriately and usefully be viewed as in some degree a drama of intention',[42] and Hart

---

[40] See J. V. Gunn, *Autobiography*, *passim*.

[41] The following list comprises, pell-mell, important studies of autobiography which seem to me to warrant this reservation: J. Olney, *Metaphors of Self*, W. C. Spengemann, *The Forms of Autobiography*, A. O. J. Cockshut, *The Art of Autobiography*; G. May, *L'Autobiographie*; R. N. Coe, *When the Grass was Taller*.

[42] F. R. Hart, 'Notes for an Anatomy of Modern Autobiography', 492. Subsequent quotations are from pp. 502 and 508.

stresses the dynamic unfolding of the autobiographical act as a process which makes it 'self-defeating for the interpreter to expect some predictable integrity or unity'. Surprisingly, however, Hart waters this down by retaining familiar categories of autobiographical intention: confession, apology, memoir. We must, he argues, seek to understand how and why a given writer oscillates between and ultimately creates fusions out of a limited range of primordial intentions: it is the dosages which are unstable, he suggests, rather than the ingredients themselves. Yet some of Hart's formulations point to the limitations of this view, for example his observation that 'Something inherent in autobiographical process calls for the continuous refocusing of expectation and intention, as each autobiographer discovers his own fluctuating mixture of confession, apology, and memoir.' What, we may ask, is the 'something inherent' if it is not simply the writing of autobiography which, of itself, destabilizes and undermines fixity of intention? Rather than analyse the particular 'mixture' of established intentional ingredients present in a given sample, as Hart seemingly invites us to do, we should perhaps seek to understand the factors which give rise to this mixing or scrambling of intentional forces. If autobiography is, as Hart suggests, a 'hybrid form', an account of its hybridity must go beyond attempts to calibrate the constituents of such species as the 'communicative-memoiristic' and the 'apologetic-exemplary'.

In the figurative sense, hybrid means 'derived from heterogeneous sources' (*OED*). If autobiographies are inherently hybrid, it is partly by virtue of their intrinsic heterogeneity. This quality can certainly be traced at the level of genre, in connection with autobiography's evolution out of, and interaction with, religious confession, memoirs, picaresque fiction, the essay, the 'journal intime', etc.; or in connection with its precarious situation on the border of fact and fiction.[43] But from the writer's point of view heterogeneity is in the first place a function of his or her materials, which are liable to be as disparate as the forms in which the past can survive into the present—memories: recent and distant, sharp and hazy, certain and suspect, verbal and visual; the first-, second-, and third-hand stories which we have heard (or invented) about ourselves; what used to be called monuments: correspondence, documents and archives, records of numerous kinds (educational, medical, juridical), journals, past writings (sometimes including earlier attempts at autobiography), and so on. Then there are the inevitable gaps: the 'missing chapter' of the unconscious; the

---

[43] On the question of the borderline with fiction see John Eakin's valuable study *Fictions in Autobiography*.

fissures, erasures, and forgeries of which the autobiographer may be acutely aware; the shadow cast by the future—and by death—which underlines the inevitable incompletion of any autobiographical enterprise. An autobiography is a patchwork assembled out of this disparateness, and a polyphony of the different kinds of discourse—historical, essayistic, psychological, ideological, factual, lyrical, investigative, conjectural—which it solicits. A further contribution to this heterogeneity is made by the diversity of contexts in which a given autobiography may be written. In many autobiographies (those of Chateaubriand and Leiris especially) allusions to events which occur in the course of composition, as the author's life continues to evolve in parallel with his or her text, play a significant role, weaving additional threads into the work's fabric of intentions. No doubt the passage of time impinges on the novelist's enterprise but rarely with the intense, deflective force it exerts in autobiography where the narrative situation, and the act of narration unfolding in the work, belong to real rather than fictive space and temporality, and where the interaction of *discours* and *histoire* involves real events and a living autobiographer. Symptomatic of this is the complex textual history, in terms of both composition and publication, of so many autobiographical texts, from Montaigne's *Essais* to Stendhal's *Vie de Henry Brulard*, Wordsworth's *Prelude*, Gide's *Si le grain ne meurt*, and Perec's *W ou le souvenir d'enfance*. Exemplary in so much else, Rousseau's *Confessions* readily furnish an example. In 1761, Rousseau's publisher asks him to write his life-story; in 1762 he sends four substantial autobiographical letters to Malesherbes; in 1764 an anonymous pamphlet (the work of Voltaire) accuses him of abandoning his children. Having begun to write his *Confessions*, he composes a substantial preface; exiled in England in 1766, he writes much of the early books at Wootton in Staffordshire, and then, in 1767, at Trye. There follows a two-year gap, after which Rousseau resumes his autobiography, probably completing it around December 1770 when he reads parts of it aloud at private gatherings; in 1771 Madame d'Epinay asks the police to prohibit such readings. Rousseau goes on to write his *Dialogues* and then the *Rêveries*, rather than continue the narrative of his life; as intended, the *Confessions* are published posthumously, in the 1780s. We should not talk of intentions without considering the pressures of such a history, the scars it may have left on the text, and the impact it may have made on the text's reception. If intentions in autobiography are fissile, if there is characteristically a 'drama of intention' in such texts, it is not simply because they inevitably involve an amalgam of genres, but because the interaction of intention and execution never ceases to be at issue—from the beginning (where, as in Stendhal, a *mise en scène* of intention may be staged) to the end (where, as in Gide or Perec, the question of the author's ultimate intention is the enigma bequeathed to the reader).

The genre's highly intertextual character also contributes to the hybrid quality of autobiographical texts. Explicit discourse concerning intentions and methodology in autobiography tends to be markedly intertextual since, explicitly or not, it implicates other practitioners and invokes the genre or canon as the author imagines it to exist before his or her contribution is made. (I set aside here the role played by books, especially accounts of early reading, in many autobiographical narratives.)[44] The autobiographer's sense of a pre-existent body of canonical assumptions and procedures constitutes one of the forms of otherness with which the autobiographer engages. This engagement is frequently agonistic, if we apply Harold Bloom's concept of a struggle between belated poet and powerful precursor.[45] For two or three generations (until at least the mid-nineteenth century) after the publication of the *Confessions*, Rousseau's text was a powerful presence and an obligatory point of reference for his successors; indeed, its spectre has never entirely ceased to haunt European autobiographers. Yet if the 'Anxiety of Influence' (especially Rousseau's influence) is all-pervasive in autobiography, the revisionary struggle on the writer's part is rarely as focused or as consistent as it tends to be in the poets studied by Bloom. Partly, no doubt, this is because Rousseau was perceived less as an exemplar to be outdone than as a deviant to be shunned and marginalized; and partly because, subsequently, the autobiographical tradition has been too sketchy, the 'strong' practitioners too few and far between. A further reason might be that the writing of autobiography often enacts the desire to carry out a task, to perform an operation, rather than to create a work. At any rate, if we think of it as an intertextual forum, marked by apprehension and anxiety, autobiography tends to be dominated less by Bloomian misprision and rewriting than by questions of style, sincerity, decorum, methodological rigour, ideological and philosophical bearing. Rousseau finds Montaigne evasive; Chateaubriand finds Rousseau unseemly; Stendhal finds Chateaubriand egotistical.[46] There is Rousseau (and Proust) in Gide; Gide in Green; Leiris in Perec. Leiris designates Nerval and Breton as precursors; Genet and Gorz write with and against Sartre; Leduc with and against Beauvoir;

---

[44] This topic is the subject of R. N. Pauly, *Le Berceau et la bibliothèque*, which unfortunately treats it in a rather tendentious manner.

[45] See, particularly, *The Anxiety of Influence*.

[46] See C. Fleuret, *Rousseau et Montaigne*, P. Berthier, *Stendhal et Chateaubriand*; R. Trousson, *Stendhal et Rousseau*; and other works of this ilk.

Sartre and Beauvoir write with and against each other and their acolytes—a number of these filiations will be pursued later in this book. In all these cases, the autobiographer's enterprise is mediated by another text or body of texts which acts as a model or *repoussoir*.

Just as important, however, is the indefinite spectre of genre, the internalized conception of what an autobiography is or should be. 'Dès qu'on entend le mot "genre",' writes Jacques Derrida, 'dès qu'il paraît, dès qu'on tente de le poser, une limite se dessine. Et quand une limite vient à s'assigner, la norme et l'interdit ne se font pas entendre: "il faut", "il ne faut pas", dit le genre, le mot "genre", la figure, la voix ou la loi du genre.' [47] The voice of genre makes itself heard in numerous ways in autobiography. For example, the autobiographer has at his or her disposal a variety of tags— *Confessions, Mémoires, Souvenirs, Vie de . . . , Autobiographie*—which, when featured on a title-page, discussed in a preface, or alluded to in passing at any stage, can be used to signal (or camouflage) intentions. By recourse to this feature the autobiographer may attempt to disclaim certain intentions, ward off certain expectations, or block anticipated interpretative strategies on the part of the reader. Equally, by eschewing such labels, and by adopting a non-committal or ironic title—*Vie de Henry Brulard*, *Le Roman d'un enfant*, *Les Mots*—the autobiographer may seek to sidestep the question of genre, and lay claim to generic indefinition. However, the hybrid character of autobiography at a generic level not only renders the question of genre extremely complex, but in fact undermines the notion, often invoked defensively by those unwilling to meet them, that autobiography places highly specific demands and obligations on the writer. In particular, it undermines two common ploys used by autobiographers: the claim that one is constrained by the conventions of a particular form (for example, Gide's remark: 'Voici la duperie des récits de ce genre: les événements les plus futiles et les plus vains usurpent sans cesse la place, et tout ce qui peut se raconter');[48] or the converse claim that the text one is writing belongs to a new genre, a claim which features recurrently from Rousseau to Robbe-Grillet.[49] While innovation is clearly possible in autobiography, a generically hybrid status makes it difficult to sustain either the view that the practitioner is bound by fixed rules or the view that he or she has invented

---

[47] 'La Loi du genre', 256.

[48] *Si le grain ne meurt*, 216.

[49] In the opening pages of *Le Miroir qui revient*, Robbe-Grillet uses the common device of setting up a normative picture of the autobiographical genre—naïve belief in the transparency of language, *'vie reçue'*, 'quelques menus souvenirs donnés pour argent comptant' (p. 118) etc.—against which he traces his own transgressive practice.

new ones, despite the fact that the parameters and limitations of autobiography are, in practice, real enough. What makes the spectre of genre so difficult to dispel for the autobiographer is its very indefinition.

In its most extreme form the threat posed by autobiographical intertextuality would be this: *my* life, in *my* autobiography, will not be *mine* if *my* text is the same as *yours*. Yet how, by another token, can it not be the same, given the power of a compulsory agenda in autobiography: early memories, initiations, education, turning points? The challenge here, as was suggested earlier in connection with the 'Tolle, Lege!' motif, is the need to strike a balance between the advantages of the archetype and the drawbacks of the stereotype. There are many cases where the autobiographer seeks to demonstrate the exemplary status of his or her life, the way it bears witness to an established cultural pattern or narrative. Moreover, all autobiography, as a public act, is in some measure a plea for recognition: thus, even if one claims to be an exceptional case, this will be in terms which others are expected to comprehend. But when, notwithstanding the desire for recognition and acceptance, the urge to declare one's difference is paramount—as it so often is in the French tradition from Rousseau to Stendhal, Gide, Leiris, and Barthes—the dead weight of the *déjà-dit* becomes oppressive and the difficulty of evading a sense of sclerosis or plagiarism in the presentation of early memories, the discussion of formative books, encounters, and places, or the stirrings of sexuality, becomes acute. Formal innovation, sometimes meretricious, often fascinating, has provided one avenue; another has been to deflect attention from the shape of a life, or the distinctiveness of a chain of experiences, by emphasizing instead the equation between selfhood and a personal voice or style. 'Mon style inégal et naturel, tantôt rapide et tantôt diffus,' observes Rousseau, 'fera lui-même partie de mon histoire.'[50] Self-consciousness, a tendency to debate openly the problems and insecurities of autobiographical writing, is also relevant in this context. When the arena in which autobiographical intentions are deployed is perceived as a hall of mirrors where one's own experience seems already to have happened to someone else, and where the face in the mirror never quite seems to be ours, it may seem expedient to point this out to the reader, even at the risk of aggravating the scepticism on the part of the Other which is one of the autobiographer's besetting fears. In this regard, self-quotation can also be seen as a facet of autobiographical intertextuality. Here the other text through which the construction of identity is mediated is one's own. The quoted fragment—letter, diary-entry, extract from a

---

[50] *Œuvres complètes*, i. 1154.

published work (and, in some twentieth-century works, the photograph)—is a part of oneself but also something which already has an objective place in the external world, which already belongs partly to the Other.[51] Self-quotation creates a particular kind of zone in the autobiographical text and inspires an interplay of past and present which dramatizes the inevitable gap between the writing 'I' and the written one. In the wider context of autobiographical intentionality it is ultimately this interface, or aperture, which must consistently be stressed: not as a formality, a consequence of certain inescapable verities, but as the arena in which a dynamic processing of intention arises by dint of the negotiations between a consciousness, a writing subject, and the heterogeneous materials out of which selfhood is made.

III

Critics seeking to define autobiographical 'truth' have often opted to set aside factual veracity: let the autobiographer's truth, they declare, be his or her 'supreme fiction'. If this helps dispose of the vexed questions of selectivity, inaccuracy, and mendacity which surround autobiography, it also tends to erode generic specificity. The more we warm to the notion that what counts is the autobiographer's self-image, *imago*, life-illusion, the greater the likelihood that *Four Quartets*, *The Scarlet Letter*, *Aurélia*, or *La Jeune Parque* will emerge as the exemplifications of what has been defined as the essence of autobiography. And why not? There is certainly something to be said for reading such works as in some sense autobiographies.[52] Yet nothing compels us to do so. Conversely, however, to read *Vie de Henry Brulard* or *Les Mots* as novels is to impoverish rather than illuminate these texts. To eliminate the question of literal truth and reference in autobiography is to pay insufficient heed to a difference perceptible to most readers and which conditions different kinds of reading. We are unlikely to respond in the same way to a writer who explicitly fabricates a poetic or mythological self-image as to one who retains a clear commitment to fact, even if we judge that the end-product of the latter's labour is no less a

---

[51] A comprehensive study of self-quotation in autobiography might take as its starting-point Antoine Compagnon's contention, in his invaluable *La Seconde Main ou le travail de la citation*, 362–3 and *passim*, that self-quotation is a subversive and aberrant practice which runs counter to the dominant logic of citation.

[52] J. Olney gives considerable space to a discussion of Eliot in *Metaphors of Self*; W. C. Spengemann, in *The Forms of Autobiography*, focuses extensively on *David Copperfield* and *The Scarlet Letter*; in *Being in the Text*, P. C. Ray considers Joyce, Proust, Valéry, and Eliot.

fabrication than the former's. However, assuming that we accept this difference, another critical manœuvre is available to us which avoids giving ontological credence to the autobiographer's reconstruction of past selfhood. This is to locate autobiographical truth not in the product but in the process of writing. One way of doing so is to posit not only that the self disclosed in autobiographical writing is that of the writer in the present,[53] but that autobiography as an 'intentional act' (in the phenomenological sense) involves a mode of consciousness which seeks to apprehend, in the act of writing, the subjectivity of the writer. Autobiographical selfhood, on this view, might be envisaged as a kind of 'secretion', a 'seepage' of subjectivity into language through the medium of style. This poses a number of problems, however. First, if it is restrictive to tie autobiography to the belief in a fetishized essence manifested in the continuity of past and present, it is no less restrictive to tie it to a fetishized essence of self 'tasted' in the act of writing. Moreover, if we do so, we must either commit ourselves to the view that there is consanguinity rather than contradiction between subjectivity and textuality, or commit autobiographers to the perpetual attempt to reconcile the irreconcilable.[54]

By contrast, Philippe Lejeune's concept of autobiography as a contractual genre, based on a pact, has the advantage of placing process and *énonciation* in the foreground while avoiding tendentious presuppositions. In his essay 'Le Pacte autobiographique' generic definition comes much closer than usual to being neutral with regard to overall intentions or beliefs about the self. An important factor is the adoption, in the first instance, of the reader's rather than the writer's viewpoint. What is it, Lejeune asks, that binds us to read a particular text as an autobiography, whatever its formal identity (first or third person), its reliability, and so on? It is the fact that author, narrator, and protagonist are 'one and the same' and that this is indicated, explicitly or implicitly, by the text itself. At one level the pact simply refers to any feature which tends to establish the relations of identity essential to autobiography. Thus, as regards author and narrator, the title, or the repetition in the text of

---

[53] The classic statement of this position is J. Starobinski, 'Le Style de l'autobiographe'.

[54] For a wide-ranging interpretation of autobiography along these lines see Louis A. Renza's important essay, 'The Veto of the Imagination'. Arguing that the act of writing inevitably fictionalizes the life it seeks to trace, Renza considers various strategies by which autobiographers try to 'mitigate' the split entailed by their undertaking and to divert the reader's attention from an alienated, 'public' self-image to the authentic experience of self engendered in, but always threatened by, writing. Renza's portrayal of autobiography as an anxious textual practice performed in defiance of 'the generalizing power of language' is highly evocative, and includes some suggestive remarks on the hybrid quality of such texts, but his account of autobiographical intentionality seems narrow and over-generalized.

the author's name on the cover, can each constitute a pact. But Lejeune also uses this word to designate more substantial portions of text which serve this function: prefaces setting forth the aims, commitments, or principles of a work, methodological asides or excursuses in the body of the text, and ultimately all signs of authorial discourse. From the standpoint of generic identity, the role of this material is purely functional: it tells us what we are dealing with; it marks the difference between one kind of text (an autobiography) and other kinds, and presents this as the difference between one kind of undertaking, and one kind of reading, as against others. The autobiographical pact is referential but only to the extent that it refers us to the extra-textual existence of the author present as a name on the cover. The great advantage of Lejeune's definition is that it ties autobiography to *reference* but not *resemblance*; to the interaction of textual 'I' and extra-textual counterpart, but not to any specific kind of relationship between them. The pressure to tie autobiography to a particular form of intentionality is greatly reduced; at the same time, anything which occurs in the space defined by the relations of author, text, and reader becomes 'of the essence': 'le terme ultime de vérité (si on raisonne en termes de ressemblance) ne peut plus être l'être-en-soi du passé . . . mais l'être-pour-soi, manifesté dans le présent de l'énonciation'.[55]

Lejeune's emphasis on 'énonciation', the *act* of narration, supports the emphasis we have placed on the dynamic play of autobiographical intentions in the space between a writing 'I' and the materials out of which its textual embodiment will be formed. The notion of contract itself, however, beyond a general orientation towards reception, is not intended to bite deeply into the issues this raises. What it does is to differentiate autobiography, resisting its absorption into other literary forms, maintaining the possibility of a plurality of intentions. To explore more fully this difference is to move, perhaps, from a contractual framework to a transactional one. In this regard one should not lose sight entirely of the sense that autobiographers share a common predicament. It may be that autobiography, considered as an activity, neither presupposes a particular vision of identity nor commits the autobiographer to one *de facto*. Nevertheless, the autobiographical act may be seen to confront the practitioner with a range of problems and constraints similar enough to allow for some generalization on the question of

---

[55] *Le Pacte autobiographique*, 39. Cf. E. Benveniste, 'L'Appareil formel de l'énonciation' in *Problèmes de linguistique générale*, ii. 79–88. Lejeune's contribution to the study of autobiography is of course far wider than is suggested here. It is no exaggeration to say that, where France is concerned, serious attention to the genre *begins* with Lejeune's pioneering work of definition and exegesis in the 1970s (*L'Autobiographie en France, Le Pacte*

autobiographical subjectivity. The most straightforward would be that selfhood or subjectivity in autobiography is always a function of the constraints, limits, boundaries, and orders which are made pertinent by the particular nature of a given autobiographer's undertaking: the self in the text is always a self in context. Given this, and granted certain *données* in the context shared by autobiographers—the fact of writing for one—it seems permissible to talk, again in the most general terms, of an autobiographical *subject*. The point is not to smuggle back a global identity or intention, but rather to suggest that there is something irreducible about the 'self' constituted in autobiography, which differentiates it not only from the *état civil* outside it, but also from the 'rapport à soi' behind it. The subject of autobiography is a hybrid, a fusion of past and present, self and other, document and desire, referential and textual, *énoncé* and *énonciation*—not a product but a process. To talk of a subject rather than a self is not helpful if we sever autobiographical subjectivity from any ground in reference, in *Erlebnis*, in desire; if we confine it to the notion of a compulsory alienation brought about by textualization, or to the sheer polarization between a formal 'sujet de l'énonciation' and an object-like 'sujet de l'énoncé'. To sentence the autobiographical subject to the prison-house of language, or to place it outside the law by dint of a *non-lieu* on the grounds that it has no case to answer, to subordinate it, in short, to post-modernist commonplaces will not do. The 'death' which befalls subjectivity in writing is also a 'coming alive' in a new domain, in a mobile context of relationships whose configuration is constantly modified as the play of intentions redefines the parameters of the autobiographical act. No single structure of intentions can hold sway over the field in which the autobiographical subject is articulated. To talk of the autobiographical subject is already to think of the individual as being constituted by, subject to, different orders of meaning defined by different discourses. We are dealing, in fact, with a plural subject—or a plurality of subjects: a subject of memory, of ideology, of desire; a subject oriented towards communication, towards death, towards the body. The process of autobiography does not resolve this diversity into unity so much as provide a context for the interaction of a plurality of strands and forces. Whatever the aspirations of the work, the autobiographical subject—often to the writer's avowed dismay—always retains a certain heterogeneity. To

autobiographique, Je est un autre) and has been sustained by the critic's indefatigable efforts, since then, to demonstrate the diversity and versatility of autobiography (*Moi aussi*). Lejeune's classic studies of Rousseau, Gide, Sartre, and Leiris, and his more recent work on Sarraute and Perec, are immensely stimulating and will frequently be referred to in subsequent chapters.

be brought together under one roof is not necessarily to find unity. It is to find, under the auspices of the time and space of writing, and particularly of narrative, a context of inter-relationship, a time and place of transaction.

IV

If narrative is the elective medium of the autobiographer, we must now ask what kind of accommodation it offers for the subject of autobiography. There is a clear link between the rise of critical interest in autobiography as a literary (rather than a merely documentary) genre, and the modernist and formalist view of narrative as an agency which promotes shape, order, and artifice. As long as autobiography is construed in terms of structural unity, *Gestalt*, and the achievement of quasi-aesthetic form, narrative—considered as capable of just these accomplishments—seems eminently hospitable to it. However, this alliance has at its root the fictive status of the 'life' which acquires meaningful form; it therefore endorses the gap between living and narrating discovered by the hero of Sartre's *La Nausée*. Roquentin, it will be remembered, discovers that for the slightest of events to become an adventure all one need do is recount it. The effect of incorporating lived experiences into a narrative sequence is to allow the end (which is already known rather than unforeseeable) to confer logical necessity and concatenation on the beginning and the middle. However, this is to uncover the guilty secret of the biographer (Roquentin's profession) and, by implication, the autobiographer, both of whom illicitly confer form on what is formless. Abandoning biography, Roquentin decides that we have to choose between living and narrating ('vivre ou raconter, il faut choisir'), formlessness and form; and he concludes that the only honest way to opt for the second is knowingly to embrace fiction itself.[56] Life aspires to the condition of art, and narrative is our best ally in this enterprise. If this view, grounded in the modernist aesthetic with its emphasis on the redemptive character of form, drives a wedge between life and art, existence and narrative, the same can be said of a very different aesthetics of narrative—the narratology inspired by structuralism, and by the rediscovery of the Russian formalists, which sees narrative as a modelling-system where meaning is primarily a function of form.[57] But if the critical fate of autobiography is likely to depend on

---

[56] *La Nausée*, 58–62, 244–9.
[57] See e.g. R. Barthes, 'Introduction à l'étude structurale du récit', and G. Genette, 'Frontières du récit'.

prevailing views of narrative, a corollary is that any moves towards a rehabilitation of narrative's mimetic, heuristic, or pragmatic functions are likely to support comparable shifts in the way autobiography is regarded. In this light it could be argued that many of the directions in which narrative theory has evolved in the aftermath of structuralism (often inspired by the aim of remedying the over-static, autotelic complexion of the structuralist model) have opened up opportunities for the reappraisal (and re-evaluation) of autobiography. With regard to the 'transactional' view of autobiography to which our discussion has led, two recent contributions to the debate on narrative seem especially pertinent—those of Paul Ricœur and Peter Brooks.[58]

Paul Ricœur and Narrative Identity

The view of narrative expounded in Paul Ricœur's *Temps et Récit*[59] is mimetic not because it renders the relationship with reality straightforward but because it envisages narrative as a vital process, a 'travail de pensée' (iii. 9) which articulates a dynamic relationship with experience. The narrative act is a refiguration which, as it emplots events, serves to mediate between a private, pre-reflexive level of understanding and an objective public world.[60] On this view, to tell a story, to construct a narrative, is not, as Roquentin supposed, to impose artificial coherence on what is formless.[61] Narrative is a response to the aporetics of temporality, to the discordances between the inner time of consciousness, cosmic time, and the objective time of clocks. The point is not that time is formlessnesss, pure flux, but that it confronts human consciousness with problems which cannot be resolved intellectually; and the response of narrative is not to 'plaster over the cracks' but, by

---

[58] Also relevant in this context are T. Cave, *Recognitions*; C. Prendergast, *The Order of Mimesis*; A. Jefferson, *Reading Realism in Stendhal*; P. J. Eakin, *Fictions in Autobiography*.

[59] Three vols., 1983–5: i. *Temps et récit*, ii. *La Configuration du temps dans le récit de fiction*, iii. *Le Temps raconté*. References to this work are incorporated in the text.

[60] Narrative ('le récit') involves a 'triple mimésis': the narrative act ('l'acte de mise en intrigue', i. 103) is 'configurational' in that it turns a succession of events into a global structure; this is *mimésis 2*. But it is only made possible in so far as narrative 'est enracinée dans une pré-compréhension du monde et de l'action: de ses structures intelligibles, de ses ressources symboliques et de son caractère temporel', i. 87: this is *mimésis 1*. *Mimésis 3* (the third dimension or condition of narrative) derives from the act of reading or understanding it presupposes. For Ricœur narrative configuration is ultimately rooted in its 'application' to the everyday world.

[61] See the discussion of Frank Kermode's *The Sense of an Ending*, ii. 39–48, where Ricœur raises objections to the idea of 'consoling plots': 'il faut trouver au besoin de configurer le récit d'autres racines que l'horreur de l'informe' (ii. 47). See also i. 111 ff.

virtue of its own essentially *hybrid* constitution, to provide a forum in which
the disparate dimensions of time can relate to each other dialectically.[62] If,
argues Ricœur, there are 'deux grands modes de récit', namely history and
fiction, this reflects the fact that narrative inherently partakes of both these
modes; indeed, its essence resides in their 'entrecroisement'.[63]

Since autobiography can itself be conceived as an 'entrecroisement' of
history and fiction, Ricœur's discussions of the fictionality of history, and
the historicity of fiction, offer much food for thought. For example, the
concept of *lieutenance* (from 'tenir lieu'), which denotes the relation of
history to the 'reality' of the past, illuminates the autobiographer's relation
to his or her materials.[64] History does not restore the past but constructs
something in its place: *lieutenance* has divergent yet interacting modes
which relate to the status of various 'connecteurs' between past and present.
One of these is the trace. Historical events leave traces—settlements,
buildings, ruins, battlefields, documents—which signify—without
resurrecting—the agencies or circumstances in which they originate. If
history can be described as a 'connaissance par trace' (iii. 204), the
knowledge in question combines two forms of interpretation, two
causalities, and two dimensions of time. On the one hand, to decipher a trace
is to reconstruct the chain of events which 'left their mark'; on the other
hand, it is to deal with the temporal and intellectual gap between the past
event and the present. Historical understanding, and *lieutenance*, involve a
'temps hybride' (elsewhere Ricœur talks of a 'tiers-temps')—an overlapping
and stitching-together of time zones which is the work of narrative. Seeking
to be his or her own historian, the autobiographer, it will be said, is in a
privileged position, does not depend on traces but on first-hand knowledge
of events that have been 'lived through'. Yet the privilege is perhaps more
apparent than real; for, after all, the autobiographer has also 'lived on': some
events are remembered, but their traces are now faint; some traces seem
indelible, but their origin is now uncertain. What Ricœur calls the *signifiance*
of the historical trace—its way of confronting the interpreter with a thing-
like enigma, *out there*; and its way of disclosing meaning only within the
context of a complex narrative act to which it remains tied—seems
applicable to autobiographical traces (autobiography, too, is a 'connaissance
par trace') and points to the specific, irreducible character of autobiographical subjectivity and knowledge. Moreover, if 'lieutenance', the narrative

---

[62] The goal or achievement of narrative is a 'synthèse de l'hétérogène' (i. 103, 241, 319), a
blending together of different kinds of event and causality.

[63] On the 'entrecroisement' of history and fiction see iii. 264–79 and 354–9.

[64] See iii, 2, ch. 3, 'La réalité du passé historique', 203–27.

construction prompted by the trace, is history's moment of fictionalization, fiction, in this context, has nothing to do with sheer invention or untruth: it connotes the controlled elaboration of hypotheses, an indirect mode of reference 'par le moyen d'une rectification sans fin de nos configurations'.

Fiction, for its part, shows its purchase on time in its ability to offer imaginary variations on the discrepancies between different time-scales (often presented simultaneously in a given work). Ricœur also highlights the interplay between the time of narration and that of narrated events, arguing that this interaction, realized in the compressions, dilations, flashbacks, and anticipations wrought by narration, has as its *enjeu* 'le vécu temporel'. In responding to these devices as novel-readers we apprehend not only a sealed-off fictional universe, but a specific writer's relation to time, and a potential relationship to real time on our own part. Ricœur's argument, against Genette, that the temporal dimension of the act of narration must be given its due is especially valid in the sphere of autobiography where the interaction between the two time-scales of narration and past events generates authentic meaning because the autobiographical act necessarily involves the confrontation of two temporal levels—present and past. It is, however, in the inscribed act of *reading* that fiction's equivalent to *lieutenance*—its 'moment quasi-historique'—occurs. The reader's place in the text, realized in different ways (through an implied reader, a narratee, the orientation towards 'reception', or the prominence of epistemic desire) marks the point of 'application' through which the fictional world engages with and encompasses the real.

Ricœur's analyses culminate in a concept which brings autobiography into the foreground as the perfect embodiment of narrative's *entrecroisement* of history and fiction. Narrative may be understood in part as a response to a 'demande de récit': it answers to a need for stories. One of the contexts of this need is the question 'Who?', which an individual may ask with respect to him- or herself, in response to what Ricœur calls 'la requête d'une authentique reprise de l'héritage que nous sommes à l'égard de nous-mêmes' (iii. 201). Without the aid of narrative, Ricœur argues, the problem of personal identity involves an intractable opposition between 'un sujet identique à lui-même dans la diversité de ses états' and the atomized subject of Hume and Nietzsche, a bundle of sensations, emotions, and desires, lacking a central core. In the face of this, the concept of *identité narrative* conceives of identity not in terms of the same (*idem*), but in terms of 'un soi-même' (*ipse*). Here identity rests on a dynamic temporal structure, akin to the composition of a narrative text, and is thus compatible with 'le changement, la mutabilité, dans la cohésion d'une vie':

Le sujet apparaît alors constitué à la fois comme lecteur et comme scripteur de sa propre vie, selon le vœu de Proust. Comme l'analyse littéraire de l'autobiographie le vérifie, l'histoire d'une vie ne cesse d'être refigurée par toutes les histoires véridiques ou fictives qu'un sujet raconte sur lui-même. Cette refiguration fait de la vie elle-même un tissu d'histoires racontées (iii. 355–6).

'L'identité narrative' is, then, an identity which derives from our recourse, in the act of living, to narrative as a source of answers to the questions which arise when we situate ourselves in relation to the disparate levels of our past and present experience. The concept has clear affinities with Dilthey, as is evident from Ricœur's use of the expression 'la cohésion d'une vie'.[65] Yet there are important differences. 'L'identité narrative' does not reduplicate and externalize a process inherent in consciousness: prior to the act of narrative is only the need and demand for narrative understanding, akin to the patient's need for the work of analysis.[66] Narrative identity is not the product of organic unfolding based on passive, intuitive understanding, but a dynamic modelling process driven by active, constructive processes at work in our engagement with the vestiges and enigmas of temporal experience. True, in Dilthey the cohesiveness of a life (*Zusammenhang des Lebens*) is not a fixity: it changes as new experiences are assimilated; but it is always conceived as a pattern, an organic equilibrium. Ricœur's 'identité narrative' is far more conjectural and precarious in its foundations; as the product of a 'rectification sans fin d'un récit antérieur par un récit ultérieur, et de la chaîne de refigurations qui en résulte' (iii. 358), it is inherently unstable:

D'abord l'identité narrative n'est pas une identité stable et sans faille; de même qu'il est possible de composer plusieurs intrigues au sujet des mêmes incidents (lesquels, du même coup, ne méritent plus d'être appelés les mêmes événements), de même il est toujours possible de tramer sur sa propre vie des intrigues différentes, voire opposées. A cet égard on pourrait dire que, dans l'échange des rôles entre l'histoire et la fiction, la composante historique du récit sur soi-même tire celui-ci du côté d'une chronique soumise aux mêmes vérifications documentaires que toute autre narration historique, tandis que la composante fictionelle le tire du côté des variations imaginatives qui déstabilisent l'identité narrative. En ce sens, l'identité narrative ne cesse de se faire et de se défaire . . . [Elle] devient ainsi le titre d'un problème, au moins autant que celui d'une solution. Une recherche systématique

---

[65] Ricœur explicitly links 'l'identité narrative' with Dilthey's notion of 'la cohésion d'une vie' (*Zusammenhang des Lebens*), iii. 201.

[66] The parallel is made by Ricœur: 'On y voit [sc. in psychoanalysis] comment l'histoire d'une vie se constitue par une suite de rectifications appliquées à des récits préalables . . . un sujet se reconnaît dans l'histoire qu'il se raconte à lui-même sur lui-même' (pp. 356–7).

sur l'autobiographie et l'autoportrait vérifierait sans aucun doute cette instabilité principielle de l'identité narrative. (iii. 358)

All these observations suggest that Ricœur's 'identité narrative' is very much germane to our discussions of the autobiographical subject and of autobiographical intention. Whatever the autobiographer's goal, autobiographical identity is the construct of intentions embedded in the activity of narrative itself—the transfusions between *énonciation* and *énoncé*, documentary referentiality and fictional speculation—and it is marked by an 'instabilité principielle'. In Ricœur's terms it remains a problem as much as a solution.

Peter Brooks and Narrative Transference

In Peter Brooks's *Reading for the Plot: Design and Intention in Narrative*, the dynamics of the psychoanalytical process, and particularly Freud's accounts of how the analysand negotiates with his or her past in the context of the relationship to the analyst, provide models for a thought-provoking rehabilitation of the cognitive function of narrative. Here the emphasis on the desires at work in narrative, and on the relationship to the Other, provide illuminating insights into the activity of autobiography. Like Ricœur, Brooks sees narrative as a dynamic process: 'plot' is force as well as form, 'not a matter of typology or fixed structure, but rather a structuring operation . . . the instrumental logic of a specific mode of human understanding' (p. 10)[67] which mediates and connects through the *act* of narration. Autobiography is frequently invoked in Brooks's readings because, if the 'recovery of the past can be said to be the aim of all narrative', the crucial paradigm of the narrative act is the individual's relationship to the potential meaningfulness of his or her own life. Concluding an analysis of the famous 'stolen ribbon' episode in Rousseau's *Confessions*, Brooks writes:

The question of identity, claims Rousseau—and this is what makes him at least symbolically the *incipit* of modern narrative—can be thought only in narrative terms, in the effort to tell a whole life, to plot its meaning by going back over it to record its perpetual flight forward, its slippage from the fixity of definition (p. 33).

In the radical upheavals to which they submit orthodox chronology and causality, Freud's case histories, seen as direct descendants of Rousseau's inaugural act of self-narrativization, lay bare the foundations, in human

[67] References to *Reading for the Plot* are incorporated in the text.

desire, of the double drive—backwards and forwards—of narrative. As the vehicle of desire's ultimate object, the quiescence and resolution of death, narrative moves towards the definitive closure of meaning; but, just as desire can never achieve its aim, so narrative also provides a medium of diversion and postponement. The reworkings and repetitions of plot, its progress-ive–regressive movement, sustain the 'pleasurable possibility (or illusion) of "meaning" wrested from "life"' (p. 108), but narrative resolution never quite effaces the dilatory loops and complications which precede it. The burden of narrative lies in the 'Remembering, repeating and working-through' (the title of one of Freud's papers) to which it subjects its materials. The characteristic of modern narrative understanding, epitomized by Freud's case history of the Wolfman, is the recognition of its own precarious basis, the awareness it betrays that the overt project of 'enchainment' is simultaneously commanded and subverted by a covert logic of desire. In the layerings and hesitations of Freud's account of the Wolfman, the customary logic of cause and effect, and distinctions between real and fabricated, are brought into question. The fundamental concept of deferred action (*Nachträglichkeit*) according to which the causative role of an event is conferred on it retroactively, creating a meaning which did not originally exist, emphasizes that

the way a story is ordered does not necessarily correspond to the way it *works*. Indeed, narrative order, sequence as a logical enchainment of actions and outcomes, must be considered less a solution than part of the problem of narrative explanation. How we narrate a life—even our own life to ourselves—is at least a double process, the attempt to incorporate within an orderly narrative the more devious, persistent, and powerful plot whose logic is dictated by desire (pp. 280–1).

If, for Brooks, the dynamism of plot is driven by the contradictions of desire, narrative is not merely a mirror but an arena in which the truth of desire may be articulated. For narrative is itself the expression of desire's wish to be 'heard, recognized, understood' (p. 54): in, or as, narrative the subject's transactions with desire are conducted by proxy of the relation to another postulated subjectivity. Here Freud's account of the 'dynamism of transference' in the relationship between analyst and analysand provides a model:

In the transference, desire passes through what Lacan calls the 'defile of the signifier': it enters the symbolic order, where it can be reordered, reread, rewritten. While other 'transactional' models of reading could be proposed, the model of the psychoanalytical transference has the advantage of imaging the productive encounter of teller and listener, text and reader, and of suggesting how their interaction takes place in a special 'artificial' medium, obeying its own rules—those of the symbolic order—yet vitally engaged with the histories and intentions of desire. In other words, the transference, like the text as read, becomes the peculiar space of a deadly serious play, in which affect, repeated from the past, is acted out as if it were present, yet eventually in the knowledge that the persons and relations involved are surrogates and mummers (pp. 234–5).

Like Ricœur, Brooks places the anticipated act of reading, of exposure to the Other, at the heart of an account of the way narrative functions, and of the purposes it serves. But Brooks's model grounds narrative in the play of an intersubjective transaction, no less compelling for being artificial. 'Framed narratives' and first-person texts provide his examples, but much of what Brooks says applies *a fortiori* to autobiography. Specifically engaged with the 'histories and intentions of desire' referred to in the paragraph quoted above, the autobiographer re-enacts past affect in the present. But the context of this act—verbal articulation in a public medium—makes the reader a narratee, and the author's discourse dialogical in Bakhtin's sense, 'whereby discourse internalises the presence of otherness, becomes marked by the alterity inherent in any social use of language' (p. 283).[68] Unlike the analyst, the reader cannot intervene, cannot even signify assent or demurral like the silent (silenced) listener in Camus's *La Chute*; surrogacy and mummery, in Brooks's metaphors, remain his lot, shared of course with other protagonists: fathers, mothers, rivals. Nevertheless, the recognition of the instance of the Other makes narrative transitional and transactional, a space where past desires are restaged *in effigy*, as Freud put it.

Brooks is concerned primarily with the power and pertinence of fictions. To find in Rousseau and Freud models for a relation to the past where the discourse of truth 'is radically allied to the fictional, since its causes and connections depend on probabilistic constructions rather than authoritative facts' (p. 284) is, in some measure, to derive support for the truth of fiction by the stratagem of defining fiction as a form of truth. Autobiography can readily accommodate fiction of this kind, but we must not underestimate the constraints under which autobiographical 'plotting' exists. Brooks describes Rousseau's response to the awareness of contradictory desires at work in his past (and in his present's designs on that past) as the production of 'more narrative', a potentially indefinite extensibility of the interpretative process, akin to the interminability of analysis evoked by Freud. This is just; and indeed we shall see in Rousseau, Stendhal, or Leiris that an autobiographer

---

[68] See M. Bakhtin, 'Discourse in the Novel' in M. Holquist (ed.), *The Dialogic Imagination*.

always has another memory, another incident, up his sleeve, ready to supply a demand produced by the logic of his narrative. Yet, at the same time, 'what comes next', or 'what remains to be covered' is to a significant degree always spoken for in advance in autobiography; and, most importantly, its claim to attention derives not from the internal exigencies of a narrative but the external ones of an extant, but looser plot. Perhaps this difference is more apparent than real. Brooks certainly insists that most narrative involves the reordering of a 'given' past. And if the truth of fiction, in Brooks's sense, does not lie in how it measures up to an independent reality, the fictional in autobiography is best understood not as departure from fact but as hypothesis and construction. What counts in both cases is therefore the act of narration. Brooks's theory of narrative is of particular significance from the point of view of autobiography because his analyses lead to the implication 'that the ultimate subject of any narrative is its narrating' (p. 305); and narrating is 'an enterprise apparently nostalgic, oriented towards the recovery of the past, yet really phatic in its vector, asking for hearing' (p. 312). The orientation towards the recovery of the past may be construed in sufficiently broad terms to encompass, in our context, the range of intentions and constraints we have encountered in the autobiographer's situation; whatever the impulses behind a given autobiographical act, their field of play is the process of telling, a continuous and indefinite present where the past negotiates its future.

2

Rousseau and the Chains of Narrative

Où est l'homme assez stupide pour ne pas voir la chaîne de tout cela?

(*Emile: ou de l'éducation*)[1]

I

Partly thanks to Rousseau's *Confessions*, autobiography has come to suggest all but irresistibly the idea of connections, the perception of some sort of pattern and linkage in the disparateness of past experience. Narrative therefore seems its natural ally, since narrative implies connectedness: beginnings, middles, and ends, causes and effects, origins and consequences. The *Confessions* teem with references to links, connections, causes, origins, threads, modifications, developments, anticipations. Indeed, one of the key words in Rousseau's text, as I shall argue throughout this chapter, is *chaîne*, along with its cognate *enchaînement*, its near-relation (at least metaphorically) *fil*, and other related words and concepts. 'Je vois le fil de tout cela', 'enchaînement d'affections secrètes', 'la chaîne de mes malheurs': such expressions play commanding roles in Rousseau's account of himself. In his pronouncements on method Rousseau often asserts that he is making chains: linking one experience, one feeling, one event, with others. In composing his story he seems constantly to be showing us how one thing led to another—how being spanked led to masochism, how stealing a ribbon led to life-long remorse, how being badly treated led to behaving badly. And yet one often hears that Rousseau was not at home in the world of causes, links, and chains. His real ambition, his heart's desire at any rate, was unmediated, timeless self-awareness; not explanations, causes, and origins, not narrative, but transparency, the immediate apprehension of subjective being, which he celebrated in the *Rêveries du promeneur solitaire*:

Un état où l'âme trouve une assiette assez solide pour s'y reposer tout entière et

[1] *Œuvres complètes*, iv. 262.

rassembler là tout son être, sans avoir besoin de rappeler le passé ni d'enjamber sur l'avenir; où le temps ne soit rien pour elle, où le présent dure toujours sans néanmoins marquer sa durée et sans aucune trace de succession, sans aucun autre sentiment de privation ni de jouissance, de plaisir ni de peine, de désir ni de crainte que celui seul de notre existence, et que ce sentiment seul puisse la remplir toute entière (p. 1046).[2]

Beyond thought, outside time, the 'âme' evoked in the Cinquième Promenade finds immunity from reason and history. In this state the 'sentiment de l'existence' is clearly beyond the pale of narrative connections. Is it appropriate, however, to make this the touchstone of Rousseau's conception of self? The fact that it chimes with a persistent anti-historical strain in all his thought would seem to encourage us to do so. And so would the remarkable prestige this view of selfhood was to enjoy in the subsequent history of European culture. Moreover, the prevailing consensus among some of Rousseau's most attentive readers, particularly those associated with the phenomenologically oriented Geneva school, has been that, despite the concern with causes and explanations, the *Confessions* are permeated throughout by an unhistorical sense of self, remote from causality. Marcel Raymond, for example, sees memory as the key to Rousseau's alliance with an original experience of self, a 'présence à soi', rooted in childhood experience, which belies the chaotic discontinuity of his mental life, and which is essentially unchanging: 'cette unité de base est plus qu'une hypothèse de l'esprit ou un postulat philosophique; elle est éprouvée, tant que l'existence dure, comme une tonalité fondamentale toujours mieux perceptible au travers des discordances'.[3] Significantly, in our perspective, Raymond repeatedly identifies this 'tonalité fondamentale', or 'résonance affective absolue', with Rousseau's notion of an 'enchaînement d'affections secrètes'. Yet rather than see this in terms of a temporal, successive, and causal unfolding, Raymond views the 'enchaînements' as primordial linkages between feelings and sensations which formed the sensibility at an early stage, and whose repercussions are felt throughout life in the form of a pressure shaping the encounter with new experiences. If Rousseau adopts

---

[2] *Œuvres complètes*, i. *Les Confessions. Autres textes autobiographiques*. Refs. to this vol. are incorporated in the text (spelling modernized).

[3] *Jean-Jacques Rousseau*, 47. In similar vein, Georges Poulet argues that, ideally, Rousseau's 'conscience de soi' involves a 'rassemblement' in which the past, recaptured through a quasi-Proustian 'mémoire affective', contributes to an intense experience of self-presence. Memory of this kind, Poulet asserts, is not temporal or historical: 'par le souvenir affectif Rousseau prend une conscience plus profonde d'un moi qui n'appartient à proprement parler ni au passé, ni au présent, ni même à la durée', *Études sur le temps humain*, i. 185.

narrative in the *Confessions*, it is not out of any commitment to an historical view of the self but in order to show how an established matrix resembling a genetic invariant acted globally on all the situations he encountered.[4] Jean Starobinski echoes the notion that Rousseau's autobiographical narrative involves the presentation, piecemeal and *seriatim*, of what is essentially instantaneous,[5] but he suggests a different motive for Rousseau's adoption of narrative in the *Confessions*, interpreting it as a reluctant complicity with an alien order, imposed by the dictates of rationality and the demands of others, a complicity in 'le triste univers des enchaînements, des consé-quences, de la pensée raisonnable'.[6] In the critical perspective I have sketched, the narrative, historical, causal dimension of the *Confessions* is an obstacle Rousseau had to circumvent, a challenge he had to overcome, an alien protocol he observed for contingent reasons. Yet whilst there seems little doubt that the ahistorical, sovereign 'présence a soi', which has been analysed with such finesse, can claim to be fundamental to Rousseau, it nevertheless seems legitimate to ask whether this is the sole criterion by which to evaluate his project in the *Confessions*. Given the notoriously multi-faceted and unsystematic character of Rousseau's thought, one must always be wary, in emphasizing one strand, of undervaluing another with which it may in fact have coexisted or alternated. Must we not, in this case, also give its due to a genuine if ultimately frustrated desire—emblematized by the ambiguous concept of 'enchaînement', and central to the subsequent history of autobiography—to give expression to a historicized self, a selfhood inseparable from the twists and turns of its story?[7]

To pursue this further, a first step must be to ask whether the idea of

[4] *Jean-Jacques Rousseau*, 208: 'Rousseau ne cesse de réagir globalement à la nouveauté, en fonction de tout son passé et de tout son espoir.' Acknowledging that one of Rousseau's aims in writing *Les Confessions* was 'faire intervenir comme élément générateur la durée ... dessiner le mouvement d'une destinée', Raymond none the less treats this as a separate motivating factor which did not involve the desire to manifest a process of *enchaînement* but rather 'mettre au jour les liaisons et les enchaînements formant la texture de son être'.

[5] *Jean-Jacques Rousseau*, 226: 'il va étaler dans la durée biographique une vérité globale que le sentiment possède d'un seul coup.'

[6] 'Jean-Jacques Rousseau et le péril de la réflexion' in *L'Œil vivant*, 180, 183: 'La tâche que s'impose Jean-Jacques comporte toutes les opérations qui lui pèsent, qui lui paraissent liées à un malheur essentiel et pour lesquelles il s'est déclaré inapte: s'astreindre à exprimer la succession, l'enchaînement, les développements, les liens qui rattachent les effets à leurs causes'. Cf. J.-B. Pontalis, 'Lieux et séparation', in *Entre le rêve et la douleur*, 139–57.

[7] It has often been pointed out that in narrative technique, Rousseau's *Confessions* are indebted to developments in 18th-cent. fiction (on this see P. Stewart, *Imitation and Illusion in the French Memoir-Novel*; J.-L. Lecercle, *Rousseau et l'art du roman*). Yet there is nothing to suggest that Rousseau considered the 'dimension romanesque' of his autobiography to be in conflict with the project of self-revelation.

'enchaînement' is in fact necessarily incompatible with Rousseau's 'sentiment de l'existence'. Both concepts are closely related to sensualist epistemology.[8] It has often been pointed out that, while he was wont to celebrate the immediacy of sensation, Rousseau frequently criticized sensualist doctrines on the grounds that they gave too passive a picture of the process and scope of cognition. It is in this context that the notion of a 'sentiment de l'existence' emerges. What we know, and what we are, is not simply the product of the sensations we receive, but of an active 'processing': 'Vivre n'est pas respirer, c'est agir; c'est faire usage de nos organes, de nos sens, de nos facultés, de toutes les parties de nous-mêmes qui nous donnent le sentiment de notre existence.'[9] In this conception, the 'sentiment de l'existence' is not only a state but a faculty (resembling Dilthey's *Erlebnis*), a synthesis of feeling (or intuitive consciousness) and sensation, a 'sentiment sensoriel',[10] an active principle which, while it may not have a permanent content, can be conceived as having a history.[11] Indeed, it is the history of his 'sentiments'—of the 'chaîne de mes sentiments'—which Rousseau will, he declares, attempt to provide in the *Confessions*.

Like 'sentiment', the term 'enchaînement', in Rousseau's usage, encompasses both the mechanisms of sensation and the realms of thought and feeling. The 'chain' figures prominently in sensualist writing. According to Condillac, for example, human needs are interlinked and our perceptions form chains of ideas 'dont la force serait entièrement dans l'analogie des signes, dans l'ordre des perceptions et dans la liaison que les circonstances, qui réunissent quelquefois les idées les plus disparates auraient formée'. By postulating an analogical relationship between different sensory registers Condillac accounts for our ability to link and

---

[8] See R. Mercier, 'Sur le sensualisme de Rousseau', which provides a useful definition: 'le sensualisme, . . . doctrine qui fait dépendre la connaissance des opérations du sujet pensant, et celles-ci à leur tour des sensations et plus spécialement de la constitution physique des organes des sens', 21.

[9] *Œuvres complètes*, iv. 499. Earlier Rousseau had asked 'comment puis-je savoir si le sentiment du moi est quelque chose hors de ces mêmes sensations et s'il peut être indépendant d'elles?' Rousseau will constantly be tempted to locate the 'moi' above and beyond the treadmill of sensations, but in the *Confessions* at least this tendency is kept in check.

[10] Coining this hybrid term, Basil Munteano defines it as a 'faculté mixte, faculté-charnière, faculté psycho-physique, à support intérieur, mais à référence sensorielle, délibérément orientée vers l'extérieur, et chargée d'insérer le "moi" dans le circuit universel', *Solitude et contradictions de Jean-Jacques Rousseau*, 76.

[11] Rousseau refers to 'cette force dans mon esprit . . .', *Œuvres complètes*, iv. 594. For a useful discussion of this aspect of 'sentiment' see J. Macleod, 'Rousseau and the Epistemology of "Sentiment"'.

compare experiences, to remember, and so forth. Were it not for this faculty, based on instinct, we would, bereft of innate ideas, possess visual, aural, and other chains of experience but be incapable of co-ordinating them. On this hypothesis there is of course, designedly, no sense of subjective 'space': cognitive force is restricted to the perception of analogy which ensures that our experiences can form 'une seule et même chaîne dont les chainons se réuniraient à certains anneaux, pour se séparer à d'autres'.[12] The chain image underlines the essentially impersonal and mechanical nature of such an epistemology.

At times Rousseau's pedagogical system in *Emile* seems to endorse this kind of sensualism, especially in its mechanistic, proto-behaviourist aspects. Yet the acquisition of knowledge seldom seems quite so automatic or abstract. Although Rousseau argues that feeling and judgement are distinct, the learning process involved in *Emile* often seems to involve a logic of feelings rather than pure sensations. Rousseau contrasts the 'chaîne de vérités générales' of purely abstract, scientific knowledge, with a more practical and immediate chain 'par laquelle chaque objet particulier en attire un autre et montre toujours celui qui le suit'.[13] By perceiving such associations the child can learn to understand the mechanism of cause and effect. More surprisingly, the inculcation of moral notions involves the same approach. For example, an elaborate *mise en scène*, involving the deliberate wrecking of the child's bean-plot, and later his incarceration for breaking a window, is devised in order to instil at one go the notions of ownership and injustice. Concluding this double object-lesson in pedagogical technique, Rousseau writes: '*suivez la chaîne de tout cela*. Le petit méchant ne songeait guère, en faisant un trou pour planter sa fève, qu'il se creusait un trou où sa science ne tarderait pas à le faire enfermer' (my italics).[14] Above Emile's head the reader is asked to observe, in the first place, the logical coherence of

---

[12] Condillac, *Essai sur l'origine des connaissances humaines*, 125. For a discussion of this passage and of the 'espèces de chaînes' see the commentary by J. Derrida in the above edn., 64 ff. Derrida points out that Condillac's epistemology is essentially semiotic: in order to lend themselves to analogical permutation sensory data need to have the character of abstract signs, and thus to be devoid of interiority. See also G. Bennington, *Sententiousness and the Novel*, 220.

[13] *Œuvres complètes*, iv. 436. Elsewhere in *Emile*, where the word occurs frequently (see E. Brunet, *Index-Concordance d'Emile ou de l'éducation*) Rousseau refers in the context of love to an affective chain which could link a 'première impression' to 'de longs effets dont on n'aperçoit pas la chaîne dans le progrès des ans mais qui ne cessent d'agir jusqu'à la mort', iv. 777.

[14] *Œuvres complètes*, iv. 329–33. The coercive 'enchainment' of the pupil by the pedagogue's discourse in *Emile* is brilliantly analysed by Joan Dejean in *Literary Fortifications*, 137–61.

an argument, to ratify a chain of reasoning viewed from the *outside*. This clearly refers, in the second place, to a process of cause and effect through which shifts in mental attitude and understanding are wrought in Emile by the agency of external 'occasions'. It is hard to judge how passive Emile is in this process. What should be noticed, however, is the ambiguity of the 'chain'. There are potentially three chains involved here: of ideas, of feelings, and of sensations; the relative status of the three, and the problematic nature of their interaction, will be important in the context of 'enchaînement' in the *Confessions*. In *Emile* the chain of feelings is embryonic or hypothetical—the pedagogue's concern is to get results. But just as the notion of 'sentiment' extends beyond sensation to active process, so the idea of 'enchaînement', when it is not confined to reason, extends beyond purely semiotic or mechanistic relations to an active linking of one impression with the next. To pursue further the common ground between these two notions, let us look briefly at Rousseau's musical theory.

Rousseau's preference for melody over harmony contrasts two kinds of 'enchaînement'. In the case of harmony, which involves a closed system of formal relationships, 'enchaînement' is purely sensory and intellectual. Melody, however, reveals the fundamentally temporal nature of music, and involves a successiveness which is seen as the condition and not the antithesis of unity: 'il faut un sens, il faut de la liaison dans la musique ainsi que dans le langage; il faut que quelque chose de ce qui précède se transmette à ce qui suit, pour que le tout fasse un ensemble et puisse être appelé véritablement un'.[15] The melodic line involves a type of succession which is akin to that of discourse in its open unpredictable progress: 'la musique, étant un discours, doit avoir comme lui ses périodes, ses phrases, ses suspensions, ses repos, sa ponctuation de toute espèce'.[16] Here we have a form of 'enchaînement' which is conceived as open, active successiveness rather than as a function of abstract laws (though it depends also on these), and which is clearly linked to 'sentiment'. What, however, of narrative and temporality? Rousseau's ideas on music have often been invoked in connection with what could be called an 'anti-narrativist' view of his autobiographical writing. Jean Starobinski, invoking Rousseau's remarks on style in the Neuchâtel preamble (p. 1154), suggests that in surrendering to the flow of discourse Rousseau made writing the externalization of sentiment. To write 'musically' was to escape from history by making the past primarily a sounding-board for present emotion: the 'good' *enchaîne-*

---

[15] *Dictionnaire de musique*, quoted in J. Derrrida, *De la grammatologie*, 299. In the *Essai sur l'origine des langues*, Rousseau notes, 'Le champ de la musique est le temps', 160.

[16] *Dictionnaire de musique* (see n. 15). Cf. *Essai sur l'origine des langues*, 91.

ment of discourse offered redemption from the 'bad' *enchaînement* of past concatenations (the existence of which, Starobinski insists, Rousseau fully recognized).[17] Paul de Man, in contrast, argues that Rousseau's musical theory indicates his understanding that successiveness, in its essentially narrative and temporal modality, is inherently fictional; accordingly, for Rousseau to write his life as a narrative was knowingly to make it fictional rather than historical.[18] Arguing along similar lines, but dropping the emphasis on Rousseau's clearsightedness, Huntington Williams suggests that the congruence of music, language, and narrative in Rousseau's thought explains his attempt to employ an essentially successive medium to distil the timeless essence of his being; but for Williams, as for de Man, the nature of narrative makes this necessarily fictional.[19] For these critics the musicality of narrative *enchaînement* is a sign either of its consecration of the present of *énonciation*, or of its essentially fictive status; a sign, therefore, in either case, of its anti-historical character. A contrary view is provided by Lionel Gossman and Suzanne Gearhart. Gossman stresses Rousseau's 'acute

[17] When Rousseau, in writing of the past, consigns himself to language, 'le passé n'est plus ce lien et cet enchaînement qui paralysent l'instant présent, . . . la "source" est ici même, et non dans la vie révolue . . . Ainsi au lieu de se sentir produit par son passé, Rousseau découvre que le passé se produit et s'émeut en lui, dans le surgissement d'une émotion *actuelle*', *La Transparence et l'obstacle*, 233. For an interesting discussion of musicality and the self in Rousseau see P. Robinson, *Jean-Jacques Rousseau's Doctrine of the Arts*, 447–70.

[18] Against those who interpret Rousseau's ideas on musical language as confirming his belief in 'unmediated presence', de Man claims that Rousseau recognized the non-mimetic character of music, language, and narrative: 'Like music, language is a diachronic system of relationships, the successive sequence of a *narrative* . . . a succession of discontinuous moments that create the fiction of a repetitive temporality', *Blindness and Insight*, 131. De Man's critique centres on Derrida's discussion of the *Essai sur l'origine des langues* in *De la grammatologie*, especially 298 ff. Where Derrida sought to show how Rousseau's writings on music in fact conflict with his desire for immediate self-presence, de Man argues that Rousseau's preference for melody over harmony did not indicate a desire for representation and presence but a recognition that 'musical signs are unable to coincide; their dynamics are always oriented towards the future of their repetition, never toward the consonance of their simultaneity'.

[19] Williams argues that in the *Confessions* Rousseau sought by means of narrative to amalgamate a timeless sense of self—the self of suspended time and reverie—with the temporal dimension of his past existence. The role of narrative is not causal; Williams asserts that Rousseau's explanations undermine rather than foster causality and ultimately produce 'the very opposite of a narrative' (*Rousseau and Romantic Autobiography*, 133) but are allegorical and non-referential: 'Without regard to what it is actually "about", the narrative line of the text can be abstractly considered as the indeterminate, temporal boundary between two heterogeneous levels of the self', 145–6. For Williams narrative is temporal not because it manifests a commitment to the temporality of real events but because, by unfolding successively, it becomes 'a textual equivalent to the movement of time in the author's life' (p. 146). On this account narrative is eminently compatible with the 'sentiment de l'existence', but it is essentially an instrument of fiction.

awareness of history as the mode of being of all things', contending that the
Confessions constitute 'the application of the historical method to
understanding of the self', and that 'Rousseau seeks the unity of his
personality in the very pattern of its change and development'. Citing
Rousseau's theory of melody, Gossman observes: 'it is almost as though we
were listening to Rousseau talk of his *Confessions* and of the underlying unity
and meaning which are to be looked for in the history of the self', and he
suggests that we must resist the temptation to interpret Rousseau's
expression of a desire to escape from time as a denial of time and history.[20]

Figurative uses of 'chain' have been ubiquitous in European thought
since the seventeenth century. From Descartes and Hobbes to Saussure and
Lacan we find numerous uses of expressions such as 'chain of reasoning',
'chain of discourse', 'chain of proof', 'chain of events', 'chain of being',[21]
'chaîne parlante', 'chaîne des signifiants'. Three main areas—rationality,
physical and mental events, discourse—recur in these usages, and no doubt
the power of this figure derives partly from the fact that to use it in one field
is to allude implicitly to the others: the chain of discourse is closely related to
the events on which discourse bears and the rationality which makes
utterances comprehensible; to talk of a 'chain of events' is to see them as
logically related, and so on. Yet these orders remain relatively independent
and autonomous—at any point the gap between them may become
pertinent or perceptible: discourse can be perceived as independent of its
referents and as having its own rationality; rational categories can seem
heedless of empirical states of affairs, etc. A figure of connectedness, the
chain is, perhaps by that very token, also associated with disconnection, with
the artificial or arbitrary 'chaining off' of an area of reality by the illicit
independence of a particular ordering system. If one were Marshall

---

[20] L. Gossman, 'Time and History in Rousseau', 323. In *The Open Boundary of History
and Fiction* Suzanne Gearhart applauds de Man for showing that Rousseau was not a
'deluded primitivist', obsessed with a nostalgic longing for 'original' wholeness, but she
questions the critic's own denial of history and the way he extends it to Rousseau.
Demonstrating Rousseau's 'theatrical . . . conception of historicity' (at the 'origin', there is
always a 'scène'—one example is the 'bean-plot' in *Emile*—in which Nature and History
interact), she argues that 'As Rousseau describes it History . . . has two irreconcilable
meanings: it is both degradation and progress, and thus its movements cannot be described
by any continuous line, or even by several disparate series'; *Open Boundary*, 280. Essentially
paradoxical and problematic, Rousseau's sense of history is in no way incompatible with the
workings of narrative.

[21] In *The Great Chain of Being* H. Lovejoy argues that in the 18th cent. a new
consciousness of historical process was grafted on to the long-established notion of a static,
immutable 'chain of being' in which all things had their places. Cf. M. Raymond:
'Introduisant le temps en toute chose, le 18e a été fortement préoccupé par l'idée de genèse',
Œuvres complètes, iv, p. xii.

McLuhan one might say that the chain is at once a warm figure, connoting the suavity and comforts of organic concatenation, and a cool one, suggesting the rigid, lifeless order of the inorganic. As we shall see, these overlaps and ambiguities are all present in Rousseau's use of the word and indeed the ambivalence of the concept of the chain will emerge increasingly in what follows.

What, then, does Rousseau mean when he proposes to reveal an 'enchaînement d'affections secrètes' (p. 1149)? On the face of it the phrase verges on oxymoron, a scandalous yoking together of quite different terrains: public with private, rational with emotional. Yet these antitheses are already encompassed within, and ideally neutralized by, Rousseau's concept. 'Enchaînement' is double: rooted in the mechanical causality of sensualism, in the abstraction and impersonality of reason, in teleology, it connotes acknowledgement of external judgement, the perspective of the pedagogue, of the Other; associated with the successiveness of melody, the fluid, mobile fusion of difference and unity in the movement of music, it connotes the self's inner history and historicity. 'Enchaînement' is at the heart of Rousseau's project in the *Confessions* because it represents the possibility, the hope, that the two perspectives or contexts it combines could be reconciled in the form of a narrative. True, the balance it implies could scarcely be more precarious, and Rousseau no doubt found it impossible to maintain. But before we contemplate his ultimate failure we must attend fully to what may be regarded as his initial success.

II

Whatever its vicissitudes in the evolution of Rousseau's text, and whatever status we ultimately decide to give it, a coherent method, based on a developmental theory of individual life-history, is articulated in the *Confessions*. Expounded in methodological passages, as well as in the treatment of specific incidents and sequences of events, the method is portrayed and applied with gusto rather than diffidence, and represented, notably in the work's original preamble,[22] as one of the text's major originalities.

---

[22] The 1764 Neuchâtel MS of the early books of the *Confessions* began with a fascinating methodological discussion which Rousseau subsequently excised, *Œuvres complètes*, 1148–55.

Two passages set out Rousseau's principles particularly clearly:

Je n'ai qu'un guide fidèle sur lequel je puisse compter, c'est la chaîne des sentiments qui ont marqué la succession de mon être, et par eux celle des événements qui en ont été la cause ou l'effet . . . Je puis faire des omissions dans les faits, des transpositions, des erreurs de dates; mais je ne puis me tromper sur ce que j'ai senti, ni sur ce que mes sentiments m'ont fait faire; et voilà de quoi principalement il s'agit. L'objet propre de mes confessions est de faire connaître exactement mon intérieur dans toutes les situations de ma vie. C'est l'histoire de mon âme que j'ai promise, et pour l'écrire fidèlement je n'ai pas besoin d'autres mémoires: il me suffit, comme j'ai fait jusqu'ici, de rentrer au dedans de moi (p. 278).

Comme en général les objets font moins d'impression sur moi que leurs souvenirs, et que toutes mes idées sont en images, les premiers traits qui se sont gravés dans ma tête y sont demeurés, et ceux qui s'y sont empreints dans la suite se sont plutôt combinés avec eux qu'ils ne les ont effacés. Il y a une certaine succession d'affections et d'idées qui modifient celles qui les suivent, et qu'il faut connaître pour en bien juger. Je m'applique à bien développer partout les premières causes pour faire sentir l'enchaînement des effets. Je voudrais pouvoir en quelque sorte rendre mon âme transparente aux yeux du lecteur, et pour cela je cherche à la lui montrer sous tous les points de vue, à l'éclairer par tous les jours, à faire en sorte qu'il ne s'y passe pas un mouvement qu'il n'aperçoive, afin qu'il puisse juger par lui-même du principe qui les produit (pp. 174–5).

Making no reference to the existence of an original 'nature', Rousseau points to the interdependence and interaction of two chains: a chain of feelings and a chain of events, involved in a complex two-way process of causation, jointly underlie and attest what he calls 'la succession de mon être'. To the extent that feelings are the effects of events, we have to appreciate the situations Rousseau has been in to understand the feelings produced. But events themselves can be the effects of the chain of feelings, as well as causative agents (in the first passage, Rousseau refers to 'événements qui ont été la cause ou l'effet'). What counts above all is the process of combination and reciprocal modification, and this means that there can be no clear precedence of feelings over events, of origins over history, or vice versa:

Pour bien connaître un caractère il y faudrait distinguer l'acquis d'avec la nature, voir comment il s'est formé, quelles occasions l'ont développé, quel enchaînement d'affections secrètes l'a rendu tel, et comment il se modifie, pour produire quelquefois les effets les plus contradictoires et les plus inattendus. Ce qui se voit n'est que la moindre partie de ce qui est; c'est l'effet apparent dont la cause interne est cachée et souvent très compliquée (p. 1149).

When Rousseau talks of establishing a 'cause interne', or 'premières causes', he seems to have in mind a situation where an event constitutes neither an absolute beginning nor a simple catalyst for a pre-existent disposition, but some kind of fusion of the two—an original modification or disequilibrium. The idea of the 'trace' ('les premières traces de mon être sensible'; 'chaque trace entrée pour la première fois') expresses this ambiguity or doubleness: the event both makes and reveals a trace which can then be modified through combination with other feelings and events. Without the event there would be no opportunity for feeling and being to manifest themselves; without a prior surface there would be nothing for the event to modify or mark. This appears to be how Rousseau approaches the question of an original nature. Something original or prior is entailed by the transformative, dynamic, historical mechanism of 'enchaînement', but this 'something' only really comes into being in so far as it is modified. Human beings may possess an innate capacity for feelings, but without events to manifest (but also modify) them this capacity could theoretically remain in abeyance: 'Quoique cette sensibilité de cœur, qui nous fait vraiment jouir de nous, soit l'ouvrage de la nature, et peut-être un produit de l'organisation, elle a besoin de situations qui la développent. Sans ces causes occasionnelles, un homme né très sensible ne sentirait rien, et mourrait sans avoir connu son être' (p. 104). An event which functions as a 'cause occasionnelle' does not simply allow nature to reveal its hand, it may set off a process of continual modification. As Rousseau says (in the second of our initial quotations), he needs not only to identify 'les premières causes' but to retrace the chain-reaction they set in motion ('bien développer ... pour faire sentir l'enchaînement des effets'). The 'real' Rousseau is not, in terms of this theory, to be found underneath, to be reconstructed, even *ex hypothesi*, by filtering out the impurities and adulterations which have corrupted him; there is really no first edition to be purged of subsequent emendations and corruptions, only a palimpsest produced through the constant interaction and modification of new by old and old by new. Rousseau, in short, is his history. Moreover, 'Nature'—whatever is innate in Rousseau—may be *one,* but history, shaped by the haphazard occasions which determine what will be actualized and developed, makes the self plural, various. Rousseau implies that the dual master-chain of feelings and events is actually made up of a series of separate, interacting chains: by dint of the contingency of occasions, different aspects of what may have been given develop independently to differing degrees. If the product is still unified, it has the unity of a specific history, a particular combination, a 'bizarre et singulier assemblage' as Rousseau calls it. The phrase occurs in a passage from the Neuchâtel preamble where Rousseau asserts that he will need to invent 'un langage aussi nouveau que mon projet' if he is to untangle the 'chaos immense de sentiments si divers, si contradictoires' that he finds in himself; a multitude of details will be required if he is to follow out 'le fil de mes dispositions secrètes' and show 'comment chaque impression qui a fait trace en mon âme y entra pour la première fois'. Every detail is necessary, 'tant tout se tient, tant tout est un dans mon caractère, et tant ce bizarre et singulier assemblage a besoin de toutes les circonstances de ma vie pour être bien dévoilé' (p. 1153). The 'dévoilement' of this heterogeneous, historical unity demands the stylistic versatility and innovation appropriate to a task which could be identified as that 'synthèse de l'hétérogène' through which narrative, according to Paul Ricœur, is capable of enacting identity.

Before we turn to its application, a number of general observations can be made about the theory under discussion. First, as most of the passages I have quoted show, its articulation serves specific strategic purposes: it justifies the scandalous attention to extremely trivial or unsavoury details; and it offers an explanation of how, notwithstanding possible defects in Rousseau's memory of events, his record is reliable since, in so far as Rousseau is its product, the chain of feelings which is his first guide is still extant. Second, Rousseau's theory is *ad hoc* and *sui generis*: it applies first and foremost to his own, possibly unique, case; it does not depend on the application of general laws; and what it seems to derive from, say, Malebranche (the phrase 'causes occasionnelles'), or from the sensualist tradition, is transformed and absorbed. Third, in espousing the language of causality and induction (but not determinism or teleology) Rousseau is enthusiastic; to demonstrate 'enchaînement' is to perform a heuristic task of heroic proportions. When it is working smoothly, a euphoric concatenation of inner and outer, past and present is the writer's prize. Fourth, we need to recognize the innovatory power and potential validity of Rousseau's theory: the emphasis on the way early experiences remain alive within us, in modified and paradoxical forms, the way stress is placed on the balance between nature and nurture in the ontogenetic scheme, and on the difficulty of telling this complex story, are among the features which make Rousseau the great precursor that he is.

Thus, if we ignore for the moment factors which will tend ultimately to undermine and subvert the logic of 'enchaînement', we can admire the remarkable analytical skills Rousseau brings so often to the exploration of his history. For example, in accounting for the effects of precocious childhood reading (pp. 8–9) Rousseau carefully attends to a number of circumstantial factors—that there were two types of reading matter; that one kind, romances, had belonged to his mother but were read to him by his still mourning father; that this occurred just at the point when the child had reached the stage of individual self-consciousness—which make early reading the origin of a fundamental contradiction in his make-up, or else the point at which it first made itself manifest.[23]

The notion that the same elements can, in different combinations and circumstances, produce radically opposed effects is commented on in a passage which bridges two of the most notorious incidents in the *Confessions*: the spanking by Mademoiselle Lambercier which is held to have formed his sexual inclinations, and the unmerited beating by her father to which Rousseau traced the emergence of his sense of injustice (he had, falsely he claims, been accused of breaking a comb):

En remontant de cette sorte aux premières traces de mon être sensible, je trouve des éléments qui, semblant quelquefois incompatibles, n'ont pas laissé de s'unir pour produire avec force un effet uniforme et simple, et j'en trouve d'autres qui, les mêmes en apparence, ont formé, par le concours de certaines circonstances, de si différentes combinaisons, qu'on n'imaginerait jamais qu'ils eussent entre eux aucun rapport. Qui croirait, par exemple, qu'un des ressorts les plus vigoureux de mon âme fût trempé dans la même source d'où la luxure et la mollesse ont coulé dans mon sang? Sans quitter le sujet dont je viens de parler, on en va voir sortir une impression bien différente (p. 18).

Two very different things, corporal punishment and sexual pleasure, formed a bond which time has strengthened, producing 'uniformly' a powerful effect, colouring in fact the whole of Rousseau's sexual and sentimental life. Conversely, two superficially similar things, a spanking and a caning, have, owing to different circumstances, produced radically different effects: a vigorous sense of moral indignation as against a masochistic sexual persona.[24] The passage is striking for its characterization of the narrator as a prospector reporting on his finds ('je trouve', 'j'en trouve'), and for the power it attributes to the causal mechanism, especially perceptible in the word 'force'.[25] No less paradoxical than the alleged effect

[23] Rousseau hedges his bets when summing up the survey of his 'premières affections': 'ainsi commençait à *se former ou se montrer* en moi ce coeur à la fois si fier et si tendre' (12, italics added).

[24] The passage is brilliantly analysed in P. Lejeune's wide-ranging essay on the incident, *Le Pacte autobiographique*, 49–85. Also interesting is E. S. Burt, 'Developments in Character'.

[25] A version of the incident in the original MS (pp. 1155–8) makes no attempt to link it to the second beating except with reference to this very factor: 'La *force* qu'ont souvent les moindres faits de l'enfance pour marquer les plus grands traits du caractère des hommes' (p. 1157, italics added). Furthermore, this version, less elaborate in many respects, also refers more directly to the discovery process and the differential 'strength' of the causalities it establishes. The 'sensualité précoce' manifested so spectacularly in the incident is rather

of the spanking itself in determining Rousseau's sexual identity are its actual repercussions on his sexual behaviour. Contrary to what one might 'naturally' have expected ('ce qui devait s'ensuivre naturellement') Rousseau does not become debauched and sexually precocious. Too ignorant to recognize that his desires belong to the category of sexuality, desirous only of repeating the pleasure of being spanked, yet too timid to request this favour, Rousseau remained chaste and sexually inexperienced for far longer than boys with more normal desires. What ought to have spelt the end of innocence in fact prolonged it. 'Je vois le fil de tout cela' (p. 1155): Rousseau bemuses or irritates his readers by presenting as discovery and excavation what may seem more like invention and construction. Yet while we are eminently justified in attending to the present psychic needs at work in Rousseau's reconstructions, we need also to acknowledge his desire to understand the past. Whatever the ambiguities of 'enchaînement', Rousseau's treatment of sexual etiology, and of the interaction of sexuality with other aspects of human experience, in a host of incidents, compels admiration not only for its ingenuity but for its cogency.

Admirable, too, is Rousseau's ability to demonstrate the multiple pathways of causation at work in a given phase of his existence. A good example is the account of his apprenticeship as an engraver (pp. 30–43), which is at once circular, in that it traces a rapid degeneration followed by a return to some sort of norm; linear, in that it traces a chronological succession of phases each growing logically out of what precedes it; and static, in that it treats the whole period, and Rousseau's character in general, as a block, and analyses dialectically its constant tensions. Rousseau's initial response to the memory of how rapidly his personality changed during his spell with Monsieur Ducommun invokes 'la nature': 'Il faut que j'eusse un grand penchant à dégénérer' (p. 31); but the burden of the account places the blame firmly on the environment. The theme of covetousness emerges in the superb paragraph (p. 31) where Rousseau outlines the transformations in his character, and attributes them to the qualitative difference between a free environment and any form of enslavement. Coveting is associated with eating, talking, and looking, and these motifs will be maintained when covetousness gives way to theft. No longer among equals, Rousseau loses his tongue: both his verbal spontaneity when in a familial context, and his right to open his mouth at table are denied him. Privation leads him to covet

tentatively linked back to the 'lecture des romans', but its connection with the narrator's current self is powerfully affirmed: 'ce que je sais c'est qu'elle [la sensualité] influa sur le reste de ma vie, sur mes goûts, sur mes mœurs, sur ma conduite. Je vois le fil de tout cela' (p. 1155).

everything he sees, and this in turn leads to surreptitiousness and then to larceny.[26]

The account of his thefts proceeds in stages: stealing to please a companion, then other thefts of food, then of forbidden, and therefore coveted, articles. The escalation is partly prompted by the discovery that stealing is easy, and then, once he has been caught and punished, by the fact that the punishment itself seems to sanction the crime. Considerable space is devoted to a complex analysis of why Rousseau was never tempted to steal money. In the ardour of his desires Rousseau seeks immediate gratification; to have to ask for something is to create a fatal gap between desire and gratification which his imagination can fill with endless perils. Money implies a social transaction which forces desire into the open. How can others be the agents of my satisfaction: surely *they* will want to thwart its accomplishment, or to mock me for betraying my desire? Rousseau's account of his tribulations in a cake shop (p. 37) is both amusing and chilling.[27] Although it leads him away from his apprenticeship, Rousseau's account of his neurotic relationship with money is justified here since he shows that, although it has no specific origin or determining force, it stands at the intersection of various significant strands––his relation to others, to desire, to freedom, and so forth.

In the last 'movement' of the 'apprentissage' sequence (pp. 39–41) Rousseau's moral identity is reinvigorated by the rediscovery of the pleasures of reading. Another trait is postulated––that his passions and enthusiasms are as fickle as they are intense: one seemingly stable 'habitude d'être' can rapidly be replaced by another. In this case, circumstances (boredom) lead to the revival of a 'goût' (reading) which has survived Rousseau's decline to the status of 'vaurien'; a psychological tendency (the fickleness of Rousseau's passions) accounts for the fact that the activity of reading cures him of theft. As such, reading closes off a stage of Rousseau's life, completing a circle by fostering at least a partial moral regeneration. There is, however, a twist. Reading does not simply resurrect an old dispensation but, intervening in a new conjuncture, it sponsors another transformation of his character. Rousseau is now an adolescent tormented by his 'naissante sensualité', but incurious about the standard ways of

---

[26] The tendency to covet in silence and to be secretive about his desires is, we are told, a feature which will permanently mark Rousseau's character even when other traits manifested in this period have been liquidated. This assertion is typical of an analysis which frequently points to such indelible marks in the midst of what is otherwise transitional.

[27] I am indebted here to J. M. Coetzee's splendid analysis in his lecture *Truth in Autobiography*, 1–3.

assuaging it. This is owing to the peculiarities of his precocious experience of pleasure, and a timidity which even leads him to eschew salacious reading-matter because his supplier, La Tribu, hints off-puttingly at its delights. In the event his sensuality finds an outlet when Rousseau's imaginative faculty, stimulated by avid reading, and then starved by the exhaustion of La Tribu's supplies, 'prit un parti qui me sauva de moi-même', prompting him to find sublimation by placing himself in an 'état fictif' modelled on the kinds of situation he had read about. This does not determine, initially at least, a literary vocation, but 'un goût pour la solitude qui m'est toujours resté depuis ce temps là'. What starts off as the solution to a local problem ends up as a permanent character trait which will have the power to determine other events, characteristics, and (apparent) paradoxes. The affectionate, tender-hearted man, in adopting a diet of fictions, ends up looking like a lumpen misanthrope. This permanent effect brings the sequence to a close. The 'amour des objets imaginaires' is a penchant which has modified all Rousseau's passions, and in tracing the last phase of his 'apprentissage', Rousseau has brought to our attention its 'origine et première cause'.

III

What is so striking in the 'apprentissage' sequence is the subtle, complex hierarchy of relations it establishes between covetousness, theft, existence in the eyes of others, moral identity, the work of imagination; the interplay between inner and outer, immediacy and mediacy; the intricate structure of explanation erected around the intractable mixture of change and fixity in the self. Fixity arises less in terms of a desired self-image, an undialectical 'sentiment du moi' which Rousseau wishes to derive from and transpose back into his past experience, than in the way an individual's passage through time is apprehended both as a process of constant adjustment, mutation, malleability to external impressions and pressures, *and* as a constant circling around, and repetition of, basic structural patterns, fashioned in early experience, which recur at different points in the spiral of an existence. Rousseau's ambivalence about the relative weight of natural and acquired factors is itself a recognition of the temporal and composite character of personal identity. The 'apprentissage' exemplifies the strength and the vulnerability of Rousseau's narrative 'enchaînement'—the explicit tracking of causal processes—as theory and practice. Before looking at the maladies which may beset it, let me summarize what its healthy functioning depends on. First it depends on the maintenance of Rousseau's untrammelled authority over his discourse through the postulation of an unthreatening reader, a compliant narratee willing to remain *in statu pupillari*, as docile witness to the coherence of what is narrated. Second, it depends on the achievement of a fluid interplay of 'sentiments' and 'événements', and on Rousseau's confidence in being able to reconstruct the 'succession de [son] être' from this dual chain. Third, it requires that the act of narration, and the changing narrative situation in which Rousseau writes, remain relatively stable—good 'conductors' of the past rather than channels of present psychic turbulence.[28] If the well-being of Rousseau's project depends on these factors, each is also a risk area liable to health hazards.

As many episodes in the *Confessions* show, self-disclosure, the urge to get his story told, ran deep in Rousseau. But the spark to write came from a desire to exonerate himself in the face of accusations all the more wounding for being to a large extent imaginary. Rousseau confesses, and justifies himself, but God is not his true interlocutor. If at the outset he poses book in hand before the Almighty (p. 5), this is a first attempt to intimidate his potential accusers and to chasten his all-important imaginary audience, us, his readers, who must have a proper sense of our responsibility in the matter since for Rousseau the stakes are high. *He* is asking for a 'fair hearing', he wants the facts to 'speak for themselves': quasi-legal expressions of this sort seem appropriate to the ever-latent forensic, juridical framework which remains submerged for much of the time in the *Confessions* but emerges clearly, and painfully, in the later books. 'Je voudrais pouvoir en quelque façon rendre mon âme transparente aux yeux du lecteur' (p. 175): to be totally visible to the reader's eye; this is certainly a plea for immediacy, but its implication—Rousseau's basic innocence despite sometimes damning appearances—underlines the fact that, as the context makes clear, what needs to be made visible is the 'histoire de mon âme': an unbroken chain of

---

[28] A fourth factor needs to be considered separately. The cyclical structure of the 'apprentissage' sequence, a decline and fall followed by a 'resurrection', is a clear instance of the mythic or archetpyal patterns critics have identified in Rousseau's text, especially in the 'Livre premier' whose structure can be shown to have affinities with the myth of the 'Four Ages' (see especially M. Raymond, *La Quête de soi et la rêverie*, 91–115; P. Lejeune, *Le Pacte autobiographique*, 87–163). This aspect can evidently encourage us to read the *Confessions* as a fictional rearrangement of the past, modelled exclusively by the needs of the writing self. Yet it seems equally valid to see the mythic dimension of Rousseau's text—predominantly concerned with evolutionary phases—not simply as the outcome of ready-made schemes superimposed on the past but as the product of the narrative process itself, a product of 'enchaînement'. It would be one expression of the inescapable 'moment' of order and coherence which can never entirely fuse with, but does not obliterate, the stray threads and loose ends, the 'work' of interpretation.

experience with no gaps, no dark spaces, for Rousseau to hide in. Only a temporal, successive medium will do; but a medium, alas, in which what is on view is, first and foremost, the consistency of a discourse about the self. Unable to make his inner being manifest, as if in an anatomical diagram, Rousseau must conduct the anatomy lesson himself, and this leads to a first model of his relation to the reader: 'il y a une certaine succession d'affections et d'idées qui modifient celles qui les suivent, et qu'il faut connaître pour en bien juger. Je m'applique à bien développer partout les premières causes pour faire sentir l'enchaînement des effets' (p. 174). In this model Rousseau shoulders the burden of explanation and concatenation. His role is conveyed through active verbs ('bien développer', 'faire sentir'), while the reader's role is that of passive witness: the word 'juger' is here equivalent to 'convenir' and signifies informed assent. But a shift begins to occur in the last sentence of this paragraph:

Je voudrais pouvoir en quelque façon rendre mon âme transparente aux yeux du lecteur, et pour cela je cherche à la lui montrer sous tous les points de vue, à l'éclairer par tous les jours, à faire en sorte qu'il ne s'y passe pas un mouvement qu'il n'aperçoive, afin qu'il puisse juger par lui-même du principe qui les produit (p. 175).

Here the reality of the act of reading—as gaze, scrutiny, judgement—begins to exert its pressure. Rousseau's role is still cast in active terms ('rendre' seems to have active force; 'lui montrer'; 'l'éclairer') but this is now balanced by the reader's need to exercise independent judgement ('par lui-même') and by the advent of a new criterion of self-revelation, that of comprehensiveness: 'tous les points de vue . . . sous tous les jours . . . pas un mouvement'. The reader's act of judgement will involve the intellectual act of inferring the single spring ('[le] principe') which underlies and explains the diversity of 'movements'. The next paragraph carries the transfer of the burden of responsibility a stage further, as the opening words suggest. 'Si je me chargeais' implies 'je m'en décharge':

Si je me chargeais du résultat et que je lui disse: tel est mon caractère, il pourrait croire sinon que je le trompe, au moins que je me trompe. Mais en lui détaillant avec simplicité tout ce qui m'est arrivé, tout ce que j'ai fait, tout ce que j'ai pensé, tout ce que j'ai senti, je ne puis l'induire en erreur, à moins que je le veuille: encore même en le voulant, n'y parviendrais-je pas aisément de cette façon. C'est à lui d'assembler ces éléments et de déterminer l'être qu'ils composent: le résultat doit être son ouvrage; et s'il se trompe alors, toute l'erreur sera de son fait. Or il ne suffit pas pour cette fin que mes récits soient fidèles, il faut aussi qu'ils soient exacts (p. 175).

Here Rousseau gives a rather different picture of his role in the matter:

comprehensiveness has become his principal mission, while the duty of concatenation, as well as the burden of synthesizing the diverse into unity, now devolves on the reader. Comprehensiveness itself is conceived less in terms of diversity of viewpoints and approaches than of simple abundance and enumeration; the possibility of error on Rousseau's part is thus excluded. It is now the reader's business to construct a whole out of disparate parts ('assembler ces éléments') and to perform the tasks of moral assessment and analysis ('déterminer l'être qu'ils composent'). The symmetrical reversal suggested here, by which the active role of sense-making crosses over to the reader, while Rousseau takes on the passive one of simply providing *all* the evidence, is immensely revealing, and we shall return more than once to Rousseau's dealings with his imaginary audience. At this point two observations must be made. First, Rousseau's recognition of the reader owes its distinctive power to the fact that it involves a zone where his writing comes into contact with the real. Initially the reader is the anticipated and therefore internalized instance of the Other's perspective— a product of doubt and insecurity. But the reader in the text, accompanying the act of writing, is an ambivalent externalization of this instance: an object of seduction whose approval is desired, but also a demonized, malevolent agent to be neutralized. Second, Rousseau's authority over his discourse is threatened by 'molestation'[29] at the hands of a reader conceived as witness to the coherence of a discourse about the self. The greater the acknowledge-ment of the reader, the greater the fear that 'enchaînement' will be exposed as no more than a discourse, a product of reason, text rather than interiority.[30] The risk, which is at the heart of all the threats to Rousseau's project, must now be examined in the context of a second danger-area, Rousseau's treatment of incidents.

Rousseau clearly felt that comprehensiveness, the claim that nothing material had been omitted, was amply attested by the minute attention he paid to seemingly trivial incidents, a feature of the *Confessions* which has, for various reasons, amazed and frequently scandalized successive generations of readers. As he piles on the detail Rousseau proceeds as if nothing could better validate the fundamental coherence ('tout se tient') of his history than the demonstration of intricate continuities between remote events and his mature self. There are of course various kinds of incident in the *Confessions* and, as the work evolves, different rhythms arise from the mix of incidents

---

[29] The term was coined by E. Said in *Beginnings*, 83–4.
[30] A general treatment of the role of the reader will be found in R. J. Ellrich, *Rousseau and his Reader*. See also J. Voisine, 'Le Dialogue avec le lecteur dans *Les Confessions*'.

and analysis, singulative and iterative styles of narration, and from the different degrees to which incidents are analysed. To some extent, narrative rhythm or choreography reflects the influence of the fictional styles Rousseau adapted to his purpose. Yet in the *Confessions*, even at their most picaresque, incidents—of whatever kind—rarely seem merely colourful, illustrative, or factitious; they always tend to serve recognizable sense-making functions, revealing some aspect of the author. Rousseau specifically mentions this as a principle when, after the rigours of the 'fessée' and 'peigne cassé' episodes, he departs from it and offers us the gratuitous incident of the 'noyer de la terrasse' (p. 22). This is cited as an example of something that *we* do not need to know, but which Rousseau cannot resist telling us. Later autobiographers will often use this device to convey the spell of a long-lost past whose enduring enchantment is reactivated as it is recreated in writing. Rousseau displays here, as he often does in the early books of the *Confessions* (for example in his concern that he is rather too fond of remembering the lascivious charms of Mademoiselle Goton (p. 27)), an awareness that desire—the desire to repeat—propels autobiographical narration. But the suggestion that the reader's interests might be different from his own is perhaps wishful thinking, disguising the recognition that *we* need to know things to the very degree that *he* needs to tell them to us: the telling is what is revealing. Thus if the 'noyer de la terrasse' is no less interpretable than any other incident, the question it prompts is not whether a narrated event is revealing or not, or even how much of what an incident reveals is a function of how it is told, but rather how far Rousseau explicitly tries to control, through explanation, the meaning the incident is supposed to have. Later we shall consider incidents which are given considerable space and detailed attention without being drawn into the labyrinth of explanation, but at this point our concern is with those incidents which involve a close anaylsis of motive and disposition, which tend to disrupt rather than enhance continuity, and which draw attention to a potential gap between explanation and event rather than to their natural interaction.

Incidents in the *Confessions* often take on the character of self-contained narrative loops where the internal logic of an event, as much as its relation to what came before or after, seems to be what is at issue. At such moments, Rousseau often seems to be dealing with a knot of conflicts and unresolved feelings which block his path towards self-understanding, and the desire to engage with what perplexes him, to scrutinize these foreign bodies in his past, is central to the seminal originality of his autobiography. But if his aim at such points is to dissolve the obstacle, to liquidate it by dilution in the fluidity of narrative 'enchaînement', and in the seamless interplay of events and feelings, this absorption may be retarded or impeded to the extent that the desire to excuse prevails over the desire to understand. At times, the drive towards disavowal and self-exculpation becomes self-incriminating. Within the confines of the incident Rousseau's discourse swells up and becomes the inevitable focus of the reader's attention, with the result that what Rousseau finds hard to digest, the reader finds hard to swallow. Rather than restoring a hidden chain of feelings, Rousseau presents an elaborate chain of reasoning which, instead of closing the gap between event and disposition, turns it into a gaping hole. Feeling obliged to begin by separating appearances from meanings, Rousseau gives us, under the guise of the 'inside story', what seems more like a strategic defence against anticipated accusations. The explanation takes on the character of a plug trying to stem the flow, or a bandage to staunch a wound it succeeds only in reopening.

The classic instance is of course the incident of the stolen ribbon (pp. 84–7). Rather than reopen a dossier which has been investigated on numerous occasions,[31] I want to focus on one detail. Rousseau's submission is that while appearances condemned him, consideration of his 'dispositions intérieures' must lead to acquittal. Blaming the servant Marion for the theft he acknowledges he had committed looks like expediency, a ploy to get himself out of a tight corner and to overcome the terrible shame of being publicly accused in an unfriendly environment. But in fact, the explanation goes, Rousseau blurted out her name mechanically because it was the first thing that came into his head ('Je m'excusai sur le premier objet qui s'offrit' (p. 86)); and the terrible irony of the situation is that the reason why her name 'came to mind' was because he had intended to give the ribbon to her. Rousseau and Marion are both victims of pure coincidence: a benign link between the theft and Marion turned into a lethal one because of what happened when Rousseau was put on the spot. What is disturbing here is not so much the explanation as the fact that Rousseau thinks it excuses him. Moreover, if the explanation is of compelling interest and potential validity from a psychological point of view, it only conforms to Rousseau's aim of indicating his inner disposition in so far as it points to a radical incoherence. What we may see as an expression of unconscious desire for Marion, Rousseau is forced to present as an unfortunate associative process where two trains of thought fatally collide. Rousseau does not really incorporate his act as a symptom of his mental life; rather, he tries to expel it as a foreign

---

[31] See especially P. de Man, *Allegories of Reading*, 278–301; M. O'Dea, 'The Double Narrative of the Stolen Ribbon'; P. Lejeune, *Le Pacte autobiographique*, 52–6.

body: he was not himself at this moment, the action was other and must remain so.[32] The incident, in other words, does not foster Rousseau's project of demonstrating the fluid interplay of inner and outer so much as subvert it, pointing to an uncontrollable logic whereby inner and outer meanings can only be reconciled by attributing a malevolent power to the circumstantial.

IV

It follows from what we have said about the reader, and about incidents, that the discourse of explanation itself, in its potential autonomy, is a danger area for the project of 'enchaînement'. From the start, as Rousseau sets out to explore the 'labyrinthe obscur et fangeux' (p. 18) of his past, there is a fear that the abstract language of causalities, the chain of pure reason, will develop its own momentum. From Rousseau's point of view at least, this tendency is kept in check for much of the time in the early books of the *Confessions*. In the case of the 'fessée', the 'peigne cassé', or the 'apprentissage', explanation, even as it ramifies into complex patterns, seems a natural outgrowth of the narrative reappropriation of the past. Yet this depends on a precarious equilibrium which, as is amply demonstrated in the later books of the *Confessions*, to which we must now turn, could easily be upset.

The ninth book of the *Confessions*, which concerns Rousseau's stay at L'Hermitage in 1856–7, offers striking testimony, although sadly *a contrario*, that the 'enchaînement' of feeling and event was vital to his autobiographical project. Here Rousseau is unable to give a coherent account of events and, as a result, is unable to reconstruct an inner chain of feelings. The various strands of his narrative—factual, analytical, emotional—seem to come apart and, instead of blending, to evolve independently of each other. The facts are in one sense straightforward. Rousseau settles at L'Hermitage in spring 1756 with his wife Thérèse and her mother, and initially finds an agreeable balance between solitude and social existence after the turbulent years in Paris. However, a disastrous infatuation with his patron's sister Sophie D'Houdetot, and the personal intrigues surrounding the affair, disrupt this serenity, lead to his departure from the house after a relatively brief stay, and mark the beginnings of what Rousseau will come to

---

[32] This is of course not the only occasion when Rousseau disavows his actions, claiming that he was 'not himself' at the time. Cf. e.g. the 'Vaussore de Villeneuve' episode where Rousseau alludes to 'des moments de délire inconcevable où je n'étais plus moi-même' (p. 148).

see as a widespread plot against him. Facts, in this conjuncture, harden into impenetrable clues, and a massive edifice of speculation grows on their slight foundations. As a visible manifestation of this process, Rousseau's text comes to be cluttered with relics of the period in the form of notes and letters exchanged by the protagonists, arrayed for the reader's perusal in the hope that he or she might explain what the author cannot.

Appropriately enough, both the theoretical dimension of Rousseau's discourse and its novelistic aspects underline separation and autonomy rather than fusion. Rousseau's account (pp. 408–9) of his projected treatise, *La Morale sensitive*, provides an ironic parallel to his current situation. Based on the postulate that force of circumstance often makes human beings 'dissemblables à eux-mêmes', the treatise would have outlined a 'régime intérieur' designed to help us recognize and avoid the sensory stimuli which can dominate our feelings in ways antithetical to our true identities. Causality here seems like a virulent force against which we need to inoculate ourselves. Ironically, Rousseau goes on to describe a chronic, and possibly incurable, outbreak of 'dissemblance' in himself. One of its symptoms, the affair with Sophie, is said to stem from over-exposure to the power of fictional emotions engendered through imagining and writing *La Nouvelle Héloïse*. To encounter Sophie in these circumstances was to be drawn fatally to satisfy in reality feelings which until then had seen fruition only on paper (p. 440). Rousseau's use of novelistic devices in his account of the episode— suspense, *mise en scène*, the language of passion and destiny—does not so much illuminate the events as cast them in an ironic light. Self-dissociation emerges as the central theme of this period, and is consistently used as a device in Rousseau's attempt to reconstruct it. With his arrival at L'Hermitage all seemed set for Rousseau to become himself again after years of 'dissemblance' in the role of writer on the Parisian scene. However, thrown back on himself, he sought consolation in the world of imagination, and this disposed him to fall madly in love: the sober 'citoyen' becoming a 'berger extravagant'—every bit as unlike himself as the writer 'enivré de vertu'. The evolution of Rousseau's feelings is given the character of a self-propelling machine, producing a Rousseau who is not himself. Like a jack-in-the-box he is continually expelled from himself (by the 'vifs et continuels élans que fait hors de lui-même un cœur sensible' (p. 468)), then fleetingly reintegrated ('Je revins à moi' (p. 441)) when alone.[33] The recurrent words

---

[33] He externalizes and personifies his passion as a crafty agent able to profit from a knowledge of his weaknesses: 'Coupable sans remords, je le fus bientôt sans mesure et, de gràce, qu'on voie comment ma passion suivit la trace de mon naturel, pour m'entraîner enfin

'folie', 'ivresse', 'délire', 'extravagance', punctuate an account which demonstrates how a variety of factors, internal and external, conspire to transform a wholly unpropitious and unrequited infatuation into a passion without precedent in Rousseau's life. The 'révolution' in his existence, which ought to have restored him to himself, does no such thing:

> Si la révolution n'eût fait que me rendre à moi-même, et s'arrêter là, tout était bien; mais malheureusement elle alla plus loin, et m'emporta rapidement à l'autre extrême. Dès lors mon âme en branle n'a plus fait que passer par la ligne de repos, et ses oscillations toujours renouvelées ne lui ont jamais permis d'y rester (p. 417).

If Rousseau's 'âme en branle' will now experience perpetual motion, it is partly owing to the fact that what he dubs a 'revolution' was a climacteric which, he believes, transformed his existence. He is unable to separate his emotional trajectory in the months at L'Hermitage from an obsessive sense that everything he did at this time was a false step, that he was the ignorant plaything of malevolent manipulators, and that the game led to what, at the time of writing, he regarded as a wretched and definitive state of victimization. Rousseau's account here constantly points to an interaction between feelings and events, but of a sort which makes both ultimately unfathomable. It is by turns comic and painful to watch him rake over his memories trying to find, like the needle in the haystack, the point at which his downfall became irrevocable. The identification of turning points is a prominent feature of the *Confessions*. But here, so pronounced is his retrospective sense that every step he took was probably a *faux pas* responsible for subsequent misfortunes, Rousseau constantly designates acts and omissions which he thinks may have been harbingers of disaster, originators of 'la longue chaîne de mes malheurs'.[34] His uncertainty as to exactly which moment or action to designate as the first cause of his later misfortune may be contrasted with his absolute conviction that the subsequent course of his life, up to and including the time of writing,

---

dans l'abîme' (p. 442). Taking advantage of its knowledge of his character, passion adopts the guise of humility, and even spoilt pride, the better to enmesh the poor 'citoyen' in its nets.

[34] He even blames his idleness, once he had completed his study of the Abbé de Saint-Pierre: 'cet intervalle de désœuvrement fut ma perte' (p. 424). The tendency becomes chronic in the account of the last phase of the stay, which is heralded by these ominous words: 'mais il est temps d'en venir à la grande révolution de ma destinée, à la catastrophe qui a partagé ma vie en deux parties si différentes et qui d'une bien légère cause a tiré de si terribles effets' (p. 474). The catastrophe referred to here (relating to Rousseau's failure to accompany Mme D'Epinay to Geneva) is by no means the first claimant for the title of *the event* which changed everything, after which nothing was ever the same again: the announcement of the Dijon prize, the adoption of the 'réforme personnelle', the events of spring 1756, have all already been labelled the origin of the chain of Rousseau's misfortunes.

constitutes a continuous fabric ('tissu'), a closely knit causal and successive entity, in other words a *chain*. Yet the uncertainty about its origin, or its 'première origine', is reflected in Rousseau's inability to follow through and reconstruct this chain. If this is primarily a chain of events, feelings are certainly entwined with it, but in this case Rousseau cannot unravel the two strands. In a sense the point Rousseau is seeking to identify in his past life has as its (equally elusive) correlative the point when the *Confessions* cease to be conceived as the confident reconstitution of a hidden chain of feelings, and become the anguished attempt to unravel a secret chain of misfortunes—secret now, not because Rousseau alone (prior to the act of writing) has access to it, but because crucial links are kept secret from Rousseau himself. There could scarcely be a fitter symbol of his sense of a total reversal of destiny than the way in which the same word is the emblem of self-knowledge and transparency, and of self-loss and opacity. If the figure of the chain still expresses the conviction that, beneath the surface inconsistencies, the apparent haphazardness and unruliness of the individual's existence, there lies a fundamental coherence, Rousseau's fate will be to experience the obverse of his own law, and to know exclusion from, and by, the chain he has postulated.

To write autobiography, for the Rousseau of the *Confessions*, is to engender a chain-reaction which keeps meaning moving from link to link as blood circulates in a healthy organism. Sickness may be defined as the state when meaning no longer circulates, when the chain breaks, disappears, or changes its status. Of course there is paranoia here, and a grating tone which alienates easy sympathy, if it provokes pity. But there is great poignancy in a passage such as the following:

En narrant donc les événements qui me regardent, les traitements que j'ai soufferts, et tout ce qui m'est arrivé, je suis hors d'état de remonter à la main motrice, et d'assigner les causes en disant les faits. Ces causes primitives sont toutes marquées dans les trois précédents livres; tous les intérêts relatifs à moi, tous les motifs secrets y sont exposés. Mais dire en quoi ces diverses causes se combinent pour opérer les étranges événements de ma vie; voilà ce qu'il m'est impossible d'expliquer, même par conjecture. Si parmi mes lecteurs il s'en trouve d'assez généreux pour vouloir approfondir ces mystéres et découvrir la vérité, qu'ils relisent avec soin les précédents livres; qu'ensuite à chaque fait qu'ils liront dans les suivants ils prennent les informations qui seront à leur portée, qu'ils remontent d'intrigue en intrigue et d'agent en agent jusqu'aux premiers moteurs de tout, je sais certainement à quel terme aboutiront leurs recherches, mais je me perds dans la route obscure et tortueuse des souterrains qui les y conduiront (pp. 589-90).

This extraordinary invitation to a form of reader participation in which one would help the author prove his case by securing the information he suspected but could not prove, and by completing the chain he could imagine but not reproduce, offers striking testimony to the power of the idea of causality in Rousseau's mind. Here things have fallen apart: causalities abound, but because the interconnections between them cannot be grasped, the various causal chains—actions or events, 'sentiments', theories or axioms, reasons, the code of the *romanesque*—are like autonomous circuits. Each is coherent in its own terms, and theoretically compatible with the others, but there is no aggregate, no Jean-Jacques, only a series of Rousseaus. What has brought this about? What is missing? Why is Rousseau unable to make the connections on which his narrative depends?

As the passage just quoted poignantly shows, the question of the Other is at the heart of this. The place of understanding, the line of perspective, has abandoned Rousseau to become the prerogative of the threatening crowd. This is partly for circumstantial reasons (the idea of a plot), and partly a consequence of trying to report on a relatively recent period. Rousseau tells us (pp. 114–15) that for him understanding is linked to rumination rather than spontaneous revelation. Experience becomes comprehensible when there is no more input, when he can close down the shutters and allow connections to form. The sifting and decanting which, for Rousseau, are the offices of memory require a significant lapse of time; more recent events, still alive in the present, fall outside the realm of remembrance.

With the period covered in book 9, recapitulation has no firm point at which to begin or end, and surveys a terrain strewn with the impenetrable machinations of others. The 'enchaînement' of narrative no longer offers a way of negotiating the treacherous border area between a subjective intuition of self and its objective history. The chain is broken: the possibility of a narrative identity derived from a 'synthèse de l'hétérogène' is suspended. Rousseau's project falters and founders when he attempts to deal with a situation in which he is denied a sense of the compliance of the Other. He needed to imagine the collusion of a pre-defined reader, and therefore to submit the Other to his control; but he also depended on the illusion that the reader was a free agent, exercising independent judgement. Writing about a period dominated by the unfathomable designs of others, Rousseau loses control over his narrative; his narrative identity loses its foundations, and the heterogeneity of its ingredients—theory, fiction, psychological analysis, narrative shape—becomes apparent. The paranoia which accompanies this shift may be peculiar to Rousseau, but the factors which underlie it are perhaps endemic to the genre he is inventing: inscribed in the small print of the autobiographical contract, which he is the first to draw up explicitly, is the codicil that, from the point of view of the practitioner, autobiographical narrative requires the sanction of the Other; the sense of the compatibility, the fluid interplay, of an inner chain of feelings and an outer chain of causally linked events, is ultimately dependent on an intersubjective paradigm, a scene of mutual recognition in which the self *I* vouchsafe already acknowledges (and assumes that it is in turn acknowledged by) *your* scrutiny. When this is lacking, narrative risks grinding to a halt; unsanctioned, it becomes rigid and arbitrary, wholly the province of the Other: a chain *out there* which shuts out a subjectively determined self, condemning it to autistic entrapment and paranoia. This is the drama played out with increasing intensity in the last pages of the *Confessions*.

While Rousseau occasionally clings to the coat-tails of a potentially beneficent reader, his narrative comes increasingly to record the sway of a 'ligue', a 'système' (p. 492) pitted against him—specific individuals and groups who personify a generalized hostile otherness which checks Rousseau's every move and prevents him from being himself. Ultimately the text can no longer sustain this deadlock: only a direct confrontation can answer Rousseau's desire for self-ratification (and absolution). As his text itself threatens to become another bone of contention between the author and his imagined accusers, he must provide it with the ultimate sanction of its truth: his own living presence as the voice which animates it. Curtailing his narrative abruptly, Rousseau arranges to read his text aloud to small circles of admirers and patrons, but succeeds only in provoking embarrassment: 'J'achevai ainsi ma lecture, et tout le monde se tut. Mme. Egmont fut la seule qui me parut émue; elle tressaillit visiblement, mais elle se remit bien vite et garda le silence, ainsi que toute la compagnie. Tel fut le fruit que je tirai de cette lecture et de ma déclaration' (p. 656).

The *Confessions* end with this curt (and infinitely ironic) account of their first reception; the text was never to be resumed. Rousseau will not abandon autobiography, but non-narrative strategies will predominate in subsequent works. The imaginary dialogues of *Rousseau juge de Jean Jacques* build the reader/Other into the textual edifice,[35] and lay on for his benefit a *mise en scène* over which Rousseau exercises total control, a 'scène' designed to demonstrate and thus eradicate the possibility of conflicting views of his character. Finally, in the *Rêveries*, Rousseau relaxes his control: the past and

---

[35] On this see Williams, *Rousseau and Romantic Autobiography*, 149–65, 205–14. Williams also has some excellent remarks on the hostile 'ligue'—the 'chain-like configuration of malevolent individuals' (p. 210)—in the *Confessions*.

the world of others become distant satellites as the *promeneur* loses himself in the present, striving to be a man without a history.

v

In putting the case for an historical sense of self, rooted in temporal processes, and relatively congenial to narrative, as an essential feature of the *Confessions*, I have also sought to demonstrate how difficult it was for Rousseau to sustain his project on this basis. Although the concept of 'enchaînement' was not narrowly based on mechanical causality, its inherent ambivalence, and the precarious balancing-act its successful application required, ensured the ever-present risk that it might ultimately be diverted into an obsession with causes and effects. The device which helped Rousseau to construe his early years as a complex process of modifications became, when applied to a period dominated by the imagined designs of others, instrumental in the depiction of Rousseau's experience as a nightmare zone of coercive but impenetrable causal chains. The wholesale adoption of a sense of self located outside causality, and beyond narrative, can be seen as an attempt to cast off those chains.

But there is, I now want to suggest, another side to the story, another variation or development of 'enchaînement'—deriving from the attenuation rather than the exacerbation of its causal aspect—which plays a significant role throughout the *Confessions*. The relation between past episodes and present being, the interaction of feelings and events, and the successiveness of narrative are still essential, and the historicity of the self is still implied. But in the passages I have in mind the event is responded to not as something to be explained causally, or reorganized analytically, so much as described in detail, attended to in its own unfolding. In one of his critiques of causal explanations, Wittgenstein suggests that these are often a poor substitute for what he calls 'perspicuous presentation' which 'makes possible that understanding which consists in seeing the connections'.[36] A passage in Rousseau's autobiographical 'Lettres à Malesherbes', which predate and anticipate the *Confessions*, is relevant here. Of two contradictory components in his character (an 'âme paresseuse' and an excessive sensibility) Rousseau notes that while he is unable 'de résoudre cette

---

[36] 'Remarks on Frazer's *Golden Bough*', 36. For the application of Wittgenstein's notion to speculation about lives I am indebted to Frank Cioffi, and especially to his article, 'When Do Empirical Methods Bypass "The Problems Which Trouble Us"?'

opposition par des principes', 'J'en puis donner par les faits une espèce d'historique qui peut servir à la concevoir' (p. 1134). This is the kind of historical understanding through description which must now be investigated with reference to two of Rousseau's encounters with women.

The episode concerning Madame Basile in the 'Livre second' (pp. 75–7) is given a temporal context and a diagnostic status by virtue of being presented, on the one hand, as an initiation ('les prémices') into 'les plus doux ainsi que les plus purs plaisirs de l'amour' (p. 73), and, on the other hand, as a first manifestation of what was to be the very form of Rousseau's subjectivity as a lover, marked by 'une . . . folie romanesque dont jamais je n'ai pu me guérir . . . j'aimais trop sincèrement, trop parfaitement, j'ose dire, pour pouvoir aisément être heureux' (p. 77). But it is the precise description and contextualization of the incident which give it its global meaning and power. Rousseau describes how, initially, the mixture of coquetry and modesty in Madame Basile, coupled with timidity and inexperience on his part, resulted in the boy's ardour being exclusively channelled into the act of *looking* without being observed: 'Je dévorai d'un œil avide tout ce que je pouvais regarder sans être aperçu: les fleurs de sa robe, le bout de son joli pied . . . etc.' (p. 74). These intermittent glimpses of parts of the body have a powerful physical effect on the boy, accentuated when his accompanying sighs seem echoed by the woman's, but no explicit communication of any sort acknowledges anything between them. It is this embargo which is broken in the central incident Rousseau reconstructs. He had followed her up to her room, found the door ajar, entered without being seen, observed her sewing by the window and, finding her charms particularly overwhelming, had thrown himself on his knees, with arms outstretched, certain that he could neither be seen nor heard (because of the noise of the street below). In fact Madame Basile had observed him in a mirror over the chimney-piece, and without word or glance she had pointed to the mat at her feet. Rousseau sprang up and knelt beside her but found himself unable to press his advantage, while she too was incapable of further action. Only when 'cette scène si vive et muette' is about to be interrupted by the maid is the silence broken: Rousseau seizes her hand and kisses it twice, detecting on her part a slight pressure of the fingers on his lips.

What is striking about the incident is how much is communicated and how little actually stated. If it demonstrates the expressive power of a tiny silent gesture—Madame Basile's 'petit signe du doigt'—it also shows how expressive an incident can be when allowed to speak for itself. Every detail of the central scene is crucial to its meaning, but the details are not enveloped in an explanatory discourse so much as placed exactly in their succession. The body language of the two protagonists—movements, gestures, postures—is rendered with great accuracy, and accompanying nuances of feeling are conveyed with precision. The interpretation of emotions is closely tied to, and implicitly deduced from, silent gesture.[37] Although the context enables us to read it in terms of Rousseau's life-history as a whole, the incident is treated in a way that encourages the reader to continue the process through which meaning is intuited from action and gesture. The silent language of the body, and the tacit communication between subjectivities which bears meaning and solicits interpretation, leaves a margin for further interpretation. Yet it also creates a limit: what the reader may continue is not so much speculation around the incident as further attentiveness to what is given in it, to its suggestiveness. The process I am seeking to describe is not inconsistent with the exploration of causality. An incident rendered in a way which prompts us to scrutinize it attentively certainly draws us towards something irreducible in it, but it does so by inviting an exactitude in our perception of the relationships between one moment or detail and the next, between parts and whole, and thence to extrapolate from these relations internal to the incident to the continuous process of the life of which this is a moment.

My second example is Rousseau's fiasco with the Venetian courtesan Zulietta (pp. 317–22).[38] A fairly straightforward explanation is supplied: Rousseau's 'mauvaise tête', his restless, suspicious mind, made him suspect some defect in Zulietta: when she proves to have a 'téton borgne' he overreacts, sees her as monstrous, and thus deprives himself of the 'jouissance' which awaited him. But if the psychological mechanism (a tendency to find obstacles to desire, amply attested in other episodes) is

---

[37] The interplay of feelings is superbly expressed: the mixture of fervour and excruciating embarrassment in the adolescent: 'j'étais muet, immobile, mais non pas tranquille assurément: tout marquait en moi l'agitation, la joie, la reconnaissance, les ardents désirs incertains dans leur objet et contenus par la frayeur de déplaire sur laquelle un jeune cœur ne pouvait se rassurer'; the suggestion of the way gestures betray the woman's disquiet at having, perhaps unpremeditatedly—'d'un signe parti sans doute avant la réflexion'— provoked a response she finds herself unable to reciprocate. On gestures in Rousseau see J. Starobinski's admirable analysis of the 'Dîner de Turin' (*Confessions*, 94–6) in *La Relation critique*, 105–52.

[38] The episode seems greatly to have appealed to the most illustrious of Rousseau's immediate successors in the field of autobiography. 'Je me dis: je suis en Italie, c'est-à-dire dans le pays de la *Zulietta* que J. J. Rousseau trouva à Venise, en Piémont dans le pays de Mme Bazile': Stendhal, *Vie de Henry Brulard*, 421. 'Ma scène du matin à Venise me fait encore souvenir de l'histoire du Capitaine Olivet et de Zulietta, si bien racontée' (followed by extensive quotation): Chateaubriand, *Mémoires d'outre-tombe*, iv. 360. See also P. P. Clément, *J. J, Rousseau: De l'éros coupable à l'éros glorieux*.

revealing, the way it manifests itself in this concrete instance is even more so. In fact everything about the event is revealing, as Rousseau implies in the remarkable paragraph that he places on the brink of the crucial scene:

S'il est une circonstance de ma vie qui peigne bien mon naturel, c'est celle que je vais raconter. La force avec laquelle je me rappelle en ce moment l'objet de mon livre me fera mépriser ici la fausse bienséance qui m'empêcherait de le remplir. Qui que vous soyez, qui voulez connaître un homme, osez lire les deux ou trois pages qui suivent: vous allez connaître à plein J. J. Rousseau (p. 320).

The bluff tone contrasts comically with the bathos which is to come, but despite this the reader is not summoned to assent to a demonstration so much as to witness the unfolding of an event. 'Connaître à plein J. J. Rousseau' will here involve attention to a detailed synoptic presentation which will combine several threads of meaning. This is borne out by Rousseau's close attention to the context and framing of the incident. The sequence begins with two minor episodes which prefigure what is to come: captivated by the beautiful voices of the *Scuole*, Rousseau is horrified to find the girls, without exception, afflicted by some physical defect. But a train of thought reverses this reaction and he ends up finding them beautiful despite their ugliness. His first visit to a courtesan in Venice is the fruit of 'une de ces inconséquences que j'ai peine à comprendre moi-même' (p. 317). Although it has been arranged by his 'enemy', Vitali, Rousseau keeps his assignation with La Padoana, '*per non parer troppo coglione*'. He is also forced to keep up appearances when La Padoana refuses to take money for nothing; cursing his rashness, convinced he has contracted the pox, Rousseau is eventually reassured by one of the doctors he consults. Again most of the action takes place in his mind ('Je ne pouvais concevoir qu'on pût sortir impunément des bras de la Padoana'): preconceptions, misgivings, afterthoughts leave little room for much else to happen.

The circumstances in which Rousseau encounters Zulietta hardly seem auspicious. Invited to dine on board ship by a French sea captain, Rousseau is put out that, as ambassadorial secretary, he is not accorded a ceremonial salute. As he sulks during the meal, a gondola draws up bearing a beautiful woman; in no time ('en trois sauts') she is seated beside Rousseau, talking, eating, and making eyes at him. Suddenly she kisses him on the mouth and, addressing him as 'mon cher Brémond', says how thrilled she is to see him again. Everything about the scene is ambiguous. Rousseau is clearly aware that he has been set up by Captain Olivet and his companions, and that the mistake over his identity may be a ruse to speed up the proceedings. At this point the intensity of his desire clearly predominates over any wish to acknowledge the reality of the situation—all the more so since his tastes as a lover are generously catered for by its equivocal nature. The description emphasizes Zulietta's vivacity and the power of her assault on Rousseau: he has no time to think as she takes command, turning him into a submissive puppet: 'Elle prit possession de moi comme d'un homme à elle, me donnant à garder ses gants, son éventail, son *cinda*, sa coiffe; m'ordonnait d'aller ici où là, de faire ceci ou cela, et j'obéissais' (p. 319). If this appeals to Rousseau's taste for the passive role in amorous relationships, the confusion about identities also creates the kind of situation which stimulates his desires. Rousseau is already 'ivre ou plutôt furieux' with desire by the time Zulietta chooses to explain her mistake, and the terms in which she does so maintain its essence: she adopts Rousseau as a substitute for the man she claims to have taken him for, and describes the role he will have to fulfil. Rousseau's summary of her breathless, dizzying tirade, with its astounding range of tenses, makes it clear why her words achieve the desired effect: 'Ce qui fut dit fut fait' (language is highlighted throughout the episode). All this takes place in front of Captain Olivet and Carrio, the Spanish secretary, but in this context the presence of others seems to intensify rather than inhibit desire, perhaps because, while he is unable to do other than play his appointed role in the scenario laid on by his host, the very intensity of his desires gives Rousseau a sense of imaginary authority, particularly since the point of the scenario seems to be to put his virility to the test. Captain Olivet had heralded Zulietta's arrival with the enigmatic words 'Voici l'ennemi', and the courtesan's whispered confabulation with Carrio (at which Rousseau does not bridle), where she perhaps takes fresh instructions, is followed by her warning that a good performance will be expected of the French Ambassador's secretary, whom she addresses familiarly as 'Zanetto' (thus adding to the list of pseudonyms Rousseau aquires in the *Confessions*). Rousseau plays up to these expectations when, after an excursion to Murano, he spies a pair of pistols on Zulietta's dressing-table: 'Ah! Ah! dis-je en en prenant un, voici une boîte à mouches de nouvelle fabrique; pourrait-on savoir quel en est l'usage? Je vous connais d'autres armes qui font feu mieux que celles-là' (p. 319). The fatuous, cocksure tone, uncharacteristic of Rousseau, again draws attention to language and places the scene squarely in a novelistic register, as does Zulietta's spirited rejoinder to the effect that she will shoot the first man who does not satisfy her.

Apparently undaunted by this intimidating prospect, Rousseau eagerly keeps his personal appointment with Zulietta, who greets him in a 'déshabillé plus que galant' decked with pink pompoms he remembers only too well. The description underlines the idyllic prospect. What goes wrong? A striking feature of Rousseau's account is that his rationalizations are never allowed to invalidate the complex, ambiguous evidence provided by his detailed reconstruction of the event. Before we know what happened we are told, rather vaguely, 'la nature ne m'a point fait pour jouir. Elle a mis dans ma mauvaise tête le poison de ce bonheur ineffable dont elle a mis l'appétit dans mon cœur' (p. 320). But as is implied in the paragraph quoted earlier, which immediately follows, the revelatory character of the episode transcends any straightforward verdict. If the general idea of a compulsive psychological proclivity to self-conscious suspicion and doubt is asserted unequivocally, its *modus operandi* is shown to involve a range of psychological, physiological, and social factors which embrace many other aspects of Rousseau's make-up as progressively delineated in the *Confessions*. If Rousseau gives hostages to fortune, making room for interpretations other than his own, this is here a consequence of a willingness to pursue—descriptively—the ramifications of an episode, suggesting paradoxical and irrational aspects of his character. Thus, Rousseau's description of his initial 'défaillance' ('Tout à coup, au lieu des flammes qui me dévoraient, je sens un froid mortel courir dans mes veines, les jambes me flageolent, et, prêt à me trouver mal, je m'assieds, et je pleure comme un enfant') has prompted suspicions that the fiasco should be attributed to sexual incontinence rather than psychological malaise. Rousseau certainly does not acknowledge this, but in focusing on the practical applications rather than the aetiology of his psychological mechanism, and in showing it to take the form of a compulsion to find an obstacle to the consummation of his desire, to find fault with Zulietta, he reveals a desire to displace the blame from himself to another.

The transcript of 'ce qui me passait par la tête' at the moment of 'défaillance' ('Je me disais: cet objet dont je dispose est le chef-d'œuvre de la nature . . .' (p. 321)) is unconvincing as an explanation of what caused it, but in its hollow rhetoric and *ad hoc* rationalization, it rings true as a symptom of the transfer of blame. As such it suggests that, throughout the episode, both at the time and in the reconstruction, Rousseau's access to 'what went through his head'—his 'dispositions intérieures'—comes in the wake of the physical evidence which is primal: gestures, tones of voice, bodily signals, including of course the malformed nipple which irresistibly catches his attention and thus prompts the sexual fiasco. Rousseau interprets his unfortunate fixation on the 'téton borgne' as an expression of his need to find a 'défaut', and he emphasizes the expenditure of mental energy ('me voilà cherchant dans ma tête . . .'; 'à force de tourner et retourner cette idée . . .') which leads to the idea that Zulietta is a freak. To some degree one may feel that Rousseau is thereby sterilizing the incident, diverting attention from the truth of desire. Yet he makes it plain that the tendency he is depicting manifests itself when 'jouissance' is in prospect, and indeed that it works in close interaction with the movement of desire. He portrays his 'inquiétude' both as a 'défaut'—an ineradicable taint or congenital defect like Zulietta's malformed nipple, and thus an unimpeachable alibi for sexual failure—*and* as an intermittent pressure in the psychophysiological arena of sexual exchange. The thoughts which run through his head impede only the consummation of a desire which resurges after each fiasco, and even survives Zulietta's memorable put-down: '*Zanetto lascia le donne, e studia la matematica*'. Having solicited a second rendezvous, Rousseau goes along confident that he will make amends ('réparer mes torts'), but he is spared what he darkly calls this 'épreuve' (p. 322) since Zulietta sensibly finds it preferable to be elsewhere.

Wittgenstein suggests that what we often want, rather than explanatory hypotheses, are ways of sorting out 'the crush of thoughts' prompted by something that bothers us. As Frank Cioffi puts it: 'What we want with respect to certain phenomena are not their causes but their bearings. The lack of closure, the sense of unfinished business that we experience with respect to them, is not always a matter of factual ignorance, to be relieved by the discovery of causal relations.'[39] The 'perspicuous presentation' which answers this need is, I believe, Rousseau's achievement in episodes such as those we have been examining. The quotient of causal language is low, and it is not so much a logical chain which is held to contain the episode's meaning as a network of internal relationships discovered and divulged through narrative re-enactment. It has often been observed that in episodes such as the stolen ribbon, Rousseau tells the story twice, splitting apart (if we employ the terminology of Barthes's *S/Z*) the proaretic dimension of actions and the hermeneutic dimension of understanding, in the interests of exculpation. This does not happen in the episodes we are now considering where rationalization and causality play their parts within the context of a single process of narrative understanding. My point is not to deny perspicacity to the Rousseau who investigates the case of the stolen ribbon, or who analyses what happened to him under the tyranny of Monsieur Ducommun. Nor do I wish to suggest that Rousseau necessarily shows superior wisdom in his account of Madame Basile or Zulietta. What he does show, however, is how advantageous it may be, in the general context of

---

[39] 'Empirical Methods', 171.

autobiography, to play down the desire for (logical) closure. In these episodes the reader, rather than being led by the nose, accompanies Rousseau through the re-enactment of events; it is as if, here, Rousseau confined his need for the reader to the desire to be watched, inviting a beneficent gaze to witness the replay of past perceptions.[40] Yet if the stakes are not as high as in, say, the 'fessée', the ribbon, or the comb incidents, more is involved than self-indulgence or the pleasures of anamnesis. In 'Zulietta' the epistemic need seems to be to find bearings among the contradictions of past desires, to open channels between the event, its antecedents, and its pertinence to Rousseau's subsequent history. Staging the event is a way of keeping it in play, scanning its latent topography through a transaction which makes it an 'intentional object of reminiscence and rumination'[41] but also, by proxy of the reader, a space of 'transference'—where desire accedes to knowledge—and, by virtue of narrative, a mobile synthesis of conflicting perspectives. Vital to 'Zulietta' is the interaction of narrating voice and narrated event, manifested in switches of tone and register, the use of quoted speech, the overdetermination of meaning produced by implicit allusions to earlier phases of Rousseau's development. To some degree it may be appropriate to see in this the 'langage aussi nouveau que mon projet' which, according to the Neuchâtel preamble, will be as much part of Rousseau's self-revelation as the manifest content of what he has to tell:

En me livrant à la fois au souvenir de l'impression reçue et au sentiment présent je peindrai doublement l'état de mon âme, savoir au moment où l'événement m'est arrivé et au moment où je l'ai décrit; mon style inégal et naturel, tantôt rapide et tantôt diffus, tantôt sage et tantôt fou, tantôt grave et tantôt gai fera lui-même partie de mon histoire (p. 1154).

---

[40] Thought-provoking in this general context is W. Lyons's argument, in *The Disappearance of Introspection*, that the traditional view of introspection as involving 'direct, immediate and reportable knowledge of inner states and processes and their information content' (p. 90) should be supplemented by a model based on the *replay* of perception: '"Introspection" is not a special and privileged executive monitoring process over and above the more plebeian processes of perception, memory and imagination; it is these processes put to a certain use' (p. 113). Lyons argues that 'folk psychology', models and notions based on the surrounding culture, play a preponderant part in our assessments of our own motivations, intentions, wishes, etc., in regard to which we enjoy no special privileges, beyond the ability to 'replay' edited highlights of past events which we consider to be relevant. Lyons's model helps us to grasp the conflict, played out in many autobiographies, in the treatment of incident and memories, between an introspected self in the traditional sense—a 'self' we can 'look in on' and catch fleeting sight of—and a self evidenced only in edited (and thus unreliable) replays which require interpretation from a point of view which is no less 'other' for being our own.

[41] Cioffi, 'Empirical Methods', 169.

Style, Rousseau suggests, will be the instrument of a 'double vision' through which past and present interact. For Jean Starobinski this confers on the dimension of style—the activity of writing in which Rousseau surrenders himself ('en me livrant') to the flow of past and present feeling— the status of a *parole* which extricates Rousseau from 'ce nœud inextricable de déterminations qui nous condamnent à subir notre sort'.[42] The tempo and *allégresse* of some moments of the *Confessions* certainly warrant such a diagnosis. But in the passages we have been considering the attenuation of causal discourse does not dispense with 'enchaînement', with the sense, if not of a distance, then of a problematic interface between present and past. Rousseau may describe his fiasco as a 'circonstance qui [peint] bien mon naturel', as an event where he recognizes himself 'as he is', but what is recognized does not have the character of a timeless essence. Recognition bears, rather, on a self embedded in its history, in the interplay of feelings and events. If the real action takes place in the narrating present, the past remains something to be negotiated with, and on terms partly dictated by the imagined exigencies of others. Often, in the *Confessions*, those exigencies become tyrannical, and the desire to demonstrate, to control and regiment the past, asserts itself. Ultimately the flight from the Other will drive Rousseau away from his history. But it is part of the comprehensiveness of Rousseau's legacy to subsequent autobiographers that it should include not only a cautionary tale about the nightmare of causal explanations (which will frighten off many of his successors) but also a demonstration of how autobiography might find its truth in an open transaction with past desires.

[42] *La Transparence et l'obstacle*, 233.

3

Diagrams in Stendhal's *Vie de Henry Brulard*

Language shows clearly that memory is not an instrument for exploring the past but its theatre. It is the medium of past experience, as the ground is the medium in which dead cities lie interred. He who seeks to approach his own buried past must conduct himself like a man digging. This confers the tone and bearing of genuine reminiscences. He must not be afraid to return again and again to the same matter; to scatter it as one scatters earth, to turn it over as one turns over soil. For the matter itself is only a deposit, a stratum, which yields only to the most meticulous examination what constitutes the real treasures hidden within the earth: the images, severed from all earlier associations, that stand—like precious fragments or torsos in a collector's gallery—in the prosaic rooms of our later understanding.

(Walter Benjamin, 'A Berlin Chronicle')[1]

I   IMAGES AND EXPLANATIONS

Mais le lecteur, s'il s'en trouve jamais pour ces puérilités, verra sans peine que tous mes *pourquoi*, toutes mes explications peuvent être très fautives. Je n'ai que des images fort nettes, toutes mes explications me viennent en écrivant ceci, quarante-cinq ans après les événements (p. 66).[2]

Written at great speed between December 1835 and March 1836 while the author was languishing in a dull administrative post at Civitavecchia, pining for the good conversation of Milan or Paris, Stendhal's autobiography, *Vie de Henry Brulard*, constantly plays down the construction of causal hypotheses. Where Rousseau sought to marshal his memories to reveal the 'enchaînement d'affections secrètes' which can both explain particular actions and account for the emergence of a specific personality, Stendhal adopted an interrogative stance, seeking to find out rather than demonstrate who he was. Conscious of eventual readers (publication was to be posthumous), he wished to spare them the self-justifying 'emphase' of Rousseau (p. 310), and the self-glorifying 'effroyable quantité de *Je* et de

---

[1] *One-Way Street*, 314.
[2] References, which will be cited in the text, are to the 'Folio' edn. ed. by Béatrice Didier.

Moi' of that 'roi des *égotistes'* Chateaubriand (p. 30).[3] Instead of keeping to a
pre-ordained plan or imposing a particular order, he adopted the same
procedure as in the *Souvenirs d'égotisme*, a short memoir of a period of his
adult life written three years earlier: 'Pour tâcher de ne pas mentir et de ne pas
cacher mes fautes, je me suis imposé d'écrire ces souvenirs à 20 pages par
séance, comme une lettre' (p. 68). Conducting himself 'like a man digging', in
Benjamin's phrase, though writing fast and spontaneously, he made daily
forays back into the layers of his childhood. This results in 'de terribles
digressions' for which the author frequently apologizes: 'Mais je m'égare'
becomes a sort of refrain. But it also pays dividends in that fresh discoveries
are made in the process of writing. One of the work's great originalities is the
way it quickly takes the form of a 'journal de fouilles'[4]—bulletins on an
ongoing process of discovery. The discoveries are, however, of two distinct
kinds:

> En écrivant ma vie en 1835, j'y fais bien des découvertes, ces découvertes sont de
> deux espèces: d'abord, 1° ce sont de grands morceaux de fresques sur un mur, qui
> depuis longtemps oubliés apparaissent tout à coup, et à côté de ces morceaux bien
> conservés sont comme je l'ai dit plusieurs fois de grands espaces où l'on ne voit que
> la brique du mur . . . 2° En 1835, je découvre la physionomie et le pourquoi des
> événements. Mon oncle (Romain Gagnon) ne venait probablement à Grenoble, vers
> 1795 ou 1796, que pour voir ses anciennes maîtresses et pour se délasser des Echelles
> (142).

The distinction is a radical one. First: sudden reapparitions of past scenes
which are compared to the surviving portions of a fresco because, along with
what is remembered, comes an acute sense of what has been forgotten, just
as the luminous patches of detail in a fresco subsist beside blank areas which
time seems to have destroyed.[5] Stendhal calls these apparitions *images*: they
are discontinuous, undated, acausal, visual, emotional. Second: 'la
physionomie et le pourquoi des événements', the whys and wherefores.
These also arise in the process of writing, but their relation to past events is
quite different. Stendhal's *pourquoi(s)*, as he will reiterate frequently, are
retrospective rationalizations which usually depend on later knowledge and
experience. For example he has distinct images of his uncle's visits to
Grenoble from his country estate, but it is only at the time of writing that he

---

[3] Stendhal makes frequent reference to his precursors in autobiography. Of the twenty or
so references to Rousseau, see esp. pp. 246, 385, 417, 428. On the relationship between the
two writers see R. Trousson, *Stendhal et Rousseau*. For Chateaubriand see pp. 225, 245, 274,
and P. Berthier, *Stendhal et Chateaubriand*. See also B. Didier, *Stendhal autobiographe*.

[4] P. Lejeune, 'Stendhal et les problèmes de l'autobiographie', 32.

[5] The fresco image occurs several times, e.g. pp. 130, 187, 308, 338.

realizes what prompted them. A couple of pages later (p. 143) he will deduce that his first trip to Les Echelles must have occurred in 1790 or 1791 because the sudden recollection of the route he had taken suggests that it must have been prior to the annexation of Savoy by General Montesquiou. However spontaneous, discoveries such as this are products of the intellect, of writing as an analytical process. Stendhal is, accordingly, extremely wary of them because they fall outside the sphere of memory proper: 'Je ne puis voir la physionomie des choses, je n'ai que ma mémoire d'enfant. Je vois des images, je me souviens des effets sur mon cœur, mais pour les causes et la physionomie néant' (p. 187). The authentic return of a past emotion or sensation is likely to be sudden and disruptive: 'En écrivant ceci l'image de l'arbre de la Fraternité apparaît à mes yeux, ma mémoire fait des découvertes' (p. 326). In many cases the resurrected image plunges Stendhal back into the world of his childhood and adolescence, when he was unaware of motives and clear-cut explanations and when his relation to experience was primarily via sensations and emotions. This was exacerbated by the circumstances of his upbringing, since he was cut off from other children, 'élevé sous une cloche de verre' (p. 331), with the result that at 15 he felt deeply but lacked psychological insight. 'Ainsi je n'ai pas grande confiance au fond dans tous les jugements dont j'ai rempli les 536 pages précédentes. Il n'y a de sûrement vrai que les *sensations*, seulement pour parvenir à la vérité il faut mettre quatre dièzes à mes expressions' (p. 331).

Images, related to unverbalized emotional experience, raise the problem of expression: Stendhal is less concerned with explaining them than with the danger of being unable adequately to render them in words. Moreover, the emotional context in which images originate is also responsible for their relative paucity and discontinuity: 'J'étais tout émotion et cet excès d'émotion ne m'a laissé que quelques images fort nettes, mais sans explication des comment et des pourquoi' (p. 350). As he writes, Stendhal frequently has occasion to observe that strong emotions tend to obliterate his memories. The most exciting and moving moments of his life have either left no living trace or can only be recaptured partially through disconnected images. Another feature of the image is that it can only be explored from within its own framework: 'Mais pourquoi ce monde? à quelle occasion? C'est ce que l'image ne dit pas. Elle n'est qu'image' (p. 72). The image can be interrogated but it cannot reply. Like an old photograph, it can be pored over, speculated on, compared with other images, examined in different lights, but it is impervious to explanation.

There is undoubtedly a powerful tendency for Stendhal to revel in images and to spurn explanations. Yet the repudiation of all explanatory manœuvres would not only have been unfaithful to the other kind of genuine and spontaneous discovery he found himself making as he wrote, but would also have amounted to a denial of the process of change and maturation; pushed to its limits, it represented a regression into total identification with past emotions and infantile conflicts. As Michel Crouzet has argued, *Vie de Henry Brulard* is a work in which Stendhal not only relives the emotional struggles of his youth, experiencing again in all their fury his antagonistic feelings towards his father and his Tante Séraphie and his incestuous desires for his mother, but also comes to terms with these feelings by externalizing and comprehending them, making autobiography a process of therapy and acting out (Stendhal's word is 'mimique'), and working through: 'Dès lors, il *voit* son passé, comme image et comme image réfléchie, retouchée selon sa vraie signification, il voit et il sait, il corrige l'imagination, l'obsession enfantine. Il sentait; maintenant il distingue.'[6] Crouzet perhaps exaggerates the extent to which Stendhal achieves the sort of clarity and serenity implied here but if the burden of his diagnosis is correct we must ask how this therapeutic effect is achieved, given that the polarization we have identified seemingly excludes any easy synthesis or dialectic of images and explanations.

One solution would be to credit Stendhal's remarkable style, with its digressions, italicizations, anglicisms, parentheses, addresses to the reader, consistent irony—in short the numerous features which make it very difficult to identify a stable authorial stance—with the capacity to constitute a space in which antagonistic modes of self-understanding find a way of asserting themselves in an unhierarchical and open manner, and where the lure of images is not made to surrender to or to exclude the powerful sway of *comment* and *pourquoi*. Yet it is doubtful if what is at stake in a relation to self so strongly vested in the image could ever be articulated fully within the confines of discourse alone. It is consequently at this point of our enquiry that we need to take into account the many plans, diagrams, and drawings which give Stendhal's text a persistent but enigmatic visual dimension. Here perhaps, in these peculiar combinations of words and visual signs, is the dimension in which the image and the *pourquoi* are jointly articulated in a way that maintains their inherent ambivalence. Here, perhaps, the dead hand of explanation, and the danger of imaginary regression to childhood images, are both neutralized allowing divergent yet complementary apprehensions of selfhood—entailed by the resurrection of past moments and the achievement of understanding dependent on change and temporality—to find a *modus vivendi*.

[6] *La Vie de Henry Brulard ou l'enfance de la révolte*, 142.

It is not clear what generic name is most appropriate for the 170 or so instances in Stendhal's manuscript where the autobiographer's pen, instead of forming letters and words, starts tracing lines and shapes which, usually in combination with words, can, after some effort, be deciphered as diagrams, drawings, sketches, and plans.[7] This is partly owing to their variety but it also stems from their essentially ambiguous and hybrid quality. French critics tend to call them 'croquis', which suggests rapidity of execution but could imply the notion of a preparatory sketch. In English 'drawing' might be suitable although it tends to connote mimetic representation. 'Diagram' is better.[8] It often implies accompanying verbal material, it can refer to the 'graphic representaton of the course or results of any action or process' (*OED*), and it does not exclude schematic representation: we talk, for example, of the diagram of a house or a car. The two essential components of Stendhal's diagrams are the purely graphic aspect and the verbal aspect. But their inherent ambivalence is present not only in the combination of these divergent factors but in each of them.[9]

The adoption of lines in the place of words is in one sense a move out of discourse in the direction of precision and specificity. It is a way of avoiding discursive description by the adoption of a more direct mode of communication.[10] But this pragmatic, no-nonsense element is undermined by the fact that drawing for Stendhal is clearly a pleasurable activity, a gestural performance, associated with childhood itself, which activates the memory in particular ways and embodies a specific form of attention.[11] The move from description to inscription is only apparently a move towards order and control. Words also function in two fundamentally different ways. The diagrams are often conceived with reference to the positions of people or objects designated by letters of the alphabet whose meaning is given in

---

[7] Printed versions of *Vie de Henry Brulard* enforce a separation between forms of graphic inscription barely distinguishable in the MS, a point which must always be borne in mind when Stendhal's performance as an autobiographer is assessed. On the MSS of *Vie de Henry Brulard* see Serge Sérodès, 'Les Blancs dans les manuscrits de la *Vie de Henry Brulard*', 135–50.

[8] 'Figure' is obviously tempting because of its suitable ambiguity, but in practice this word is too diffuse in its meaning not to be misleading in some contexts.

[9] Discussions of the diagrams may be found in M. Crouzet, 'Écriture et autobiographie dans la *Vie de Henry Brulard*'; F. Coulont-Henderson, 'Remarques sur la mémoire et les croquis de la *Vie de Henry Brulard*'; B. Didier, *Stendhal autobiographe*; M. Reid, 'Représentation d'Henry Beyle'; L. Marin, *La Voix excommuniée*.

[10] The first instances of diagrammatic presentation, the initials of past loves inscribed on the sand at Albano, explicitly accompany an effort to distance and discipline past emotion: 'Je cherche à détruire le charme, le *dazzling* des événements, en les considérant ainsi militairement' (p. 40).

[11] Drawing is also associated with the mother, cf. p. 162.

the text or in a caption below the diagram. Here words serve a controlling function, tying down and curtailing the ambiguity of the graphic sign.[12] But there is generally another layer of words which do not label things already embodied but enlarge the scope of the diagram, dilating rather than contracting its meaning. These are often written directly over the image and they invoke features of the scene which had not originally been destined for inclusion. Like the graphic sign itself, words in Stendhal's diagrams enact a tension between a desire to order and control and a desire to explore and open.

As a general example of these features we may take the diagram concerning an early bout of amorous jealousy which took place on Stendhal's first visit to his uncle's estate outside Grenoble. Stendhal has a clear visual memory of the surroundings and the sequence of actions, and of his own emotions, but he can recall neither the object of his affections nor the rival who provoked his jealousy:

Peut-être cela me reviendra-t-il comme beaucoup de choses me reviennent en écrivant. Voici le lieu de la scène que je vois aussi nettement que si je l'eusse quitté il y a huit jours, mais sans physionomie.

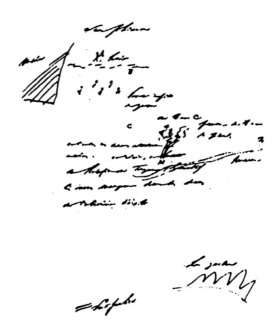

[12] On the interactions involved here see R. Barthes, *L'Obvie et l'obtus*; N. Bryson, *Word and Image*, ch. 1.

Après ma révolte par jalousie, du point A je jetais des pierres à ces dames. Le grand Corbeau (officier en semestre) me prit et me mit sur un pommier ou mûrier en M, au point O, entre deux branches dont je n'osais pas descendre. Je sautai, je me fis mal, je m'enfuis vers Z (p. 147).

The diagram duly has points marked A, M, O, and Z as well as a 'stick-figure' with outstretched arm (H.B. throwing the stones), a schematic tree, a triangular area of hatching representing a house, and five blobs representing the ladies who were victims of the attack. There are also a few labels appended to items not referred to in the text. More significantly, another inscription has been written over the image, introducing further reference points, B and C. Here the words do more than decode the letters, they also add a degree of precise and evocative detail which had presumably not initially been recollected: 'De B en C pente de huit ou dix pieds où toutes ces dames étaient assises. On riait, on buvait du ratafia de Teisseire (Grenoble), les verres manquant, dans des dessus de tabatière d'écaille' (p. 148). The diagram can be seen as the enactment of a memory process in which, at a crucial point, the attempt to reconstruct material already (re)visualized turns into an active generation of memories and feelings. The capacity to function in this manner depends on the diagram's crucially ambiguous status, on the border between the verbal and the non-verbal, the present gesture and the past one, the realm of the image and that of discourse.

The roles played by diagrams in *Brulard* are complex and various. The many plans of Grenoble serve to orientate the subject in past space and time, giving the text a significant historical dimension. Plans of interiors— especially those of rooms in Stendhal's grandfather's house on the Place Grenette—often accompany a process of working through past conflicts, especially between the solitary child and the father of whom he was so contemptuous. Many diagrams re-enact past emotions relating particularly to art, death, and desire. They also have a more general function relating directly to the textual status of visual/verbal communication and involving consideration of a central issue raised in Stendhal's autobiography: the status of strategies which seem to play down narrative causality, articulating, at least potentially, an alternative, non-causal sense of self. Each of these functions draws on the possibilities opened by the crossing of visual and verbal modes of signification, bearing out the suggestion that such activities permit an 'exponential growth in meaning', allowing 'written language [to traverse] different fields of semiotic potential'.[13]

---

[13] P. Florence, *Mallarmé, Manet and Redon*, 4.

II   PUBLIC AND PRIVATE SPACES

In a pioneering study which makes substantial reference to *Vie de Henry Brulard* the French sociologist Maurice Halbwachs argued that memory is not solely a private phenomenon but a collective one. Remembering, he suggested, involves not simply negotiation with mental traces but, very often, a process of reconstruction whereby memories are resituated in the wider context from which their significance may in part derive. Submitted to scrutiny, a remembered incident, image, or impression will often disclose an interlocking network of experiences, rooted in particular places and social groups (the spatial configurations of memory are often vital in this respect). Whilst our memories are fragmentary it often turns out that the fragments can be related to larger 'ensembles'. 'Le souvenir', notes Halbwachs, 'est une image engagée dans d'autres images, une image générique reportée du passé.'[14] Even our most isolated memories may have a living historical dimension which recollection can uncover. Halbwachs remembered as a child seeing groups of Russians with long fur garments and flowing hair in a certain quarter of Paris. Years later he learnt that they were Siberians suffering from wolf-bites who had come to take advantage of Pasteur's recent discovery of vaccines.

Stendhal's aims are scarcely sociological, but the social, spatial, and historical dimensions of memory have a significant place in *Vie de Henry Brulard*. One of the functions of the diagrams seems to be to capture fleeting images by attempting to revisualize their contexts, one image frequently acting as bait for others. The memory of being taken to the theatre by his uncle centres on an incident when the actor playing Le Cid injured an eye with his sword. By means of the letters A and H and accompanying captions a small diagram shows the positions of the actor on the stage and the young boy in the second box on the right in the auditorium. This stirs up Stendhal's ambivalent feelings towards the 'infâme salle de spectacle de Grenoble' (p. 64), with its unpleasant smell, which he had venerated in his early teens, particularly at the time of his passion for Mlle Kubly of which the reader will learn in a later chapter. A second diagram locates the theatre near the river Isère and pinpoints the box-office (p. 63). The vista of

---

[14] M. Halbwachs, *La Mémoire collective* [1950], 60. For Halbwachs a 'courant de pensée sociale' (p. 23) will often be detected in the most 'individual' memories: the hardest things to remember are those which seem to involve ourselves alone. Yet there can be no rigid opposition between individual and historical memory, 'Ce n'est pas sur l'histoire apprise, c'est sur l'histoire vécue que s'appuie notre mémoire' (p. 43)—we grow up and live in an ever-changing constellation of events, groups, beliefs, and places: to remember is to reconstruct our situation within this vanished field.

mountains on the far side of the river is indicated, and this prompts Stendhal to recognize how this view has recently been altered by General Haxo's fortification of the Bastille. A building near the theatre is tentatively identified as the former palace of the 'Connétable de Lesdiguères', the words 'je pense' injecting an air of uncertainty into the demonstrative idiom of the plan.

The interaction of objective and subjective viewpoints, and the incorporation of detail relating to disparate moments, are consistent features of the diagrams of Grenoble. Certain landmarks in the Place Grenette, such as the two trees planted in honour of the Revolution, the old pump, the spire of Saint-André, the chestnut tree, the Rue Montorge, are often featured, whether or not they have a role to play in a particular memory: they serve as 'figurants' enlisted to create the basic space. We can link most diagrams to particular passages in the main text, but quite frequently a diagram develops an insignificant detail—such as the passing allusion to the Didier cousins who lived near Saint Laurent (p. 66)—and explores its independent ramifications, thus becoming a self-contained branch-line, an additional, optional loop in the text. Diagrams may be the repositories for details and narrative threads not found elsewhere: for example, some feature a house in the Grande Rue apparently associated with the recollection of memorable sexual bouts with a certain Mme Galice. On the first occasion a caption reads 'Là je m'élevai jusqu'à 7 avec Mme Galice' (p. 186); thereafter Stendhal generally uses the characteristically cryptic abbreviation '7 fois' (p. 270). This memory never figures in the text proper and of course belongs to a much later period than the events which initially stimulate the diagram.

At a cursory glance, the numerous (over twenty) street-plans of Grenoble, particularly those which focus on the Place Grenette and environs, where the houses belonging to Stendhal's father and grandfather were situated, may seem almost identical; but in each case the crux of the diagram—its *punctum*, to use Roland Barthes's term for the feature (often a detail) which arrests us in a photograph—is different.[15] Each diagram is the trace of a separate act of reconstruction: the streets of Grenoble are not a rigid framework but an evolving organism which needs to be visualized afresh each time Stendhal feels his way back to a particular moment. Each diagram is the residue of a mental journey. To read *Vie de Henry Brulard* is to be escorted by these recurrent emblems of the author's native city and to be a party to the interplay between, in Baudelaire's words, 'la forme d'une ville' and 'le cœur d'un mortel'.

[15] See *La Chambre claire*, 47 and *passim*.

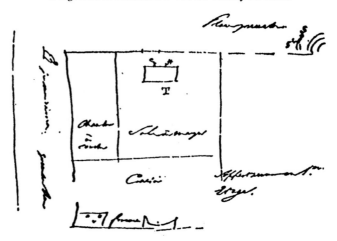

Stendhal was 6 in 1789. One of his early memories concerns the *Journée des tuiles* when he claims he saw the first bloodshed occasioned by the Revolution (p. 73). The family was roused from the dinner table with their guest the Abbé Chelan; the young boy saw a journeyman hatter fatally wounded by a bayonet thrust in the small of the back. A first diagram, commented on in the main text, shows the table positions of boy and priest, the man outside and the exact location of his wound. Other details include the kitchen with its furnace and, in the Grande Rue running alongside the house, a human figure and the words 'Je me révorte'. Before this is explained, Stendhal evokes the background to the incident, basing his account on later information, and provides a digression on the officer Bernadotte who subsequently became King of Sweden. Recognizing that he has switched to second-hand information, Stendhal then resolves that he will henceforth confine himself to what he had actually seen: 'ce que *j'ai vu*'. We are then given a second, more detailed and somewhat different account

of the incident. The child had been alone (his parents having already interrupted their meal) at a window—not in the dining-room but in another room—and had first seen an old woman holding her worn shoes in her hand and shouting with all her might: 'Je me révorte!' (p. 75). It was just after she had disappeared round the corner that he had seen the 'spectacle tragique' at point O. This refers us to a second diagram which indicates the old woman's path with a dotted line and, once again, the position of the hatter. This memory has altered too. The origin of the wound is now uncertain: he had not seen it inflicted. What Stendhal does remember clearly ('Je le vois encore') are the man's shirt and pale buff or white trousers soaked with blood, and the wound itself in the small of his back, opposite the navel.

The second diagram marks a shift from the temptation to expatiate on this moment in Grenoble's history, checking dates in an almanac and so on,[16] to the realization that it is in reconstructing precisely what he saw that Stendhal truly engages with what Halbwachs calls 'l'histoire vivante'. In a subsequent episode relating to the revolutionary period—the plot by Stendhal and some accomplices to deface the inscription on the Arbre de la Fraternité (pp. 317–27)—the initial reconstruction (three diagrams) is followed by a second (three further diagrams) which both repeats and revises. Yet Stendhal, focusing on precise visual recollection, never reassembles the event as a whole, gaps and uncertainties remain. By contrast, the eye-witness account of another participant, Stendhal's cousin Romain Colomb, while full of remarkable detail, offers a more rounded and coherent narrative, but tends to rationalize and distance the event, the tone adopted—referring to the boys with ironic self-indulgence as 'ces trois

---

[16] The question of documentation regularly arises as Stendhal writes. Early on he is inclined to complain that in Civitavecchia he lacks the materials which would help him establish precise chronology and topography. At various points he considers: purchasing a plan of Grenoble next time he is in France (p. 462); consulting the register of the criminal court to establish the date when two priests were guillotined (p. 175); consulting the registrar's list to see exactly when Séraphie died (p. 219); looking up the *Journal du Département* in connection with the list of suspects established by the Revolutionary authorities (p. 125); checking the *Archives de l'Administration départementale* to establish the year the *École centrale* was opened (p. 237). He did have a copy of Loeve-Weimar's *Table chronologique* which tells him that Lyons fell on 9 Oct. 1793; but, perhaps because he found its precision unhelpful and unstimulating where his own memories were concerned, he used it very little: 'Je n'ai aucun livre, et je ne veux aucun livre. Je m'aide à peine de la stupide *Chronologie* . . . Je ne prétends nullement écrire une histoire' (p. 214). Stendhal seems to have grown increasingly aware as he wrote that to try and square his own images of past events, even public ones, with the impartial official record of history was otiose. Towards the end he states outright that he is glad not to have more reference books: the book he is writing will not be based on other books, but on memory alone (p. 394). There is no reason to believe that Stendhal intended to revise his manuscript when more documentation became available.

grands coupables' and 'ces amis'—conveying the impression of an insignificant schoolboy prank viewed from the standpoint of middle age.[17] Stendhal's jerky hops from one intensely remembered moment to another avoid the pitfalls of a more psychological reconstruction and serve to recover past events in their immediacy. The high degree of identification—but with emotions and sensations rather than motives—in fact curtails sentimentality and helps to unearth forgotten memories such as the one which abruptly follows the Arbre de la Fraternité incident. Stendhal had witnessed at close quarters the guillotining of Jomard, a priest who had murdered his stepfather, and he suddenly recalls the man's unshaven face, the red cape of the parricide, and the drops of blood on the blade, a sight which had put the young boy off boiled beef for some time!

Retrospection in *Vie de Henry Brulard* frequently involves the perception of links and associations between the politics of the family and the politics of the nation. The child's situation in the dynamics of the family structure takes on a political colouring, while historical events—the overthrow of absolute rule, the blows to privileged groups such as the clergy—are portrayed in terms of family conflicts. The interaction of public and private history comes to the fore in a number of scenes where news from the outside world—for example the assassination of Louis XVI, the guillotining of two priests, the siege of Lyons in 1793—impinges on the family unit, and the child's reaction is shown to be quite different from that of other family members, notably his father. Part of the focus in such scenes is on the passion and spontaneity of the child's reaction; when Stendhal's father tells him of the king's death: 'je fus saisi d'un des plus vifs mouvements de joie que j'ai éprouvés en ma vie' (p. 121). Stendhal makes it clear that the child's jubilation is intensified by the awareness that his 'contrary' response inflames the wrath of his father and aunt, though he regrets that it might sadden his esteemed grandfather; the child's relationship to politics is mediated through the family, and vice versa. Moreover, in these scenes, Stendhal tends to identify strongly with the child, fending off potential accusations of hypocrisy or heartlessness on the part of readers who are, in this regard, placed *in loco parentis*. Observing, in connection with the regicide, that a similar realism and lack of sentimentality had characterized his feelings in 1830 (when, in his view, the failure to deal promptly with the promulgators of the 'Ordonnances' led to Revolution) Stendhal notes: 'mon caractère était absolument le même qu'aujourd'hui' (p. 123).

[17] Romain Colomb was Stendhal's literary executor; his annotations to the MS of *Vie de Henry Brulard* are quoted in the notes to most edns., including the 'Folio'. The passage referred to is on p. 488.

However, the return of forgotten emotions, and the desire to express solidarity with the child, do not have a total monopoly. The mature perspective of the adult enables Stendhal to go beyond his immediate reactions to a more global appraisal of his situation and his past identity. Political parallels reflect not only the incursions of politics into the family circle ('Bientôt arriva la politique', p. 110) but a retrospective awareness of conflicts and alliances, and of the child's position: 'J'étais absolument comme les peuples actuels de l'Europe, mes tyrans me parlaient toujours avec les douces paroles de la plus tendre sollicitude, et leur plus ferme alliée était la religion' (p. 112). Such comparisons indicate a more detached assessment of the child's attitudes; Stendhal shows a willingness to be more understanding towards his family and more critical of himself, even acknowledging traces of bloody-mindedness and posturing in his ferocious republicanism, and conceding that he was to some extent unjust towards his father, and indeed towards the much maligned Abbé Raillane (p. 104).

Diagrams tend to feature prominently in the kinds of scene which concern us here, reflecting Stendhal's desire to home in on a strictly localized event and to uncover its wider ramifications. Rather than aiming at a synoptic vision of the past, and fitting remembered events into a fixed pattern, Stendhal, by constantly changing his angle and range of vision, tries to elicit the patterns and forces which may be detected in the memory of a specific moment. News of Louis XVI's assassination reached Grenoble at seven o'clock one evening. A diagram (p. 120) records the spatial and emotional configuration of the event: remote from one another, father and son are in the study at the Rue des Vieux-Jésuites, the boy sitting in his own space, 'séparé de mon père par une fort grande table', pretending to work but surreptitiously reading Abbé Prévost's *Mémoires d'un homme de qualité*, while Chérubin Beyle is at a small desk in the corner. The diagram plays a part in the retrospective mapping of intersubjective space: reconstruction favours re-enactment, and the generation of details and digressions leads towards more complex, multi-faceted understanding. Stendhal's memory of the period when his father had, to the child's satisfaction, been classified as 'notoirement suspect' by the revolutionary commissioners Amar and Merlino, and had gone into hiding at the grandfather's house in Place Grenette, is dominated by memories of the scorn and 'aigreur' inspired in the child by his father's hypocritical indignation and pathetic apprehensiveness. But as the memory crystallizes in a diagram of the house showing the room father and son had shared at this time, a detail floats back which inspires a more charitable attitude: a mark indicates the spot where Chérubin would sit reading Hume's *Life of Charles Ist* and other works about the fortunes of the monarchy in place of his customary diet of devotional works, as approved by Tante Séraphie. At the time, Stendhal notes, this lightning transformation into a political animal struck the child as ridiculous; but 'aujourd'hui je vois le pourquoi': the father's single-mindedness in adopting a new passion to the exclusion of all else reveals aspects of his character which command respect.

In the 'Billet Gardon' episode (p. 132), where Stendhal forges a letter of invitation to join a revolutionary youth brigade (among other things this is interpreted as an attempt to break out of his isolation—'sortir de cage', p. 135), two diagrams retrace the event. The first focuses on the spot where Stendhal placed the forged note; the second, far more elaborate, centres on the child's come-uppance, and in particular on his misfortune in accidentally inflicting an unsightly mark on his grandfather's map of the Dauphiné just when he was steeling himself for the showdown with his family who had discovered his forgery. The diagram pinpoints the incident with a wealth of detail, and the 'considérations' which then flow from this concentration of attention embrace a wide range of character traits (inability to maintain his resolve to be angry, tendency to put himself at a disadvantage in a quarrel, etc.); in the account of the aftermath of the incident these reflections inspire an acute analysis of family alliances, culminating in the recognition that in his hostility to his father he had been in part motivated by Oedipal rivalry for his mother's love.

A final example is provided by the chapter which juxtaposes two disparate events: Stendhal's similarly jubilant reaction to the postman's vivid account of the siege of Lyons and to the news that Tante Séraphie had died. In the first case, two diagrams (pp. 213–15) contextualize the child's feelings—'les plus vifs transports d'amour de la patrie'—in a dense texture of detailed memories: summer breakfasts in grandfather's 'cabinet d'études naturelles', excellent *café au lait* served with 'griches', the postman's broad-brimmed hat (just identifiable in the diagram), the view towards the village of Méaudre which Stendhal would contemplate at sunset because he had been told that canonfire from the siege might be heard there at that time. Stendhal then switches abruptly and anachronistically to his immediate reaction to Tante Séraphie's death—he had gone down on his knees to thank God for this great deliverance!—and draws a diagram showing him in this posture at 'point H' in the kitchen, indicating various stray details including a box of powder which exploded (presumably on a quite different occasion). He then cuts to a scene, reconstructed in two diagrams (one providing more details, including a snatch of speech), which gives a more objective view of Tante Séraphie's insufferable character since it involves a sally addressed to the grandfather whose response, 'Elle est malade', implies that Stendhal was perhaps not alone in finding her death a deliverance.

Stendhal's ideological passions are placed in a wider field of sensations and experiences by virtue of the form of attention manifested in the diagrams. These do not serve simply to intensify the recollection of specific emotions but they act as conduits for emotional ambivalence and for a cluster of disparate desires. Diagrams locate private memories in communal spaces—interior and exterior—and in the wider context of family and public history. Although they address events in their specificity, avoiding rather than favouring psychological generalization, they are not simply *instantanées* which pin down lost moments like butterflies. They also encourage an anachronistic process of association which discovers the layered quality of events and attests the multi-faceted nature of the truth they disclose.

III DEATH, DESIRE, AND LOOKING

The switch from a verbal to a visual regime in the process of memory engages a different mode of attention to the past's traces. While the verbal chain articulates memory as a temporal process, unfolding in present and past time, the visual enacts it as a process of returning, searching, and scanning. In the first case truth is at the end of the line, waiting to be uttered; in the second it is already there in the image, waiting to be noticed. The combination of visual and verbal modes in Stendhal's manuscript, and in the diagrams themselves, seems particularly attuned to the working through of past experiences where elements remain unresolved, or to understanding how conflicts that are still vividly remembered came effectively to be resolved and absorbed in the individual's development towards his current identity. Scenes of pleasure, desire, death, and aggression figure promi-nently, and often the incursion of the visual can be linked to the presence of *looking* as a factor in the incident.

Death arises in the first place as the punishment for desire. Having deferred what he refers to as one of the two or three 'récits' which may make him abandon his autobiography, Stendhal, in a famous passage (p. 51), owns up to having passionately desired his mother physically, and moreover to being able still to identify, as an adult, with his childhood way of 'making love'. But, he hastens to add, she died, and his 'vie morale' was inaugurated by her death: death makes desire innocent, sublimating it into the emergence of moral identity. This confession leads into a central incident from his early childhood. He had been put to bed on a mattress on the floor of her room, and his mother had jumped over him to reach her own bed. The presence of desire is not directly stated but implied since this brief paragraph is supposed to exemplify the criminal 'fureur' of the child's ardour. Louis Marin is surely right to suggest that desire here, apart from erotic proximity, and the connotations of the bedroom scene, involves the glimpse—real or imagined—of what is forbidden from sight: the mother's vagina.[18] But death asserts itself once more. The mother's room was kept locked, the next sentence reminds us, for ten years after her death; when it was reopened for the 18-year-old Stendhal to set up his blackboard and work at his maths, only *he* was allowed the key: in retrospect the mature author sees that this concession was to his father's credit. The working-through of desire for the mother, death, and feelings towards the father, focuses in an elaborate diagram of the mother's room depicted on the night of the incident. The terseness of the diagram echoes the terseness of the brief paragraph. There are no words, only numbers on the image, with

[18] L. Marin, *La Voix excommuniée*, 37.

explanatory captions beneath it. But the diagram does not just repeat, it licenses vision: it is not because of what it shows that the image matters, but because of the switch into vision which it permits. The diagram does not show us mother and son (a schematic child is shown on the mattress but no one else is there), it shows us, in the form of a graphic trace, the signs of a mental act of revisualization.

In the next chapter, which recounts the circumstances of his mother's death in childbed, Stendhal focuses particularly on the morning of the funeral, using a diagram to reconstruct the scene in his father's dark study (lightened only by the bright-blue spines of his volumes of the *Encyclopédie*), where relatives and friends foregathered. The scene is connected with the child's sense that social proprieties seemed to exclude any true recognition of death or the deceased. The adults chatted quite normally and were merely embarrassed when the clatter of a coffin was heard from the landing. The event, Stendhal says, marked the end of his complicity in social existence: 'ce fut là ma dernière sensation *sociale*' (p. 60). Not allowed to mourn properly, or to arrive at any real comprehension of death, the child experienced at the funeral a particular feeling of despair—'une tristesse morne, sèche, sans attendrissements . . . tristesse voisine de la colère' (p. 60)—a feeling subsequently associated with the sound of the cathedral bells, even when he revisited the town in 1828.

The self-contained chapter (the fourteenth) concerning the death of the servant Lambert makes implicit and explicit comparisons with the death of the mother.[19] While the grandfather was a 'camarade sérieux et respectable', Lambert was 'mon ami' (p. 155), the person in whom he could confide—in some respects clearly a substitute mother. When Lambert died after falling from a ladder, the child experienced a new kind of emotion: not the cold frenzy his mother's death had provoked, but 'la douleur comme je l'ai éprouvée tout le reste de ma vie, une douleur réfléchie, sèche, sans larmes, sans consolation' (p. 156). The difference has partly to do with looking. The maternal body was only to be glimpsed: in death it is quickly enveloped in a cumbersome and socially embarrassing coffin. Lambert however is seen to die. Ten times a day the child entered his room and looked at his dying friend. Contemplated and reflected on, this death provokes an emotion in which inconsolable grief is allied to a strong sense of the order of reality, the way of things, a type of melancholy which has a redemptive and aesthetic

[19] The account of the funeral of Maréchal Vaux (ch. 5), which the child attended in the company of Lambert before his mother's death, presents an image of death's sublimity which the child could not perceive when his mother died. Lambert's death will be presented as a fusion of the domestic and ordinary with the sublimity of aesthetic experience.

character. It is a feeling which in later life has been elicited by painting: an Italian picture of St John mourning Christ; by music: certain accompaniments in Mozart's *Don Giovanni*; and, evidently, by words such as those quoted from Virgil: *Sunt lacrimae rerum* (p. 159).

Having initially repeated the emotion via the recognition of these associations, Stendhal seeks to recall the nature of his feelings towards Lambert, recognizing that the response to his death must have paralleled the feelings he had experienced for him alive. Here diagrams play a major role. The first shows the position of Lambert's room and adjacent portions of the house, but the crucial detail is a point, at the edge of the courtyard, marked L, with a note identifying it as the place from which he had forced himself to remember Lambert by *staring* at the 'tops' (the unexpected word 'toupies' is illustrated by a drawing) of the woodshed. This is elucidated by three further diagrams which constitute a primal scene in Stendhal's recollections of Lambert. The memory of mourning him by staring at the woodshed brings back the fact that his warmest moments ('mes plus doux épanchements') with his friend had occurred when he was sawing, separated

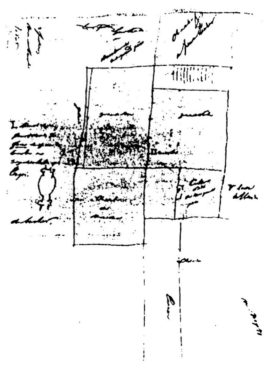

from the courtyard by a railing ('cloison à jour') formed of walnut-wood posts shaped on a lathe as in garden balustrades (p. 160). It was the carved capitals of these posts which, to Stendhal, resembled spinning tops. A large-scale diagram indicates in close-up the position of the woodshed, the 'cloison à jour', and the uncle's room overlooking the courtyard from the first floor. But the next diagram manifests the paradoxical emotional and psychological currents which seem to underlie these memories.

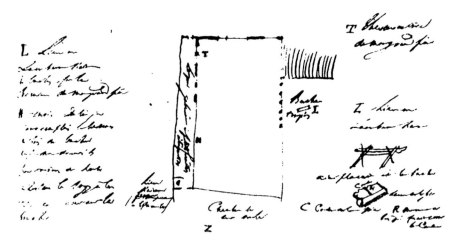

From the ideal position in which a diagram places the viewer we look straight down on the courtyard—an empty rectangle of white paper. On the right we are shown the woodshed, the spot where Lambert would saw, his sawing-horse, saw blade, and other tackle, the 'toupies': *Lambert is alive.* On the left we are shown the upstairs gallery, 'à petites fenêtres élégantes', a lavatory 'réservé à la famille' (thus presumably out of bounds to servants), and a 'point H' captioned 'Moi. De là, je contemplais les barreaux de bois du bûcher et je me donnais des paroxismes de douleur en portant le sang à la tête en ouvrant la bouche' (p. 160): *Lambert is dead.* The diagram is placed between Lambert alive and Lambert dead, between the 'doux épanche-ments' and the 'paroxismes de douleur'. Radically anachronistic, it superimposes divergent moments, and amalgamates disparate feelings. Yet it seems to mark not so much emotional contradiction or tension, as if memory were confronted by the choice of adopting the positions of love or loss, but—in its centring around a vacancy, and in the way the caption, as in the earlier diagram, registers a wilful act of recollection, 'je me donnais des paroxismes'—to suggest that memory's true burden lies elsewhere.

When the main text switches to the memory of contemplating the

woodshed from the gallery, it picks up the recollection of staring at the 'barreaux du bûcher' and of being struck by their resemblance to tops: this prompts another diagram consisting of two attempts to depict with greater accuracy the precise shape of the posts, and particularly the portion of them which resembled tops (a line with an arrow presumably indicates rotation). Then, a significant transformation occurs: the 'paroxismes de douleur' which accompanied the staring at the posts, become 'paroxismes d'amour': 'Les paroxismes d'amour que je me donnais au point H sont incroyables. C'était au point de me faire éclater une veine. Je viens de me faire mal en les *mimiquant* au moins quarante ans après. Qui se souvient de Lambert aujourd'hui, autre que le cœur de son ami!' (p. 161). At this point one is prompted to ask: who is staring at what? How can we reconstruct the logic of the child's gaze relayed (replayed, mimicked 'quarante ans après', drawn) by the adult?

Somewhere here, one feels, is the gaze of the infant at its mother's body. In the diagram the 'toupies', whose roundness is emphasized, have a comforting maternal air, the air of transitional objects, as well as evident connotations of regression to early childhood.[20] Of course many details in the text imply that Lambert was a substitute mother. But, like the mother's, Lambert's body is forbidden; during their 'doux épanchements' the servant saws logs, attends to the techniques of his craft: 'Ainsi plaçait-il la bûche'. Still, Lambert can be looked at; looking at Lambert can be a substitute for the forbidden and now impossible desire to gaze at the mother. And when Lambert dies the child goes up to the gallery by his maternal uncle's room

---

[20] Blin observes that Stendhal is 'au fond moins curieux de relever en lui un centre où ensuite il eût dû rester épinglé . . . que de manier . . . ces bibelots appelés "souvenirs"', *Stendhal*, 576. D. W. Winnicott's concept of the transitional object (see *Playing and Reality*) seems relevant here. Barthes cites it in connection with the 'Italy' of Stendhal's travel writings: 'Telle est, me semble-t-il, l'Italie de Stendhal: une sorte d'objet transitionnel dont le maniement, ludique, produit ces *squiggles* repérés par Winnicott et qui sont ici des journaux de voyage', *Le Bruissement de la langue*, 341. This aspect of the diagrams is also greatly illuminated by some of the perspectives adopted by A. Ehrenzweig, *The Hidden Order of Art*.

and looks out of the small panes of glass. What does he see? His gaze falls diagonally down, across the courtyard to the 'cloison à jour': a screen rather than a wall which permits intermittent glimpses of the woodstore within: that is where Lambert sawed. But the gaze lingers, is drawn to the posts, to their shape, their connotations of infancy, their rotundity. The gaze is both restricted and permitted. What the child remembers, what the adult wants to remember, is a certain experience of looking.

Considerable emphasis falls on the physical effort of memory. Rather than receiving spontaneous images of his dead friend, the child seeks to procure a particular physical sensation, a kind of seizure. The self-inflicted 'paroxismes de douleur' are brought on by an effort both mental and physical which sends the blood rushing to the face and leaves the mouth agape ('en portant le sang à la tête en ouvrant la bouche'). Transmuted into 'paroxismes d'amour' such efforts nearly burst a blood-vessel ('éclater une veine'). In one sense the effort is that of raising the dead: perhaps by staring hard enough at these quasi-human posts—the top-like parts also resemble heads with blank faces—he will resurrect his friend. Resurrect, but also appropriate, incorporate. The effort is partly one of identification, of making oneself the same as the other. And it is also sexual, as the shift from *douleur* to *amour* recognizes. A generalized sexuality, incorporating homosexual feelings for Lambert, but addressed unmistakably to the mother's body by the infantile echoes of tops, and of primarily oral satisfaction (the mouth agape).

The effort is also in a sense moral and aesthetic. The gaze aims not only at the mother's body but at her death. The child had been unable to mourn her: the premature experience of emotional loss, and the family conflicts it reanimated, made mourning impossible. In the case of Lambert Stendhal is able to brave Séraphie's anger and cry. Up in the gallery the child uses the death of the valet to mourn the mother properly, to transform loss into emotion and presence, performing an act of the imaginative will which externalizes but controls feeling, creating a chain of displacements and substitutions—grief, pain, desire, mother, Lambert, the 'toupies', the 'cloison', the woodstore. Emotion is stimulated from within rather than imposed from without. Stendhalian 'douleur'—described as being at the very core of his being, his 'cœur'—takes on forms recognized by the adult. The act of the child at the gallery window, reinscribed and located by the diagram, can be identified with totally via an act of mimicry: 'Je viens de me faire mal en les *mimiquant* au moins quarante ans après. Qui se souvient de Lambert aujourd'hui, autre que le cœur de son ami!' A 'douleur' which is now an inalienable part of the mature individual can relocate its childhood origin and celebrate a euphoric capacity to incorporate, to remember, in an emotional space, that which it has lost. This applies not only to Lambert but also, as a similar passage at the end of the chapter claims, to lost loves, such as Alexandrine and Métilde. Those remembered in this way are truly his, 'à moi, moi qui les aime mieux que tout le reste au monde' . And behind or through them, and in the music of Mozart, the poetry of Virgil, Italian painting, the mother too—*amour* and *douleur*—is briefly glimpsed again. What the adult identifies with, mimics forty years on, is a particular act of attention: bearing on remembered experience it finds its physical expression in a fervent act of vision, but one which looks through rather than at; a vision which is directed outwards but works on what is inner.

Nowhere does this act find a clearer analogue or embodiment than in the diagram, the graphic work of memory, which enables a work of remembrance that achieves something of the humanization of desire Leo Bersani sees as a central function of literature:

> ... scenes of desire in literary works are surrounded by and submitted to *developments* which compromise but which also humanize desire. On the one hand literature hallucinates the world in order to accommodate desire. On the other hand, it illustrates the ways in which we learn, in time, to make what Melanie Klein called reparations to the world for our imaginary devastations of it. Literature thus makes a double argument. It invites us to return to that variety of scenes of desire which is stifled by the interpretive tracing back of all desires to a single, continuous design in a supposed maturing of desire. The literary imagination reinstates the world of desiring fantasies as a world of reinvented, richly fragmented and diversified body-memories. But, at the same time, it also gives ample space to those processes by which we make a continuous *story* of our desires, processes which also teach us to give up the intensities of an infinitely desirable hallucinated world for the somewhat disappointing enjoyments of fulfilled desires.[21]

The reinstatement of desiring fantasies in the 'richly fragmented and diversified body-memories' evoked by Bersani is, as we have seen, precisely what Stendhal's text so frequently engenders. And we have also observed the balancing tendency to contain and understand desire rather than simply repeat it. The diagrams have been crucial to both. Yet Stendhal seems to avoid, in *Vie de Henry Brulard*, the narrativization of desire identified by Bersani as literature's characteristic act of reparation, at least to the extent that he seems unwilling to settle for the 'somewhat disappointing enjoyments of fulfilled desire' which narrative resolution would foster in a fictive work. In Stendhal's autobiography the humanization of desire seems

[21] L. Bersani, *A Future for Astyanax*, 314.

to involve an acceptance of self as a desiring subject, a wish to remain in the orbit of desire and to continue to enjoy its mobility, if the pitfalls of infantile regression are circumvented.

IV   THE RHYTHM OF SELFHOOD

Two-thirds of the way through his manuscript Stendhal notes: 'Mais au fond, cher lecteur, je ne sais pas ce que je suis: bon, mauvais, spirituel, sot. Ce que je sais parfaitement, ce sont les choses qui me font peine ou plaisir, que je désire ou que je hais' (p. 280). Commenting on this passage, and others like it in *Vie de Henry Brulard*, Georges Blin rehearsed the various forms of Stendhal's refusal to be defined by his attributes. The Stendhalian *moi*, he argued, was fundamentally future-oriented: 'pas une substance ni un support, mais une intention, un "désir"'. Looking back on his past, Stendhal was less interested in self-defining features than in signs of past desires which tended towards the future in which he was now writing:

> Il a vu, en effet, que pour comprendre un vivant, il sied d'en interroger non la part consommée de son destin, mais la destination où il se rend, et encore non son but, mais la manière dont il le négocie: les voies par lesquelles il y tend et l'allure—'style', à la fois, et 'rythme'—que soutient son pas.[22]

A self conceived as a 'style', a 'rhythm', a 'stride', more akin, as Blin suggests, to bodily gesture than to intellectual assertion, cannot readily find expression in a narrative work dominated by content and causality, character and significant incident. Many stylistic features of *Brulard* which subvert the categories of linear narrative clearly serve to pre-empt the imposition of an alien order of selfhood, yet few can be said directly to articulate an alternative conception of the self.

This is hardly surprising. It may well be, as Louis Marin suggests in a series of rich and fruitful (if somewhat elliptical) studies,[23] that Stendhal's mode of autobiography reflects a recognition of the *aporias* inherent in the autobiographical text—its incapacity to deal adequately with its own founding presuppositions and referents, the birth and death of the subject, a subjectivity present to itself ('le "Je" dans l'instant unique et ponctuel de sa présence') in the moment of utterance which the text can only alienate. In the face of this an autobiography becomes necessarily a fictive structure made up of 'simulacres', 'machinations d'écriture', sleights of hand which

---

[22] Blin, *Stendhal*, 589.
[23] Marin, *La Voix excommuniée*, 152. See also 'Images dans le texte autobiographique'.

may seek to consecrate the illusion of a self encountered, encompassed, and transmitted, but in fact constitutes a screen behind which the authentic pulse of the subject may be heard to beat. The autobiographical text, argues Marin, 'sera travaillé par une voix originaire et inaudible et se constituera d'en être l'écho de ses signifiants'. A writer as lucid as Stendhal knows that selfhood is received and transmitted on a frequency outside the range of the narrative text, legible only between its lines; accordingly he constructs 'son propre espace d'écriture . . . pour laisser entendre une voix qui serait au-delà de toute voix, laisser voir une image au-dela et en-deça de toute image'.[24] In some writers, as Philippe Lacoue-Labarthe has suggested,[25] music is a privileged motif for rendering the ineffable flavour of subjectivity. Stendhal certainly detects in his response to music, particularly Mozart's *Don Giovanni*, a fundamental part of his identity, but the visual field is nevertheless predominant in his apprehension of his scattered subjectivity; and, moreover, for the mature writer, the verbal realm is also inseparable from his apprehension of self. Michel Crouzet has amply demonstrated Stendhal's multifarious attempts to create a 'langage-self', creating a 'sabir' of coinages and borrowings, anagrams, abbreviations, and cryptograms. At one extreme of course this apparently leads beyond language itself, into non-linguistic forms of communication which occur frequently in the novels. But language is only briefly lost sight of. It would seem in fact that what counts for Stendhal is the interference between semiotic systems, the clash of codes. If the verbal is sometimes ostracized by the writer's manœuvres it is also refreshed, 'Stendhal joue avec soi, il singularise ses expériences par un dépaysement linguistique, rafraîchit le vécu'.[26] Equally, pure visuality, the frozen and inert, or rather immobilizing and dazzling, quality of the visual image whose fascination is in part deathlike, has little appeal for Stendhal. The Stendhalian rhythm is quintessentially a transit between word and image, verbal and visual, the frozen image and the warm flow of discourse. Denying exclusive privileges to one or the other, Stendhal conducts his self-investigation as a constant switching between codes. The diagrams of

---

[24] Marin, *La Voix excommuniée*, 55.

[25] P. Lacoue-Labarthe, 'L'Echo du sujet', in *Le Sujet de la philosophie*, 217–303. Following Theodore Reik, Lacoue-Labarthe argues that *style*, oral or graphic, is also *character*: 'le caractère: l'incisé et le gravé, le prescrit (ou le pré-inscrit), le 'programmé d'un sujet—soit . . . l'inconscient comme système de traces, de marques, d'empreintes', 151. Although this is the object of the autobiographical quest it is naturally inaccessible, hinted at in such things as Reik's 'haunting melody'. Following Lacoue-Labarthe, to whom he expresses a debt, Marin analyses *Vie de Henry Brulard* in terms of such impossible objects. I prefer to emphasize what is positively manifested, partly through the diagrams, in the process of writing.

[26] M. Crouzet, *Stendhal et le langage*, ch. 15. The passage quoted is on p. 390.

Brulard are clearly a crucial symptom and it is to these that we must turn once again.

Given that the emergent 'rhythm' of Stendhal's subjectivity in *Brulard* is essentially related to pleasure ('Je ne puis que noter le degré de bonheur senti par cette machine', p. 378) and especially *visual* pleasure, one might expect recourse to a visual medium, as an adjunct to the written, to involve the consecration of vision.[27] But even when euphoric vision is involved, as in the case of the momentary glimpse of Camille's leg: 'sa peau blanche à deux doigts au-dessus du genou' (p. 143), the diagram reconstructs the conditions of seeing rather than the vision itself. Stendhal draws the bridge over the Drac and a figure 'au point A' on one side with a solid line which runs from its eye tracking the path of vision across the bridge but stopping at its object: what was seen remains invisible, buried in the whiteness of the page.

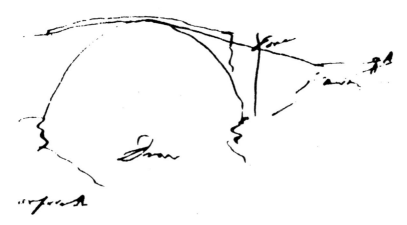

Homing in on the singular moment of vision does reflect the shift in *Brulard* from an attempt to construe the past as a total panorama, a unified field of vision where relationships are perceived and a past self is excavated,[28] to a subjectivity constituted by discrete momentary flashes of memory and insight.[29] However, drawing a diagram is an attempt not only to capture the

[27] On the investment of the visual in Stendhal see J. Kristeva, *Histoires d'amour*, 433.

[28] I am thinking, naturally, of the book's opening with its famous *mise en scène* of 'Toute la Rome ancienne et moderne' visible to the ideally positioned observer. The diagrams will offer the past a very different kind of visibility.

[29] Stendhal constantly stresses that it is past *sensations* which interest him, although he is only too aware that 'Toute sensation, si l'on veut respecter sa vivacité et son acuité, induit à l'aphasie': Barthes, *Bruissement*, 338. The absolute singularity of past events, as opposed to their typicality, is what is most resistant to language.

fleeting moment, outside the parameters of narrative, but to hold it steady so that it can be scanned and 'X-rayed'. And it is this process which manifests the rhythm of subjectivity in Stendhal: the moment of recognition in the autobiographical process is not the identification with and repetition of past desire, nor its incorporation into narrative frameworks, but the engendering of a rhythmical motion encompassing past moments, the subject's history, and his present being. As an act performed in the present the diagram aims to regulate as much as to consecrate vision. Rather than remaining spellbound, blinded by imaginary identification with past desire, Stendhal's approach to such memories will involve a *modulation* which befitted his emerging sense that his own *caractère*—by which progressively he came to mean not the answer to the questions 'suis-je bon, suis-je méchant?', but a person's 'manière d'aller à la chasse du bonheur'—was a compound of acute pleasure and reflective emotion, and that the 'signes de vie de mon âme' which he picked up from the past characteristically involved a blend of comedy and tragedy, heroism and buffoonery, self-approval and self-disdain.

The account of his youthful passion for the actress Mlle Kubly is markedly concerned with Stendhal's retrospective understanding of the emergence of his subjectivity, and the theme of pleasure is prominent. But the central incident, which is recreated by diagrams, involves a flight from pleasure's intensity, its intolerable 'brûlure'.

Un matin, me promenant seul au bout de l'allée des grands marronniers au Jardin de Ville, et pensant à elle comme toujours, je l'aperçus à l'autre bout du jardin contre le mur de l'intendance qui venait vers la terrasse. Je faillis me trouver mal et enfin *je pris la fuite*, comme si le diable m'emportait, le long de la grille par la ligne F; elle était, je crois, en K et j'eus le bonheur de n'en être pas aperçu. Notez qu'elle ne me connaissait en aucune façon. Voilà un des traits les plus marquants de mon caractère, tel que j'ai toujours été (même avant-hier). Le bonheur de la voir de trop près, à cinq où six pas de distance, était trop grand, il me brûlait, et je fuyais cette brûlure, peine fort réelle (p. 244).

The first diagram locates the initial glimpse in a detailed plan of the Jardin, and we can see that Mlle Kubly's position is originally given as within the 'jardin planté par Lesdiguères, dit-on', not far from the railings indicated by a dotted line. But her name is crossed out there, and reinscribed in a totally different position, by the wall which, we are told, was destroyed in 1814. The mistake may be explained by the fact that the railings clearly figure in Stendhal's initial recollections of the event. Executing the diagram seems to have helped him remember that it was *he* who took flight via the Lesdiguères

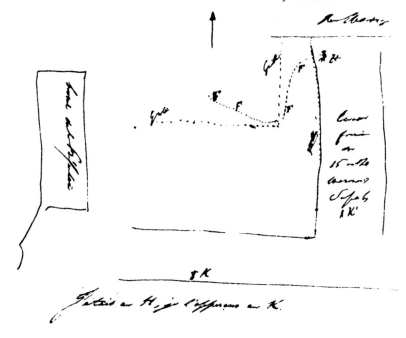

gardens and their railings. A second diagram, pared down to essentials, and corresponding to the second sentence of the paragraph just quoted, marks the boy's line of flight (F for 'fuite'), an ellipse, seemingly prompted by a gap in the railings but which gives a graphic impression of panic and disarray.

What the diagrams give us is a *mise en scène* of a glimpse followed by a flight from the embarrassment of being seen, a move with which the mature narrator clearly identifies. But the diagrams make pleasurable what was experienced as excessive *jouissance*. As the second diagram emphatically shows, Stendhal can now be in more than one place at a time, can occupy 'subject positions'[30] which experientially were in conflict. The diagram constitutes a repetition in which the pleasure of seeing Mlle Kubly ('J'étais en H, je l'aperçus en K') can be reactualized simultaneously with the rout of the adolescent whose flight is so vividly plotted by the scattered 'F's.

A few sentences further on Stendhal observes that his conduct as a writer differs from his conduct as a lover. In the latter sphere he is inclined to a

[30] For this concept see J. Kristeva, *La Révolution du langage poétique*. At one point in *Vie de Henry Brulard* Stendhal declares 'Voilà un des grands défauts de ma tête: je rumine sans cesse sur ce qui m'intéresse, à force de la regarder dans des *positions d'âme* différentes je finis par y voir du nouveau, et je le fais *changer d'aspect*' (p. 292).

melancholic character, whereas 'je ne suis ni timide ni mélancolique en écrivant' (p. 244). Writing enables a different part of his psyche to relive (and perhaps compensate for) the lover's vicissitudes. But this seems to be the fruit of a process which depends on, or at least is deeply rooted in, the experience of the visual. Visual enactment is a crucial stage in a repetition which accommodates the disparateness of desiring subjectivity.

To understand more fully what is involved in this, it is useful to draw on Jean-François Lyotard's investigation of the difference between the verbal and the visual. Challenging the notion that we read the visual, Lyotard contrasts reading written characters with responding to and understanding the graphic line. The act of reading, he argues, is essentially a form of hearing, which is not fundamentally different from speech itself in the relation it proposes between subject and discourse. The process of interpreting, or apprehending line, on the other hand, involves the encounter with a crucial resistance, an opacity which slows us down, forcing on us patience, passivity, effort:

Cette lenteur requise par le figural vient de ce qu'il oblige la pensée à abandonner son élément, qui est le discours de signification, où le tracé n'est pas accueilli pour lui-même . . . Il lui faut sortir de la transparence communicable; la façon dont le sens est présent dans la ligne (dans tout constituant de la figure) est ressentie comme opacité par l'esprit habitué au langage. Un effort presque sans fin est exigé pour que l'œil se laisse capter par la forme, se laisse communiquer l'énergie qu'elle détient.[31]

Art and discourse involve different 'positions'; what Lyotard calls the *figural* implies a relationship, partly physical and corporeal, between the mind and something intrinsically exterior and unassimilable to itself, while discourse dissolves difference into meaning. This should not be taken to mean that we can escape from discourse into the silent, maternal realm of the figural; rather, the figural is a horizon of discourse itself which becomes manifest in modes where the relation of discourse to the absolute exteriority of its object is maintained:

. . . de l'intérieur du discours, on peut passer à et dans la figure. On peut passer à la figure en manifestant que tout discours a son *vis-à-vis*, l'objet dont il parle, qui est là-bas, comme son désigné dans un horizon: vue bordant le discours. Et on peut passer dans la figure sans quitter le langage parce qu'elle y est logée . . .[32]

The biform, ambivalent discourse of Stendhal's autobiography is just such a mode, bearing many hallmarks of the figural. Lyotard's descriptions

[31] J. F. Lyotard, *Discours, Figure*, 218.
[32] Ibid. 13.

illuminate in particular a central paradox of Stendhal's diagrams which are not, in practice, evasions of discourse so much as devices through which discourse functions in a different way. Slowing down attention; requiring and imposing bodily movement as executant and decoder shift and tilt the paper, move the eyes up, down, and around; insisting on the absolute particularity of objects and events, out there and back then; interrupting or punctuating the flow of language; the diagrams nevertheless remain explicitly in the orbit of discourse and constitute those passages 'à et dans la figure' referred to by Lyotard. Yet these do not occur 'à l'intérieur du discours' (Lyotard is thinking primarily of metaphor here) but in a process where the figural dimension of writing itself, present in the graphic motions of the pen, is manifested explicitly when letters abruptly give way to lines and shapes. It is the radical continuity of the verbal and the visual in Stendhal, a tendency for the figural and the discursive to subvert and qualify each other in a constant dance of difference, which is so striking and effective. Far from abolishing words, the diagrams attract a swarm of annotations and emendations; far from providing a short cut to vision they hijack the process of visualization inspired by the kind of description they expunge and, *depriving us of vision*, insist instead on the 'lenteur' of the figural which curtails the metonymic extrapolation from descriptive item to imagined whole, and enforces an attention to the graphic sign as an icon of the particular, as ideogram.

To look at the manuscript of *Brulard* is to contemplate what at first glance resembles an undifferentiated mass of black marks on white paper. Even when, at a second stage, we categorize these marks as words and images, problems remain. Is this squiggle an illegible word or the branch of a tree? Is this a sentence crossed out or the edge of a street? The continuity of the graphic process, across the divide between verbal and visual communication, reflects in Stendhal the continuity in the autobiographical process between the adult and the child whose experiences are progressively rediscovered. Equally, the pictures in Stendhal's manuscript are like holes in a tattered fabric, manifesting the inward gaze of the 'subject of recollection' who suddenly stops, breaks the chain of discourse, and makes a clearing in which the past is attended to in a different way.

Fresh from the glory (commemorated by two diagrams) of having shot his first thrush, the young Beyle went fox-hunting on the steep mountain slopes around Comboire. Day-dreaming, he suddenly caught sight of a fox a few yards away, fired—and missed. The fox ran off but the boy experienced 'une peur complète' because of the precipitous paths he had to negotiate on his homeward journey. Returning to this incident Stendhal remembers that he had looked at his watch: 'Je regardais à ma montre qui était d'or comme je fais dans les grandes circonstances pour avoir un souvenir net au moins de l'heure' (p. 315). As a precaution against the tendency for strong emotion to dissolve memory, Stendhal imprints the moment in his mind, making a kind of mental inscription which does not aim at a descriptive record or encapsulation but at the preservation of the absolute singularity of a moment in time. Thus inscribed, the event calls subsequently for a form of repetition which resurrects not only its form but its force. As a figural inscription, externalizing and propitiating a specific form of mental act, the diagram clearly answers this call. With their provisional and pragmatic air, their 'one-off', 'to-hand' quality, diagrams aptly match the 'morcellement' of a subjectivity vested in the motions of desire enacted in the disorderly details of memory. Yet, as we have seen, diagrams, unlike dreams, are not pure expressions of desire. We should perhaps think of the Stendhalian diagram as an area of transference, in Peter Brooks's sense, 'a special "artificial" space for the re-working of the past in symbolic form',[33] a kind of half-way house betweeen past desires and present realities.

Responsive to desire, pleasure, and a disseminated subjectivity, Stendhal's diagrams are also symptoms and agents of a need to distance and deter these agencies. Yet this is precisely what makes them so central an expression of Stendhalian subjectivity, which discovers itself in *Brulard* to be an amalgam in which *jouissance* is modulated by *douleur*, comedy by the *lacrimae rerum*, Italian ecstasy by the reflectiveness of the Dauphinois temperament. Stendhalian subjectivity is not pure difference, unblinking vision, the inaudible voice or proximate body of the mother. Manifesting itself, rather, in the modulation and filtering of desire, the intermittences of vision and recognition, the perpetual historialization of experience—which, whatever his repudiation of a cause-bound, definitive self, available to introspection, and his rejection of the narrative devices which bolster such a conception, Stendhal never entirely loses sight of—it has no more characteristic emblem than the remarkable 'squiggles' which are the most original and visible feature of his autobiographical enterprise.

---

[33] 'Psychoanalytic Constructions and Narrative Meanings', 57.

4

Autobiographical Incidents

... as a man divinely abstracted and self-absorbed into whose ears the
bell has just drummed the twelve strokes of noon will suddenly awake
with a start and ask himself what hour has actually struck, we
sometimes rub our ears after the event and ask ourselves, astonished
and at a loss, 'What have we really experienced?',—or rather, 'Who are
we, really?'

(Nietzsche, *The Genealogy of Morals*)[1]

Augustine steals some pears, Montaigne falls off his horse, Rousseau steals a
ribbon, Stendhal drops a knife, Gide meets Wilde, Sarraute stabs a sofa . . .
Incidents figure prominently in the autobiographical tradition, but the kind
of significance they are granted varies considerably. Before Rousseau
incidents play, by and large, a supporting role; they may be credited with
exemplary, allegorical, or emblematic sense, but they are not treated as
relatively autonomous centres of meaning influencing the framework of
particular lives. In the *Confessions* of St Augustine the transcendent
viewpoint alone confers meaning on his life as a whole, and incidents are
therefore meaningful in the full sense only when considered as part of a
providential scheme.[2] In the spiritual autobiographies of the seventeenth
and eighteenth centuries typology (the interpretation of events in terms of
their analogies with earlier ones—especially those in the Bible, or the Life of
Christ) frequently provides the framework in which particular events are
given meaning in a person's account of his or her life.[3] Another kind of
typology, deriving from classical models, is found in early biography and
also in Montaigne. The author of the *Essais* admired the concrete details in
Plutarch's *Lives* and became progressively bolder at incorporating personal
details into his self-portrait. None the less, when Montaigne quotes an
incident from the life of Socrates or Alexander he has in mind principally its
emblematic and illustrative status, its power to exemplify a particular

[1] *The Birth of Tragedy and the Genealogy of Morals*, trans. F. Golfing, 149.
[2] See W. C. Spengemann, *The Forms of Autobiography*, ch. 1.
[3] For an illuminating general discussion of typology see A. C. Charity, *Events and their
Afterlife*. On the English 17th cent. see J. N. Morris, *Versions of the Self*; on the use of

character trait. The remarkable evolution of self-writing in Montaigne, which takes him from a reverential dependence on ancient exemplars to a bold personal dialectic of selfhood and writing, does not involve a marked change in the status of incidents. To be sure, it is Montaigne who falls from a horse, not Alexander, but the derivation of meaning from this occurrence, recorded in 'De l'exercitation',[4] while it involves detailed attention to circumstances and feelings, does not ultimately rest on its specificity as an event. In any case this is a fairly exceptional instance; the price Montaigne places on what we learn from experience is inestimable, but its elucidation does not rest on the analysis of life-events in their historical and circumstantial dimensions. For this to occur it will require not only that self-disclosure be cleared of the taint of moral unseemliness but that the more or less realistic depiction of everyday events should become relatively familiar, as it is not to any great extent until the rise of the novel in the eighteenth century.[5]

There is no doubt as much folly in taking Rousseau's *Confessions* to be the inevitable product of a congeries of historical developments, as in seeing it as a work wholly without precedent. However, where incidents are concerned, it would be difficult to deny Rousseau's originality, or the awesome example he set his successors. Rousseau treats incidents teleologically and forensically—as evidence in a court of appeal where he exhibits himself in the form of episodes from his past. There may be strong traces of the confessional here,[6] but incidents do more than illustrate and exemplify: they have become authentic centres of contentious meaning which need to be explored in their concrete circumstances, and understood within the historical framework and empirical context of the individual's life. The construction of causal chains constitutes one of the principal avenues of such understanding. But 'enchaînement' in Rousseau is perceived as being at odds with an acausal 'sentiment de l'existence'. In the *Confessions*, therefore, we also find an alternative attitude to incidents, which maintains their inherent importance but attenuates the compulsion to convert them into an explanatory currency. A similar tension in Stendhal's *Vie de Henry Brulard*—between 'images' and explanations—engenders a strategy which, if anything, augments the importance of specific incidents but treats them

typology in Victorian autobiography, L. H. Peterson, *Victorian Autobiography*. On example as a rhetorical figure see J. D. Lyons, *Exemplum*.

    [4] *Essais*, ii. 6. 41–51.
    [5] The narratives of memorialists such as Retz, Bassompierre, and Saint Simon also belong to this process of development. See M. Fumaroli, 'Les Mémoires au 17ᵉ siècle au carrefour des genres en prose'.
    [6] On this see J. Tambling, *Confession*.

less as the ingredients of a coherent narrative of the past than as forces still very much alive in the present. On the strength of what we have observed in Rousseau and Stendhal, a fruitful way of looking at the general question of autobiographical incidents might be based on a polarity between two basic models. On the first model, rooted in causality, and in the teleological aspect of narrative, the incident serves as a sponge which, as it soaks up virtual meanings flowing through the text, becomes itself saturated with meaning. Changing the metaphor, this approach turns the incident into a provisional point of anchorage where a cargo of meanings, in transit through the text as a whole, can be unloaded. But clearly, to allot such a role to an incident—to construe it, that is, as an origin, a climax, or a turning point—is to credit it with considerable diagnostic power. Employed in this way, often in support of a fixed view of the past self, incidents, however detailed, risk becoming at best largely emblematic, at worst crude instruments of a deterministic view of human reality. Consequently, on our second model, the incident is 'denarrativized' (if for a moment we identify narrative with cause and effect). This does not mean, as Stendhal's example shows, that it is withdrawn from the historical ground of individual existence, but rather that its specificity is affirmed through the attempt to neutralize—by fragmentation and other means—the potentially derealizing, distortive power of a cause-based approach to human experience.

The poetics of the autobiographical incident—the various ways in which incidents can be made to make sense—could certainly be explored in terms of the polarity I have indicated. It enables us to perceive the sharp differences between Rousseau and Stendhal, and it offers an illuminating perspective on the broadly anti-narrative tendencies to be found in much twentieth-century autobiography, from Leiris to Sarraute. Yet this polarity misses something essential: it masks the fact that what these two models have in common—a sense of the power and particularity of incidents—may be more important than what distinguishes them. To pursue this further we need to look more closely at the question of what constitutes an incident.

An incident is a kind of event, and an event ('événement'), if we consult Lalande's dictionary, is: 'Ce qui advient à une date et lieu déterminés, lorsque ce fait présente une certaine unité, et se distingue du cours uniforme des choses de même nature.'[7] Distinctiveness, unity, specificity of time, place, and action are the characteristic features of the event when this notion is credited with ontological validity. However, in recent years the traditional metaphysics of events (which would include, say, Leibnitz on 'individual

---

[7] Lalande, *Vocabulaire technique et critique de la philosophie.*

accidents') has been attacked from a number of quarters. In the Anglo-American analytical tradition, for example, the status of events has become a focus of controversy. On one side are those who argue that the notion of the event is purely 'supervenient', a construction we superimpose unnecessarily on facts, states of affairs, the changing properties of substances, and so forth.[8] On the other side we have the kind of position taken by Donald Davidson who, whilst acknowledging the shortcomings of the traditional metaphysical view, nevertheless puts forward a case for 'the individuation of events', for 'events as particulars'. Davidson concedes that there is 'something scandalous about events' in as much as the sentences which describe them make do with a language lacking singular terms, and he stresses the great difficulty in arguing that events are individual. But, having considered the claims of time and place, he ultimately finds his criterion for the individuation of events in the role of causality: 'it is easy to appreciate why we so often identify or describe events in terms of their causes and effects. Not only are these the features that often interest us about events, but they are features guaranteed to individuate them in the sense not only of telling them apart but also of telling them together.'[9] By the last phrase Davidson suggests that what makes an event individual is the particular way it relates to other events. An event is not simply a state of affairs, or a fact, but a causal nexus. If 'events as particulars' are basic to our understanding of the world it is because the same action is often susceptible of a number of descriptions and evaluations. Davidson's defence of events is, therefore, based on multiple causalities rather than rigid causality, and it is in keeping with an open-ended conjectural stance.[10]

In structuralism and post-structuralism the ontological status of events is challenged in the first case by the abolition of fixed terms in favour of formal oppositions, and in the second case by the displacement of 'presence' in the endless play of difference. In his essay 'Signature événement contexte' Jacques Derrida questioned the distinctiveness of any action or event on the grounds that an unlimited iterativity—the capacity to be inserted into an endless series of contexts—undermined stable descriptions or distinctions.[11] However, unlike those of analytical philosophers, Derrida's

---

[8] In *Events and their Names*, J. Bennett argues for this view and summarizes the ideas of other proponents. Another important context in which events have come under suspicion is in the attack on 'l'histoire événementielle' mounted by proponents of the *nouvelle histoire* in France (on this see P. Ricœur, *Temps et récit*, i. 138–59 and 287–313).

[9] *Essays on Actions and Events*, 179.

[10] See, however, Ricœur's critique of Davidson on events in *Soi-même comme un autre*, 93–108 (cf. n. 15 below).

[11] *Marges de la philosophie*, 365–93.

critique, as he develops his position in other writings, tends to enhance rather than dispel the mysterious aura of events. Through the aporias into which thought and language are led in the attempts to circumscribe it, the event comes to shine with a kind of negative, ghostly radiance. Like a kinetic sculpture which exists only in movement, the event is sustained solely by the movement of interpretation and redescription, yet as such seems all the more irreducible.[12] A more explicit negative theology of the event, at an experiential level, may be found in the writings of Maurice Blanchot, and in Clément Rosset's concept of an 'ontologie négative du réel' which points to an absolute singularity of the *real*, barely accessible to historicity and rationality.[13] Similarly, in his monumental study *L'Être et l'événement*, the philosopher Alain Badiou argues that only mathematics (along with poetry) can provide the key to the ontology of events, which he defines as 'multiple(s) indécidable(s)'. For Badiou the problematic essence of the event, its absolute singularity, resides in the 'undecidable' nature of its relation to situational factors—time, place, unity—for which he coins the phrase 'site événementiel'.[14] Finally, more pragmatically, Paul Ricœur seeks to reclaim the specificity of events beyond their subordination to generalized frameworks of meaning. An event can be seen as a disruption in an existing state of affairs which thereby poses a demand for meaning and order which can be met by assimilation into existing systems: the laws of nature for physical events, the rules of language for linguistic events (utterances), various explanatory frameworks in the case of actions. However, in each of these areas Ricœur identifies a factor in the event which exceeds the boundaries of law and abstract explanation. In the physical universe this is located in the more or less metaphysical questions which still subsist when we have exerted our explanatory powers; in the sphere of language it is the intersubjective character of the communicative situation which 'opens' the event. Where actions are concerned, Ricœur insists on the necessity of assigning such events to their agents, and thus to their place in the agent's history—the narrative of his or her identity. The irreducible quality of the event is tied, for Ricœur, to the irreducible specificity of an individual's narrative identity.[15]

---

[12] See e.g. *Limited Inc.*, Derrida's riposte to a critique of 'Signature, événement, contexte' by the American philosopher John Searle.

[13] See e.g. Blanchot's 'Le Demain joueur', and Rosset's *L'Objet singulier*.

[14] For Badiou, Mallarmé's *Un coup de dés* provides an image of the paradoxical character of the event because it joins 'l'emblème du hasard à celui de la nécessité, le multiple erratique de l'événement à la rétroaction lisible du compte . . . quelle plus belle image de l'événement, à la fois impalpable et crucial, que cette plume blanche sur la mer . . .', 215–16.

[15] See *Soi-même comme un autre*, esp. 73–108 and 157–80. Endorsing Davidson's emphasis

What emerges from this sample is that, for those contemporary philosophers disposed to entertain it, the category of event is problematic and refractory. This highlights the fact that if events are among the autobiographer's prime raw materials, the challenge they pose does not stem exclusively from their pastness (problems of memory), or from their hybrid character, but from their status *as* events. Moreover, the tendency to locate 'events as particulars' outside the range of clear-cut explanatory frameworks suggests that the polarity outlined above—the opposition between the incident as part of a chain of causes and the incident considered to some degree independently—should be at least partly revised so that the emphasis is placed more squarely on the kinds of meaning they are granted. To explore this further it is useful to ask first why the word 'incident' rather than 'event' seems appropriate in autobiography. To the ingredients of Lalande's definition of 'événement' (which distinguishes events from simple facts or states) the notion of the incident brings a greater connotation of adventitiousness—an incident befalls someone, and may prompt reflection on that account. Moreover 'incident' places more emphasis on the self-contained quality of certain events with, in some cases, the implication that they fall outside the range of the predictable. Further, 'incidents' lack the trappings of what is generally considered important or significant: whilst events can easily be momentous, we more readily think of incidents as minor or trivial.[16] Lastly, the notion of the incident tends to connote discourse: an incident is an event which has been identified as susceptible of being recounted, of forming the basis of, for instance, an anecdote.

In the light of these remarks the following definition seems appropriate: an autobiographical incident is a minor event to which the autobiographer's discourse ascribes a heavy payload of meaning. This suggests how our earlier criterion might be reformulated. Instead of opposing (*a*) the incident as plenum, crossroads of causalities, narrative peg, or 'embrayeur' (e.g. the stolen ribbon in Rousseau), with (*b*) the incident as fragment, resistance,

on 'events as particulars', Ricœur argues, however, that the American philosopher's causal theory involves an 'occultation de la question *qui?*' (p. 77), and thus makes events abstract and impersonal (the same criticism is levelled at Derek Parfit's *Reasons and Persons*). If for Ricœur the status of the event is 'la pierre de touche de l'analyse de soi' (p. 169) it is because of the crucial difference between events considered under the aegis of the configurational process of narrative and events considered purely in terms of (or entirely independently of) causality.

[16] For Leiris the notion of the incident is closely linked to that of the *fait divers* (cf. *L'Age d'homme*, 112), while in his later work Barthes uses the word 'incident' to designate 'tout ce qui tombe comme une feuille' (*Roland Barthes par Roland Barthes*, 153), in other words tiny events which attracted his attention but which seemed immune from any kind of exemplariness. In this connection see Barthes's *Incidents*, and cf. Ch. 8 below.

moment in writing (e.g. the death of Lambert in Stendhal)—a polarity based on the role of causality—we could take as criterial whether the meaning allotted to an incident accrues (*a*) by virtue of its incorporation into a larger framework, so that the incident becomes a working part in the smooth running of a narrative machine, or (*b*) by virtue of its autonomous power, explanatory (i.e. rooted in causality) or not, and its capacity either to disrupt the smooth progression of a narrative (as in the case of Rousseau's ribbon), or to require a 'customized' form of textual organization or device (such as Stendhal's diagrams, Chateaubriand's superimpositions, or Leiris's collages). In this polarity the emphasis is on how the incident functions, and it suggests an opposition between two species which, for convenience, could be labelled 'domesticated' and 'wild'.

Domesticated incidents

Their essential characteristic is that, whatever weight they are given, their meaning derives principally from the narrative line which 'puts them in their place'. The domesticated incident not only exemplifies something other than itself (all autobiographical incidents do this to some degree), but is very largely subordinated to a transcendent logic. Rousseau's thefts during his apprenticeship, his desertion of M. Le Maître, his first encounter with Mme de Warens exemplify the author's views on tyranny, his self-exculpating theory on moments when we are 'not ourselves', the decanting of experience in memory. This is not to suggest that such incidents are denied authentic power and density, but that these qualities derive less from features inherent in the event itself than from the use to which it is put in the narrative.

Amidst the numerous types or degrees of domestication one important distinction needs to be drawn. In many cases the subordination of incidents to a dominant 'discours' involves external validation by a particular ideological framework, or a pre-existent code of verisimilitude. This is almost invariably the case in routine or popular autobiography where the use of incidents tends to implement one of the cultural functions of narratives—the reinforcement of dominant patterns and assumptions.[17] But it is also to be found in more sophisticated autobiographies which readily adopt the assumed conventions of the genre. A case in point would be the *Mémoires* of the composer Berlioz. By his declaration 'ma vie est un roman

[17] On this point see the exceptionally lucid account given by J. Hillis Miller in F. Lentricchia and T. McLaughlin (eds.), *Critical Terms for Literary Study*, 66–79.

qui m'intéresse beaucoup', Berlioz sounds the keynote for a vivid recasting
of his past experiences which borrows its language from the myths of the
Romantic period, and from the conventions of narratives which mix the
picaresque and the introspective (at one point the author promises 'quelques
mots sur les orages de mon intérieur'). Rousseau's *Confessions* naturally
provide one of the principal models here (although Berlioz is faithful to the
custom among autobiographers of the period of disclaiming any wish to
emulate Jean-Jacques).[18] The numerous incidents in the *Mémoires* serve as
stepping-stones which enable the narrative to move forward at a brisk pace.
They are signalled in advance by chapter-digests which encapsulate the
narrative in miniature—'On me présente à Miss Smithson. Elle est ruinée.
Elle se casse la jambe. Je l'épouse'—and by the stereotyped lingua franca of
personal narratives: 'je touche ici au plus grand drame de ma vie'.[19] The
point here is not to carp at literary shortcomings, but to identify a particular
narrative regime in which a consistent self-image is communicated by
incidents whose meaning is regulated not only by intratextual self-
consistency, but, more dominantly, by consistency with established cultural
paradigms. This is not, however, the only type of domestication. Whilst all
narratives depend to some degree on existing paradigms, the *vraisemblable*
which ties incidents down may be created, to a considerable extent, by the
text itself; and in such cases (exemplified, as will presently be demonstrated,
by the autobiography of Julien Green) the discourse which subordinates
incidents and regulates their meaning 'from the outside in' is that of the
author.

'Wild' incidents

An autobiographical incident is 'wild' when, rather than being allotted a
specific role in the text (and remaining constrained by that role), it is
endowed with a certain autonomy which underlines its specific and
irreducible qualities. In becoming a centre of interest in its own right, the
wild incident tends to jeopardize conventional, linear, narrative order, and
in some instances to instigate alternatives to it. Rather than swift absorption
into the text's bloodstream, the wild incident occasions a kind of clotting
which may (more or less provisionally) invert the customary hierarchy of
textual part and textual whole. Here—picking up an earlier stage of the
argument—we can identify various divergent possibilities: in some cases

[18] *Mémoires*, i. 39.
[19] Ibid. i. 283, 125.

clotting occurs because the incident—Rousseau's ribbon, for example—becomes an overdetermined nexus of possibly incompatible meanings. In other cases it is because the incident—like so many in Stendhal, Chateaubriand, or Leiris—is represented as being meaningful precisely in the degree to which it resists assimilation by wider frameworks. Of course a wider framework—the identity of the autobiographer—is always present. However, the wild incident does not relate to that framework by dint of its position within the metonymic chain of the subject's story, but rather by virtue of becoming the metaphorical embodiment of a global subjectivity—the rhythm of selfhood in Stendhal's case. The ontology of the incident involved here makes it a particular type of 'site événementiel', whose basic characteristics must now be further elucidated.

First, it is the *quiddity* of the incident which is addressed. The wild incident compels particularly intense scrutiny, eliciting a quality of attention which is often highlighted or 'acted-out' in the text itself. The effect will often be that the incident splits, unfolds, or mutates; like cells under a microscope, what seemed inert will reveal itself to be in perpetual motion. The plasticity of the event may become the prime focus, underlining the extent to which its problematic character is held to reside in the difficulty of aligning it with other experiences. A striking example would be the famous 'Spots of Time' in Wordsworth's *Prelude* which, in successive versions of the poem, undergo a series of remarkable adjustments and modifications as the poet seeks to pin down the meanings these incidents hold for him.[20]

Secondly, wild incidents draw attention to discourse and to the moment of writing. The elaboration of hypotheses and the positing of alternative descriptions may explicitly display the constructive process involved in autobiographical writing, while devices such as juxtaposition (Leiris) or superimposition (Chateaubriand) may, implicitly, point to the text as construct. Moreover, wild incidents tend to vivify the channel of communication with the reader—explicitly, through a discourse which stresses the imponderable, the ineffable, the ineradicable; or tacitly, by confronting the reader more squarely than elsewhere with his or her interpretative role. A third facet is the relationship to temporality. In becoming a textual moment the wild incident 'stops the clock', suspends the relay of past time, questions the natural link between causality and temporal flow, asserts its own temporal coordinates. This enhances rather than diminishes its status as an irreducible event: while its pastness or otherness

---

[20] On this see D. Ellis, *Wordsworth, Freud and the Spots of Time.*

is not denied, the writer's confrontation with the past becomes a real event in the present, and the past incident, instead of being incorporated into the abstract time of narrative causality, comes to partake of the temporality of narration. (That this temporality is itself fictional will provide a further level of irony in an autobiographer such as Leiris.) Fragmentation becomes a sign of the incident's relative autonomy, its own temporality. As a fragment it may have the character of something incomplete, torn from a context to which its restoration is sought, or of something absolute, its fragmentariness rooted in the quality of the instant, the moment 'outside time', the 'souvenir sans date'.

More generally, wild incidents displace the question of truth. In the domesticated variety the overall framework of meaning determines truth, whereas with wild incidents the question of truth is less one of veracity than of 'power': as a result, texts which feature such incidents deal more successfully with the problematic character of autobiographical memories, the possible inescapability of an element of fictionalization, and the fact that the onus for creating a particular regime of meaning rests firmly with the autobiographer. To focus more concretely on the issues raised by the discussion so far, we shall now examine in turn works by three autobiographers: Chateaubriand, Julien Green, and Michel Leiris.

CHATEAUBRIAND: *MÉMOIRES D'OUTRE-TOMBE*

A famous passage in the *Mémoires d'outre-tombe* concerns an incident when the song of a thrush abruptly transported the author back to his childhood at Combourg, stimulating him to resume the evocation of his past after a three-year gap.

Montboissier, juillet 1817

Depuis la dernière date de ces *Mémoires*, Vallée-aux-Loups, janvier 1814, jusqu'à la date d'aujourd'hui, Montboissier, juillet 1817, trois ans et six mois se sont passés. Avez-vous entendu tomber l'Empire? Non: rien n'a troublé le repos de ces lieux. L'Empire s'est abîmé pourtant; l'immense ruine s'est écroulée dans ma vie, comme ces débris romains renversés dans le cour d'un ruisseau ignoré. Mais à qui ne les compte pas, peu importent les événements; quelques années échappées des mains de l'Eternel feront justice de tous ces bruits par un silence sans fin.

Le livre précédent fut écrit sous la tyrannie expirante de Bonaparte et à la lueur des derniers éclats de sa gloire: je commence le livre actuel sous le règne de Louis XVIII. J'ai vu de près les rois, et mes illusions politiques se sont évanouies, comme ces chimères plus douces dont je continue le récit. Disons d'abord ce qui me fait reprendre la plume: le cœur humain est le jouet de tout, et l'on ne saurait prévoir quelle circonstance frivole cause ses joies et ses douleurs. Montaigne l'a remarqué: 'Il ne faut point de cause, dit-il, pour agiter notre âme: une reverie sans corps et sans subject la régente et l'agite'.

Je suis maintenant à Montboissier, sur les confins de la Beauce et du Perche. Le château de cette terre, appartenant à Mme la comtesse de Colbert-Montboissier, a été vendu et démoli pendant la Révolution; il ne reste que deux pavillons, séparés par une grille et formant autrefois le logement du concierge. Le parc, maintenant à l'anglaise, conserve des traces de son ancienne régularité française: des allées droites, des taillis encadrés dans des charmilles, lui donnent un air sérieux; il plaît comme une ruine.

Hier au soir je me promenais seul; le ciel ressemblait à un ciel d'automne; un vent froid soufflait par intervalles. A la percée d'un fourré, je m'arrêtai pour regarder le soleil: il s'enfonçait dans les nuages au-dessus la tour d'Alluyes, d'où Gabrielle, habitante de cette tour, avait vu comme moi le soleil se coucher il y a deux cents ans. Que sont devenus Henri et Gabrielle? Ce que je serai devenu quand ces *Mémoires* seront publiés.

Je fus tiré de mes réflexions par le gazouillement d'une grive perchée sur la plus haute branche d'un bouleau. A l'instant, ce son magnifique fit reparaître à mes yeux le domaine paternel; j'oubliai les catastrophes dont je venais d'être le témoin, et, transporté subitement dans le passé, je revis ces campagnes où j'entendis si souvent souffler la grive. Quand je l'écoutais alors . . . (i. 101–3).[21]

The passage displays many features of Chateaubriand's handling of autobiographical incidents. First, the temporal span of the text's composition is shown to parallel and interact with historical time. The *Mémoires d'outre-tombe* were written over a long period (intermittently between 1811 and 1846) and Chateaubriand is therefore able to point to the constantly changing contexts in which he writes.[22] The first two paragraphs play ironically on the fact that cataclysmic changes—Napoleon's downfall, the 'Cent Jours', Waterloo, the Restoration—have occurred between the composition of successive chapters of his book, and thus in what for the reader is a hiatus between two blocks of print: 'Avez vous entendu tomber l'Empire?' enquires the author, 'non, rien n'a troublé le repos de ces lieux'. But these events have reshaped Chateaubriand's life. He has rapidly lost royal favour: Louis XVIII does not approve of his conception of a constitutional monarchy and has stripped him of his ministerial post (a

[21] References are to the 4 vols. of the Édition du Centenaire by M. Levaillant, reissued by Garnier-Flammarion. Proust greatly admired the passage quoted, and refers to it twice in *A la recherche du temps perdu*.

[22] There is clearly an element of artifice here. Chateaubriand rewrote the *Mémoires* completely from 1832 onwards but retained the dates of first drafts at the heads of the chapters.

reversal of fortune typical of Chateaubriand's public career). With his political illusions (provisionally) behind him, he now writes from a different perspective which modifies his outlook on the past. Although this turbulent period will one day need to be covered by the *Mémoires* (so that the passage is partly proleptic) its repercussions already, explicitly, make themselves felt in the writing.

Secondly, the incident becomes a point of intersection for disparate historical contexts whose divisions reflect the discontinuities of individual experience. In addition to the split already noted (before and after Napoleon) the flashback to Combourg gives us another division—before and after 1789—manifested emblematically by the fact that Montboissier (which recalls the château at Combourg) was destroyed during the Revolution: the gardens retain traces of the *ancien régime*, but in a ruined state. The surviving Alluyes Tower then takes us further back since it is associated with Henri IV's mistress Gabrielle d'Estrée, who, Chateaubriand muses, must like him have seen the sun set behind it. The hands of the clock then spin forward to a point in the future when Chateaubriand's memoirs, always understood to be posthumous, 'd'outre-tombe', will have been published, and he will be united with Gabrielle in death *and* in the book which links them. Thus the resurrection of a past epoch, that of Henri IV— the first Bourbon, associated for Chateaubriand with an acceptable monarchy—links to a future in which he will be resurrected in his book: pushed out of history at the level of events, Chateaubriand reinserts himself into historicity by an act of imagination and fantasy. The marginal, insubstantial instant is converted into a nexus of relations and representations, involving the superimposition of six temporal levels.

Thirdly, there is the *mise en scène* of time as a psychological reality, a kind of psychotemporality in which the sudden translucence of an earlier moment in a present one disrupts the linearity of time and introduces the subject into an associative space, an 'entre-deux'.[23] If the bird-song transports Chateaubriand back to Combourg, the account of adolescence which follows is strongly marked by the interaction of temporal planes rather than the restoration of lost unity. The remarkable descriptions of the father as a ghostly revenant from the medieval past ('ma mère, ma sœur et moi, transformés en statue par la présence de mon père . . .', etc. (i. 111)) contrast with the evocations of adolescent desire (incarnated by the *Sylphide*, a syncretic representation of the eternal feminine constructed out

---

[23] Stimulating reflections on this theme will be found in André Vial, *Chateaubriand et le temps perdu*.

of fleeting sexual intimations), setting up a conflict between past and future which dislocates the temporal framework.

Deeply characteristic of Chateaubriand, the device of superimposition, as employed in the passage we have considered, makes him to some degree an exponent of the 'wild' incident. Interrupting a broadly linear narrative, the incident draws attention to the act of writing and imposes its own temporal coordinates; it summons up a particular kind of attention which discloses a nexus of temporal relationships amalgamating the personal and the historical. Meaning is located in the dialectic of past and present rather than in the reconstruction of a past causality, and the incident is seen as a global metaphor for the subject's identity rather than as part of a totality. At the same time there are elements of the tendency we labelled 'domestication'. The very alacrity with which Chateaubriand shuttles back and forth between one moment or context and another indicates that while incidents do not serve a purely illustrative or instrumental function, they never fully accede to autonomy as centres of interest before being assimilated by an overarching logic; this derives in part from the Romantic ethos Chateaubriand himself helped create, but also, more specifically, from the text's relatively stable thematic emphases.

Very often, in *Mémoires d'outre-tombe*, Chateaubriand's sense of history provides the key to his past experience. This fact, together with his discretion regarding personal relationships,[24] masks to some extent the considerable interest and originality of his contribution to French autobiography. This lies in the interaction of the individual and history, and the presentation of the self in terms of images and echoes. Jean-Pierre Richard refers to 'le caractère essentiellement projectif de l'intériorité chateaubrianesque' and comments: 'incapable de se saisir directement lui-même . . . il se poursuivra donc à travers ses reflets ou ses échos'.[25] For Chateaubriand an encounter or a memory immediately prompts a connection with an earlier or later experience. So obsessive is this trait that, borrowing a word Nabokov invented to describe himself, we might call Chateaubriand a chronophiliac.[26] After one of the coincidences so frequent in the *Mémoires* (just as he is composing the narrative of his journey to America, thirty years after the event, he receives a letter from a fellow

---

[24] Chateaubriand makes it clear on several occasions that he disapproves of Rousseau's indiscretion and that he has no intention of emulating the author of the *Confessions* (cf. i. 164).

[25] J.-P. Richard, *Paysage de Chateaubriand*, 9 and 93.

[26] Chateaubriand would also no doubt have approved of Nabokov's assertion that 'the following of . . . thematic designs through one's life should be . . . the true purpose of autobiography', *Speak, Memory*, 23.

voyager who turns out to be his next-door neighbour in London) Chateaubriand reflects that, even if they are rarely brought back by chances such as this, one's past years are not irretrievably lost: 'lorsqu'il en fait la revue et qu'il les nomme, ils répondent "Présents". Aucun ne manque à l'appel' (i. 276). What bothers him is not the inaccessibility of the past but its profuse life, accompanied by an acute sense of loss. So pervasive are the past's echoes that they can make the present seem insubstantial, 'notre vie est si vaine qu'elle n'est qu'un reflet de notre mémoire' (i. 69), but past reflections and echoes are disparate, contradictory, and discontinuous. Several times Chateaubriand uses the image of geological strata to convey this: 'Nos ans et nos souvenirs sont étendus en couches régulières et parallèles, à différentes profondeurs de notre vie déposées par les flots du temps qui passent successivement sur nous' (iv. 308). Elsewhere he remarks 'L'homme n'a pas une seule et même vie: il en a plusieurs mises bout à bout, et c'est sa misère' (i. 137).

In the light of this, autobiography becomes euphoric chronophilia, a revel amidst coincidences, repetitions, thematic variations, the exploitation of a whole 'rhétorique de l'existence', as Richard puts it.[27] Discontinuity is reinforced rather than mitigated: as one memory finds its echo in another, as analogies are discovered between diverse planes of experience, the effect is not so much to affirm as to fragment and disrupt identity. Chronological order gives way to potentially endless substitution: 'ma mémoire oppose sans cesse mes voyages à mes voyages, montagnes à montagnes, fleuves à fleuves, et ma vie détruit ma vie. Même chose m'arrive à l'égard de la société et des hommes' (iv. 237). The notion of a kind of self-destructive quality in the repetitions and parallels of recollected experience is elsewhere expressed in terms of erasure: 'les événements effacent les événements, inscriptions gravées sur d'autres inscriptions, ils font des pages de l'histoire des palimpsestes' (i. 43–4). Past inscriptions subsist, memories remain 'présents à l'appel' but what is effaced is the distinctiveness and specificity of the individual moment as it becomes part of an anachronistic series, a structural element in an endless 'bricolage'. Writing from Dieppe in 1836 Chateaubriand observes:

Dieppe est vide de moi-même: c'était un autre *moi*, un moi de mes premiers jours finis, qui jadis habita ces lieux, et ce *moi* a succombé, car nos ans meurent avant nous. Ici vous m'avez vu sous-lieutenant au régiment de Navarre . . . vous m'y avez revu exilé sous Bonaparte: vous m'y rencontrerez de nouveau lorsque les journées de juillet m'y surprendront. M'y voici encore; j'y reprends la plume pour continuer mes confessions (ii. 10).

---

[27] *Paysage de Chateaubriand*, 121 ff.

The grip of the past on Chateaubriand's self-imaginings may be illustrated with reference to the account of his first steps in Parisian society in the years 1786–7 where it is not the analysis of specific events which animates the narrative, but their infiltration by parallels and digressions involving other moments, personal and historical. A prologue characteristically resituates the moment of writing: we are in 1821, Chateaubriand is now ambassador to Berlin, and he turns to his memoirs when the secretaries have gone home. The autobiographer withdraws from actuality but does not remain for long at any specific temporal level. Each of the main events he covers is drawn into a montage involving disparate levels of history. In its original context the death of his father had little impact. But by juxtaposing his death certificate, with its florid, feudal rhetoric, 'Le corps du haut et puissant Messire René de Chateaubriand . . . époux de la haute et puissante dame Appollonie-Jeanne-Suzanne de Bédée', with that of his mother in 1812, 'décédée le 12 prairial, an six de la République française, au domicile de la citoyenne Gouyon', Chateaubriand vividly portrays the gulf between pre- and post-revolutionary France. 'Dans l'extrait mortuaire de ma mère, la terre roule sur d'autres pôles: nouveau monde, nouvelle ère' (i. 158).

In more whimsical vein, Chateaubriand's account of his solitary existence in Paris focuses on his search for a pretty laundress mentioned in one of the escapades of the seventeenth-century nobleman Bassompierre. Following the directions in Bassompierre's *Mémoires*, 216 years later, Chateaubriand was disappointed to find a modern house at the specified address, but pursued the matter as far as enquiring whether a young girl answering the memorialist's description had been seen in the neighbourhood (i. 165–8). There is more to this than the strong element of historical fantasy which anticipates Nerval. By superimposing Bassompierre's experience on his own, reading his own past through someone else's, Chateaubriand reinforces rather than closes the divisions between the writing self and the past self; rather than retrieving a past identity, he reinscribes his past image in a hall of mirrors where a variety of moments reflect and displace one another without fusing. Similarly, in the account of his presentation at the court of Louis XVI, Chateaubriand narrates the events with wry detachment: 'Le roi plus embarrassé que moi, ne trouvant rien à me dire, passa outre' (i. 169). The incident was of little significance, particularly since, as Chateaubriand explains at length, he was temperamentally incapable of turning it to his advantage. But a massive increment of meaning arises when this brief encounter is placed in the context of Chateaubriand's subsequent relationship to the French monarchy, and especially when it is linked to the extraordinary moment in 1815, frequently referred to in the

Mémoires, when Chateaubriand was charged with the gruesome task of identifying the remains of Louis XVI and Marie-Antoinette so that, after being scattered on common ground at the revolution, their bones could be reburied at St. Denis. Here the narrative comes alive: 'Et ce nouveau courtisan qu'il [Louis XVI] regardait à peine, chargé de démêler les ossements parmi les ossements, après avoir été sur preuves de noblesse présenté aux grandeurs du fils de Saint Louis, le serait un jour à sa poussière sur preuves de fidélité!' (i. 169). Further on, Chateaubriand will claim somewhat implausibly that his brief glimpse of Marie-Antoinette's smile in 1789 enabled him to identify her skull in 1815. In both cases there is a striking disproportion between the fleeting incident and the booming resonances it is given in a textual montage. Chateaubriand maintains a chronological narrative of past events, but plays down any inherent significance they may have had in their original context, prizing them rather for their echoes of past and future time. In so doing, he rarely employs an idiom of foreshadowing or presentiment which would maintain and bolster some form of continuity. His mode is, rather, that of juxtaposition and discontinuity so that it is generally across a gulf, a temporal abyss, that past, present, and future moments find in the text a place of reverberation.

From the point of view which concerns us here, the later sections of *Mémoires d'outre-tombe* (prior to the general conclusion) are of particular interest. Books i–x of the 'Quatrième partie' dealing with Chateaubriand's abortive missions to the exiled Charles X on behalf of the Duchesse de Berry were originally written quite soon after the events they record, at the beginning of the period which then saw the complete rewriting of the earlier parts of the text, as well as the composition of much of the account of 1800–30 which occupies parts ii and iii. The style and perspective of the 'Quatrième partie' therefore strongly influenced the text as a whole. This is where the notion of writing 'd'outre-tombe'—the adoption of an imaginary narratorial position beyond history, and the conception of the work as a 'temple de la mort élevé à la clarté de mes souvenirs' (i. 15)—fully takes grip. At this stage Chateaubriand knew that his political career was over. Having resigned from the Chambre des Pairs with a resounding speech (reported verbatim), he has no place in Louis-Philippe's regime. Yet, as his account amply shows, he does not really believe in the machinations of the *légitimistes*. He recognizes that his relation to the monarchy is paradoxical since he sees it as responsible for its own downfall and acknowledges that he has little in common with other royalists. He sees the acceptance of the Duchesse's mission—to liaise with the exiled Charles X in Prague, knowing that her manœuvres were wholly anachronistic—as the act of a man who has cast himself as 'l'homme dédaigné de la légitimité', and who has forsaken praxis for melodrama, grandeur for *grand guignol*. Going to Prague is a sort of *acte gratuit*, an 'ego-trip' based on images rather than realities—the apotheosis of the marginal. Chateaubriand's carriage becomes a time-capsule in which he travels forwards, to a French king at a foreign court, and backwards into an imaginary vision of the French monarchy.

On the first of two visits to Prague, with a long detour to Venice, the ageing writer sets off in 'ma calèche délabrée comme la monarchie de Hugues Capet' (iv. 210). The carriage had once belonged to Talleyrand and is therefore, he snidely remarks, ill-used to being faithful to royalty. Associations soon come thick and fast: 'Matière de songes est partout' (iv. 182). One of his antennae is acutely sensitive to signals of his own notoriety. Delighted when a schoolboy rushes up and pays homage with a quotation from Virgil, Chateaubriand archly claims to be put out at his treatment by a surly customs guide: 'il existait sur terre un homme qui n'avait jamais entendu parler de moi' (iv. 197). Later he comes across a hotel dining-room papered with scenes from *Atala* and notes that she too is getting older and fainter. Forced to halt in the Bavarian village of Waldmunchen Chateaubriand translates everything he does and sees into metaphors and mythic self-images. Spying a man with some pigs he observes: 'Je m'aperçois que cette partie de mes Mémoires n'est rien moins qu'une Odyssée; Waldmunchen est Ithaque, le berger est le fidèle Eumée avec ses porcs, je suis Ulysse, revenu après avoir parcouru la terre et les mers' (iv. 203). Chateaubriand revels in the theatricality of his mission: he carries a message from the Duchesse to the Dauphine written in lemon juice, and at Carlsbad he helps her heat it over a flame. A couple of months later when he goes to meet the Duchesse at Ferrara he notes: 'nous ne ressemblions pas mal à une troupe ambulante de comédiens français jouant à Ferrare, par la permission de Messieurs les magistrats de la ville, *La Princesse fugitive* ou *La Mère persécutée*' (iv. 432).

The encounters with the royal family have a fantastic air. In the Hradschin Palace with its empty corridors and muffled sounds they huddle like strange creatures from another planet. The royal children are compared to gazelles hiding among ruins, while banal exchanges with the elderly Charles X are made to seem monstrously weird—as if a waxwork figure had suddenly acquired the power of speech. The climb up the steep hill to the castle provides an archaeological vista in which the historical past and Chateaubriand's own are simultaneously brought to light:

A mesure que je montais je découvrais la ville au-dessous. Les enchaînements de l'histoire, le sort des hommes, la destruction des empires, les desseins de la Providence, se présentaient à ma mémoire en s'identifiant aux souvenirs de ma propre destinée: après avoir été appelé au spectacle des ruines mortes j'étais appelé au spectacle des ruines vivantes (iv. 216).

This total internalization of what he sees is conveyed three times through the image of memory as a camera obscura which immediately transposes the outer scene on to an inner screen. Throughout his travels Chateaubriand describes people, landscapes, monuments, nature. Birds often trigger associations: at Bischofsheim a nightingale perches on the dining-room windowsill and Chateaubriand translates its twittering into a speech in which the bird reels off a list of ancestors who have accompanied him at various times in his life from Combourg to America, London, Berlin, and Rome. A particularly beautiful superimposition concerns Murano where Chateaubriand made a point of visiting the glass-factory where the mirrors in his mother's bedroom at Combourg had been made. A glass-blower spins a sliver of glass—'comme le temps file notre fragile vie' (iv. 355)—which reminds him of a glass nose-pendant worn by a Native American girl he had seen at Niagara. A chapel in Venice recalls St Christopher carrying Christ across a river, and prompts Chateaubriand to note, exquisitely, 'Et moi aussi j'ai voulu porter un enfant-Roi, mais je ne m'étais pas aperçu qu'il dormait dans son berceau avec des siècles: fardeau trop pesant pour mes bras' (iv. 353).

From time to time Chateaubriand reminds us that 'ces mémoires que je barbouille en courant' (iv. 275) are the jottings of an old man scurrying across Europe in a carriage. He draws attention, semi-apologetically, to his digressive style ('un mot me mène à l'autre. Je m'en vais en Islande et aux Indes . . . Et pourtant je ne suis pas encore sorti de la vallée de la Tèple' (iv. 272)). At one point he even craves our indulgence by reminding us that the author is dead: 'Lecteurs, supportez ces arabesques; la main qui les dessina ne vous fera jamais d'autre mal; elle est séchée. Souvenez-vous, quand vous les verrez, qu'ils ne sont que les capricieux enroulements tracés par un peintre à la voûte de son tombeau' (iv. 308). The awareness of writing under the aegis of death, of converting the immediate into the posthumous and of writing 'd'outre-tombe', runs through the text as a particular way of enunciating existence. The devices I have outlined—superimposition, the *mise en scène* of time, the assimilation of writing and travelling, the obsession with disparate images, and above all the massive preponderance of a multitude of small incidents over any long-term causalities—serve to displace the protagonist from history to the perpetually anachronistic sphere of memory. Still enmeshed in temporality, Chateaubriand injects the fluid of memory into the hardened arteries of historical time. This displacement matches the espousal of the marginal and anachronistic, so prominent in the journeys to Prague. Chateaubriand's desire to present himself as 'l'homme dédaigné de la légitimité', as a 'Cassandre inutile', as a ruin among ruins, as the last subject of the last king (iv. 522), the self-image which permeates the *Mémoires* as rewritten from the mid-1830s onwards, goes hand in hand with the text's narrative dynamics, so much so that it is ultimately in the dialectic of writing and existence, as exemplified supremely in the journeys, that one can see Chateaubriand simultaneously adopting the reading of his political career that will cast its shadow over the whole text, and creating the narrative voice which haunts it.

Stendhal may have been right to call Chateaubriand 'le roi des égotistes',[28] but if self-apotheosis was one of the author's goals in constructing the extraordinary funerary monument of the *Mémoires d'outre-tombe*, what he communicates is by no means the secure 'présence à soi' of a sovereign, transcendent subjectivity. In its monumental aspect the massive textual edifice is in theory a bulwark against death and dissolution, yet it also acts as a reminder of these agencies: the text is a 'temple de la mort', and throughout the *Mémoires d'outre-tombe* monuments are associated with emptiness, ruin, and impermanence.[29] If in Chateaubriand the movement of autobiographical memory tends to void the given moment of autonomous meaning, and to destroy its specificity, the compensatory replenishment it derives from being serialized depends essentially on the perpetual motions of associative memory and, ultimately, on the 'empty' miracle of writing itself.[30] Yet it is the animated semiotic ambience he engenders through the *mise en scène* of self-images in time, and the effects produced by a constantly shifting and dramatized narrative present inflected by the consistently paradoxical *gageure* of writing, hypothetically, 'd'outre-tombe', which serve to make Chateaubriand's way with incidents as revisionary, *vis-à-vis* Rousseau, as Stendhal's.

Each member of this great triumvirate developed new potentialities in the poetics of the autobiographical incident. Rousseau, with the benefit of his incomparably fluid style, placed incidents at the heart of autobiography, demonstrating not only how readily they could serve the interests of a

---

[28] *Vie de Henry Brulard*, 30. On the relationship between the two writers see P. Berthier, *Stendhal et Chateaubriand*.

[29] For a closely argued discussion of the functions of the monument motif see M. Riffaterre, 'Chateaubriand et le monument imaginaire'.

[30] 'Le *fait* de l'écriture, dans le moment même qu'elle énonce une destruction, représente la victoire du monument sur la ruine', Riffaterre, 'Chateaubriand', 80.

dominant narrative line, but also how, less subserviently, they could become relatively autonomous and potentially subversive centres of interest. In playing down narrative teleology and stressing the process of autobiographical attention, Stendhal gave incidents a different kind of evidential status rooted in pleasure and desire conceived as the channels of subjectivity. By contrast, the ontology of the incident in Chateaubriand may seem superficial: no sooner attended to than the incident deflects attention away from itself towards its avatars and antecedents. But here the very real power of incidents to determine rather than to be determined by autobiographical meaning does not lie in their *quidditas* but in the perpetual motion engendered when the accent is placed on echoes and parallels.

There is no need to underline further the ways in which incidents in the *Mémoires d'outre-tombe* conform in other respects to our profile of the 'wild' incident: the stress on temporality, and the dramatization of the moment of writing are clearly the most important features. A word should be said, however, about Chateaubriand's legacy. As I suggested earlier, narrativized (and domesticated) incidents became autobiography's staple in the course of the nineteenth century. Followed in the letter but not in the spirit, Rousseau's example—edulcorated and sanitized (sex and paranoia are suppressed)—fostered in Romantic writers such as Sand, Lamartine, and Berlioz a genuine if sometimes perfunctory attention to childhood, and a concern with the interplay of inner and outer, public and private facets of experience. The success of the *roman intime*, from Constant's *Adolphe* to Flaubert's *Novembre* and Fromentin's *Dominique*, further consolidated the subservience of incident to overall narrative coherence and also offered, in the age of realist fiction, a convenient substitute for fully fledged autobiography. In this context Chateaubriand's deviant approach appears to have had little impact prior to its enthusiastic endorsement by Proust. Indeed, for an autobiography which unmistakably bears his stamp we have to wait until the publication, a century after the *Mémoires d'outre-tombe*, of the work of another writer-politician (and self-mythologist), André Malraux.[31] Yet Chateaubriand's strong sense of the permeability and permutability of experience, which makes the fleeting, marginal, insignifi-

---

[31] The superimposition of disparate moments in time on the basis of analogies between them is the basic structural principle in Malraux's *Antimémoires* (originally published in 1967, then incorporated into the 2-vol. *Le Miroir des limbes*), where the juxtaposition of incidents from widely scattered phases of his life (and, as in Chateaubriand, from earlier writings) occurs continually (for an excellent discussion of Malraux's technique see Riffaterre, *Essais de stylistique structurale*, 286–306). As in Chateaubriand, the self is conceived primarily in terms of roles and self-images profiled against the background of

cant character of certain incidents a central part of their fascination and power, is echoed in the para-autobiographical writings of Nerval, and in a range of twentieth-century works—from Apollinaire and Breton to Butor—where the creation of a personal myth occurs in the context of a close reading—thematic and structural—of the text of experience.[32] By this time, of course, the impact of Stendhal's approach to autobiography, and to the autobiographical incident, had also made itself felt (*Vie de Henry Brulard* remained unpublished until 1890), and in the course of the century the modernity of both writers has gained increasing recognition.[33]

JULIEN GREEN: *JEUNES ANNÉES*

Early in the first volume of his autobiography Green writes: 'Ce qui importe, ce qu'il faut essayer de saisir et de bien retracer, c'est le passage de Dieu dans la vie d'un homme, et c'est ainsi que peu à peu j'entrevois le sens de ce livre' (i. 41).[34] And then, further on: 'Je voudrais retrouver le fil plus fin qu'un cheveu qui passe à travers ma vie, de ma naissance à ma mort, qui guide, qui lie et qui explique' (i. 76). Although there is no necessary contradiction between these statements they refer in practice to divergent paths of understanding: (*a*) the identification of a transcendent dimension in past experience; (*b*) the reconstruction of links in a chain of causalities. With regard to the latter, Green sometimes fears that his expertise as a novelist has led to excessive coherence (i. 286), and he consequently insists from time

---

death which is seen to pervade all experience. In Malraux's case the device of superimposition stems from a hostility to introspection. On this point see the chapter on Malraux in R. Elbaz, *The Changing Nature of the Self*.

[32] Riffaterre argues, with reference to Malraux (*Essais de stylistique structurale*, 296) that the device of structural superimposition is fundamentally poetic, and the point would certainly apply to Chateaubriand. On Nerval and autobiography see N. Rinsler, 'Nerval's *Promenades et Souvenirs*: The Structure of Chance'.

[33] It is interesting to note, among the later works of Barthes, enthusiastic appreciations of the autobiographical writings of both Stendhal and Chateaubriand: see 'On échoue toujours à parler de ce qu'on aime' in *Bruissement*, 333–42, and 'Pour un Chateaubriand de papier' in *Le Grain de la voix*, 321–5.

[34] Green's autobiography originally consisted of 4 separately published vols.: *Partir avant le jour* (1963), *Mille chemins ouverts* (1964), *Terre lointaine* (1966), *Jeunesse* (1974), which were subsequently brought together, with the addition of a certain amount of new material, in vol. v of his *Œuvres complètes* in the Bibliothèque de la Pléiade, ed. by Jacques Petit (1977). In 1984 a 'nouvelle édition augmentée' was published by Éditions du Seuil under the collective title *Jeunes années*; this comprises 2 vols. subtitled *Autobiographie* i and ii. The main addition was a new concluding section, 'Fin de Jeunesse'. References, incorporated in the text, will be to this edn.

to time on the fragmentary nature of his recollections,[35] conceding that
perhaps 'l'essentiel me demeure-t-il caché' (i. 55). This in turn is reflected in
his ambivalent treatment of narrative focus. At times Green insists that, by
dint of 'une sorte de substitution de personne' (ii. 504), the adult writer is
dictated to by his younger self and that the child's viewpoint prevails.[36] Yet
Green also makes frequent references to the child's ignorance and lack of
perspicacity (e.g. 'les petits événements de la vie semblaient ne rien
m'apprendre sur moi-même' (i. 416)), contrasting this with the writer's
retrospective insights and discoveries. On this view what the child
'provides' is not a dictation to be taken down but, at each stage, a fresh crop
of untarnished incidents for the writer to work on (Green in fact often
stresses the revelations that occur as he writes, recognizing that they derive
from what Georges Gusdorf calls 'une seconde lecture de l'expérience [qui]
en est la prise de conscience').[37] In fact *Jeunes années*, which is organized not
in chapters but in short two- or three-page sections divided by asterisks, is a
mosaic of incidents. These are of numerous kinds: decisive moments,
epiphanies, encounters, actions, and many are given vital roles in Green's
account of his past. However, the treatment of incidents is characterized by
a variety of tensions and oppositions including those we have so far
identified. To explore this further, three narrative levels will be examined
successively: the point-to-point movement of narrative logic; an overarching theological perspective, the putative 'passage de Dieu'; and the act of
narrative 'énonciation' itself.

In spite of a certain amount of scene-painting, and the occasional air of an
impressionistic evocation of time past (turn-of-the-century Paris, an
American family very aware of its roots in the *ante-bellum* South), Green's
autobiography is narrowly focused on the emergence of the writer's sexual
identity (ultimately his homosexuality), its interaction with his religious
sensibility, and with his aesthetic vocation. *Partir avant le jour*, centred on
childhood, establishes a number of strands, each constituted largely by a
series of incidents. First, sex is associated with evil through such episodes as
his mother's threat to cut off his penis (i. 26) (the exclamation 'Alcotétof'

---

[35] Stressing e.g. the 'blancs' he keeps encountering, and drawing attention to the memory
process or the role of forgetting (cf. i. 63, 410, etc.).

[36] Perhaps the most striking expression of this idea is the following: 'Se promener dans un
passé aussi lointain, c'est suivre l'enterrement d'un jeune homme et courir après son fantôme.
Il ne dira que ce qu'il veut, gardant son secret' (ii. 418). The adoption of this view is linked to
the question of whether the writer should pass judgement on his past or simply express
solidarity with the child he once was, and with the state of childhood itself (cf. i. 40).

[37] 'Conditions et limites de l'autobiographie', 227.

became proverbial among family servants!); a boy exposing himself at school (i. 78); his mother's veiled references to Uncle Willie which culminate in the revelation that he died of syphilis (i. 158). Secondly, Green imbibes a rich brew of religious influences from his mother who, after a lifetime of staunch Episcopalianism, was edging towards the Catholic Church in her last years. Soon after her early death, a key event in the narrative, Green, aged 14, discovers a guide to Catholic doctrine amongst his father's laundry (i. 182) and is officially converted shortly afterwards. Thirdly, works of art and the activity of drawing figure prominently in the many incidents relating to sexual feelings. At age 6 Green discovers Doré's depictions of the 'corps souffrants et splendides' (i. 40) in Dante's *Inferno*, and these are held to have determined his sexual tastes ('fixaient à jamais mes goûts' (i. 41)). A little later, the painting of a pharaoh and slaves at the Musée du Luxembourg engenders 'le tourment d'une faim qui ne peut s'assouvir . . . Une frustration aussi douloureuse ne peut se décrire. Elle me marqua profondément, à jamais' (i. 43).[38] The identification of desire with hunger and lack will be definitive, and the effect of the image will be reinforced when he finds it in a book at home. Green's own drawings ('gribouillages') become an outlet for his embryonic sexual fantasies. A further twist in his sexual evolution is prompted by the discovery of erotic paintings by Giulio Romano which instil both 'le plaisir de la chair' and a sense of sin (i. 223). A fourth strand—separation from other people—runs through incidents involving the birth of self-awareness (i. 22); private rituals reflecting the fear of contact and the feeling of inhabiting a 'zone interdite' centred on his body (i. 101); a sense of the unreality of the external world and of personal inviolability (i. 249).[39]

The same themes recur in the three subsequent parts of *Jeunes années*[40]— concerning, respectively, Green's service with the American army, his three

[38] The painting, which has been identified as *Les Porteurs de mauvaises nouvelles* by Lecomte de Noüy, is conveniently reproduced in R. de Saint Jean and L. Estang, *Julien Green*, 12.

[39] The four strands I have identified are of course interlinked, and some incidents involve specific connections between them. For example, Green takes his crucifix off the wall when he masturbates (i. 213), and at one point secures Père Crété's permission to confess to an unknown priest, thus instituting a system where sin is followed by immediate exoneration behind the olive-green curtain at Saint Honoré d'Eylau (i. 217). Religion and sexuality become connected in the context of a visit to Genoa where Green experiences a 'griserie étrange' which will become persistent (i. 223); and religious fervour takes on a narcissistic, self-enclosed character when he becomes obsessed with his 'saintly' demeanour. These connections will have further repercussions when, in later vols., the homosexual character of Green's sexuality emerges.

[40] i.e. *Mille chemins ouverts, Terre lointaine, Jeunesse*.

years at the University of Virginia, and the period following his return to
Paris when he began to write in earnest—which focus increasingly on the
progressive recognition of his homosexuality. Religion continues to be
important. At times, religious fervour panders to the interests of a repressed
sexuality, providing the alibi required by a love reluctant to acknowledge its
name: 'La sensualité avait changé d'étage, mais elle habitait toujours la
même maison' (i. 338). Religious preoccupations perpetuate Green's
naïvety about sexual matters and also encourage self-absorption rather than
human contact: 'mon cerveau devenait un mauvais lieu' (i. 335). Religion
also figures in an increasingly enervating oscillation between acknowledgement and disavowal of sexuality and thus helps to exacerbate the obsessional
character of Green's sexual conflicts. 'Il y avait alors dans ma vie deux forces
contraires, je le vois bien, et l'une tenait l'autre en échec' (i. 330). The
existence of 'un conflit entre le spirituel et le charnel' (ii. 270) becomes
established as a key to Green's predicament. His tendency to feel cut off
from the world intensifies as his sexual drama unfolds. There are many
incidents involving mirrors or polished surfaces in which he pays anxious
homage to his physical charms.[41] The recurrent images of the 'cercle
magique' (ii. 17) and the 'cellule portative' (i. 373) express his mental
isolation. Drawing still sometimes serves as a channel for obsession, as does
writing: 'En une seconde, je rejoignis les hallucinations de ma sixième année
et le mal se glissa dans mon cerveau comme dans les couloirs d'un palais
dont il avait retrouvé le chemin. Peut-être n'y a-t-il pas eu dans ma vie de
minute plus décisive' (i. 310).

Incidents involving sexual encounters are, as one would expect,
abundant. *Jeunes années* features a large cast of prurient *lycéens* and boy
scouts, American college boys with classical features, soldiers and sailors,
and, later on, anonymous street pick-ups. The stages on Green's way to
acknowledging and then acting on his homosexual desires are numerous and
varied.[42] A particularly striking incident concerns a Greek statuette of

---

[41] Scenes involving mirrors will be found on i. 157, 234, 247, 309, 337, 341, 347, 368, 389,
408; ii. 63, 263, 345, 469.

[42] Dalliance with a girl in Milan which, if consummated, might have changed his sexual
history (i. 302); the overwhelming impact of a soldier glimpsed outside the American
embassy (i. 410); the lewd inscriptions at Pompei (Green is prevailed upon to purchase
reproductions, but is inspired to throw them overboard when a young man does the same
with a copy of Zola's *La Terre* exclaiming: 'saletés', i. 429); embarrassment at the classical
statues which adorn the neo-classical University of Virginia (ii. 27), and at posters for
underwear (ii. 121); a lecture on the 'boy-love' of the ancients (ii. 42) followed by a reading of
Havelock Ellis (ii. 168, 174) which finally opens his eyes; his durable infatuation for the 'ange,
Mark S.' as well as his feelings for Ted, cousin Bill, Nicholls, etc.

Narcissus in the museum at Naples: 'tout ce que j'avais en moi de religion batailla pour me faire quitter cet endroit dangereux, mais je ne bougeai pas' (i. 416). The museum-attendant, observing Green's rapture, presses him to order a reproduction of the statue, which could be shipped to America at little cost. Green acquiesces, and the consequences are momentous:

de toutes les rencontres que j'ai jamais faites sur terre, la rencontre de cet homme me fut certainement la plus néfaste. Je n'insinue pas que j'avais eu affaire au diable en personne! Sans doute ce gardien était-il parfaitement innocent dans toute cette histoire dont je raconterai la suite dans un autre volume, mais il est certain que, s'il ne se fût pas trouvé là, le cours de ma vie eût peut-être changé (i. 418).

As so often in Green, the causative power of the incident is affirmed in hyperbolic terms, yet no attempt at substantiation is made before we move on to yet more incidents. True, there is a sequel in this case: to Green's consternation, the statue, with its 'nudité insolente', duly arrives at his aunt's house in Savannah, eliciting admiration for his cultivated tastes (ii. 83), and prompting the young man, who tries not to look at it too often, to plunge into St Paul and become, temporarily, 'un autre homme'. But this does nothing to ratify the incident's credentials as a major turning point. Even if we choose to diagnose a failure of the will to resist temptation as the gist of the event at Naples, we lack grounds for seeing the event as anything more than a symptom of Green's retrospective reading of his past experience.

Green is by no means uncritical of the posturings to which his contradictions led him ('je voulais être à la fois un dieu grec et un saint catholique', ii. 281), particularly in his American period. Equally, his indulgence towards the tortured young man who, on his return to Paris, inaugurates an active sexual life 'dans les rues de la ville nocturne' (ii. 335) seems entirely justified. The Jekyll and Hyde alliance between the 'religieux manqué' and the 'cheval fou' (ii. 255), the accounts of studious days laced with licentious nights on the prowl, 'ligoté de nouveau par l'ancien désir' (ii. 325), racked by a 'faim sexuelle ne me laissant presque aucun répit' (ii. 334), are powerfully evocative. Religion is seen to have provided some cover at the price of sophistry: 'Si la nuit, en effet, je devenais le gibier de Satan, le jour j'étais autre, et l'autre était sauvé. Ce raisonnement douteux ne pénétrait pas jusqu'à ma conscience, mais, si je puis dire, flottait autour d'elle, cherchant à l'endormir' (ii. 346). And religion plays an unexpected role in some of his sexual encounters. In one incident (ii. 342) Green is suddenly prompted to ask one of his partners if he is a believer: 'D'où venait l'irrésistible tendance à voir dans le prochain quelqu'un à sauver? Il y avait en moi une dame de l'Armée du Salut avec son tambourin et ses questions indiscrètes. Peut-être même est-ce elle qui écrit ce livre étrange!' (ii. 342).[43]

What we have established so far can be summed up as follows. Throughout *Jeunes années* a multitude of incidents provide the energy which propels a markedly linear narrative forwards in perpetual motion. The reader is borne along from point to point on a frequently dizzying ride, as each incident delivers its cargo of causal material and then fades into the distance. Hyperbole repeatedly underscores the enduring power or long-term effects of particular moments. Declarations such as 'Cette minute fut peut-être la plus importante de ma vie' (i. 18), or 'Peut-être n'y a-t-il pas eu dans ma vie de minute plus décisive' (i. 310) are recurrent. The word 'minute' is especially favoured, and although it often identifies moments of pure exhilaration or mystery, there is usually a causal implication.[44] The same applies to the frequent use of prolepsis. Green often suggests that a given event portended a later (usually unspecified) development, sometimes imminent but quite often located at a very much later stage in his narrative.[45] Whilst in some respects these devices emphasize concatenation—the links between events, and between past and present—they also undermine it by presenting the incident in absolute terms as a pure distillation of Green's 'essence'. Moreover, if incidents in *Jeunes années* are nevertheless bound together thematically, and thus create the various strands we have identified, the absence or incompletion of an overall structural design, and the lack of a clear hierarchy of incidents, deny resolution. If each one seems to have a clearly defined significance at the point when it occurs, the accumulation of incidents, the thematic parallels and oppositions they engender, encourages open-endedness. As a result we may conclude that, despite their predominance, incidents are not in themselves the prime sources of autobiographical meaning, and that their significance is in fact regulated at another level or in another dimension of the text.

The first dimension to which the reader is likely to turn is the theological—the traces of 'le passage de Dieu dans la vie d'un homme'. In fact, where the experience of theological reality is concerned, it is God's implacable rival—'le diable', 'le malin', le 'démon', 'satan', 'le prince de ce monde', 'l'ennemi', l'autre', 'celui qui veut nous perdre'[46]—who predomi-

---

[43] Green will suggest more than once that a sexual activity he could never entirely condone helped him emerge from narcissistic self-imprisonment and to engage with *le prochain*. But this was at the cost of a definitive separation between love and sex.

[44] Among the many minutes the following are of particular note: i. 18, 39, 64, 87, 168, 182, 221, 277, 425; ii. 30, 74, 265, 462.

[45] Cf. i. 323, 363, 418; ii. 63, 120, 124, 242.

[46] All these appellations figure more than once in the text.

nates. It is the Devil who inspires the child to ogle Dante's wretched sinners
(i. 40), or to feel impure stirrings at the sight of horses outside the 'Grands
Magasins du Louvre' (i. 72). As he executes his lurid drawings he feels that
'Il y avait quelqu'un avec moi' (i. 48, 72). An eternal opportunist, the Devil
takes advantage of our instincts and exploits '[les] circonstances et [le]
mécanisme délicat des causes et des effets' (i. 134). Titillated by the
lascivious Jeffries in the ambulance corps, young Green had experienced 'le
sentiment d'être devenu tout à coup une proie' (i. 322). On the fateful night
when he springs from his armchair, announcing 'je vais sortir' to his startled
father and sisters, it is 'le démon [qui] me lança dans les rues de la ville
nocturne' (ii. 335). The nature of the Devil's role is, however, far from clear.
On one hand he represents a transcendent agency which might appear to
make other explanatory strategies superfluous. But on the other hand the
devil's interventions are generally treated as *experiences*—as incidents—
within the wider context of Green's destiny. And of course they contrast
with the experiences of numinous deliverance, if not divine intervention,
which also feature in the text. As a result, the Devil, and the notion of a
struggle or oscillation between the diabolical and the divine, become little
more than a thematic element, a 'manner of speaking' about the conflicts
Green perceives in his life.[47] This is especially clear in a page from 'Fin de
jeunesse', the epilogue to Green's autobiography (to which we shall return
presently) where he reviews the diabolical excesses he perpetrated through
his drawings, and, once he had discovered 'les sortilèges des mots', in
writing:

Si je m'étends sur ces aspects de ma vie secrète, c'est que jamais peut-être une âme
n'a été livrée à l'esprit du mal comme le fut la mienne en ces heures lointaines. Un
miracle était nécessaire pour me dépêtrer du filet de rétiaire que l'ennemi lançait sur
moi, et le miracle se produisait tôt ou tard. Je comptais dessus (ii. 466).

The child played a Manichaean game, letting the Devil have his way,
knowing that God was waiting in the wings. But to put it that way is to
devalue these players as agents in his mental life, as Green seems to
acknowledge: 'On me dira que c'etait la nature et je pense que la
psychanalyse aurait aussi voix au chapitre. J'ignorais ces explications' (ii.

---

[47] On this point (the paradoxical role and status of the Devil), as on many others, an
interesting comparison could be made between Green and Gide. Although homosexuality is
as central to *Jeunes années* as it is to *Si le grain ne meurt*, Green is manifestly less concerned
with self-defence than Gide. Nevertheless like Gide's, his handling of autobiographical
narrative, and particularly of causes, origins, and consequences, tends to problematize rather
than clarify. There is a dismissive reference to Gide's *Corydon* in *Jeunesse* (ii. 439). For a
discussion of Gide see Ch. 6 below.

466). This seems to make the hypothesis of the Devil, and the notion of being vulnerable to 'l'esprit du mal', a function of the child's ignorance. By indicating his willingness to consider other 'explications' Green denies any definitive validity to a theological reading of his past.[48]

This brings us to the narratorial dimension of *Jeunes années*. Does the narrator's discourse remove the difficulties we have encountered and provide the perspective in which incidents 'make sense'? The straightforward answer is 'no'. Whatever its validity, Green's insistence that it is the protagonist who 'dictates' makes him reluctant to vitalize the 'moment de l'écriture', and to refer us to the present act of narration as the locus of truth. By default it becomes the site of unresolved oppositions, anxieties, resistances, and desires. True, the narrator's presence in the text—through hyperbole, prolepsis, the ecstatic celebration of past moments and their return in writing—could scarcely be more strongly marked. Yet, for all that, the narrator remains a shadowy figure who reveals relatively little about the connections between his past and present selves.[49] Symptomatic of this are Green's evident difficulties in concluding his autobiography. *Jeunesse* ends abruptly with the encounter heralding a relationship which is to bring 'des années de bonheur . . . les plus belles de ma jeunesse' (ii. 456). However, the epilogue, *Fin de jeunesse*, tells a somewhat different story.[50] Here we gather that the relationship which had begun in 1924 had perpetuated Green's conflicts in the form of what he describes as an inexplicable inability to reconcile love and desire. At the outset, 'Je n'entrevoyais même pas les complications infinies que contenait en germe un amour aussi violent en l'absence de toute sexualité' (ii. 484). This leads to the elaborate account of an incident in 1929 when Green, who had condemned himself to chastity, had confessed his desires to his beloved 'compagnon' and found that the

---

[48] A number of the words he uses regularly, notably 'faim', 'chemin', 'amour', and 'mystère', are Janus-faced, connecting at once the all too human and the sphere of spiritual election, and thereby blurring the dividing-line between psychological causality and religious destiny.

[49] The same is true of Gide, perhaps for similar reasons. Like Gide Green was a diarist and a novelist before he was an autobiographer. In Green's case the inauguration of his *Journal* in 1926 (to be published regularly—14 vols. to date—from 1938 onwards) provided a *terminus ad quem* for his autobiography. Inherently discontinuous, the diary form enabled Green to record his life without providing a synthesis (on the relations between the autobiography and the diary see P. Lejeune, *L'Autobiographie en France*, 32 ff.)—a habit difficult to overcome when he adopted autobiography. The strongly autobiographical character of Green's fiction is well-known (see the discussion of this issue in the Pléiade edn., pp. 1584–5).

[50] Appended to the 1984 Seuil edn., 'Fin de jeunesse' is a 50-page coda substantially made up of material already published in the prefatory essays Green appended to the reissues of his principal novels, particularly *Adrienne Mesurat* and *Léviathan*, in the late 1970s.

other was beset with the same guilt-ridden obsessions. There follows the surprising account of their hasty departure for the flesh-pots of Germany where each sates himself in the 'bains publics' of Hamburg and Berlin. Yet Green's redemption quickly follows, although it is not religion but humane culture, in the guise of Signorelli's *Pan* and Goethe's house at Weimar, which restores him to what he now calls 'ma vraie nature', and to the recognition that with German youths, 'J'assouvissais une faim qui me révoltait' (ii. 492).

This is a conclusion of sorts. Referring to the years 1919–38 as a whole, Green indicates that, although he continued to be 'le jouet de Satan', he was no longer spiritually tormented. He had gained self-understanding: Body and Soul were not rival claimants as he had once thought; rather, as he had put it earlier, 'Il fallait faire du corps un esclave sourd et aveugle, obéissant jusqu'à la mort à toutes les royales injonctions de l'âme' (ii. 445). But he also hints that the struggle was protracted and terrible: 'l'idolâtrie de la beauté faisait de moi une sorte de malade' (ii. 441). This echoes one of a handful of remarks which incorporate the present, when, much earlier, he had referred to 'un grand combat dont je n'ai pas encore vu la fin' (i. 184). Implicit here are the consequences of the revival of his Catholic faith at the end of the 1930s. In making no direct reference to this or to other later developments Green, writing thirty years later, makes it more difficult for the 'présent de l'énonciation' to become too manifestly the origin of meaning. To pass judgement on the past from the vantage-point of the present would necessarily be to acknowledge everything that had happened up to this point. Avoiding this, Green frequently reminds us that his purpose is to focus on his 'jeunes années', to 'listen' to the youth he once was—the 'enfant torturé d'amour'—and to identify with his viewpoint.

One form of identification involves the recrudescence of past desire. Green's own body becomes a privileged object of the autobiographer's gaze—in the reconstruction of 'mirror scenes', in the emphasis on clothing, in the insistent concern with his looks. In addition, the *jouissance* of redirecting one's gaze at past bodies, through writing, is at the centre of numerous incidents, though what gives the desire its power is precisely that it is a repetition of frustration and lack. At one point Green admits that he regrets the opportunities he missed in America by reason of his shyness and ignorance (ii. 120). The obsession with past scenes of desire is well illustrated by an episode from his long infatuation with a young American named Mark. The incident is described twice, in more or less identical terms, in different volumes (*Terre lointaine*, ii. 236; *Jeunesse*, ii. 370). Green is accompanying Mark and a travelling-companion on a tour in Normandy.

At Rouen two rooms are available: who will share with Mark? Green tosses a coin—'La seconde qui suivit dura des années, dure encore' (ii. 236); Mark grabs the coin and nominates Green; they share a bed but Mark suddenly opts to sleep on the floor. 'Avec le temps', Green observes, 'je finis par voir toutes les significations qu'on pouvait donner de cet acte. A mes yeux, il demeure indéchiffrable et c'est mieux ainsi' (ii. 370). The incident's indecipherability—bearing on the question of whether Green's love was reciprocated, but also on that of whether love and desire could be reconciled—determines the enduring power manifested in its repetitions.

Narration is the place of enduring divisions and abiding desires. Like the text's theological dimension, the narrator's discourse in *Jeunes années* fails to provide a coherent overall perspective. The effect of this is to deny incidents the full 'domestication' which they appear to require. Yet, as we saw earlier, incidents in *Jeunes années*, despite their preponderance (but perhaps in part because of their very multiplicity) do not display in full measure the qualities which would make them 'wild'. While they are fully accredited as authentic carriers of autobiographical meaning, their significance seems to derive less from a density and autonomy evidenced or established in the context of writing, and capable of determining the trajectory of sense, than from their place within a closely wrought teleological pattern of causes and effects. The type of domestication this might lead one to anticipate would not involve subordination to a dominant extra-textual cultural paradigm but to a relatively stable, *ad hoc* network of meaning established by the text as a whole. However, in *Jeunes années*, the dimensions of the text susceptible of doing so do not serve to corroborate or elucidate the causalities advertised at the level of incidents: the theological dimension is never given full credence, and the narrator's discourse remains shadowy and ambiguous. As the text progresses, therefore, the dominance of incidents is progressively reinforced rather than undermined, even though the returns, so to speak, appear to diminish; their proliferation comes to have a compulsive quality which, in literary terms, is hypnotic and compelling. Incidents take on the air of fetishes, substitutes for a totality which (though never put in doubt) remains imperfectly explored—as fixation on the past progressively triumphs over comprehensive elucidation.

It would be rash to describe so elaborate and idiosyncratic an autobiography as in any sense typical, but the tension between wildness and domestication we have detected in Green's treatment of incidents, and the kinds of uncertainty it sponsors, are not unique to it. In a general sense Green's practice reflects a hesitancy shared notably by autobiographers of considerable literary sophistication (Gide would be an example) whose sense of the individual past precludes them from peremptorily laying down the law (or meekly invoking the law by which they abide) but who are unable or reluctant to make autobiography a radical gesture of self-investigation or self-mythologization.

LEIRIS: *L'AGE D'HOMME*

Consider the following incidents from *L'Age d'homme*. (1) Leiris's mother falls while carrying him and injures her forehead; her brother (Leiris's uncle) is unable to help because he has an arm in a sling (p. 76).[51] (2) Demonstrations by the 'Secouristes français': a man walks briskly across the stage and then suddenly collapses; two 'secouristes' appear and promptly apply appropriate first-aid techniques (p. 112). Leiris does not comment on the significance of his mother's fall. In the case of the 'Secouristes', he recalls the anguish he felt, the second time, at the prospect of the man's collapse; uncertain whether to link this to another memory, he connects it with the apprehension 'faits divers' (especially accidents which happen out of the blue) have always inspired in him, and with his tendency to fret when things go too well. Yet, in the case of both incidents, the reader is liable to make further connections—between the mother's fall and other episodes where she figures; between the first-aid display and the importance of theatricality in *L'Age d'homme*; between these instances of people falling (there are other examples in the text), and so on. To make such links is, we may feel, our role as readers of autobiographies. What is it, though, that makes 'connecting' so irresistible here, so particularly incumbent on us? How does it relate to the way *L'Age d'homme* is structured? What does it tell us about the status of incidents in this text?

In the case of our samples it is noticeable that classification predominates over interpretation. These incidents do not arise in the course of a chronological narrative but a thematic structure based on associations.[52] If

---

[51] Originally published in 1939 (but composed in 1930–5), *L'Age d'homme* was reissued in 1946 with an important prefatory essay, 'De la littérature considérée comme une tauromachie', and some additional notes. A further note, on Puccini, was added in the 1964 edn. References here, incorporated in the text, are to the Folio reprint.

[52] In 'De la littérature considérée comme une tauromachie' Leiris compares his technique to 'une sorte de collage surréaliste ou plutôt de photo-montage' (p. 16). The extensive critical literature on *L'Age d'homme* frequently touches on Leiris's methodology. See in particular P. Lejeune, *Lire Leiris* and *Le Pacte autobiographique*, 245–310; R. Bréchon, *L'Age d'homme*; J. Sturrock, 'The New Model Autobiographer'; S. Hand, 'The Orchastration of Man'; R. Simon, *Orphée médusé*.

in the first instance, however, the meaning of the incident is tied to its structural position, the nature of the structure is far from simple. The mother's fall belongs in the series *femmes blessées*, incidents which include a school play where a vestal virgin (played by a boy) was punished, and a lurid episode in Cardinal Wiseman's *Fabiola*; but the category 'femmes blessées' (p. 76) is a sub-set of another theme, indicated by the chapter title 'Lucrèce'. The image of the virtuous Roman heroine has led Leiris to locate in his memory-bank any deposits concerning injured or suffering women. Yet the pertinence of Lucretia for Leiris's investigation is itself contingent on her association with the figure of Judith, since it was the discovery of the Elder Cranach's diptych of these two which sowed the seeds of *L'Age d'homme*. And if the juxtaposition of the violated heroine who takes her own life, with the woman who used her powers of seduction to kill a tyrant and defeat her people's enemy, proved seminal for Leiris, it was specifically as a key to the features of his psycho-sexual makeup.[53] Thus, the associative network inspired by these figures is necessarily slanted towards the investigation of sexuality, and commandeered to some degree by Leiris's identification with the third 'figure' in Cranach's painting, the decapitated Holophernes. Moreover, in the case of 'femmes blessées'—and the mother's fall—the figure of Lucretia already involves another associative framework stemming from a chapter where Leiris had explored the strong aura of sexuality which the notion of antiquity—its 'côté salle de bains'—had exerted on him since childhood. Consequently, in the memories featuring injured women, the reader is likely to notice the references to antiquity when they are explicit, and perhaps supply them when they are not.

An earlier passage (pp. 64–7) has established a strong link between the mother and antiquity, and we may be tempted to relate the memory of her fall to the child's tendency to see events in larger-than-life terms, and in this case to see his mother as a tragic heroine. But we also need to take into account another aspect of the way the incident is framed. The fall occurs under the rubric 'Mon oncle l'acrobate' (pp. 76–80), in which far more space is given to Leiris's memories of his uncle than to the incident itself.

---

[53] Leiris indicates that the discovery of the Cranach painting in 1930 occurred in the context of his experience of psychoanalysis from which he emerged uncured and somewhat sceptical but nevertheless convinced that 'il y a une unité dans une vie et que tout se ramène, quoi qu'on fasse, à une petite constellation de choses qu'on tend à reproduire, sous des formes diverses, un nombre illimité de fois' (p. 201). His reaction to the juxtaposition of Judith and Lucretia suggested that it had a bearing on his particular 'constellation', and *L'Age d'homme* was initially conceived as a therapeutic investigation which might liberate him from 'un certain nombre de choses dont le poids m'oppressait' (p. 41).

Leiris's admiration for, and partial identification with, his uncle opens out on to other networks in *L'Age d'homme* (the theme of art, the prestige of what is 'nu et authentique', the willingness to sacrifice bourgeois comfort for passion's sake) and these lead us away from the fall: until we recognize that in the original incident the uncle was perhaps as important as the mother; her plight—and her status as a 'femme bléssée', a Lucretia—was partly a function of the uncle's inability to help; it is his impotence which makes her a victim, and it is with this impotence that Leiris identifies.

To spell out these connections is to be flat-footed and long-winded. Leiris's method, by contrast, is remarkably economical: setting up frames within frames it creates a context where minor incidents accumulate manifold meanings. The atmosphere surrounding incidents is reminiscent of Freud's case histories in which childhood experiences, whatever their original context or significance, are regarded as raw materials which may have been mobilized and transformed at any point in the subject's mental history. But if, for Freud, the memory of an incident will 'make sense' in the light of a network of associations uncovered (or supplied) in the work of analysis, for Leiris it is the process of textual construction which engenders meaning. In Freud meanings are assigned by the analyst, in Leiris they are largely a function of the interplay of themes and structures, and therefore remain virtual and unofficial: it is for the reader to collaborate in the work of analysis, even if in doing so he or she is unlikely to go beyond the possibilities foreseen by the author.

The 'Secouristes' incident belongs to the class 'hommes blessés' which derives from the identification with Holophernes (the chapter is entitled 'La Tête d'Holopherne'). But here, too, a subheading,[54] 'Cauchemars', provides a different frame through which the first-aid display is linked to another terrifying performance Leiris had witnessed in the same premises: recitations (notably a poem on nightmares) by a woman with a deep voice. Beyond unity of place, this may seem to have little connection with the falling man, until we speculate that in this case Leiris himself is the 'homme bléssé'—recoiling in terror at Medusa, the 'femme castratrice', incarnated by the statuesque woman 'drapée dans une robe à l'antique' (p. 113).[55] A further connection comes into view when the woman's nightmarish voice is identified with the snores of Leiris's father (and then his death-rattle) as

---

[54] It is interesting to note that in the table of contents Leiris chose to list these subheadings or rubrics, and to exclude the chapter titles, thus drawing attention to competing systems of organization, or rhythms, in his text.

[55] The figure of Medusa (cf. the chapter entitled 'Le Radeau de la Méduse') and the fear of castration (p. 202) play a prominent part in *L'Age d'homme*.

something which troubled the boy's sleep. In the light of this, Leiris's disquiet at the man's sudden fall might be interpreted as a displacement of the Freudian 'primal scene' (remembered or imagined glimpses of parental intercourse) or, more generally, as an aspect of the Oedipal scenario which figures prominently in *L'Age d'homme*.[56] Leiris, however, is not inclined to give exclusive rights to explicitly Freudian explanations, but tends, rather, to play them off against a more metaphysical perspective.[57] In the case of the falling man he makes a speculative link with the memory of his first erection which had occurred at the sight of ragged children climbing a tree. This memory recurs several times, coated on each occasion with different layers of meaning. Initially it figures in a series of incidents, referred to as 'le cadre—ou des fragments du cadre—dans lequel tout le reste s'est logé' (p. 41), connected with Leiris's first intimations of death, age, the soul, and so forth. In this framework, which constitutes what Leiris calls 'La métaphysique de mon enfance' (p. 29), his 'éveil viril' is interpreted as a first intuition of the division between subject and object, self and other. Sexuality becomes a metaphysical affair, located in Leiris's primordial relation to the world, and present, more or less diffusely, in a range of feelings such as apprehension (whence the connection with the 'secouristes'), separation, and pity (Leiris was especially conscious of the children's bare feet against the rough bark). Over and above potential connections with other memories, any incident in *L'Age d'homme* is potentially framed by Leiris's childhood metaphysics, by his relation to psychoanalysis, and by the opppositions between the two.

The same is true of the discussion of intentions, motives and models which features both in the text and in its prefatory essay.[58] The reader's developing awareness of Leiris's overall aims, and particularly the conflicts between them—catharsis and liquidation versus narcissistic self-absorption or mythologization, documentary authenticity versus formal beauty—is

---

[56] Lejeune interprets an earlier incident (pp. 64–7) in terms of the primal scene: on this and, more generally, the links between Leiris and Freud see *Lire Leiris*.

[57] Cf. 'Que les explorateurs modernes de l'inconscient parlent d'Oedipe, de castration, de culpabilité, de narcissisme, je ne crois pas que cela avance beaucoup quant à l'essentiel du problème (qui reste selon moi apparenté au problème de la mort, à l'appréhension du néant et relève donc de la métaphysique)', p. 153. Notwithstanding this, Leiris delivers a very Freudian diagnosis of his fears—in terms of a castration complex (p. 202)—only to query it in a note appended in 1946 (p. 211).

[58] As its title suggests, 'De la littérature considérée comme une tauromachie' develops the analogy between writing and bullfighting sketched out in the original (1939) 'prière d'insérer' for *L'Age d'homme* which is quoted in full at the beginning of the 1946 essay. Leiris's discussion of whether or not *L'Age d'homme* succeeds in being an *act*, as opposed to just

liable to contribute to the meanings which accrue to any incident or sequence. *L'Age d'homme* is punctuated by methodological bulletins through which Leiris keeps the process of construction in the foreground, reminding us (e.g. pp. 56, 121) that he is pursuing themes and associations identified through the Cranach painting, and that since incidents are often there simply because they come to mind in one context or another, they are items in an open dossier rather than a closed file. More than once, however, Leiris suggests that *L'Age d'homme* may owe its form to his fondness for allegories, images, and metaphors (cf. p. 55), and that this fact may undermine the heuristic status of his associative method. Noting at one point that his digressions have made him lose his thread (p. 128), he wonders if he has succumbed to self-indulgent aestheticism. Locally and cumulatively such scruples and hesitations complicate the texture of *L'Age d'homme*, intensifying the pressures to which incidents are subjected without necessarily deflecting the text's progress or subverting its overall designs. The book is nevertheless pervaded by an atmosphere of potential disaster, a sense that the mission might abort before reaching fruition, which comes to a head at the beginning of the penultimate chapter. In the light of an incident (an encounter with a woman) which has taken place while he is writing the book Leiris wonders if he will be able to continue:

Nos deux destins ne se joignirent qu'en une tangence extrêmement brève; mais, pour limités—voire à peine ébauchés—que furent nos rapports, cette rencontre toute récente m'a révélé à moi-même d'une manière si abrupte que c'est tout juste si je peux continuer à rédiger cet écrit, tant j'ai maintenant conscience de me trouver au pied du mur, dans un état de dénuement excluant toute possibilité de me forger des mythes, ou de ces pôles à demi légendaires auxquels—si ardemment qu'on aspire à la sincérité—l'on se réfère toujours, parce qu'eux seuls permettent de vivre (p. 156).

An experience which prompts real (as opposed to simulated) self-confrontation lays bare the self-mythologizing basis of Leiris's autobiographical writing and its roots in the need to remedy a sense of absence, to fill a void. Acknowledging his desire to address this (now absent) woman, and to write in order to compensate for her lack, Leiris recognizes that 'il ne peut, tout compte fait, s'agir d'écrire que pour combler un vide ou tout au moins situer, par rapport à la partie la plus lucide de nous-même, le lieu où bée cet incommensurable abîme' (p. 157). Ultimately, this implies, writing

another literary work (on this issue see Ch. 7 below), lays bare and reinforces a number of conflicts which have a bearing on the status of incidents since they underline the ambiguous status of all the ingredients, and all the methodologies, in the text.

cannot bring about change (it involves fixation rather than liquidation);[59] nor can it successfully replace lack with plenitude. Indeed, its main product may be lucidity concerning its own, possibly culpable, designs. The fact that this recognition, provisional as it may be, arises by dint of an incident which occurs in the context of the act of writing itself, is indicative of that shift in the centre of gravity of autobiography, so decisive and influential in *L'Age d'homme*, from the reconstructed past to the reconstructing present.

Another sequence (pp. 120–31) involving the theme of the 'homme blessé' displays something of the full complexity of the structures engendered by Leiris's treatment of incidents and it will therefore be examined in some detail. The passage culminates with the second of three incidents which are said to illustrate Leiris's 'façons de réagir' in the face of suffering or injury, two of which involve the younger and more likeable of his elder brothers, hence the subheading 'Mon frère ami'. The incident is said to be 'bien minime', and so in a sense it will prove, although by the time we reach it, after seven pages of elaborate *mise en scène*, it will have accumulated by proxy a strong charge of meaning. The fact that it took place in Le Havre leads Leiris to pursue, in advance, two paths of association: subsequent memories of that port and memories of sea-crossings. The first 'souvenir du Havre' consists in a nostalgic evocation of its 'quartier chaud', in particular the long-vanished Silver Dollar Bar. The first sea-crossing concerns a storm in the channel when (or so he claimed to his family) Leiris had seen a St Elmo's fire. The next crossing to be considered was Leiris's first real 'départ', a fugue to Egypt early in his marriage which anticipated the abortive attempt to cure his malaise by an expedition across Africa. In this case the crux of the memory is the 'minute de plénitude déchirante' he had experienced as he watched the gap widen between ship and quay at Marseilles, and the sense of being 'debout devant les choses', able to 'prendre sa propre mesure'. As Leiris winds from incident to incident, tacking from one current of association to another (Le Havre, 'souvenirs maritimes', self-confrontation), arrival at the promised destination is deferred; and we still do not reach it with the next incident, another 'souvenir du Havre', but this time of recent vintage since it concerns a visit made in the course of writing *L'Age d'homme*. This highly elaborated incident seems, rather, to be the product of its precursors, which it echoes in many particulars, but to which it adds the ingredients of identification and allegory which will be to the fore when the main incident is eventually reached. Leiris recounts that he had revisited the night-spots of Le Havre

[59] For a brilliant discussion of this issue see B. Pingaud, 'L'Écriture et la cure'.

the previous Whitsun, and that he had once again been struck by the sense of 'humanité profonde' experienced in 'mauvais lieus', exemplified by a charming young prostitute with whom he and his companions had conversed. The next morning, in the course of a recuperative walk on the Ste Addresse cliffs, he had found himself looking down on a small creek where a sound buoy bobbed out to sea, while on the shoreline a mother was supervising two neatly dressed schoolboys one of whom was taking rock samples with his geological hammer. As the scene transformed itself into a 'tableau vivant', Leiris had found himself 'face à face avec moi-même' (p. 127). A complex movement of identification occurred: Leiris identified (negatively) with the more studious schoolboy to the degree that he (positively) identified the plangent ringing of the bell on the buoy with the poignancy and authenticity of the young prostitute condemned to a harsh life. The dutiful boy exemplifies for Leiris the prosaic 'mesquinerie' of his professional life as a 'fonctionnaire', while the plaintive sound of the buoy embodies, via the link with the prostitute, 'quelque chose de si brûlant qui délire, qui crie tout seul, demandant simplement qu'on l'entende et qu'on ait assez de courage pour s'y dévouer tout entier' (p. 128). Turned into allegory the scene confronts Leiris with a *mise en scène* of his inadequacies, particularly his inability to surmount the fears and scruples which impede his devotion to the poetic intensity and authenticity he craves. As in the case of the encounter with a woman (commented on above) a recent incident provokes a crisis in the writing of the text. In this case Leiris, noting how far he has drifted from the point of departure, wonders whether his associative method has become no more than an aesthetic formula. Setting aside these doubts he at last comes to the long-deferred incident.

On his first sea-crossing, an excursion from Trouville with his parents and brothers, a sea-fog had forced an impromptu night in a hotel at Le Havre. Leiris and his 'frère ami' (then schoolboys) had been enlivening the outing by pretending to be jockeys travelling with their trainer; taking advantage of the unexpected turn of events they had spiced their fantasy with an adulterous sub-plot involving one of the jockeys (Leiris) and the trainer's wife (their mother). The Oedipal implications are further underlined by the depiction of Leiris's father on the return crossing the next day—stricken with sea-sickness, slumped in a corner, top hat over his eyes. But the burden of the incident is yet to come. The boys' unruly behaviour in the cramped hotel-room had led Leiris's brother to break a window overlooking a crowded street; the mother's reaction to this (her 'façon de réagir') is what is crucial: she jumps up, but then, thinking she has heard screams, she *hesitates* before finally looking out to check that no one has been injured. It is Leiris's own identification, *at the time of writing*, with his mother's hesitation, which emerges, at the incident's finale, as the core of its meaning and—through the themes of self-confrontation, identification, intensity—as its link with the incidents which preceded its narration:

J'ai parlé de chose brûlante, de prostituée d'une douceur inimitable, de feu Saint-Elme, de cloche geignant sur une mer sans tempête. Pourquoi faut-il que, de plus en plus, cette ardeur délirante m'échappe et que, telle ma mère posant une main craintive sur l'espagnolette à l'Hôtel de l'Amirauté, j'ose à peine lancer un brief regard à travers la fenêtre, de peur de trouver seulement un peu de sang sur le quai? (p. 131)

What this remarkable sequence demonstrates, as it moves from detail to detail, generated by memories secreted within memories, is that often in *L'Age d'homme* the contribution individual incidents make to the history of an identity is less important than what they bring in their wake as they are reconstituted in writing. What counts here is the movement of meaning through incidents: the movement of an allegorical imagination which turns events into polarized structures, and which is driven by a powerful tendency towards identification. Meaning collects in overlaps and interstices. One incident provides a temporary frame through which others are 'read': a visit to Le Havre in 1924, the scene on the Ste Adresse cliffs in the 1930s, become screens through which we view an incident from 1912 which, as it arrives on the horizon of Leiris's text, sends up a number of advance flares lighting up avenues of meaning to be negotiated before it can be reached. The process of deferral, so emphatically marked here—the deferred return to Trouville, the delayed look at the pavement, the narrative we have to wait for, the circumlocutory style, the delay in getting to the point—allegorizes the path of autobiographical meaning where truth resides in the journey rather than the destination.

Yet deferral is also symptomatic of Leiris's discovery about himself: not to get to the point is to put off definitive self-confrontation and commitment. In this respect, equally, Leiris's collage method could be seen as a means of defence rather than discovery. In the creation of networks where overdetermined meanings coagulate rather than flow, as well as in the sometimes overtly manipulative 'staging' of events, we may diagnose Leiris's aspiration to turn his life into a 'bloc solide' (p. 20), a bulwark against death or dissolution, and his desire that writing should fill rather than explore the void, that it should compensate for a feeling of emptiness (the 'toujours trop peu que je ressens') without genuinely transcending it through the adoption of new directions. But since it is Leiris himself who intermittently points to such a diagnosis, the reader cannot adopt it wholesale without denying the restless, self-revising energies at work in *L'Age d'homme*, the constant reframing which, as we pass from incident to incident, upsets stability and insists on plurality of meaning as a variety of frames of reference—Freudian, metaphysical, poetic—interact in the text.

It is in this connection that we should consider the last two chapters where, having completed his 'X-ray' of the Cranach painting, Leiris adopts a seemingly more conventional narrative method. Does this move away from collage, fragmentation, and thematics mark the collapse of Leiris's project? In some measure, perhaps; but it is also evident that if the balance between chronology (the ever-deferred movement towards an elusive manhood) and thematics tips towards the first it does not abolish the second. When we read Leiris's account of his liaison with Kay, his links with the surrealists, his marriage, and the 'marasme' which led him to psychoanalysis, travel, and then autobiography, we inevitably detect a multitude of connections with the thematics of Leiris's identity established earlier on. Yet the change in approach, from juxtaposition to narrative continuity, creates a distance which temporarily opens the text, offsetting the impression of excessive and obsessional thematic coherence, and indicates a more objective appraisal of the tensions, possibly inescapable, which have emerged from Leiris's endeavours.

The last chapters reflect a triple recognition: that the aesthetic drive, as it vainly seeks to remedy the lack at the core of experience; the sexual drive, which flirts with and flees from the fear of castration; the metaphysical drive, which courts and cowers from death—all present in the affair with Kay and its dissolution—are so intertwined as to be endlessly convertible into each other. The last chapters of *L'Age d'homme* display a mixture of freewheeling openness—we are now moving briskly forward through Leiris's curriculum vitae—and deadly closure as he exhibits the same symptoms in different contexts. Rather than reaching any conclusion, the text ends abruptly with two consecutive 'récits de rêve', saturated with Leirisian imagery: the reader embarks on the second of these, expecting a return to the main text, but is left suspended at the end, in the midst of Leiris's 'monde imaginaire'. Collage and juxtaposition thus return to underline the fact that the last chapters do not represent a fundamental change of method or outlook. If Leiris's escape from himself seems unlikely to materialize, his past remains a fertile reservoir of incidents whose meanings, however restricted in scope, will remain mobile as long as they are framed and reframed by the multiple frameworks of the text.

No autobiographer before Leiris had made the issues of order and

structure so central or so patent. Yet in *L'Age d'homme* incidents, despite
their subordination to thematic patterns, despite their status as data to be
marshalled and processed in the interests of predetermined schemes, have
authentic power. Here—as in Stendhal and Georges Perec, more than in
Chateaubriand, and by other means—the autobiographical incident, one of
the genre's most significant ingredients, achieves a certain sovereignty. How
is it that despite the elaborate literariness of Leiris's style, and the fact that
these are scarcely, as in Stendhal, incidents relived, we have the sense of
dealing with fragments of lived experience whose power to unsettle seems to
be enhanced rather than diminished by becoming counters in a textual
game? One of the virtues of Leiris's methods, in this respect, is that they
enable him to assemble materials which lack evident interest or dramatic
import, and which therefore display, unmistakably, the character of what is
purely incidental. True, it is a Leirisian obsession, revealed and interrogated
in *L'Age d'homme*, to confer a possibly spurious glamour on what is
otherwise unremarkable—'Je porte dans mes doigts le fard dont je couvre
ma vie' (p. 155) reads the opening of a diary entry quoted as epigraph to one
of the chapters.[60] Ultimately, however, it is not the transmutation of the real
which counts in *L'Age d'homme* but the fact that the intrusive work of
classification and structuring is never seen to achieve mastery. Indeed it is
perhaps the perpetual struggle between the desire for control and finality
and the desire to keep meanings in circulation which gives Leiris's devices
their paradoxical strength. If incidents here maintain an undomesticated
'wildness' it is because strategies which seem destined to bind and constrain
in fact serve to liberate, and thus authenticate, the existential force of the
incidental.

[60] The epigraphs at the head of each chapter, which comprise quotations from
encyclopaedias, literary works, and, as in the instance cited, Leiris's own past writings, add
another frame, and contribute further to the vertiginous sense of infinite regression which
had so impressed Leiris when as a child he contemplated the illustration on packets of cocoa
(p. 36).

5

Dealing with the Reader

Cet ouvrage terminera ma carrière, et lorsque tu le tiendras, Lecteur, je
ne serai plus. Mais je vivrai cependant avec toi par le mélange de mes
pensées avec les tiennes; je remuerai encore ton âme, et nous existerons
ensemble.

Restif de la Bretonne, *Monsieur Nicolas*[1]

What do autobiographers want? Beneath the official motives they readily
own up to—putting their lives on record, offering a sincere account of their
formation, discovering who they are—we often find a swarm of less explicit
desires which may or may not be acknowledged: confession, exculpation,
self-justification, self-transformation, self-acceptance; the desire to turn a
life into a fable, a fetish, or a monument; the desire to liquidate the past, to
embalm it, to exorcise it, to glamorize it, to dramatize it, to bowdlerize it; the
desire to set the record straight, to falsify it; to correct false impressions, or
to propagate them; to evade all definitions and images or to generate them.
As a literary act usually leading to publication, autobiography obviously has
a public dimension; it involves a rhetoric and implies a reader.[2] But it is
when we pursue the autobiographer into the darker recesses of his or her
undertaking, its seemingly more private motivating forces, that we truly
encounter the inescapably public face of this activity. The things
autobiographers find they really want, as they write, often involve an
engagement, an imaginary negotiation, not only with the conventions of a
particular kind of discourse, but with an imaginary Other, an interpolated
subjectivity which receives and responds to their utterances.[3]

'Cher lecteur': direct address to the reader is clearly a prominent

[1] *Monsieur Nicolas*, ii. 49.
[2] This dimension of autobiography has been examined, from the perspective of speech-act
theory, by E. Bruss in *Autobiographical Acts*. See also P. Lejeune, *L'Autobiographie en
France*, and *Le Pacte autobiographique*; and B. Mandel, 'Full of Life Now'.
[3] The role of the reader has attracted considerable attention in post-structuralist criticism,
and much of this work is very germane to autobiography. For a useful general survey which
discusses the ideas of Iser, Fish, Culler, *et al.*, see E. Freund, *The Return of the Reader*. Two
useful anthologies are J. P. Tompkins (ed.), *Reader-Response Criticism*, and S. R. Suleiman
and I. Crosman (eds.), *The Reader in the Text*.

symptom of this aspect of autobiography, and here a little goes a long way. A few passages explicitly bending the reader's ear can lay down particular terms of reading (though nothing forces the reader to accept them) and have the power, in theory at least, to tie down long sequences of narrative where the reader's role is not directly referred to. Characteristically, autobiographers pay *intermittent* attention to the reader, but in doing so betray an awareness which pervades the autobiographical act—and text—as a whole. As readers we may be tempted to dismiss these symptoms of the autobiographer's manifest designs on us; we may be inclined to see them as purely conventional, a routine feature of the poetics of autobiography: no more than an *hors d'œuvre* or an optional *amuse-gueule*. If so, we neglect something important about the genre: its referential basis, the fact that here it is not the minion of a fiction-maker who stands behind the pronoun 'I', but someone we could have bumped into in the street. When an autobiographer betrays his or her awareness of a reader, we potentially become aware of ourselves as readers in a different way than when a novelist uses this device. When a narrator in fiction addresses a reader we are confronted with an intratextual phenomenon. We may be led to read differently, to feel that our alignment to the text has shifted; in some cases we may feel that 'Laurence Sterne' or 'Philip Roth' has invaded the fictional space; an enriching complexity may ensue. The narrator nevertheless remains an emanation of the fictional world, and the reader or narratee likewise remains a fiction addressed by a fiction. But when an autobiographer addresses a reader something of his or her uncanny palpability, lent by the aura of the proper name, seems to communicate itself to us. The text becomes a boundary between two zones, both of which hover between the fictional and the real. Of course as 'readers' we are no less abstract, notional, impalpable, textual than we are in fictional discourse, yet somehow the space marked for us in the text seems to embrace more of the real space in which we live and breathe. In an autobiography the author is at only one remove from his text, and so it is with the reader.

A scene in Wim Wenders's film *Paris Texas* may provide a shiver of recognition in this regard. The characters played by Nastassia Kinski and Harry Dean Stanton are eventually reunited in a place situated away from familiar horizons—a back-street whorehouse with individual booths for the voyeuristically inclined. Kinski speaks into darkness: she knows she is seen but can see only her own reflection; Stanton watches her silently, uncertain of how he is seen. The woman's words cross a space where the conditions of speaking, seeing, and knowing are problematic. The conditions in which the man listens are inflected by his uncertainty as to the context of utterance.

Reading autobiographies can feel like looking in on something resembling this unstable, disquieting space, and the interface with the reader, in its uncertainties and paradoxes, often seems to be where some of the most interesting action in autobiography takes place. The writer–reader relationship, whether it is handled with *hauteur* and *sang-froid*, or in fear and trembling, tends to make autobiography an anxious activity—and one that can provoke discomfort.

Symptomatically, the relationship is often explicitly manifested at points of critical self-consciousness. It is when questions of methodology, protocol, intention, and disavowal are broached that the reader tends to get a look in. At such moments, often marked by a discourse of lucidity and far-sightedness, the writer temporarily disengages from the act of narration, as well as from the protagonist. Symmetrically, a potential mutation occurs in the reader's role. From being cast as the passive consumer of the tale, he or she is summoned to a certain vigilance about the prevailing conditions of reading. The writer vicariously crosses the boundary that separates writing from reading and tries to anticipate and incorporate in advance the reader's reception. Correspondingly, the reader has to cross over the other way and imagine what it was like to write the text—and what it would have been like to be concerned about its reception. We 'ourselves', of course, are never the readers designated in the text: indeed, we are made aware of ourselves as readers at the very point when the writer, in venturing to frame or portray a reader, reveals that, like Kinski in the whorehouse booth, he or she cannot see us. The writer designates a fictive reader with whom we cannot coincide. To be addressed by an autobiographer is a bit like being nabbed in a game of blind man's buff; we know we cannot be seen, and yet this may not prevent correct identification.

The role created for the reader in the autobiographical text may be seen as the outer manifestation of an inner presence—the Other who inhabits all acts of self-scrutiny: 'C'est nécessairement à d'autres qu'un discours sur soi s'adresse', observes the psychoanalyst J.-B. Pontalis in connection with Michel Leiris.[4] Or, from another angle, the figure of the reader may be seen as the inner manifestation, in the framework of the text itself, of an outer instance: the Other on whose authority the success of the autobiographical act, as communication of and with self, ultimately rests: 'C'est l'oreille de l'autre qui signe', as Jacques Derrida puts it, nicely underlining the rather surrealist anatomy of such texts.[5] The reader is a ghost which is always

---

[4] *Après Freud*, 315.

[5] *L'Oreille de l'autre*, 47. The notion of autobiography as *Allographie*, a writing of the Other, is further developed in Derrida's *Otobiographies*.

already in the machine: this may make it a difficult role to play; but it does not alter the fact that reading autobiography can take on at least some of the characteristics of an intersubjective encounter. To investigate this further I want to suggest that the reader in autobiography, whether figured as the externalization of an inner division or as the internalization of an outer demand, represents both a threat—that of the law—and an object of desire; and, as a corollary, that the behaviour of autobiographers towards readers, however various its actual forms, comprises an oscillation between repudiation and ingratiation, rebuttal and seduction.

When autobiographers invoke readers they are often answering presumed allegations about their performances. The reader becomes the embodiment of stated or unstated laws, axioms, or assumptions by the lights of which the autobiographer imagines he or she might be found wanting. Many invocations of the reader are of the form, 'You think I'm trying to defend myself, but I'm not . . .', 'You think I'm oversymplifying, but in fact . . .'. One of the principal types of legislation in this area is that of narrative as the embodiment of laws of causality and coherence. Because autobiography tends to be governed by what Georges Gusdorf calls 'le postulat du sens',[6] autobiographers are present in their texts as architects of structures of meaning. But they are rarely content to let it be assumed that these structures derive their authority only from the author's say-so or fiat, that they are based on purely intuitive and *ad hoc* rationalization. Autobiographers know that the hypotheses they formulate about the past, the patterns they make out of their experiences, invoke general ideas about human lives—about nature and nurture, childhood and maturity, vocations and conversions, minds and bodies—and that these ideas have strong ideological implications. It is common for the reader to become the embodiment of such assumptions and laws: to invoke the reader is often to register awareness that what one says implies—or else flouts—a general belief about human affairs, an official narrative. As such the reader is identified with the demands of the law, demands which can be met either by claiming that one's text is law-abiding, or else that it is deviant, and that the lawlessness of one's narrative is the mark of one's nature. A swerving course between these options is a feature of Rousseau's autobiography, and of Gide's.

There is an uncomfortable, voyeuristic side to being a real reader of autobiographies in that, as in the Texan whorehouse, we seem to look through a transparent surface and witness the flailing gesticulations of

---

[6] 'Conditions et limites de l'autobiographie', 232.

someone who is trying to see us but cannot, who is trying to guess who we are but will never know, and yet who seems uncannily to have guessed fairly accurately what we are like. The appearance of superiority is on the reader's side: it is the writer's position which seems inherently insecure. Yet it only takes a slight alteration of perspective for the distribution of strengths to be reversed. The writer is, after all, the producer, freely able to dictate his or her terms, to switch unpredictably from one thing to another, to change the hidden agenda which impels the writing, to adopt a different guise. In short, it is the writer's prerogative to keep us guessing and on the move, to give us different roles to play in the staging of the self in the text. Nothing obliges us to play them, indeed for the reader it is perhaps never really a question of playing a role; reading is in one sense too passive an activity for that. Moreover, the reader always arrives after the event, and witnesses what has already taken place: it is too late to play an active part. What we can do, and this is perhaps what we may feel is incumbent on us *vis-à-vis* the autobiographer, is seek to understand what, at various points, the autobiographer felt he needed us to be and do in order to write the text. And if we do that we must be active, we must forgo provisionally at least the apparent security and impregnability of our position. We must be prepared to think less of our own hand than of the cards which were dealt for us, less of our own apparel than of the costumes we have been asked to put on. The roles created for the reader, which very often fluctuate as the autobiographical text progresses, remain in the space between writer and reader; they are not wholly to be believed in by either party. Yet we do cede some of our sovereignty as readers in consenting to think about the roles created for us. When we deign to notice that the role we are asked to play is not a uniform one, we involve ourselves in a game; we acknowledge the autobiographer's designs on us; we recognize that for the autobiographer the reader represents not only the threat of the law but also, and perhaps by that very token, an object of seduction. In search of love, esteem, or recognition, the autobiographer places a demand on the reader. The demand is addressed to no one in particular, but the moment we read the text it is addressed to us: like a portrait which seems to move as we do, making us the perpetual object of a vacant stare, the autobiographer seems always to have his eyes on the singular reader, even when it is humanity at large he would like to convince or convert.

I have been trying to convey something of the atmosphere created by the behaviour of many autobiographers towards their putative readers, and to indicate in general terms some of the pressures at work in a very unbalanced two-way relationship. It must be stressed that the reader is always first and foremost a spectator who observes the writer's dealings with an imaginary partner, and whose responses to the various solicitations and manipulations to which he or she is subject are always liable to remain virtual. Yet this vicarious sense of participation merits our close attention since it is the locus of important energies in and behind autobiography: the need to speak *to* someone; the need for the Other's look to substantiate our claim to selfhood; the need to 'flesh out' the 'Tu' which, as Benveniste has suggested, is always implied when we say 'Je'; the need to negotiate with a pre-existent image in the public eye; the need to engage with necessarily public or universal ideologies. The relation with the reader is the nub of all these energies. Of course in many texts it does not manifest itself in passages of reader-oriented discourse or in marked efforts at framing: the cultivation of the reader may simply be conducted in the rhetoric of narration. It follows from this that if we grasp the less elusive opportunities which seem to present themselves when the relation to the reader is explicit, when this channel runs, as it were, overground, we risk giving undue emphasis to this feature. But the risk is probably worth taking. If, following Lejeune, we choose to envisage autobiography as a contractual activity, it is important that we interpret this not only in terms of the attempt to cordon off an area in which certain general protocols of reading will apply, but as a recognition that the constant attempt to bargain, to negotiate, to engage with us is a predominant feature of the genre.

To establish a taxonomy of the numerous forms the reader–writer relationship may take in autobiography would be a vast undertaking, fraught with probably insuperable difficulties. However, before moving entirely to particular cases, I propose, with Rousseau as a sounding board, to sketch out a very broad dichotomy.

Ingratiation

This word could serve as a label for the first general attitude of autobiographers towards readers. All asseverations of the author's good faith—of which the prototype might be Montaigne's 'C'est icy un livre de bonne foy, lecteur'[7]—could be considered as belonging to a strategy of ingratiation in its simplest form, along with all more or less craven espousals of the reader's imagined views. Less straightforwardly, the author may curry the reader's favour by adopting a slight distance from the narrative:

---

[7] 'Au Lecteur', *Essais*, i. 35.

'these tedious details', 'for those who find this account unconvincing'—seeking to validate the narration by showing that he or she is not entirely its dupe. By changing the frequency and addressing the reader direct, the autobiographer seeks to lower the volume of the narrative transmitter, downplaying the tale a little lest it should seem to have a dangerous independence. For the autobiographer's besetting fear often seems to be that the story says more than he wants it to, that it tells its own story and prevents him from being 'his own man'. By ingratiating himself with the reader he tries to control the connotations of his story, to prevent it from getting out of hand. Some forms of ingratiation aim at trying to make up for the embarrassing stamp of delusion and naïvety which surrounds many kinds of autobiographical statement—particularly those involving seemingly trivial incidents or events credited with a strong determining force—and to pre-empt the incredulity with which it is feared they may be greeted. This factor in autobiography stems in some degree from the fact that explanations which subsume behaviour under obvious laws may seem banal, while those which do not may seem incredible. Excuses—so prominent in Rousseau—obviously belong to the strategy of ingratiation, though to judge by the response down the years to his painstaking dissections of long lost peccadilloes, excuses are often counter-productive and inflame the suspicions they are supposed to allay.

All these forms of ingratiation figure in the negotiations with the reader in the *Confessions*. The desire to be vindicated and exonerated leads Rousseau to appeal to the good faith of a reader willing to make common cause with him in his struggle against false witnesses. He will place all the material evidence at the reader's disposal, and make himself totally available to scrutiny. For long stretches Rousseau writes in a manner which suggests that the reader will inevitably share his own estimate of himself. His effortlessly seductive prose exudes confidence that the indulgence he is willing to show towards his past personae will not be withheld by others. But, as we saw in an earlier chapter, this is only part of the picture. There are also passages which make it abundantly clear that the reader poses a potential threat which must be neutralized; that, notwithstanding his attempt to write *d'outre-tombe*, for posterity, Rousseau's relation to the reader perpetuates his conflictual relationships with his contemporaries, and also with himself. When he seeks to place the burden of interpretation on the reader's shoulders, making him responsible not only for the final verdict but for the sifting of evidence and the construction of meaning, Rousseau is not offering the reader a more active role so much as issuing him a threat. Ingratiation turns into intimidation, as Rousseau seeks to disqualify all readers except those willing to perceive him in the way he wants to be perceived. In the later books of the *Confessions* Rousseau's attitude moves between two extremes: the reader cast as potential member of the enemy clan intent on blackening him, or as saviour who will clear his name. If the latter case could be seen as ingratiation in its ultimate form, the former can be seen as a radical expression of another strategy quite common in autobiography—that of repudiation.

Repudiation

In its simplest form this involves portraying the reader as the embodiment of norms, beliefs, and assumptions which are deemed to be inappropriate, inapplicable, or misleading in the particular case of the autobiographer. In defining the reader he repudiates, the autobiographer is able to define himself against a negative background. But the effect is also to convert the diffuse threat posed by an unknown quantity into something more localized which, having been clearly identified, can be more easily disposed of. A more complex form of repudiation occurs when autobiographers not only give a negative portrayal of the reader they repudiate but also depict the more suitable reader they seek (an example of this in Stendhal will be examined presently). In such cases repudiation may turn out to be a veiled form of ingratiation: by flattering ourselves that we resemble the positive reader, we may deny ourselves the chance to ask the questions which would occur to the negative one—or so the autobiographer hopes. In another variant, repudiation involves the suppression of contact with the reader. Few interesting autobiographies seem, so to speak, unwittingly oblivious of the reader. In certain cases, however, the autobiographer seems—wholly or for long stretches—to suppress the relationship with the reader, adopting strategies which seem to acknowledge the omission. One of these is the interpolation of a designated reader who comes between us and the author. This device may affect the text as a whole, as in Augustine where the addressee is God, or it can be intermittent but carry implications for the whole, as in the case of Wordsworth's *Prelude* which addresses his friend (Coleridge). A striking example occurs in Nathalie Sarraute's *Enfance* which will be discussed later in this chapter. Another kind of suppression can be discerned in the intricate, highly structured autobiographies of Leiris or Sartre which refrain from any explicit specification of the reader's role but succeed, through the narrator's rhetorical performance, as well as through formal design, in making the reader's positioning and repositioning an important aspect of the text. No one would be likely to suggest that the absence of reader-oriented discourse could necessarily be equated with a lack of concern for the reader. But in texts such as those just mentioned its absence has, as it were, a particularly expressive quality. However, whatever one's misgivings, it seems advisable to focus particularly on texts where the concern with the reader is advertised more openly.

Like Rousseau, Stendhal did not envisage publishing his autobiography in his lifetime. But where Rousseau, despite his occasional appeals to the long view, tends to act as if the reader might burst into the room at any moment, Stendhal, perhaps with such an eventuality somewhere in his mind (he complains of being constantly interrupted at Civitavecchia) tends to address a future reader living in 1880 or 1930—fifty or a hundred years after the time of writing. Stendhal says he will write as if he were composing a letter to a friend.[8] By this device he is able to get round the problems posed by his scepticism about introspection ('Quel œil peut se voir soi-même?' (p. 31))[9] and about sincerity. He will try and see himself from someone else's point of view, but as he does not know the person the temptation of insincerity will be lessened. Moreover, the imaginary reader he addresses is explicitly deemed not to belong to the immediate historical period in which Stendhal is writing. This makes him an object of fascination for Stendhal, who can wonder whether such a reader will understand allusions to *Les Liaisons dangereuses*, to Louis-Philippe, or to the mores of the 1830s generally. More importantly, it means that the judgements of the imaginary reader will not be restricted by the prevailing social codes, norms, and assumptions of Stendhal's time. But in adopting a strategy of repudiation towards a constituency of readers which he feels would be incapable of understanding him, Stendhal does not simply recruit a complaisant readership fashioned with regard to a specific self-image. As we saw in an earlier chapter, the self in *Brulard* is conceived in terms of rhythm, mobility, and desire rather than psychological essence. Accordingly, as Ann Jefferson has argued, the relationship with an unqualifiable reader takes on the character of an open, dialogical partnership which serves to defer and suspend the question of self-knowledge.[10] The reader is not to be cajoled or seduced, but nor is he just a blank or a question mark. By associating the reader-figure with such exemplary spirits as Montesquieu, Mme Roland, M. Gros the mathematician, or Mélanie Guibert—each cherished for the kind of discourse he or she represents—Stendhal makes the reader desirable

---

[8] *Vie de Henry Brulard*, 32.

[9] Ibid. 31.

[10] See 'Beyond Contract'. See also B. Didier, *Stendhal autobiographe* and 'L'Adresse au lecteur dans les textes autobiographiques de Stendhal'.

as an interlocutor within the field of a certain kind of discursive exchange
which can accommodate the indefinition and waywardness of subjectivity.
The important thing here, as Jefferson underlines, is that if we place
ourselves in the position carved out for the reader by Stendhal's text, we
become honorary members of the Stendhalian 'Happy Few'. Not only does
he make the reader-writer relationship a vital aspect of his project, he offers
the reader a genuinely attractive and honorific role in the proceedings, and
one which it is a pleasure to fulfil. *Vie de Henry Brulard* is relatively
exceptional in this regard. On the whole, the evidence suggests that when
autobiographers draw attention to the reader, the kinds of complicity they
invite are likely to be less flattering to the reader's self-esteem, and to involve
a stronger dose of manipulation. In such cases it becomes especially
important to understand the ways in which we are being framed and put
upon, repudiated and seduced. To illustrate this I have chosen three more
recent autobiographies which in different ways place emphasis on the
reader's role.

GENET: *JOURNAL DU VOLEUR*

Few works are as insistently reader-oriented as the *Journal du voleur*.[11]
Repeatedly, a hundred times or more, the reader is directly invoked,
sometimes several times on a single page. The reader is habitually
represented as the embodiment of norms, values, and presuppositions
which can be taken for granted, a fixed point of reference against which
Genet can trace his deviations. The reader supposedly represents a world of
fixed moral, psychological, and metaphysical bearings of which he or she is
the zealous custodian. We are presented *ad nauseam* with references to 'votre
sol' (p. 55),'votre langage' (p. 29), 'vos règles' (94), 'votre salut' (p. 94),
'votre beauté' (p. 110), 'votre morale' (p. 111), 'votre monde' (p. 292). This
dummy reader is the reverse image of Genet who, by arranging the lamps in
this way, can turn the spotlight on a clearly defined persona (criminal, pimp,
thief, etc.) who, in all he does, is an infringement and subversion of the
reader's world-view. But if it involves trapping the reader, this arrangement
is supposed to guarantee Genet his freedom: *he* knows that he does not
coincide with the image he has foisted on the reader. 'Enfin plus ma

---

[11] First published in 1948, *Journal du voleur* is generally recognized to be an authentically
autobiographical text, by contrast with such autobiographical fictions as *Miracle de la rose*
and *Pompes funèbres*. See Serge Meitinger, 'L'Irréel de jouissance dans le *Journal du voleur* de
Genet'. References, incorporated in the text, are to the Folio edn.

culpabilité serait grande, à vos yeux, entière, totalement assumée, plus grande sera ma liberté' (p. 94). Genet's freedom lies in the knowledge that he is other than the way others define him. His strategy is to use the Other's defining gaze in order both to deflect it and to make it serve his own private ends.[12]

However, this reveals Genet's dependency on the perspective he repudiates: his chosen path can only be defined in relation to what it transgresses: 'Je décidai de vivre tête baissée, et de poursuivre mon destin dans le sens de la nuit, à l'inverse de vous-même, et d'exploiter l'envers de votre beauté.' And this dependency is intensified by the fact that writing, including writing *Journal du voleur*, is now the main sphere of action within which Genet seeks to pursue his transgressive ends. By making the text a 'chant d'amour', a perverse appropriation of language, Genet strives towards 'la sainteté', a project of imaginary self-transformation which works at the level of images and involves the participation of an audience, willing or otherwise. 'La sainteté' is inseparable from the verbal performances designed to engender it, and these involve the theft and subversion of the Other's language. Yet, to the desire to escape definition it allies the desire to become an image, the pure object of the Other's gaze, a beautiful artefact whose qualities depend on the eyes of the beholder: 'Je détruirai les apparences, les bâches tomberont brûlées et j'apparaîtrai là, un soir, sur la paume de votre main, tranquille et pur comme une statuette de verre. Vous me verrez. Autour de moi, il n'y aura plus rien' (p. 234). This weird apotheosis in which Genet pictures himself as a glass statuette in the reader's hand shows how badly he needs the reader he shuns; indeed, as he himself observes, his repudiation of the reader is a measure of that need: 'A la gravité des moyens que j'exige pour vous écarter de moi, mesurez la tendresse que je vous porte. Jugez à quel point je vous aime par ces barricades que j'élève dans ma vie et dans mon œuvre . . . afin que votre haleine (je suis corruptible à l'extrême) ne me puisse pourrir' (p. 235). The reader Genet desires is a fictional entity entailed by a particular quest, a pure look, without the corrupting breath which would confine him in the real world. The reader Genet needs is the reader confounded, humiliated, stymied, dazzled, deformed by the impossible contortions he is asked to perform. In a sense Genet's apotheosis lies *in the reader* whom he creates and identifies with, a reader reduced to being nothing but Genet's own gaze at himself, the compliant avatar of 'un homme monstrueusement enlisé en lui-même'.[13]

---

[12] See the classic analysis by Jean-Paul Sartre in *Saint-Genet: Comédien et martyr*.

[13] For Georges Bataille Genet's attitude to the reader is a symptom of his reluctance to forego the imaginary sovereignty of the ego, and to engage in real communication with the

But the more he fictionalizes the reader the more Genet undermines his own aims. To a certain extent, in consenting to read *Journal du voleur* we become Genet's accomplices; we enter a space commandeered for his peep-shows; in making sense of his bizarre syntax and all the other idiosyncrasies of his style, we enter his world, as will the spectators of his later plays. But Genet cannot wholly dictate the terms on which we read: if he remains elusive and unpredictable, so do we. The text is a game which we can play by our rules as well as his; and even as he writes (which is when it counts) Genet knows this. *Journal du voleur* is permeated by the recognition that writing must inevitably fail to live up to Genet's ambitions, and after completing it he was to lapse for a number of years into silence.[14]

VIOLETTE LEDUC: *LA BÂTARDE*

La Bâtarde[15] offers a striking example of how the evolution of the relation to the reader in the course of an autobiography can enact the transformation of self-understanding which the text has brought about or wishes to simulate. Broadly speaking, we can identify three phases in which Leduc successively (*a*) gives the reader the cold shoulder while she focuses on other addressees; (*b*) draws the reader into the machinations of her relations with others; (*c*) uses the relation with the reader as a channel through which she can demonstrate (or struggle towards) a new-found commitment to the extra-textual world (the world outside her obsessions).[16] In the early sections, concerning her childhood, Leduc's extensive use of conative discourse and apostrophe involves addressees such as her mother, her grandmother Fidéline, and Isabelle with whom she had a passionate affair at boarding-school. A passage addressed to her mother begins: 'Je te raconte ton passé, je voudrais te l'expliquer, je voudrais t'en guérir' (p. 32). The passage re-enacts the emotional dynamics of the mother's seduction by a rich 'fils de famille', 'l'homme au lorgnon', who was Leduc's father. By addressing the

Other. Setting up an 'ersatz de communication' Genet condemns himself to a false sovereignty: 'le désir solitaire de souveraineté', concludes Bataille, 'est trahison de la souveraineté', *La Littérature et le mal*, 244.

[14] Ironically, perhaps, the efforts of a supremely attentive super-reader— Sartre and the monumental *Saint-Genet*—played a significant part in Genet's affliction by writer's block. *Journal du voleur* is discussed from a different angle in a later section of this book (see Ch. 7 below).

[15] First published in 1964. References, which will be cited in the text, are to the Folio edn.

[16] Many perceptive reflections on the role of the reader in Leduc's autobiographical texts will be found in I. de Courtivron's excellent *Violette Leduc* which underlines the importance of gender in Leduc's writings.

protagonists, identifying now with her mother, now with 'l'homme au lorgnon', Leduc seeks to appropriate her own origins and cast off the bonds of heredity: 'Non, je ne veux pas de toi, hérédité. Mon Dieu, faites que j'écrive une belle phrase, une seule' (p. 32).[17] Similarly, in recreating her discovery of sexual pleasure, Leduc repeatedly addresses Isabelle in the present tense. The effect is not only to revivify the past but to transform it into an active force in the present. 'Isabelle' becomes a dimension of Leduc herself which is still alive, so to speak, and capable of further mutation. Leduc's use of apostrophe bears out much of what Jonathan Culler says about the device: apostrophe tends to complicate or disrupt the circuit of communication, raising questions about the identity of the addressee; it is often a device which readers find subversive, unsettling, and embarrassing; it establishes a relationship with another object or person which in fact helps to constitute the speaker (and thus to raise the question of who is speaking); it can be read as an act of radical interiorization and solipsism; it is a device which neutralizes time and draws attention to the temporality of writing.[18] This last feature is particularly relevant in Leduc's case since the apostrophes to her mother, Fidéline, Isabelle, and later to her lover Hermine, suggest that if she is still locked in what she calls the crypt of past desires—'Isabelle, Hermine, mes candélabres lorsque je pars dans la crypte de la folie' (p. 157)—the activity of writing constitutes a process of 'working through' which has its own time-scale.[19]

In the early stages, then, the role of the reader is akin to that of someone forced to eavesdrop on a conversation which does not concern him; in the middle sections of the book we are brought into the conversation and drawn more directly into Leduc's negotiations with her past. She reconstructs a series of chronically unstable triangular relationships which reflected and perpetuated the insecurities caused by her illegitimacy. These relationships, which will be examined in more detail in a later chapter,[20] show how Leduc was constantly driven to sacrifice others to her own desires and, as a result, to make the achievement of lasting fulfilment impossible. Through writing, Leduc seeks not to repeat the past but to control it, and stylistic virtuosity, the ability to switch rapidly between tones, to laugh at as well as pity herself, to play one style off against another, become instruments of control. Style

[17] On self-generation through writing see M. N. Evans, 'La Mythologie de l'écriture dans *La Bâtarde* de Violette Leduc'.
[18] 'Apostrophe' in *The Pursuit of Signs*, 135–54.
[19] The space writing explores in *La Bâtarde* has many of the characteristics of the '*crypte dans le Moi*' analysed by N. Abraham and M. Torok in *Cryptonymie*, and further reflected on in J. Derrida's remarkable preface 'Fors'.
[20] See the section on Leduc in Ch. 7 below.

becomes performance, a display of histrionic skill, and the reader is pressed to become the audience. It is not enough for Leduc to imagine readers in the comfort of their own surroundings, free to take or leave what they read; they have to be there on the stage, and inveigled to participate more directly. A characteristic example occurs in the remarkable *mise en scène* constructed around an incident when Leduc, walking at night with Hermine in the Place de la Concorde, overheard a passer-by deliver a disparaging remark about her face: 'Moi, si j'avais cette tête-là, je me suiciderais' (p. 301). Acutely conscious of the size of her nose—a dominant theme in *La Bâtarde*—Leduc reconstructs the incident as a fantasmagoria in which her 'trompe' grows to an alarming size and takes on a life of its own. At the beginning of the passage she begs the reader to accompany her into the fantasy world which the brutal remark will destroy: 'Lecteur, suis-moi. Lecteur, je tombe à tes pieds pour que tu me suives. Mon itinéraire sera facile. Tu quittes les gouttelettes qui venaient te retrouver, tu t'achemines vers la place de la Concorde, tu montes sur le trottoir de gauche. Te voici, nous voici. Miracle du silence le long du bruit . . .' (p. 294). It is as if the reader's assistance were needed to ensure that Leduc's reconstruction of the event take on the character of a controlled literary performance rather than a recrudescence of past pain and defeat. By taking the reader with her, rather than making the journey alone, Leduc inoculates herself against a self-destructive virus to which writing is the antidote. The reader of course scarcely needs to be told to follow Leduc: we have little choice in the matter. But in their redundancy such exhortations show that Leduc's aim is not so much control of the reader as control over herself through the medium of the imaginary reader-participant.

In some instances, addresses to the reader relate directly to the context and process of writing. In a passage concerning the period after she had been deserted by Hermine, Leduc makes it clear that her efforts are directed not at remembering a past 'douleur' but at alleviating and dispelling its remains in the present. What she refers to as 'le travail de la séparation' is still to come, and will be achieved, or at least propitiated, by a controlled ritual of remembering and forgetting in which past pain is first reborn and then dispelled. The reader has a part to play in this, and so does a picture-postcard of a carving on the royal gate at Chartres, representing the philosopher Pythagoras:

Je me souviens, dans la compagnie d'une carte postale, sur la page à gauche de mon cahier. Reproduction du Portail royal de Chartres. Pythagore. Un homme tronc du XIIe siècle avec un visage rayonnant. Son porte-plume est un racloir de plâtrier, sa chevelure un univers de parallèles. Le nez est gros, mes enfants, le nez de Pythagore.

Moi si j'avais ce gros nez je me suiciderais. Non, saleté du Pont de la Concorde. Pythagore a le front mangé par les parallèles serrées. Les lignes qui ne se rejoignent pas, ô mes colombes, se rejoignent au milieu du front, en forme d'oiseau circonflexe. Je me noierais dans sa barbe toute en franges de couvre-lit. Nos dortoirs, nos couvre-lits gaufrés. Patience. J'écris cela pour me consoler, vingt-cinq ans après, de la fuite d'Hermine. Comme les mains de Pythagore sont laborieuses sur le pupitre du Portail de Chartres. Son visage chante le bonheur de compter.

Pythagore chéri, je veux dire Pythagore que je chéris sur une carte postale pour m'aider encore à accoucher de ma douleur après la disparition d'Hermine, pour m'aider à m'arracher d'elle vingt-cinq ans après. Le travail de séparation se refera pendant que je recopierai la notice:

Pythagore philosophe et mathématicien grec, né dans l'île de Samos . . . (p. 329).

The passage enacts a particular way of dealing with the past. The image which accompanies Leduc as she writes connotes order and stability: the figure of Pythagoras exudes the delights of mathematical harmony and computation, and suggests a stable, ordered past which has been classified and defined; the monumental stone of Chartres represents a period of faith and the survival of Art. Concentrating on the picture is a diversionary tactic designed to keep the revival of painful emotions under control and to allow an inner process to take place behind the scenes. Small details prompt the irresistible resurgence of negative feelings—Pythagoras' nose brings back the incident in the Place de la Concorde, his fringed beard recalls the coverlets of the beds in the dormitory where Leduc first met Hermine—but these feelings are absorbed and resisted as Leduc switches her attention to other features. Addressing the image, Leduc asks it to help her 'deliver' ('accoucher') a pain which, like a foetus, has been growing inside her since Hermine's departure. Meanwhile she keeps her eye on her principal addressees, a plural escort of readers—'ô mes colombes'—to whom she describes the picture as if she were a schoolmistress giving a guided tour. We, the readers, are now situated with Leduc as she writes and we too are to help her in the process of dealing with her past. Conscious, however, that we may find her contortions insincere, Leduc hastens at the end of the sequence to reassure us:

Non lecteur, ma douleur n'est pas fabriquée. Je m'efforce d'éclaircir cette bouillie de désespoir lorsque Hermine me quitta. Nous souffrons, après nous nous aidons du vocabulaire. Je m'efforce de déblayer ma tête, mon cerveau, cette ruche en folie précipitée sous la terre, emmurée, coincée dans les avalanches de charbon. Lecteur, tu as souffert. Pour se soulager avec ce qui a été, il faut s'éterniser (p. 330).

Playing with words, converting one's travails into an eternal textual artefact, is a way of flushing out at last the buzzing underground network of raw emotions, and thus of finding serenity. But somebody has to watch and listen, and that is our role as readers. Or rather that was our role when Leduc wrote: by the time we read it is of course too late to be of much help.

In the last section of *La Bâtarde* the relation to the reader enters a third phase. When the reader is addressed it is now usually in the context of the frequent bulletins where Leduc interrupts her narrative to draw attention to the circumstances in which she writes, and to comment on the activity of writing:

15 mai 1961 à 9 h 20 du matin dans un village du Vaucluse. Je n'ai pas changé; je cède au désir de jongler avec le vocabulaire pour être remarquée. Une trouvaille, c'est mon numéro. Je fais mon numéro, mon cahier à carreaux m'applaudit. Mon cahier ne m'applaudit pas: il est indifférent, il est avide de clarté ou de charabia. Le drame de l'incapable. Lecteur chéri, je te donnerai ce que j'ai (p. 432).

La Bâtarde tells the story of a woman who comes to terms with herself by discovering her ability to write. When we reach the stage where she recounts this discovery the reader is no longer asked to accompany Leduc on her excursions into the past but to validate her new-found persona as a writer. Writing has become the stage for Leduc's deep-seated exhibitionism—the leopard cannot change its spots—but there is more to it than that. Writing has also restored Leduc to the world, has helped her direct her attention to the beauty of the Provençal landscape in which she composes her autobiography, and has delivered her from 'engloutissement' in dead desires. The reader is asked to stand witness to this accomplishment by becoming the recipient of a gift, the beneficiary of the munificence Leduc is now capable of, after years of emotional avarice:

21 août 1963. Vite lecteur, vite, que je te donne encore ce que tu connais: ce mol océan des campagnes, le foin coupé, les vagues qui se reposent avec des distances entre elles . . . Avare je suis, avare je serai. J'aime tout sans profondeur. Pourtant, lecteur, pourtant. Je te donne sans compter l'émoi derrière la calotte de Ventoux le 21 août 1963 à sept heures et demie du soir . . . (p. 631).

What Leduc now has to offer is the expression of the person she has become through her victory over the forces unleashed and placated in the earlier parts of the book. Now that she no longer needs to involve us in her psychodrama, she invites us to share the bounties she has to offer. What Leduc now needs is our companionship, our willingness to endorse her new estimation of herself: '18 mai 1961, lecteur. Tu te dis qu'est-ce qu'elle a à m'appeler, à me racoler? Je ne racole pas. Je m'approche de toi' (p. 434). In the restaging of her past Leduc specifies a number of costume changes for the reader, to match her own transformations. Of course these stipulations have no absolute power, any more than the changes in Leduc occur literally at the moment of writing. Yet to ignore her gesticulations is perhaps tantamount to refusing to read fully; moreover, by reading at all we are *ipso facto* carrying out Leduc's designs. What mattered to her when she wrote was the sense that one day 'we' would read: in reading *La Bâtarde* we become 'her' readers': all her stage-directions qualify an *état de fait*.

The relationship with the reader belongs to the realm of 'discours': the reader's changes of costume, as he or she is dolled up to match Leduc's transformations, bear witness to a process which is conducted through the act and in the temporality of writing. The reader's final avatar in *La Bâtarde* reflects a self-image on Leduc's part which unites the therapeutic power attributed to writing autobiography and the rediscovery of natural harmony and simplicity in the village of Faucon in the Vaucluse where much of the book was written in the early 1960s. At the level of 'histoire', *La Bâtarde* is also of course the story of an evolution towards a new identity as a writer, and throughout the text we are given evidence of that transformation. Yet it is important that we recognize the fundamental gap between the narrator of *La Bâtarde* and the woman who, at the end of the book, embarks on a literary career in the post-war period. If we do not, we shall fail to appreciate the degree to which the dynamics of writing and the relation to the reader in *La Bâtarde* bear not only on the past events covered by the text but also on the early phases of Leduc's career as a writer which she recounts in her subsequent, posthumously published, volumes of autobiography, *La Folie en tête* and *La Chasse à l'amour*.[21]

What these two books suggest is that the therapeutic relationship with the reader in *La Bâtarde* is partly a remedy against the pathological relationship to her readers which had characterized Leduc's career up till then. They show how Leduc, in seeking to aspire to the glamorous status of a consecrated literary star, like her idol Simone de Beauvoir, tended to perpetuate the sense of failure and insecurity she had felt since childhood, and the narcissism which had been one of its principal symptoms. If, in the early part of her writing career, Leduc turned her life into literature, thus embarking on the path which was to culminate in full autobiography, her autobiographical fictions (*L'Asphyxie* (1946), *L'Affamée* (1948), etc.) lack the reflexive, critical dimension which could bring about real change in her relation to the past. Moreover, in desiring literary acclaim, Leduc did not

---

[21] Published in 1970 and 1973 respectively.

invite the participation of her readers so much as attempt to compel or incite them to confer on her the magical quality of the writer. In the first instance the implied reader at whom this demand is directed is a mentor-figure, an established writer in whose glory Leduc hopes to share—Maurice Sachs in the case of *L'Asphyxie*, Simone de Beauvoir in the case of subsequent books (*L'Affamée* is in fact a thinly veiled account of Leduc's obsession with Beauvoir).[22] But although she gained Beauvoir's support and esteem Leduc failed (until she published *La Bâtarde*) to find fame and fortune as a writer. Her books sell poorly, are not widely reviewed, suffer bowdlerization owing to their erotic content, and in some cases after a few years they are pulped. Denied the sense of existing in the public eye, of being the object of widespread attention, Leduc becomes obsessed with the scraps of attention she does receive, especially if it comes from unexpected quarters.

   La Folie en tête and *La Chasse à l'amour* feature a number of painful, amusing, and sometimes grotesque episodes involving dealings with real readers. One day Jean Genet introduces Leduc to a man who has read *L'Asphyxie*: 'Un lecteur . . . Un vrai . . . Près de moi';[23] the relationship which ensues will turn out to be long-drawn-out, frustrating, and psychologically damaging. Then there is Patrice, a 'jeune homme fiévreux' who starts writing to her from the provinces (*FT* 213). Leduc soon finds his attentions addictive ('quelqu'un pense à Gros Nez chaque jour' (*FT* 238); and in her replies (one of which she quotes at length) she adopts the role of an established writer proffering advice to a novice: 'Drageuse maniérée, je balance mon petit sac avec mes faux diams dedans' (*FT* 240). When Patrice announces that he is coming to see her the prospect throws Leduc into a frenzy where erotic fantasy is mingled with panic at the idea of being exposed as a nonentity, and with a sense that she is incapable of incarnating the identity she constructs as she writes. In desperation she secures a last-minute appointment to have her hair remodelled (though this involves further pretence), and is beset by thoughts of seducing her admirer. In the event she is downcast when Patrice refuses to remove his mackintosh, announces that he is staying with an uncle, and enthuses endlessly about André Breton. The pattern repeats itself with an even younger 'collégien', Flavien (it crosses Leduc's mind that a group of schoolboys has chosen to torment her). Responding to his entreaties, she takes a hotel room in the town where he lives and, while awaiting his arrival, rehearses alternative poses and gambits. He is unable to escape his parents' vigilance on the first

---

[22] On the relationship between Beauvoir and Leduc see de Courtivron, *Leduc,* and Leduc's 'Lettres à Simone de Beauvoir'.

[23] *La Folie en tête* (hereafter *FT*), 134.

evening, but arrives the next morning while his mother is at mass, and returns in the middle of the following night. Leduc describes her elaborate but vain efforts to seduce him in minute detail, and with self-deprecating irony.[24]

Leduc dwells at length on these obsessive dealings with real readers, no doubt because they are indeed remarkably revealing. It is as if she had found the customary channel to literary notoriety closed to her, and had thus been denied the vital return needed from writing: 'Un lecteur c'est un joueur de ping-pong. Il vous rend ce que vous avez envoyé';[25] in the face of this, needing a mirror in which to catch her image as a writer, she had resolved, when the opportunity presented itself, to go and collect it directly. But this strategy betrayed, at the same time, the extent to which the narcissistic need manifested in writing was a 'chasse à l'amour', a need for the Other, not just as mirror but as partner in the construction of her sexual identity. We are certainly made to feel that what Leduc wants from her readers is the consecration of a desired self-image, and its perpetuation outside the self-enclosed sphere of writing. The reader is, in other words, to be caught in the net of Leduc's narcissistic dealings with herself. Yet her desire for the reader also takes a desperately literal turn, as it taps into and lays bare the needs which underlie writing itself. Propped up in bed in a scruffy provincial hotel, sipping chilled Meursault, and reading Steinbeck as she waits for a callow youth—her reader—to cast off mother's apron-strings and come to her arms: this portrait of the artist, like something by Francis Bacon, figures a 'détournement' which, as she looks back, Leduc identifies at the heart of her pathological relationship to writing. Focusing unflinchingly on her body, its defects and demands, she portrays herself as a grotesque, and her dealings with readers as a grotesque parody of the relationship, and the self-image, she desires. The false and embarrassing scenes she recounts are seen as 'actings-out', as negative fantasies of the dark side of writing—a form of prostitution ('Écrire c'est se prostituer' (*FT* 410)) in which, rather than transmuting them into literature, she had been engaged in placing her secrets, and her body, in the market-place.

It is against this background, then, that we must place Leduc's switch to

---

[24] *La Chasse à l'amour* offers another example of these personal transactions with readers. Hortense writes Leduc a series of admiring letters and then invites her to lunch in a dreary Balzacian *pension de famille* where Leduc is to parade for the benefit of two other readers, Philomène and Victoire. The exchanges with these younger women are no less excruciating than those with Patrice and Flavien, but this does not deter Leduc from accepting an invitation to stay with them at Saint-Cirq-la-Popie, thus prolonging a futile and enervating situation.

[25] *La Chasse à l'amour*, 295.

autobiography, and the writing of *La Bâtarde*. In autobiography writing becomes something other than 'Un billet galant écrit à moi-même' (*FT* 14), it becomes a mode through which, progressively, Leduc breaks the spell of the past, rather than simply exploiting it, and exploiting herself, to literary ends. And, as we have seen, the reader Leduc builds into the text helps her accomplish this conversion. The trajectory of the imaginary reader in *La Bâtarde* figures the shift from narcissistic self-absorption towards an openness to the external world, from writing conceived as sterile posturing, through writing as therapeutic self-help, to writing as the sign and the transmission of a gift. By posing (for it is still inevitably a pose) as the reader's benefactor, offering to put her skills at our service, to become our eyes and ears, Leduc signals her sense of having, however precariously, found a new footing—for herself, her writing, and her reader. Where before she took, now she will give; where before she made demands on us, now she will be responsive to what she takes to be our demands. Of course, in having our demands dictated to us, we remain imaginary: we are still being exploited, enlisted in Leduc's gaze at herself. But it is now in a good cause. Without lifting a finger, we have helped Leduc transform herself: our ministry as autobiographer's reader is truly a sinecure.

NATHALIE SARRAUTE: *ENFANCE*

Nathalie Sarraute's *Enfance* (1983), a fragmentary exploration of her childhood in Russia and France, dominated by the emotional stresses and strains of a broken marriage, raises the question of the reader in a particularly interesting and original way. Each of its most salient formal or stylistic features seems ambivalent and could be interpreted either as a repudiation of the reader or, on the contrary, as inviting his or her participation. While it deals with new territory, *Enfance* is clearly an extension of Sarraute's fictional work; in turning to her own past, she maintains her concern with intersubjective space, and with the 'tropistic' movements she detects just beneath the surface of our everyday thoughts, words, and gestures, movements which give the lie to the settled identities and well-formed motives we like to think we possess.[26] In so far as Sarraute deploys an idiom (hesitancy, use of ellipsis, suspension marks, quoted speech) and a range of concerns (the power of words, the problem of finding

[26] For an excellent general account of Sarraute's world see V. Minogue, *Nathalie Sarraute*. On the relationship between Sarraute's fiction and her autobiography see Françoise van Roey-Roux, '*Enfance* de Nathalie Sarraute ou de la fiction à l'autobiographie'.

an adequate language to convey, without caricature or undue rigidity, the mobile paradoxical dynamism of tropism and 'sous-conversation') she has made familiar, it might seem that in *Enfance* the production of autobiographical meaning was monopolized by the author. Yet Sarraute has always stressed that her fictional mode demands the reader's collaboration and complicity, and that authorial power and knowledge are ceded rather than asserted by her way of writing.[27] The same kinds of reflection are prompted by the fragmentary character of *Enfance*. Sarraute resists narrative continuity (while chronological development is on the whole maintained, causalities are not spelt out), and divides her text into seventy brief chapters, usually centred on a single impression or incident—very often the short- or long-term repercussions of a specific phrase or verbal exchange. To some degree the effect is to reinforce the sense of authorial power, the limits of knowledge and control being underlined by the activity of fragmentation. But at the same time, by creating spacings and pauses, the device makes clearings in which the reader's creative collaboration is potentially solicited—it is for us, perhaps, to make sense of what is given, to create the continuity which is withheld, to pursue the work of interpretation and construction.

The device which raises these issues most acutely, however, is the presence, in most but not all of the fragments, of two narrating voices which engage in a dialogue with one another. The first voice is more closely identified with the child protagonist and with the primary submission to the emotional currents of the past reactivated through submission to memory. The second voice is sometimes (though not always) more detached and critical. On the whole, the first voice says most and addresses the second; while the second voice reacts to what it hears. Both use the 'tu' form, the idiom being that of old friends (perhaps a woman and a male friend of long standing: the first fragment indirectly attributes male gender to the second voice) who know each other well. But the fact that they are facets of the same person, that this is an inner dialogue with an *alter ego*, is occasionally underlined, for example when the second voice uses the 'je' form to designate the child protagonist. The dialogue between the two voices pre-empts and replaces any form of author–reader discourse: the author is screened behind the two voices, and the second voice provides the text with its narratee. Where does this leave the real reader?

In the critical literature which has rapidly sprung up around *Enfance*, much has been said about the dialogue device. Two issues have

---

[27] e.g. in *L'Ère du soupçon*, 90–1, 132, 138–47.

predominated: the characterization of the two voices, and the role allocated to the real reader. Valerie Minogue has suggested that the voices represent different attitudes towards the activity of autobiography, 'that of the burrower, who delves into and tries to merge with the recollected sensation [and] that of the critical sifter who challenges, warns of self-indulgence, exaggeration, falsification, and points to the gap between the sensation of *then* and the words and images of *now*'.[28] This view, which attributes relatively clear-cut roles to the two voices, has been adopted with differing emphases by a number of other critics. Philippe Lejeune, on the other hand, has emphasized the instability of the two voices: 'surtout [le dialogue] se déplace, se métamorphose sans cesse . . . les voix passent leur temps à changer de rôle, à faire bouger leur identité.' Rather than remaining in a relatively fixed relation to the first, the second voice 'passe son temps à osciller entre trois positions: contrôle, écoute, collaboration'.[29]

As regards the other issue (the reader's role), Minogue argues that the dialogue encourages 'the reader's critical participation, it cuts away any pretensions to bland authority';[30] the critical voice leads the way and invites further 'challenge, verification or dissent'.[31] Ann Jefferson and Yvette Went-Daoust argue, conversely, that the dialogue device distances and disempowers the reader; Jefferson writes that this 'represented reader [the second voice] within Sarraute's text does all the legwork on behalf of the postulated reader of the text, continuously validating the authenticity of the autobiographical narrative so that the reading role itself requires little more than passive assent'.[32] Went-Daoust asserts that the reader is confronted with 'un dialogue qui ne le concerne pas';[33] but since, in fact, potential reactions and objections are constantly anticipated, we are made to feel that the reader is very much on the author's mind. Lejeune, too, stresses the *mise à distance* of the real reader, and like Went-Daoust suggests that it is designed to protect the author.[34]

In emphasizing the flexibility of the relationship between the two voices,

---

[28] 'Fragments of a Childhood: Nathalie Sarraute's *Enfance*', 72. It should be noted, however, that in a further article, 'Nathalie Sarraute's *Enfance*: From Experience of Language to the Language of Experience', Minogue observes: 'The experiencer and narrator, approaching the matter dialogically, are no more fixed and immutable than the experience itself' (pp. 217–18).

[29] 'Paroles d'enfance', 33.

[30] 'Fragments of a Childhood', 82.

[31] For Minogue Sarraute's narrative as a whole is 'always reaching out to the reader, inviting participation, challenge, verification or dissent': 'Nathalie Sarraute's *Enfance*', 221.

[32] 'Beyond Contract', 56.

[33] Y. Went-Daoust, '*Enfance* de Nathalie Sarraute ou le pouvoir de la parole', 340.

[34] 'Paroles d'enfance', 32.

Lejeune underlines the artfulness of *Enfance*. The first function he identifies ('contrôle'), where suspicions regarding the authenticity of the autobiographer's performance are paraded, serves to divert attention from the fact that the text is far from spontaneous, and is indeed a highly artificial construct. The second function ('écoute') creates the illusion of a 'psychotherapeutic' process where buried truth is teased out by the need to satisfy a listener unwilling to settle for evasiveness. In its third role ('collaboration') the accompanying voice is represented as an equal and active partner; the two voices work in unison, jointly working at the resurrection of the past. For Lejeune the overall affect of this variation in the functions of the dialogue is to make *Enfance* a musical and oral work in which we hear a range of overlapping voices. In suggesting that critical attention should focus on the way in which this 'chambre d'échos' is constructed, Lejeune leaves the question of the reader somewhat in suspension, inviting us perhaps to infer that the fluctuations he has identified in the relationship between the voices do not, in his view, affect the overall attitude towards the real reader which should be seen as uniformly distanced and self-protective. Be that as it may, my aim is now to suggest that if we extend and develop Lejeune's typology of functions, we may perceive in the fluctuations of the imaginary dialogue between the narrating voices a comparable fluctuation in the role accorded to the reader of *Enfance*, as well as in the dynamics of the autobiographical 'rapport à soi' at work—in however calculated a fashion—in this text.

'Alors, tu vas vraiment faire ça? "Evoquer tes souvenirs d'enfance"' (p. 7):[35] the role played by the secondary voice in the opening fragment has no doubt done much to establish the stereotype of a critical, masculine, distanced, and censorious figure. Here the role seems largely designed to incarnate resistances which are to be defied: autobiographical explanation is thus characterized as a denial of repressive doubts and scruples: 'c'est de toi que me vient l'impulsion', says the first narrator, 'tu me pousses', 'par tes objurgations, tes mises en garde . . . tu le fais surgir . . . tu m'y plonges . . .' (p. 10). But from being the spokesman (or Devil's advocate) for a conventional view of autobiography (as a haven for elderly writers whose inspiration has dried up, etc.) the second voice rapidly takes on other roles. A sceptical note is sounded quite frequently, but this generally has the function of allowing the first narrator to identify more clearly what she is doing. Thus, when highly metaphorical language is used to render the child's stubborn adherence to her mother's instruction about proper mastication (p. 17)—an incident which anticipates many others concerned

---

[35] References are to the Folio edn.

with the child's need to establish order—the second voice mildly adverts to the fact that the terms used cannot be those available to the child. To this the first voice responds by saying that the range of feelings concerned in any case falls outside language, child's or adult's: 'c'était ressenti, comme toujours, hors des mots, globalement . . .' (p. 17). The second voice is quick to detect and censure any signs of reliance on ready-made images or clichés from the established repertoire of the 'souvenirs d'enfance' genre. But this critical, interrogative stance goes beyond scepticism and portrays an active concern for authenticity: is that picture really in *Max and Moritz*? (p. 48); isn't it called *rédaction* at primary school? (p. 207); yes, father suffered a lot when one of his daughters died in infancy, but he became ill with scarlet fever, not 'chagrin' (p. 119). Such interventions rehearse fairly standard routines in autobiographical writing, but they also produce the impression of an active engagement with the past. Sometimes the roles are reversed. In the fragment concerning the child's decision to stay with her father rather than return to her mother in Russia (pp. 172–6), the first narrator voices the fear that the reconstructed memory is purely artificial. 'Pas entièrement', intervenes the second voice, going on to note a parallel between the child's sense of independence and the ethos of the primary school system. This perspective is then gratefully adopted and developed by the first voice, stimulated by further contributions from its assistant.

In the cluster of roles we have so far considered, the second voice is essentially ancillary and subordinate. These roles encompass Lejeune's function of 'contrôle', but also go beyond it, towards prompting, interviewing, facilitating, questioning, as well as restraining ('sois juste': do not fall into the trap of blackening your mother, consider the evidence (p. 38)), and putting in plain words what the first narrator expresses through images—for example her reaction when her younger sister damaged her teddy bear (p. 175). In playing these ancillary roles the second voice undoubtedly serves to validate the autobiographical act. For example, in forcing the first narrator to concede that the evocation of the mother's voice is 'un petit morceau de préfabriqué' (p. 21), the second voice none the less enables her to insist on what is held to be unquestionably authentic in the memory. The concession serves to protect the core of the re-enacted memory from scepticism. In the fragment (pp. 83–8) recalling the cruel remark of a family friend to whom the girl had been urged to show her 'roman', the second voice recalls that Sarraute has previously used this incident in accounting for her late start as a novelist. Here the first narrator gladly accepts the implicit accusation and goes on to demonstrate that 'real' autobiographical self-analysis has now excavated a different account of the incident's repercussions, truer than the handy 'traumatisme d'enfance' trotted out earlier.

Validation takes on a somewhat different character when the sense of a hierarchy between the voices, and a division of roles, is attenuated. The ancillary voice, who represents another point of view, can always be seen as the avatar of a potentially hostile reader who must be neutralized or domesticated. This clearly associates the dialogue device with self-protection. But the effect is different in the many instances where the second voice is given the role of manifesting its complicity with the first narrator, and when the task of engaging with the past's resurfacings in memory is represented as a communal or antiphonal activity involving a generative process of collaboration, advance, and retreat. The second voice sometimes provides encouragement and reassurance: 'yes, there is a danger that your memories of Komenetz-Podolsk will read like "beaux souvenirs d'enfance", but go ahead, "laisse-toi aller un peu", the fragmentary quality of what you remember should insure against the second-hand' (p. 32). The two voices sometimes debate an issue—for example, why the young girl never complained to her father about her stepmother (p. 156)—on an equal footing, like sisters by the fireside as Lejeune and Jefferson[36] aptly note. This is particularly striking in the long fragment (pp. 247–58) concerning the mother's visit from Russia when Natasha was eight and a half. Here the first voice narrates and relives the sequence of events, sticking closely to remembered facts and emotions, while the second voice situates them in a wider temporal framework, but also provides the images and metaphors— the child as a parachutist (p. 249), the mother as a customer in a toy-shop (p. 253)—which bring to life the underlying dynamics of the failed encounter. Complicity takes another form in the fragment centred on the words 'Ce n'est pas ta maison' addressed to the child by her stepmother Vera (pp. 130–2). Here the second voice initially articulates the dangers of turning Vera into a fictional stereotype—'la méchante marâtre'—but her longest intervention picks up and develops the first narrator's desire to understand and mitigate Vera's apparent cruelty. By taking over the role of seeing the event from various perspectives, the second voice then enables the first to concentrate on the child's reactions and to express with unsentimental solemnity the devastating impact of the stepmother's words. Emotional complicity of a comparable kind is displayed in the fragment (pp. 107–8) based around the journey from Russia to France which was to mark the child's return to her father's custody. Here the second narrator,

[36] A. Jefferson, 'Autobiography as Intertext'.

having listened to the narrative without interrupting, takes up an implicit invitation to probe further the possibility that the girl had sensed an ulterior motive for the journey. But when the first narrator retreats, finding the idea that her mother could have coldly decided to abandon her impossible to accept, the second narrator performs a 'cover-up' operation, proposing an agreed *communiqué*—'ne nous suffit-il de constater . . .'—which provides an explanation for the girl's disquiet, while avoiding the emotional pain of wholly acknowledging the mother's heartlessness which in any case can only be a matter of conjecture.

The complicities we have been identifying in the two voices of *Enfance* present the reader with a kind of collaboration which goes well beyond the provision of a more detached point of view; in several instances this collaborative complicity takes on the character of an active working-through of memories and emotions. This is perceptible when we are made to feel that the gaps which divide the contributions of the two voices, the switch or relay from one speaker to another, confer a stereophonic density on the emotional spaces reconstructed in the fragments. In addition to confirming, extending, and carrying forward the explanation, or initiating another line of enquiry, the contribution of the second voice may convey the sense of a reassessment, a secondary process brought about by the acts of remembering and interpreting. This may in itself be provisional, as in the fragment (pp. 41–54) which comes to focus on a memory of how the child would react when her father tiptoed out of the room at night. The second voice queries the initial account and offers a different replay of the sequence (p. 53); but this then leads to a third enactment of the memory, more subtle and emotionally complex than the first two. Here one could certainly argue that it is the real reader who is left to adjudicate between the three versions. The trouble is that, unlike the reader in the text, the real reader cannot make more withdrawals from the memory-bank, cannot continue the open work of interpretation: the privilege we are offered is perhaps deceptive. Before we return to this issue, a further instance of working-through must be considered. The fragment (pp. 73–6), like many others, concerns rejection and the power of words. A phrase enduringly lodged in the adult's mind gives the lie to a current of memory which still perpetuates a family romance in which the child was securely incorporated in the relationship between her mother and stepfather Kolia. The second voice prompts the first narrator to recollect and narrate the occasion when the child had been rebuffed by the words 'femme et mari sont un même parti'. Acknowledging the power of this memory, the first narrator nevertheless insists initially that at the time the words did not hurt. In the face of this denial the second voice narrates the incident again, recreating the physical, gestural dynamics of the scene. This leads to a progressive shifting of ground, punctuated by further interjections—'allons fais un effort . . .', 'C'est bien, continue . . .'—which culminates in the acknowledgement that even at the time the child had felt alienated: 'J'étais un corps étranger . . . qui gênait.' When the second voice wants to go even further, suggesting that the child had realized that it would inevitably be expelled by the newly formed partnership in which it had no place, resistance is again encountered: 'Non tu vas trop loin'; to which the second voice replies, bringing the fragment to a close, 'Si, je reste tout près, tu le sais bien' (p. 76).

At one end of the spectrum of roles allocated to the *alter ego* in *Enfance* we find that of the analyst in relation to the analysand in the psychoanalytical encounter. In fact this transferential interaction, based on the dynamics of speaking, listening, intervening, or remaining silent, runs through the whole relationship between the two voices. *Enfance* can be seen as a demonstration of the way autobiographical self-understanding involves the postulation of another who is addressed and on whom the burden of understanding is partly placed. To revive and externalize past emotions, long-buried feelings, and to bring these into language and history, is to 'go public', to negotiate dialogically with a perspective which may be other than our own. But is it not precisely by virtue of being a controlled demonstration, a simulation of dialogical openness, that *Enfance* effectively fails to do more than ape the dynamics of exchange and transference? By constructing her own Other, and keeping it in the family, does Sarraute not extricate herself from the situation she appears to have placed herself in?

A number of considerations must be taken into account in approaching these questions. First, rather than judge *Enfance* by some ideal standard of autobiographical conduct, we should remind ourselves that the narratee in autobiography is inevitably a construct, a dummy, a pole used for particular purposes, and that the relationship with the reader is inevitably a simulacrum. One could argue that by making her narratee an extension of herself, by keeping the dialogue *en vase clos*, Sarraute lucidly avoids the pretence that the designated reader can be other than a figment whose sting has been removed. Yet such an argument can only take us so far. We can ask ourselves in the context of any autobiography: what kind of reader did the author feel he or she needed to imagine, in order for the text to answer the needs expressed through its writing? And cases will come to mind— Stendhal pre-eminently but also perhaps Gide, Leduc, or Perec—where we are made to feel that, for better or worse from the autobiographer's point of view, the potential collaboration of a free agent, unconstrained by specific parameters, by a particular image, was felt to be necessary. Even if such a reader remains an imaginary construct, what is anticipated and in some cases desired is precisely a figure who would escape the bounds of any imaginary portrait.

This is clearly not the kind of reader Sarraute felt she needed, but if we want to identify an attitude towards the real reader in her use of the dialogue device we must take into account the dominant themes of control and containment. Put in simple terms, *Enfance* is the story of a child who, on the one hand, becomes remarkably sensitive to the powerful forces which lie just beneath the surface of everyday words, and on the other hand successfully strives to order and control these forces, and thus partially to evade their potentially damaging effects. *Enfance* is the story of a liberation. In some respects the relationship between the two voices re-enacts the drama of submission and control. The *alter ego* helps the first narrator to dominate past feelings rather than simply repeat them; but at the same time this narrator is clearly shown to control the *alter ego*—whenever she wishes to, she can have the last word, as in the case of the fragment (pp. 113–16) concerning the relationship with her father which ends with the kind of unequivocal assertion that could easily have given rise to objections. The possibility of giving voice to the past in the present depends on a process of controlled release and containment enacted in the dialogue. The real reader is also implicated in this mechanism. Rather than being shut out or replaced by a more amenable representative, the reader's place is consistently marked as the necessary silent—silenced—witness to these autobiographical transactions. The control, manipulation, training of a reader located outside the psychological arena plays a necessary part in the delineation of what happens within it. However, the control exerted on the reader, as *Enfance* unfolds, is not uniform but always a function of the roles played out in the dialogue. The reader is not simply asked to endorse a verdict on the past, or to participate in the construction of meaning beyond what is given. To play the unwritten part we have been allocated we must understudy all the roles in the mobile dialogue between the voices, and thus appreciate the enduring fears and victories which make them a necessary part of the autobiographical process.

6

Autobiography and Ideology

L'idéologie n'est rien d'autre que l'idée en tant qu'elle domine.
(Roland Barthes par Roland Barthes)[1]

Wittingly or unwittingly the autobiographer engages with ideology, with ideas, beliefs, and taxonomies which are held to have explanatory force and wide application in human affairs. This vast domain ranges from *doxa*, or received opinion—what passes for true in a given period or milieu—to concepts in religion, psychology, or philosophy which claim to define and codify human reality. Such material becomes ideological by virtue of the representations which may be derived from it: it is the power to categorize, label, and name which is the mark of the ideological. 'L'Idéologie', in Louis Althusser's well-known phrase, 'nous *interpelle* en sujets':[2] we become subjects through ideology—'God's creatures', 'victims of society', 'workers', 'subversives', 'neurotics'.

And, indeed, 'autobiographers'. For it is possible to ask whether a particular set of presuppositions about identity, individuality, or self-coherence characterizes autobiography as a genre. Dilthey certainly thought so: for him the rise of modern autobiography represented a decisive step in the history of western selfhood; and this Whiggish view, which charts with approval the progressive fashioning of the Individual, dominated autobiography criticism until recently. To view autobiography as a culturally symbolic act is to endow it with marked ideological connotations. But if this makes it possible to launch an attack on what one takes to be the ideology of autobiography, the likelihood is that this will be from the standpoint of another ideology.[3] Rather than take such an approach I propose to focus on the place of ideology in the writing of autobiography, and to consider how

[1] *Roland Barthes par Roland Barthes*, 51.

[2] *Lénine et la philosophie*, 142. For a lucid discussion of Althusser on ideology see R. Coward and J. Ellis, *Language and Materialism*, 71 ff.

[3] As is the case of R. Elbaz, *The Changing Nature of the Self*, where the autobiographical tradition from Abelard and Augustine, through Montaigne, Descartes, and Rousseau, to the mid-20th cent. is said to involve the hegemony of a specific 'discursive formation' based on a privatized, territorial, self-sufficient selfhood. Elbaz descries the premonitory gleams of an 'extra-territorial' self—sandwiched between a medieval configuration and a post-modern

autobiographers themselves deal with the inescapable ideological dimension of their undertaking. After more general discussion, works by Renan, Gide, and Barthes will be considered in detail.

The staple ingredients of autobiography are permeated by ideology. The topic of childhood reading will provide an example. References to the books one read as a child, and the influences they are supposed to have had, are extremely common in autobiographies.[4] It can of course be argued that this points to ideological assumptions which have characterized the genre since Rousseau, for example the general assumption that the things we did as children are formative, or more specific assumptions about the role of reading in relation to other kinds of experience. However, above and beyond these assumptions, one finds that in specific autobiographies the account of childhood reading supports different kinds of explanatory manœuvre, figures in different kinds of plot, and becomes the site of different kinds of conflict. In a famous passage early in the *Confessions*,[5] Rousseau ascribes a powerful determining effect to the experience of staying up late with his recently bereaved father reading 'Romans', 'livres amusants', which had belonged to his late mother. He claims that because it coincided with his nascent self-consciousness, but preceded his full acquisition of the powers of reason, this experience not only afforded him precocious insight into passions and feelings ('Je sentis avant de penser') but definitively shaped his ways of thinking and behaving. The brief passage is riddled with presuppositions, inferences, causalities; in short, with ideology. It proposes a connection between childhood events and adult personality which implies a theory about human genesis that could be enunciated in a series of abstract propositions. More specifically, it invites consideration in the light of Rousseau's earlier treatise on education, *Emile ou de l'éducation*, where he had proscribed the uses of literary works (except *Robinson Crusoe*) in the upbringing of children, had theorized extensively on the deleterious effect the wrong kind of reading can have, and had advocated a careful vigilance and control on the part of the child's educator.[6]

one—in André Malraux's *Antimémoires*. Commending Malraux's anti-psychological bias, and his rejection of the paraphernalia of conventional autobiography, Elbaz adopts him as the patron saint of a de-territorialized subjectivity, engaged in the historical contingency from which earlier autobiographers, he claims, remained aloof. Elbaz's own ideology, it seems to me, makes him blind to the patently metaphysical and supra-historical aspects of Malraux's autobiographical stance.

   [4] On this see R. N. Pauly, *Le Berceau et la bibliothèque*.
   [5] *Œuvres complètes*, i. 8. For an extensive discussion of the passage see P. Robinson, 'The "Actor's Talent" and the "Accent of the Passions"'.
   [6] 'Je hais les livres; ils n'apprennent qu'à parler de ce qu'on ne sait pas', *Œuvres complètes*, iv. 454.

It is interesting to compare the Rousseau passage with the fifth book of Wordsworth's *The Prelude*, entitled 'Books', which is concerned with the general place of literature in the imaginative life of the child, and may in part be a rejoinder to Rousseau, and thus a contribution to an ideological debate. In some respects, Wordsworth's meditation on childhood reading chimes with Rousseau's views, particularly in its strictures against the excessive use of abstract or abstruse knowledge, 'the rank growth of propositions'. But in stressing the need to foster the child's imagination, Wordsworth suggests that teachers, 'watchful men | and skilful in the usury of time', tend to control and limit children excessively, confining them, 'Like engines', 'to the very road | Which they have fashioned . . .'. Teachers need to be taught that, outside the schoolroom, children are in the hands of 'A wiser spirit' and that 'our most unfruitful hours' are often our most profitable.[7] As an example Wordsworth adduces the kind of reading matter which had such a damaging effect on Rousseau:

> The tales that charm away the wakeful night
> In Araby—Romances, Legends, penned
> For solace by the light of Monkish lamps;
> Fictions, for Ladies of their Love, devised
> By youthful Squires; adventures endless, spun
> By the dismantled warrior in old age . . .

Like Rousseau, Wordsworth stresses the enduring power of such reading but sees it in positive terms, as supplying an essential human need:

> These spread like day, and something in the shape
> Of these will live till man shall be no more.
> Dumb yearnings, hidden appetites, are ours,
> And they must have their food. Our childhood sits,
> Our simple childhood, sits upon a throne
> That hath more power than all the elements.[8]

The point is not simply that Rousseau and Wordsworth disagree about a certain form of childhood reading but rather that the moment they seek, as autobiographers, to allocate a place to it in the narrative of their lives childhood reading becomes an ideological issue. The same will apply when Stendhal talks about reading Ariosto and Shakespeare, when Edmund

[7] *The Prelude* (1805), v. 172.
[8] Ibid. 178.

Gosse recalls the cataclysmic effect of an adventure story called *Tom Cringle's Log*, or when Sartre tells of the effects of his early immersion in the verbal world of books.[9]

To write autobiography is to place oneself, or to seek one's place, amidst ideological configurations. The history of the genre is, in part, the history of such configurations and autobiography's highly intertextual character is partly a reflection of this fact: the autobiographer's precursor is generally identified as an ideologue. The term 'intellectual autobiography' has some validity when, for example, it is applied to books which play down the personal element and focus on the evolution of a person's ideas,[10] but there is no such thing as an ideological autobiography: they all are in some respect. There is no need to quibble over whether or not a neutral inventory of facts would be ideological. No autobiography fits this description and the moment selection, evaluation, and organization are present we are in the realm—or the clutches—of ideology. It might seem as if autobiographers were forced to choose between two options: disregarding the ideological aspect of their texts and running the risk that they will thereby be perceived as all the more ideological (in the narrow, pejorative sense of being fettered to a singular vision of the world of which one is merely the instrument or mouthpiece); or taking an explicitly ideological line and risking the accusation that their lives have been viewed exclusively through the abstract medium of concepts and beliefs. If these are not in fact the only options it is because the practice of autobiography has, since Augustine at least, often been allied to an active participation in the domain of ideas. Augustine on memory, Montaigne on the limits of knowledge, Rousseau's 'morale sensitive', Leiris's dialogue with psychoanalysis, are contributions to ideological debate in the medium of autobiographical writing, and at the same time contributions to a writing of the self conducted partly through ideological debate. One of the *raisons d'être* of autobiography is as an ideological testing-ground, a place for the *mise à l'épreuve* not only of ideas about the self, but of the relationship between subjective existence and ideology, the individual and concepts of individuality. To discuss further the variety of stances autobiographers adopt towards ideology it will be useful to distinguish three kinds of strategy. In the first, the ideological dimension is viewed as a source of legitimation for a discourse about the self. In the second, the discourse of the self is pitted *against* the domain of

[9] 'L'Arioste forma mon caractère', *Vie de Henry Brulard*, 107; *Father and Son*, 171; *Les Mots*, 39.

[10] As in, say, E. Quinet's *Histoire de mes idées* (1858), Alain's *Histoire de mes pensées* (1936), or, a less clear-cut case, Lévi-Strauss's *Tristes Tropiques* (1955).

ideology as a whole. In the third, autobiography becomes the channel for a public act of personal commitment, a form of *engagement*.

Legitimation

In its earlier forms, autobiography was characteristically a genre through which an individual demonstrated the way his or her life conformed to a pre-existing pattern. Subsequently, at least since Montaigne, it has often been associated with the desire to forge new patterns of selfhood. In both cases the willingness to engage with ideology through abstract or theoretical discussion, or by other means, reflects the desire to ground what one wishes to say about oneself in a wider context. At a time when it was either unheard of or unseemly to talk about oneself, only the exemplary character of a life could justify autobiography. Augustine's narrative of his experiences prior to conversion is authorized by its exemplary and thus didactic status; the self it describes is inseparable from the ideological framework in which the meaning of events is established. In many subsequent autobiographies the narrative aims to demonstrate the exemplary quality of the author's life-history, often in terms of his conformity to a particular human type: the sinner or reprobate, the artist, the intellectual. Victorian autobiographers were particularly inclined to use Christian typology to this end, creating parallels with biblical characters and contexts, while in the twentieth century psychoanalysis and Marxism have been sources of new paradigms. The use of pre-existing models also encompasses paradigmatic situations such as the 'Tolle, lege!' scenes discussed in our first chapter, declarations of intertextual affiliation, and instances of express fidelity to the established rhetoric of the autobiographical genre. By such means, legitimation of one's own discourse—and of the self-image it seeks to articulate—is derived from conformity with an existing ideological nexus. In the simplest forms of autobiography, from the devotional works of Puritans to the ghosted life-stories of modern politicians and celebrities, conformity with a prototype may be almost total. In more sophisticated autobiography it may only be partial.

When autobiographers themselves are conscious of forging new paradigms of selfhood, ideological legitimation works in a different way. Here the writer himself seeks to redraw the wider configuration within which his or her new approach to the self is to be viewed. In Montaigne, Rousseau, Leiris, or Sartre, self-writing involves not simply the rejection of existing ideological foundations but the provision of a new set of ideological bearings, a new anthropology which extends well beyond the individual writer's case. Much of the thrust of Montaigne's self-investigation is counter-ideological. Having begun by essaying his own judgement within the context of the wisdom of the ancients, he progressively comes to pit the lessons of his own experience, and the evidence of his own self-examination, against available truths and authorities. Yet Montaigne is not content to define himself against authority; he seeks constantly to extrapolate from himself to 'l'humaine condition', to delineate a new model of human reality of which he serves as exemplar. In Rousseau's case the autobiographer constantly supplies not only the explanations which make his narrative comprehensible but the wider *ratio* which legitimates his explanations. The result is that what Rousseau, by his own account, is or was, seems to be vouched for by a framework of ideas which, even if it is supplied largely by Rousseau himself, has the authority of a certain universality. Since Rousseau autobiography has often been a vehicle for ideological testimony, debate, or conflict. In the nineteenth century this frequently involved the account of a conversion from a dominant value-system to a more personal and subjective one, an alternative ideological configuration regarded as more congenial to the subject: Mill goes from Reason towards Feeling; Renan from Catholicism to 'La Déesse Raison'; Newman from the Church of England to the Church of Rome; Gosse and Ruskin from Science to Art. In the twentieth century conversion is less common and ideological debate is more likely to consist in the playing-off of one ideology—psychological determinism, for example—against another. Where the alternative value-system is not in the public domain we encounter the second of the strategies outlined above.

Evading Ideology

The attraction of ideology as a source of self-definition and legitimation is its independence and generality; but this is also its limitation since it offers identity, sameness, at the expense of individual difference. The impulse to resist ideology may stem from a sense of one's own singularity and also from the desire to resist and repudiate alien *images*—not only specific deformations (or defamations) of our character, but the wider sense that our identity is in the hands of others. Autobiography may become an act of reappropriation through which identity is wrested from the grip of ideology. It then involves less a debate within ideology than a conflict with its alienating power, a counter-ideological practice through which the subject discovers or seeks to establish his or her uniqueness.

The process of writing may be primordial in this regard. Rousseau often conveys the impression that it is partly autobiographical writing itself which, while it spawns ideology—theorizations of how the self is formed through time—also secretes or validates a sense of self, a 'sentiment de l'existence' which is refractory to ideological categorizations. The true self is disclosed through friction with the categories which seek to circumscribe it. The strategy of legitimation seeks to contain the centrifugal movement of writing; the alternative which concerns us here makes a virtue of necessity and derives a sense of self from the break with, rather than the legitimation by, ideology. The autobiographical work comes to reside in a process of isolation, as the chemist isolates element from compound, deducing selfhood from what denies it. Stendhal, for example, cites from time to time potential assessments of his character which might be derived from the characterological science of the so-called 'idéologues', among them his friend Cabanis who defined the 'tempérament mélancolique',[11] or Destutt de Tracy who dubbed him a 'cheval ombrageux';[12] but he shows little inclination to validate such an approach, merely offering it as a contrast with his own which is exploratory, interrogatory, hypothetical, and leads away from such categorizations.[13] This might be compared with Nathalie Sarraute's device (in *Enfance*) of a second narrating voice which cites ready-made versions of herself that her autobiographical investigation tends to discredit.[14] Something similar is at work when Leiris and Sartre cite the judgements of psychoanalysts, acknowledging the partial truth of their diagnoses but also seeing them as beside the point. Leiris, like Stendhal, demonstrates through his self-conscious and constantly evolving autobiographical quest that the question of identity cannot be the prerogative of a single method. In Sartre's case it is somewhat different. *Les Mots* may be seen as the self-portrait of an ideological fall guy, a victim of ideological conditioning who has now seen through what happened to him. But Sartre makes no reference to his autobiographical method (in fact closely based on the tenets of existentialist psychoanalysis) and thus tends to evade the question of the ideological situation of the autobiographer and his practice. Nevertheless, by making no explicit bid for legitimation Sartre tends to

---

[11] See *Vie de Henry Brulard*, 37, 45, 244.

[12] Ibid. 44. Stendhal owed a great deal of his intellectual formation to Destutt de Tracy's *Éléments d'idéologie*.

[13] Acutely conscious, none the less, of the limits of introspection, Stendhal amusingly imagines a celestial rendezvous with Montesquieu (*Vie de Henry Brulard*, 31) whose judgement he admired and whose verdict on his character he would accept even if it were negative.

[14] For a discussion of this device in *Enfance*, see Ch. 5, above.

betray the desire to place his current self outside the reach of existing ideological systems.[15]

Pushed to its extreme, the tendency we are considering makes the self a negative quantity: something which lies beyond definition, outside the Other's grip, a pure difference. Already in Montaigne one has the sense that the introspective act carried out pen in hand discloses a quality which lies outside ideology. The 'forme maistresse qui luicte contre l'instruction'[16] falls outside the sway of available representations of human reality, and the more Montaigne writes the more he feels that the contours of the individual, always 'ondoyant et divers', can never be pinned down. From Rousseau onwards, resistance to ideology in autobiography is often associated with resistance to the example of existing texts, partly on the grounds of their assumed ideological foundations. While Stendhal and Chateaubriand feel the need to distance themselves from Rousseau in particular, autobiographers from Gide to Sarraute reveal a need to resist the dead weight of the genre as a whole. Generally this leads to self-consciousness about method, to formal innovation, to radical doubts about the consistency or knowability of the self, and ultimately to the view that the concept of selfhood is itself an ideological construct (although, as Barthes will suggest, this last view is as ideological as the one it opposes). There seems, then, to be a perennial link between the desire to evade ideology and the dissolution of the self. Unless they are willing to substitute a new ideology and a new image for those they discard, autobiographers have to accept indefinition and its drawbacks: that the desire for self-knowledge will be frustrated, and that the reader (and the reader's ideology) will provide the conclusions the autobiographer has spurned. While some (Stendhal, Barthes) are willing to settle for this to a considerable degree, the more general trend is towards a mixed economy where the resistance to ideology and the desire for ideological legitimation coexist in creative tension, as in Rousseau or Gide.

Autobiography as 'Engagement'

To write autobiography is to expose oneself and there is always something potentially unseemly about it. 'Le sot projet qu'il a eu de se peindre', observed Pascal of Montaigne: the 'moi haïssable' should not be flaunted but restrained.[17] However various or historically relative the criteria—

---

[15] See the discussion of *Les Mots* in Ch. 7, below.

[16] *Essais*, iii. 2. 26.

[17] An illuminating discussion of Pascal on the self, and of his strictures against Montaigne, will be found in J. Mesnard, 'Pascal et le "moi haïssable"'.

religious, ethical, aesthetic, social—by which self-writing is considered blameworthy, either in itself or in its contents, autobiographical disclosure has a transgressive potential. Autobiography has the capacity to become an act conducted in defiance of ideological authority, actual or potential, a form of commitment involving an element of personal risk, real or imaginary, immediate or posthumous. In the preface to *L'Age d'homme* (of which more in a moment) Michel Leiris explains that this is the feature which attracted him to the genre. Autobiography as commitment draws on the work's public aspect: the sense of an audience and the fact of publication itself. Instead of passively accepting these parameters the autobiographer seeks to harness them to his or her own ends: an active transformation of the relationship with others or with oneself.

Rousseau's *Confessions* are, as usual, exemplary. Stung by the accusations contained in an anonymous pamphlet, Rousseau composes his life-history as a riposte in which he will offer the unvarnished truth, however unflattering. Echoing Montaigne, he asserts that he prefers to be condemned for what he really did than praised on false evidence. His autobiography will set the record straight and its veracity will be vouched for by his willingness to reveal things one would normally keep hidden. Writing autobiography is equated with martyrdom; truth is placed above vainglory; Rousseau's text will be a sign of his commitment to a higher good than his own reputation.[18] Gide uses similar arguments with regard to *Si le grain ne meurt*, but in this case publication in the author's lifetime is crucial to the act of commitment. Revelation of his sexual identity will have an impact on Gide's subsequent life: autobiography will have been the instrument of permanent change. To present one's autobiography as an act is to confer a certain necessity on the (potentially vain or gratuitous) gesture of self-revelation; it is to imagine the text as an objective embodiment of subjective truth, a bulwark against falsehood. It also serves to give greater definition and palpability to the writer's audience: the human community is invited to stand witness to a discourse addressed in the first instance to a particular constituency. Representing himself book in hand at the Last Judgement, Rousseau defies his calumniators to dispute what he has said; by his commitment, vested in assurances of unsparing candour and absolute sincerity, the autobiographer forces the hand of his audience. Since autobiography generally involves making public what is usually private, confession is the principal mode of autobiographical commitment. For Rousseau, notoriously, confession of itself warrants or ensures exoneration.

[18] The famous opening of the *Confessions*, and the work's original preamble (see *Œuvres complètes*, i. 1148–55) are the crucial texts here.

More generally, autobiographical confession tends to presuppose its reception and to be predicated on an imaginary scene of direct confrontation where one deals with the Other eyeball to eyeball. By 'putting himself on the line' the autobiographer aims at a particular mode of textual presence.

'Faire un livre qui soit un acte': Leiris's 'De la littérature considérée comme une tauromachie', appended to *L'Age d'hommme* when it was reissued in 1946,[19] is both a manifesto for autobiography as a means of *engagement* and a critique of the illusory nature of such an idea. He explains that his aim in writing *L'Age d'homme* had been to confer authenticity on literary activity, too often anodyne and frivolous, by means of an uncompromisingly frank confession. Autobiography, he hoped, would engender a catharsis and through this a liquidation of the past. Writing and publishing the book would be an act *vis-à-vis* himself, since it would elucidate 'certaines choses encore obscures' which had been partially revealed to him through psychoanalysis; an act *vis-à-vis* others, who would be obliged to set their relationship with him on a revised footing; and a literary act which conferred aesthetic form on the remains of the past. Admitting now—a further confession—to a sense of failure, Leiris points to his recognition that confession is always in some degree a plea for exoneration; that self-depiction, however unflattering, is inevitably narcissistic; and that the effect of literary *mise-en-forme* is not to create distance but to glamorize and mythologize. Yet after largely demolishing the idea of autobiography as *engagement*, Leiris proceeds to rehabilitate it to some degree by revising the analogy with bullfighting on which he had based his case. The risk taken by the autobiographer may not be commensurate with that of the bullfighter, but in both activities the element of risk stems from the willingness to adhere strictly to rules clearly established at the outset. Leiris deduces from this that it is by taking on the character of a rite performed with unwavering exactitude that autobiographical confession can retain a certain authenticity. The commitment it involves is essentially aesthetic, and its repercussions involve not definitive transformation but the institution of a new rigour in one's dealings with oneself. Still linked to the idea of public disclosure, the element of risk now lies in the risk of failing to observe the rules of the game, of failing—publicly as well as privately—to live up to one's commitments. Viewed this way autobiographical commitment becomes essentially a long-term activity (Leiris had embarked on *La Règle du jeu* by the time he wrote his essay) associated primarily with the writer's performance.

[19] *L'Age d'homme*, 9–24.

'Faire un livre qui soit un acte': Leiris's essay demonstrates, in its tensions and doublings-back, that the notion of autobiography as commitment cannot be dissociated from the wider aesthetic dimension of the text and the array of competing motives, desires, and constraints inevitably at large in it. The attempt to harness and give precedence to the extra-literary, public, and referential dimension of autobiography is inevitably compromised and hampered by the exigences of autobiographical practice and discourse. The performative dimension of autobiography, whether it is enlisted to validate the self by confrontation with others, or to transform the self in some way through practices (confession, catharsis, the therapeutic reconstruction of a life-history) which necessitate the Other's complicity, is inevitably caught up with and constrained by other factors which always threaten to expose it as nothing more than a rhetorical illusion. Yet in this regard autobiography as commitment simply shares the fate of all other aspects of autobiographical discourse, and Leiris's example serves as an important reminder of its potency. As a stance towards ideology, it blends the two positions we examined previously since it involves an attempt at legitimation but one which bypasses, as it were, the ideological standing of the text's reconstruction of the past (and of the author's self-image) in favour of the author's presence as the originator of the textual act. No more or less deluded than other autobiographical strategies, autobiographical *engagement* inevitably exists in combination and in tension with them, just as the ideological dimension of autobiography inevitably cohabits, often uncomfortably, with other aspects. To substantiate this, let us now turn to our three examples: Renan, Gide, and Barthes.

RENAN: *SOUVENIRS D'ENFANCE ET DE JEUNESSE*

A major aim, and to some degree the *raison d'être*, of Renan's autobiography[20] is to show how his conversion to science and progress, far from representing a total repudiation of his sacerdotal vocation, was a transformation in which much—and much of value—was preserved. The difficulty of atheism, the spiritual aristocracy of the élite who have, in exemplary fashion, lived through the major intellectual crises of the age, the difficulty (but also the necessity) of maintaining a balance between spiritual and scientific values, are some of the book's major cruxes. Renan's is a

---

[20] First published in 1883. References, cited in the text, are to the edn. by J. Pommier (Armand Colin, 1959), reissued unmodified in the Collection Folio, Gallimard, 1983.

conversion narrative of a distinctly mid-nineteenth-century kind, and part of the interest of the *Souvenirs* lies in the fact that it is probably the only French example to mirror fully the major autobiographies of Britain's Victorian ideologues, and to emulate the ways in which they reflected some of the great isues of the age: Science versus Religion, History and Progress, Faith and Reason, Imagination and Objectivity.[21] Renan's 'de-conversion' is represented as the triumph of objectivity, in the shape of philological accuracy, over irrational belief. Yet Renan was reluctant to leave it at that. His autobiography was, in part, an attempt to show the ways in which, to put it in the telegraphic terms of his personal index to the *Souvenirs*, 'foi perdue agit encore' (p. 317). Subjective factors were to be given their authentic place alongside scientific and ideological ones. Whether they are or not must now be examined.

Despite the central conflict between Catholic faith and scientific truth which he records, Renan constantly emphasizes the continuity of his nature and suggests that in many respects he has never really changed.[22] He frequently portrays himself as a 'prêtre manqué', faithful to the *idéalité* of his Breton ancestors, incarnating 'la gageure paradoxale de garder les vertus cléricales, sans la foi qui leur sert de base et dans un monde pour lequel elles ne sont pas faites' (p. 196).[23] The Bretons may, according to Renan, cloak their longing for the ideal in the mantle of religion, but unlike most Catholics, religion for them is not a matter of dogma or constraint

---

[21] Personal crises connected with large issues of faith and vocation; a conscious relationship to the generic tradition of spiritual autobiography; a mixture of abstract theorizing with the detailed reconstruction of particular events; the retrospective delineation of public and private postures: these are some of the features Renan's *Souvenirs* have in common with Newman's *Apologia pro vita sua* (1864), Mill's *Autobiography* (1873), Ruskin's *Praeterita* (1899), Gosse's *Father and Son* (1907), and with related semi-fictional works by Carlyle and Butler.

[22] D. G. Charlton, *Positivist Thought in France during the Second Empire 1852–1870*, ch. 6, provides a searching account of Renan's intellectual evolution. K. Gore, *L'Idée de progrès dans la pensée de Renan*, provides a comprehensive account of the foundations and fluctuations of the idea of progress, very much at the centre of Renan's work.

[23] It is the 'prêtre manqué' side of Renan that Sartre will have in mind in *Les Mots* when he deplores the ways in which, in the second half of the 19th cent., literary culture became an ersatz religion (Sartre's grandfather is reported to be an admirer of Renan's style); e.g.: 'prélevé sur le catholicisme. le sacré se déposa dans les Belles-Lettres et l'homme de plume apparut, *ersatz* du chrétien que je ne pouvais être' (*Les Mots*, 209). But one of the ironies of *Les Mots* lies in the fact that, having analysed the ways in which his own concept of 'littérature engagée' could be interpreted as a faded copy of the humanistic 'fadaises' he thought he had repudiated, Sartre reveals his inability, at the time of writing, to purge himself of these tendencies. His stance at the end of the book is not unlike Renan's, and he might well have echoed the sentiment that 'foi perdue agit encore'.

('assujettissement') (p. 54). Renan is therefore able to indicate how his Breton idealism could have survived his loss of specifically religious faith. What, then, of his passionate adherence to rational scientific enquiry? To account for this Renan adduces another set of ancestors, on his mother's side: 'Par ma race, j'étais partagé et comme écartelé entre des forces contraires . . . Un Gascon, sans que je le susse, jouait en moi des tours incroyables au Breton et lui faisait des mines de singe' (p. 87). The idea of doubleness ('Presque tous nous sommes doubles . . .', p. 4) permeates the *Souvenirs*. Irreconcilable forces tend to pull the individual in different directions. In the 'Préface', these are labelled, on the one hand, 'la tête', 'le cerveau brûlé par le raisonnement', 'les abstractions', 'la dissection à outrance'; and on the other, 'le pôle contraire, c'est-à-dire l'irrationnel, le repos dans la complète ignorance, la femme qui n'est que femme . . .', etc. Renan does not suggest that any real accommodation between what he conceives as the warring forces of rationalism and idealism can be found:

j'étais prédestiné à être ce que je suis, un romantique protestant contre le romantisme, un utopiste prêchant en politique le terre-à-terre, un idéaliste se donnant inutilement beaucoup de mal pour paraître bourgeois, un tissu de contradictions, rappelant l'*hirocerf* de la scolastique qui avait deux natures. Une de mes moitiés devait être occupée à démolir l'autre, comme cet animal fabuleux de Ctésias qui se mangeait les pattes sans s'en douter (p. 52).

Renan is unwilling to endorse either side of his nature, to give precedence to his religious over his scientific side, or vice versa. However, in presenting himself as a 'tissu de contradictions', Renan uses the *Souvenirs* to articulate a more recent ideological position which, over and above the conversion which is at the heart of his narrative, contains elements of both strains.

We can detect this in his use of the 'Prière sur l'Acropole', one of the nineteenth century's great purple passages, which Renan claims he had written ten years earlier on the Acropolis. The 'Prière' has the air of a *mise en scène* of Renan's contradictions: a paean to 'La Déesse Raison', which also exudes a 'romantisme effrené';[24] a tribute to 'la raison toute nue' which is also a confession of inadequacy in the face of a daunting and perhaps inhuman ideal. Moved to review his past life in the light of 'le miracle grec', Renan tells us, he found that 'mes résolutions de devenir classique finissaient par me précipiter plus que jamais au pôle opposé' (p. 46). The closing words of the 'Prière' seem to consign the cult of Reason, along with Christianity, to the mausoleum of 'dieux morts', the funerary imagery

---

[24] See *Souvenirs*, 'Choix de variantes', 244.

echoing the repeated symbol of lost faith, the submerged 'Ville d'Is' whose bells, calling the faithful, still resound in Renan's ears even though there is no going back. What is asserted unequivocally is the fact of polarization. By setting Christianity and rationality back to back, insisting on his divided nature, accounting for it by his mixed ancestry, Renan betrays his disinclination to envisage any dialectical resolution of these oppositions, encouraging, rather, the sense of an enervating and ultimately sterile oscillation which cannot be resolved. Seldom inclined to render the subjective 'feel' of these divisions, Renan tends progressively to reveal that he has adopted a different ideological perspective which transcends them— the belief in 'le devenir', in 'un éternel *fieri*', in a 'souffle divin' permeating the universe.

The hypothesis of 'le devenir' had played a significant role at previous stages of his intellectual evolution, acting often as a convenient bridge between Religion and Reason, associating Science with Progress and the History of Humanity. Disillusioned with such perspectives, the Renan of the *Souvenirs* makes 'le devenir' a sort of cosmic vitalism,[25] a view he traces back to his days at Issy prior to the dawning of his historical consciousness: 'Un éternel *fieri*, une métamorphose sans fin, me semblait la loi du monde. La nature m'apparaissait comme un ensemble où la création particulière n'a point de place, et où, par conséquent, tout se transforme' (pp. 144–5). The conflict between religion and science, and its reflection in Renan's myth of doubleness, is allowed to remain unresolved in the *Souvenirs* while Renan makes for the higher ground of cosmic vitalism. The pseudo-science of cosmic speculation and the pseudo-religion of 'le souffle divin' provide a markedly ideological synthesis which seems to minimalize subjective factors—the sense of doubt or inner debate, for instance.

Renan's presentation of the successive phases through which a devout 'petit provincial' became a renowned expert in Semitic languages, and a famous writer to boot, but remained a 'prêtre manqué' in the process, keeping some sort of faith with his Breton ancestors and his teachers at Saint-Sulpice, is entertaining, often vivid, and sometimes exceedingly complicated. Renan can make us feel that he is writing *against* a cluster of possible narratives along the lines: devout naïve young Breton goes to Paris, falls prey to 'le siècle', and soon puts his faith behind him; credulous Breton finds that a few history lessons soon dispose of his totally childish beliefs, etc. Renan gives the appearance of trying at times to explain to one section of

---

[25] See Charlton, *Positivist Thought*, 112–20, on the Hegelian origins and unscientific character of Renan's notion of *devenir*.

his audience how it was that he could ever possibly have believed in Catholicism, while trying to convince another constituency that once he had abandoned the Church he did not simply turn his back on religious values. Often Renan seems to feel he is faced with admitting that either his faith or his reasons for abandoning it were frivolous. The end-product is a narrative whereby he underwent a series of radical transformations but remained basically the same: devout, serious young Breton goes to Paris, is utterly transformed by the worldliness of Saint-Nicolas du Chardonnet, modified again by the discovery of theology and biblical scholarship at Issy, further transformed by Saint-Sulpice, leaves the Church, becomes a famous teacher and writer—but remains essentially the same devout Breton he always was.

At Saint-Sulpice the close textual study of the Bible, as an historical phenomenon, inspired by the developments, mainly in Germany, of a 'science' of philology, opens totally unexpected vistas. Renan discovers an innate aptitude—'J'étais philologue d'instinct' (p. 165)—and claims to have found what he was looking for: 'la conciliation d'un esprit hautement religieux avec l'esprit critique' (p. 167). Yet the conciliation will be short-lived. Unlike his teachers, Renan cannot keep his faith and his critical faculties in sealed compartments: 'Comme je n'avais pas en mon esprit ces sortes de cloisons étanches, le rapprochement d'éléments contraires qui, chez M. Le Hir, produisait une profonde paix intérieure, aboutit chez moi à d'étranges explosions' (p. 159). Paradoxically, Renan seems to claim that he lacks Le Hir's sealed compartments precisely because of his *inherently* divided nature. For Renan's faith is already an unstable compound of romantic idealism and sober rationality. Were the former to have predominated Renan might have remained a Catholic; were it the latter, he might have become a Protestant. Instead, what happens is that Saint-Sulpice develops the rational component of Renan's religious identity to such a degree that it comes into open conflict with his romantic side. Renan, in other words, presents his loss of faith as a consequence not of the corrosive influence of an external agency but of the circumstances which led a contradiction *inherent in his faith* to reach breaking-point.

Having followed him so far, one may be surprised by Renan's account of the way the contradiction manifested itself. The passionate pursuit of philological truth, he tells us, led to the discovery of numerous contradictions between Catholic teaching and the textual status of the Bible. And a no less passionate commitment to an historical perspective based on 'le devenir' led to the realization that 'le dogme chrétien s'est fait, comme toute chose, lentement, peu à peu, par une sorte de végétation intime' (p. 163)—the last phrase, with its biological flavour, is most telling: it might aptly qualify Renan's account of the process of his loss of faith. Yet rather than attempt to reconcile the historical 'development of doctrine' with its status as the revelation of the teachings of Christ, Renan adopts a wholly dogmatic conception of Catholicism. Catholicism, he argues repeatedly in chapter 5 of the *Souvenirs*, is an edifice which stands or falls on the absolute veracity of its doctrines. In the case of the Bible, the Catholic must believe that each word is divinely inspired: 'il suffit [que l'apologétique] ait tort une seule fois pour que la thèse de l'inspiration soit mise à néant' (p. 168). Renan thus reveals the criteria of his own faith. A certain amount of equivocation is perceptible. In a passage admired by Gide,[26] Renan underlines the fact that he took Catholicism seriously, on its own terms, and that to pretend, as many liberal Catholics try to, that there is no conflict between faith and reason, is intellectually dishonest. But to suggest that in the face of philological evidence Catholic faith represents a kind of intellectual suicide is another matter. Renan refuses, it seems, to give any real force and validity to the subjective component in religious faith. His Catholic teachers at Saint-Sulpice were right, he asserts, not to make theological concessions 'puisqu'un seul aveu d'erreur ruine l'édifice de la vérité absolue et la ravale au rang des autorités humaines, où chacun fait son choix selon son goût personnel' (p. 167). For Renan the only kind of certitude is rational and objective; and there is nothing between this and the whims of the individual.

This helps explain certain peculiarities in Renan's narrative of his loss of faith. Although he refers to months of 'travail intérieur', to the anguish he felt at disappointing his mother, and although he quotes letters of 1845 which do convey the impression of an individual undergoing some sort of crisis, Renan's account tends to 'de-subjectify', so to speak, the process of loss of faith. Wishing to make it in no way a manifestation of a 'goût personnel' he portrays it as the inevitable unfolding of a purely rational process:

Les gens du monde qui croient qu'on se décide dans le choix de ses opinions par des raisons de sympathie ou d'antipathie s'étonneront certainement du genre de raisonnements qui m'écarta de la foi chrétienne, à laquelle j'avais tant de motifs de cœur et d'intérêt de rester attaché. Les personnes qui n'ont pas l'esprit scientifique ne comprennent guère qu'on laisse ses opinions former hors de soi par une sorte de concrétion impersonnelle, dont on n'est en quelque sorte que le spectateur . . . le devoir de l'homme est de se mettre devant la vérité, dénué de toute personnalité, prêt à se laisser traîner où voudra la demonstration prépondérante (pp. 169–70).

---

[26] *Souvenirs*, 171, quoted in Gide's *Journal* (1918), 300.

The contention here is that we do not (or should not) choose our opinions; these are determined for us, independently of will or subjectivity, by an impersonal process. Renan tends to deny any reflective qualities to the 'spectateur' within the psyche, who simply seems to look on as a process unfolds more or less 'hors de soi'. There seems to be no question that one side of the psyche would contest, debate, or in any way engage with the mechanical unfolding of rationality. By portraying his loss of faith largely as the working out of an objective intellectual evolution rather than a subjective process, Renan plays down any sense of personal responsibility and is thus able to forestall and ignore the question of possible external influences such as the role of his sister Henriette, the call of 'le siècle', or of sexual desire. One of his ways of trying to block any speculation on these matters is to portray himself as an unworldly man who still incarnates in late middle age the teachings of Saint-Sulpice. The only change he underwent was the loss of religious faith itself which, notwithstanding references to strenuous intellectual labour and to 'la grande lutte entre ma raison et mes croyances' (p. 170), is seen as a product of 'une force indépendante de moi [qui] ébranlait les croyances' (p. 175). Once Renan has taken the step of leaving Saint-Sulpice, the further stages of his mutation (conveyed in biological terms) occur rapidly, and his friendship with the scientist Berthelot further precipitates an inevitable process: 'quelques mois suffirent pour reléguer ces vestiges de foi dans la partie de nos âmes consacrée aux souvenirs' (p. 191). So scientific is it, that the two men's joint 'croissance intellectuelle' can be described in Darwinian terms as resembling those 'phénomènes qui se produisent par une sorte d'action de voisinage et de tacite complicité' (p. 192). Yet, in the very style of their friendship, the two friends retain distinct markings of their former evolutionary stage and look for all the world like 'deux prêtres en surplis se donnant le bras' (p. 192). So far from representing a *fall* into 'le siècle' the transformation irradiates the two men who are now expressions of 'un devoir abstrait envers la vérité' (p. 193).

The final expression of Renan's 'de-subjectification' of his loss of faith is his tendency to identify it with the workings of a 'higher' power. The erasure of subjective process is symptomatic of an overriding ideological commitment. Renan's 'Darwinism' is largely superficial. Far from being the product of a conversion to scientific rationality, his conversion is itself interpreted as the design of providence:

Si mes origines eussent été moins disgraciées selon le monde, je ne fusse point entré, je n'eusse point persévéré dans cette royale voie de la vie selon l'esprit, à laquelle un vœu de nazaréen m'attacha dès mon enfance. Le déplacement d'un atome rompait

la chaîne de faits fortuits qui, au fond de la Bretagne, me prépara pour une vie
d'élite; qui me fit venir de Bretagne à Paris . . . Je ne conclus rien de là, sinon que
l'effort inconscient vers le bien et le vrai qui est dans l'univers joue son coup de dé
par chacun de nous . . . Nous pouvons déranger le dessein providentiel dont nous
sommes l'objet; nous ne sommes pour rien dans sa réussite . . . Le dogme de la grâce
est le plus vrai des dogmes chrétiens (pp. 209–10).

By contriving to assimilate the fortuitous to the providential, hypostatizing
and personifying nature, providence, and destiny, Renan makes his own
destiny part of the 'éternel *fieri*'. Yet he also renders it circular: rather than
marking a hiatus the events of 1845 restore the continuity of Renan's Breton
nature: 'Je suis sorti de la spiritualité pour rentrer dans l'idéalité' (p. 204).
The new departure was really a return.

Ideology calls the tune throughout the *Souvenirs*.[27] Renan's account of his
Breton origins,[28] his depictions of milieux and religious styles, his treatment
of influences, decisions, turning points, are driven by stereotypes, disourses,
'beliefs' of one sort or another. Ideology here means *doxa*: that which is part
of the stock of widely sanctioned assumptions; but it also means that which
is legitimated from the outside, by transcendent categories. As an
autobiography, the *Souvenirs* are a highly wrought literary artefact which
remain closed within the boundaries of ideological thinking. Renan's text
serves to legitimate rather than to contest or examine his late ideology and
pulls together the eclectic material and mutually contradictory features he
wished to register and, as it were, to embalm. He observes in the 'Préface':
'Ce qu'on dit de soi est toujours poésie', adding: 'on écrit de telles choses
pour transmettre aux autres la théorie de l'univers qu'on porte en soi' (p. 2).
The 'poésie' of articulated selfhood, Renan concedes, is ideology. However,
before we credit him with a clear-sightedness other autobiographers might

---

[27] Although it deals with his philology rather than his religious evolution, Edward Said's
account of Renan in *Orientalism*, 130–48, provides a very pertinent commentary on the
overall ideological tenor of his work: 'Knowledge of man was poetically transfiguring only if
it had been previously severed from raw actuality . . . and then put into a doxological
straitjacket. By becoming philology the study of words [pertains] less to the senses or the
body . . . and more to a sightless, imageless realm ruled over by such hothouse formulations
as race, mind, culture and nation' (pp. 147–8). Like his Orientalism, Renan's past, as
represented in the *Souvenirs*, is what Said calls a 'discursively constructed realm' (p. 148).
Said's comments on Renan's 'peculiarly ravaged, ragingly masculine world of history and
learning' (p. 147) and on his references to the feminine are also very relevant to the recurrent
use of the feminine to characterize religion, Breton *idéalité*, etc. in the *Souvenirs*, see
especially p. 4.
[28] It is noticeable that Renan conveys little sense of childhood experience, preferring
instead to depict, in the early sections of the *Souvenirs*, the 'childhood' of Humanity itself in
the shape of a Britanny still shrouded in the mists of legend.

lack on this score we should note that in practice Renan does not treat his ideology as 'poésie', and explain how subjective and objective factors *formed* it, but tends, rather, to endow concepts such as his double nature or the 'fieri' with heuristic validity.

Of course the danger of suggesting that in Renan ideology displaces subjectivity is the possible inference that subjectivity is something quite outside or immune from ideology. The point here is that a critical sense of the interpenetration of subjectivity and ideology is wholly lacking. Renan never draws attention to the process of writing his text, to the difficulty of reaching the truth, to the slipperiness of the categories he uses: the spirit of 'critique' does not seem to apply in the arena of the self. On the other hand, the elements of self-portraiture in the *Souvenirs* lack real self-awareness and betray deep ideological prejudices with regard to women, the common herd, Catholics, and so forth.[29] The *Souvenirs* are full of tensions, contradictions, oppositions, explicit polarizations. But these are merely part of Renan's stock-in-trade from which he weaves a 'doxological straitjacket', to borrow Edward Said's phrase, a wardrobe of hand-me-downs in which to dress himself for posterity. The *Souvenirs* reveal a willing acquiescence in, rather than an oppositional stance towards, rigid ideological categorizations. And it is these which give the book the function of a ritual, a 'toilette des morts' before the author goes down to rejoin his memories in the apocryphal village of Is.

GIDE: *SI LE GRAIN NE MEURT*

Gide's references to the composition and publication of *Si le grain ne meurt* invariably give it the status of an act of personal commitment, motivated by an imperative sense of moral obligation and justified, in part at least, by its utility.[30] The need for courage and the willingness to risk martyrdom are

[29] See especially the passages in ch. 6 (197–207) where Renan reviews the character traits which prove that he has remained loyal to Saint-Sulpice (the vulgarity of tone here is aggravated by the fact that this is presented as an 'examen de conscience', and by the fact that Renan adopts, disastrously, some of the tonalities of Montaigne's 'De l'expérience'). The section on 'politesse' is particularly revealing since it betrays Renan's hankering for a strictly hierarchical social order, and supports the view that his notion of identity is primarily social rather than based on subjective reality. It is especially hard not to raise an eyebrow at this: 'Je serais assez aise d'avoir le droit de vie et de mort, pour ne pas en user, et j'aimerais fort posséder des esclaves, pour être extrêmement doux avec eux et m'en faire adorer' (p. 202).

[30] See e.g. a letter to Gosse of 16 Jan. 1927, *The Correspondence of André Gide and Edmund Gosse*, 190. For an account of the composition and publication of *Si le grain* see P. Lejeune, *Le Pacte autobiographique*, 171 ff. See also C. D. E. Tolton, *A. Gide and the Art of Autobiography*, ch. 2.

recurrent themes in his diaries and correspondence at this time. To Dorothy Bussy he wrote in 1922: 'Toutes les raisons pour ne pas [les] publier sont des raisons de lâcheté.'[31] The choice of title for his autobiography reflected the author's willingness to sacrifice his reputation, his 'figure dans le monde', for the sake of truth[32]—to accept one kind of death as the price to be paid for a truer life. The 'horreur du mensonge'[33] which prompted the work was partly disinterested and partly personal. Like *Corydon* written some years earlier but published just before,[34] *Si le grain* represented a plea for greater understanding of the nature of homosexuality, a plea made all the more pressing by the 'exemple de franchise'[35] which it gave. But in recounting his personal history Gide was also concerned with his own image in the eyes of others: 'J'ai écrit ce livre parce que je préfère être haï qu'aimé pour ce que je ne suis pas.'[36] A diary entry reveals the desire to engineer a confrontation with potential accusers: 'Je n'écris pas ces mémoires pour me défendre. Je n'ai point à me défendre, puisque je ne suis pas accusé. Je les écris avant d'être accusé. Je les écris pour qu'on m'accuse.'[37] Accused or not, Gide clearly felt that to withhold the declaration of his homosexuality constituted a form of dissimulation; publication of his 'mémoires' would remedy this; writing them, however, was to be a painful business. The *Journal* makes plain that if his autobiographical enterprise was an act directed towards others, it was also an act directed at himself, an 'œuvre de macération'[38] in which, at a crisis point in his life, Gide engaged in intense and painful self-confrontation.

---

[31] *Correspondance André Gide—Dorothy Bussy*, i. 514–15.

[32] See *Numquid et tu...?*, a section of his diary, 1916–19, where Gide comments on the verses from the Gospel of Saint John in which the title phrase occurs: 'Celui qui aime sa vie, son âme,—qui protège sa personnalité, qui soigne sa figure dans ce monde—la perdra; mais celui-là qui en fera abandon, la rendra vraiment vivante, lui assurera la vie éternelle', *Journal 1889–1939*, 594. Gide emphasizes the idea that renunciation leads to a repossession of self in the present. Cf. *Journal 1889–1939*, 612. For further discussion see Tolton, *Gide*, 24–6.

[33] See *Entretiens André Gide—Jean Amrouche* (1949), 15.

[34] *Corydon* is a defence of homosexuality written in the form of dialogues between a homosexual and an open-minded but sceptical enquirer who puts the point of view of the 'man in the street'. Written in 1911, Gide delayed publication for many years. The first accessible edn. appeared in 1922.

[35] *Correspondence of Gide and Gosse*, 189.

[36] Ibid. This was in response to Gosse's doubts: ('Was it wise, was it necessary . . . ?'), p. 188. Cf. *Entretiens Gide—Amrouche*, 15: in both places Gide goes on to quote Montaigne: 'je reviendrais volontiers de l'autre monde, pour démentir celuy qui me formerait aultre que je n'étais, fût-ce pour m'honorer'. See also Gide's abandoned preface for *Si le grain*, reprinted in P. Lejeune, *L'Autobiographie en France*, 192–3.

[37] *Journal 1889–1939*, 614.

[38] Ibid. 552.

Si le grain ne meurt, then, bears all the hallmarks of autobiography as *engagement*; and given the fact that it is centred on the question of homosexuality one would reasonably expect it to offer a legitimation, via his personal history, of Gide's homosexual identity. So indeed, to some degree, it does; and as such it was censured by many of Gide's contemporaries. Yet what makes his autobiography so fascinating is that Gide constantly appears to subvert and question the case he seems to be making, to undermine the ideological foundations on which it seems to be based, and to introduce ambiguities amidst what seemed unequivocal.

The central thesis of *Corydon* is that homosexuality is natural and innate, a deviation rather than a perversion of instinct, a condition rather than a choice; one is born a homosexual, one does not become one. If *Si le grain ne meurt* ratifies this theory it is not by explicit argument. There is scarcely any direct repetition of the case made in *Corydon* for the naturalness of homosexuality, and it is only incidentally, in a passage concerning discussion with a school-friend about education, that Gide, with a certain •preciosity, articulates one of the central postulates on which his case depends: the view that 'le natif l'emporte sur l'acquis, et qu'à travers tous les apprêts, les empois, les repassages et les plis, la naturelle étoffe reparaît' (p. 191). It is primarily by indirect means, in the way he presents his personal history, that Gide gives support to this view. In diary entries dating from the period of composition Gide reproaches himself for beating about the bush, delaying the revelation which alone warranted his undertaking.[39] But the tendency to prolong the account of his childhood and adolescence, with its often sombre tonalities, prior to the discovery of his true nature in the radiant North African sun is both dramatically effective and germane to his theme since it supports the idea that his youth was marred by self-ignorance. Sexuality features prominently in the first part of the book, but it generally has a negative aura: 'mauvaises habitudes' with the concierge's son, expulsion from school for masturbation, and so on. A number of passages concern indifference to, or repulsion at, female sexuality and Gide makes the point more than once that his puritanical upbringing allowed him to attribute this to virtue rather than to sexual orientation. In connection with the terror prostitutes inspired in him, he observes:

Mon éducation puritaine encourageait à l'excès une retenue naturelle où je ne voyais point malice. Mon incuriosité à l'égard de l'autre sexe était totale ... Je m'abandonnais à cette flatterie d'appeler réprobation mes répugnances et de

[39] See entries for 31 Mar. and 13 Oct. 1916; 11, 19, and 21 Jan., 23 Sept. 1917, *Journal 1889–1939*, 551–2, 572, 612, 614, 615, 632.

prendre mon aversion pour vertu; je vivais replié, contraint, et m'étais fait un idéal de résistance; si je cédais, c'était au vice, j'étais sans attention pour des provocations du dehors (p. 196).[40]

Just as Gide remained ignorant of his sexual make-up ('je ne voyais point malice') so the reader is kept largely in the dark: we are not at this stage told why Gide might have seen anything untoward in his reactions to female sexuality. Similarly when in his early twenties Gide succumbs again to 'le vice de ma première enfance', he tells us that he attributed a reluctance to resort to prostitutes to his upbringing: 'Mon éducation puritaine avait fait un monstre des revendications de la chair; comment eussé-je compris, en ce temps, que ma nature se dérobait à la solution la plus généralement admise, autant que mon puritanisme la réprouvait' (p. 246). If at this stage the reader has still to be apprised of the characteristics of Gide's nature, the idea has now been firmly planted in his mind that whilst Gide's puritanical upbringing did not determine his sexual orientation it provided a screen for it, enabling him to believe that his lack of sexual interest in women stemmed from repression rather than homosexuality (at no point does Gide indicate when he became aware of the existence of this sexual option). Moreover, other potential manifestations of Gide's sexuality which will turn out in retrospect to have been possible clues to his nature are not treated as such when they arise. When narrating his crushes on various boys, or explaining that in the Louvre he was sexually stimulated by colours and sounds rather than by nudes, Gide makes no link with the revelations to come in the second part of his autobiography.

The trip to North Africa with his friend Laurens is thus presented as an escape from repression rather than from the confines of sexual orthodoxy. The two friends, both virgins, had resolved to sow their wild oats, and it is in these circumstances—when nature was allowed to take its course[41]—that Gide made the discovery of his homosexuality. Gide narrates his first homosexual experience—with Ali at Sousse (p. 299)—in a way which stresses his self-detachment: no deliberation is involved; he observes his own response, and recalls principally his ecstasy. From this point on, the naturalness of Gide's homosexuality is affirmed in a number of ways. First, by accounts of his unsuccessful attempts at what he calls 're-normalisation' (he makes love to a courtesan, Meriem, but only by thinking of a boy; with En Barka, another of the *Oulad Naïl*, he experiences a fiasco, and so on).

---

[40] References, cited in the text, are to the Folio edn.

[41] Explaining their frame of mind Gide writes: 'ce qui nous dominait surtout, c'était l'horreur du mensonge, du bizarre, du morbide, de l'anormal' (p. 287).

Gide's normality, he discovered, lay in his homosexual nature: with Mohammed, for example, 'je trouvais enfin ma normale' (p. 344); his 'penchant naturel' withstands the purely cerebral experiments designed to redirect it. Secondly Gide presents his homosexual experiences in ecstatic terms. The lyrical descriptions of Ali, 'nu comme un dieu', the relaxed charm of the boys, the peaks of sensual joy achieved with Mohammed, the luminous landscape, all contrast vividly with the 'ténèbres' of Gide's childhood and the 'selve obscure' (p. 256) of the symbolist milieu from which he fled to Africa. The fact that Gide falls ill on this journey, and then regains his health in the context of his sexual liberation, provides him with the opportunity to develop the theme of the *vita nuova* through Christian images of resurrection ('un secret de ressuscité . . . Lazare', etc.), and classical images ('un Apollon nouveau', etc.), a mixture heralding the syncretist ideal Gide was led to adopt in his attempt to reconcile his experiences with his moral and religious outlook. Thirdly, Gide subtly adopts an ethnological perspective, contrasting different tribes of homosexual, dissociating his own from any kind of abnormality or inversion. The brilliant handling of the figure of Oscar Wilde serves to scotch the idea that Wilde debauched the young Frenchman, and also portrays a type of homosexuality—proselytizing, diabolical—very different from Gide's. The presentation of Bosy as a nasty 'queer' and rabid misogynist, and the chilling description of Daniel B. brutally taking his pleasure with a boy (p. 345) have a similar function and enable Gide to convey, by contrast, the human, reciprocal aspect of his own sexual behaviour. By such means Gide underlines the natural character of his homosexuality. But such legitimation (ideological in its dependence on the concept of nature and on the foundations provided by *Corydon*) is by no means given full sway; indeed it is constantly undermined by other aspects of Gide's narrative which must now be considered.

Since he avoids disclosing his theme, the many incidents, anecdotes, and portraits Gide assembles in the first part of *Si le grain* are not submitted to explicit ordering principles which would determine their pertinence. A number of strands emerge: the 'enfance ténébreuse'—torpor, dull-wittedness, and stagnation, despite the varied pursuits of a privileged child—interrupted by sudden experiences of intense nervous and emotional energy which Gide labels *Schaudern* ('tressaillement', shuddering), after a line in Goethe's *Faust*; the emergence of an aesthetic vocation; love for his cousin Madeleine (referred to as Emmanuèle). What is lacking is a clear sense of how these strands connect with each other, and how they relate to his homosexuality. We are made conscious from time to time of the mature narrator's perspective, as distinct from that of his youth, but never of how he envisages his past as a whole. There are dark hints that certain events were to have momentous repercussions but we are not told what these actually were. The period between the events covered in the narrative and the time of writing is left blank. Thus the consequences of the surprising event with which Gide chose to end the book—his engagement to his cousin in the aftermath of his mother's death and the discovery of his sexual nature—are not indicated, speculation being confined to possible explanations: that having discovered his nature Gide still felt inclined to challenge it ('mettre au défi ma nature', p. 368); that, despite a disposition (essentially ideological and intellectual) to equate the natural with the good, he was inclined to pass adverse moral judgement on the idea of simply following the path of nature; or that the very notion of having discovered his nature was an opportunistic delusion through which Gide contrived to gild his baser instincts. This last view is associated with a figure who plays a prominent role in Gide's retrospective evaluation of his homosexuality—the Devil.[42]

The Devil tempts, drives, and enslaves. In Gide, however, 'le Diable' is primarily the label for a particular mode of self-delusion and *mauvaise foi*.[43] Here, references to the Devil are connected with Gide's legitimation of his homosexuality as a natural phenomenon which it would have been wrong to suppress. The Devil becomes the name for a form of self-serving ideological blindness which, it is intermittently suggested, led Gide to justify, among other things, the separation of mind and body, and of spiritual and sensual love, thus enabling him to think he could reconcile love for his cousin with homosexual pursuits. But the association with a diabolical agency, introduced very much as a manner of speaking, tends to limit the force which such a perspective might have. References to the Devil enable Gide to raise doubts and ask questions without fully pursuing their potential implications. The Devil is an agent of ambiguity which introduces loose ends rather than tying them up.

Allusions to the Devil can be related to three main issues. The first is the possibility that Gide's homosexuality represented a capitulation to base temptation, the perpetuation of the darker side of his childhood rather than

---

[42] In a diary entry early in the period of composition of *Si le grain*, Gide writes: 'Je n'eus pas plus tôt *supposé* le démon, que toute l'histoire de ma vie me fut du même coup éclaircie; que je compris soudain ce qui m'était le plus obscur, au point que cette supposition prenait la forme exacte de toute mon interrogation et de mon admiration précédente', *Journal 1889–1939*, 609.

[43] For an extensive discussion of the Devil in *Si le grain* see P. Lejeune, *Exercices d'ambiguité*. See also E. Marty, *L'Écriture du jour*, 114 ff.

a deliverance from it. By deluding himself as to the reasons for his negative reaction to female sexuality Gide allowed himself to be ensnared by the Devil: 'Certains jours qu'il m'arrive de croire au diable, quand je pense à mes saintes révoltes, à mes nobles hérissements, il me semble entendre *l'autre* rire et se frotter les mains dans l'ombre. Mais pouvais-je pressentir quels lacs . . .?' (p. 196). If homosexuality itself was one of these snares we would have to surmise that Gide was implying that he ought to have got off the slippery slope before it was too late, that in not doing so he connived with and thus abetted the growth of a proclivity he could have resisted. Such a view plays a shadowy role in the text, but since it conflicts starkly with the hypothesis that homosexuality is natural it tends to be subordinated to a second, slightly less controversial issue: the possibility that the snare of self-delusion to which Gide succumbed lay in the positive evaluation he conferred on the discovery of what was perhaps no more than a physiological trait. Here the role of the Devil is not to lead him along illicit paths but to blind him to the fact that homosexuality, however natural, cannot really be condoned or reconciled with higher forms of love. In the opening paragraph of the second part of *Si le grain ne meurt* Gide prefaces the account of his homosexual liberation with the observation that his assessment of this event fluctuated, and that latterly he has come round to believing that 'un acteur important, le Diable, avait bien pu prendre part au drame' (p. 283). The Devil's part, it seems, was to encourage the sophistries through which Gide contrived to conflate and justify the gratification of his physical desires with the ideal of a life lived in harmony with one's own nature. The reconciliation of flesh and spirit was, Gide recalls, at the top of his agenda when he left for Algeria, and the (apparently unexpected) revelation that the way of the flesh was to be homosexual in his case did not divert him from this goal. In the grip of fervour and *amor fati* Gide found abundant reasons for believing that homosexuality was compatible with the state of harmony to which he aspired. To introduce the Devil into this scenario is to suggest that these reasons were specious and opportunistic: Gide's error, on this view, was to persist in the search for intellectual and moral legitimation, although one of the benefits of this fervent preoccupation with 'ces grandes questions' was that it kept the moral issue in the foreground and protected him from 'un hédonisme de complaisance, fait de facile acquiescement' (p. 361). This reservation, and the reluctance to pass summary judgement, typifies a stance whose thoroughgoing ambiguity reflects the fact that the issues were still live for Gide at the time of writing.

The third, and perhaps the most pervasive and damaging, of the Devil's wiles was to enable Gide to disguise from himself possible connections between his homosexuality and the quasi-mystical character of his love for his cousin. Another way of putting this would be to say that perhaps the most significant use to which Gide puts his allusions to 'le Diable' is to hint at such a recognition without ever explicitly acknowledging or exploring it. The starting-point here would again be the notion that the separation of body and mind, spirituality and sensuality, was a self-serving delusion, a view expressed unequivocally at one point, in connection with 'Emmanuelle':

aussi bien . . . mon amour [for Emmanuelle] devenait-il quasi-mystique; et si le diable me dupait en me faisant considérer comme une injure l'idée d'y mêler quoi que ce fût de charnel, c'est ce dont je ne pouvais encore me rendre compte: toujours est-il que j'avais pris mon parti de dissocier le plaisir de l'amour; et même il me paraissait que ce divorce était souhaitable, que le plaisir était ainsi plus pur, l'amour plus parfait, si le cœur et la chair ne s'entr'engageaient point (pp. 286–7).

The passage refers to Gide's frame of mind just before the revelation of his homosexual nature. If he had been able to perceive (as he subsequently did—when is not specified) that his resolve to divorce flesh and spirit was diabolically inspired, what would the consequence have been? It would hardly have averted the discovery of his nature but it might, rather, have alerted him to the fact that his desires were not in any case destined to find heterosexual expression. In which case the nature of his love for his cousin might itself have come under suspicion, as a premonitory sign of his sexual orientation. In fact, Gide's prior decision to separate body and spirit, while at the same time fervently searching, intellectually and emotionally, for a 'new order' where the claims of each would be recognized, enabled him to persist in believing that his experiences with Mohammed and his love for Madeleine were not incompatible. And of course it is this belief which justifies his engagement to Emmanuelle. The account of this event, in the last few pages, makes no direct reference to the Devil[44] but ambiguity and self-deception are well to the fore: 'en Emmanuèle, n'était-ce pas la vertu même que j'aimais? C'était le ciel, que mon insatiable enfer épousait; mais cet enfer je l'omettais à l'instant même' (p. 368)—a marriage of heaven and hell, but licensed only by the omission of the infernal pole, and thus not

---

[44] The last direct reference, in the scene (p. 340) where Gide acknowledges his desire for Mohammed, explicitly associates the Devil with Gide's succumbing to homosexual *practices*, but context and style makes this ironic since here the *deluded* party is Wilde (who thinks he has made another 'convert') while Gide's role is to acknowledge the authority and authenticity of his desires. In 'Different Desires: Subjectivity and Transgression in Wilde and Gide', Jonathan Dollimore draws an illuminating comparison but consistently overstates the alleged essentialism of Gide's view of subjective identity.

truly a reconciliation of opposites. Gide's extraordinary account of the frame of mind in which he became engaged to his cousin embraces a bewildering range of factors: that he was seeking to sublimate the discovery about himself, distilling from it a pure sense of liberation ('un élargissement sans fin où je souhaitais l'entraîner à ma suite'—shades of *L'Immoraliste* here); that he was looking for an anchor; that his main concern was his cousin's happiness rather than his own; that, unconsciously, he was being driven to defy (and thus deny) his own nature; that his mother's death had put it from his mind: 'j'étais comme ébloui d'azur, et ce que je ne consentais plus à voir avait cessé pour moi d'exister.' Once again blindness and elation are the instruments of (devilish) self-delusion. Yet the question of Gide's precise evaluation of his homosexuality remains as elusive as before.

Gide's allusions to the Devil illustrate a more general strategy of ambiguity in *Si le grain ne meurt* whereby, as Philippe Lejeune has shown, the reader is left uncertain as to the narrator's stance towards his narrative.[45] A further expression of this ambiguity may be found in Gide's reluctance to make explicit connections between the revelation of his nature in the second part of the book and earlier episodes which suggest a break with the usual run of experiences and seem to herald another side of his being. The various potential manifestations of an aesthetic vocation, for example, or the *Schaudern* incidents where intense feeling breaks through the confines of emotional indigence and takes on an oceanic character—'on eût dit que brusquement s'ouvrait l'écluse particulière de je ne sais quelle commune mère intérieure inconnue dont le flot s'engouffrait démesurément dans mon cœur' (p. 133)—are treated as separate strands rather than as parts of a potential totality. Gide tends to compartmentalize the different facets of his experience, isolating them from each other; but this denial of overall coherence, while it is occasionally alluded to ('Je suis un être de dialogue; tout en moi combat et se contredit', (p. 280), is never explored in its own right. In this respect it is interesting to compare *Si le grain ne meurt* with a book Gide greatly admired, Edmund Gosse's *Father and Son*.[46] The point of Gosse's narrative is to demonstrate how his gravitation away from the strict evangelical outlook of his father occurred not by virtue of intellectual revolt

[45] On the 'stratégie de l'ambiguité' in *Si le grain* see Lejeune, *Exercices d'ambiguité*, esp. pp. 5–10 and 99–102, and *Le Pacte autobiographique*, 179–84.

[46] In a letter to Gosse dating from Sept. 1924 (during the composition of *Si le grain*) Gide wrote: 'Ce que j'écris à présent . . . c'est un peu mon *Father and Son*', *Correspondence of Gide and Gosse*, 165. In a subsequent letter, after the publication of his autobiography, Gide noted of *Father and Son* that it was a book 'avec qui j'ai vécu, que j'ai senti écrit *pour moi* et qui put réveiller les échos les plus indiscrets dans mon cœur', ibid. 187.

but as a natural process in which his own nature progressively emerged. Thus, many of the events he relates are portrayed, allegorically, as outlets through which latent proclivities found expression.[47] In Gide's case the *Schaudern* episodes suggest a comparable process of emergence, and point to an underlying psychic energy linked, in part at least, to questions of sexuality and difference. However, rather than explore them in these terms Gide ultimately assimilates the *Schaudern* passages to what he calls 'l'état lyrique', a 'délire', prompted by the intermittent visitations of Dionysus (p. 194). They are thus drawn away from the specificity of his sexual identity, and indeed from any specific role in his personal history, towards the generalized thematics of 'ferveur' which, since it colours, in fact, the circumstances in which he came to regard his homosexual emancipation as the expression of his nature, always bears the mark of delusion and uncertainty.

Philippe Lejeune has argued convincingly that Gide's exclusive aim in writing *Si le grain* was the unequivocal revelation of his homosexuality, and that in all other respects the text betrays the writer's desire to avoid at all costs—including that of aesthetic failure—the implication that his autobiography was to be considered the definitive key to his personality.[48] To write an autobiography for Gide was to put at risk the desire that his work as a whole, in all its facets and contradictions, would reflect the ungraspable multiplicity of his personality. Hence, Lejeune demonstrates, a thoroughgoing strategy of ambiguity which blocks interpretative paths and neutralizes the potential diagnostic power of, say, the *Schaudern* episodes.

In the narrower context of the relationship between autobiography and ideology we can suggest that, in employing autobiography as a form of *engagement*, Gide makes limited, strategic use of ideological legitimation. It could be argued that Gide's autobiography supplies the materials for a plausible and coherent account of a sexual object-choice determined by a fear of heterosexuality inspired by the mother, the punishment of desire and 'plaisir' in the context of masturbation, the transfer of sexual excitement on to other stimuli of an aesthetic kind, and so forth. However, drawing on the ideological foundations of *Corydon*, Gide chooses to present his homosexuality as a natural phenomenon outside the realm of choice and conditioning. But he also shows a disinclination to explore links between his nature and his

---

[47] See e.g. the passages regarding what Gosse calls 'the sense of my individuality' (p. 58), 'a hard nut of individuality deep down in my childish nature . . . my innate and persistent self' (p. 168), 'the stream of my spiritual nature' (p. 219).

[48] This is the argument brilliantly expounded in 'Gide et l'espace autobiographique', *Le Pacte autobiographique*, 165–96.

history. His homosexuality is presented as unhistorical and non-genetic, not only because it falls outside the sphere of causes but also because it turns out to be impossible to identify its traces with any confidence outside the strictly delimited area of sexual responses and practices. Gide's nature is revealed to be simultaneously fundamental and strangely inconsequential. In quarantining his homosexuality from all other aspects of his experience, Gide makes it both the only possible key to an overall identity or 'drame', and a factor which is not judged amenable to interpretative negotiation. Homosexuality becomes the secret core of Gide's being which cannot be penetrated because it belongs to the undialectical sphere of nature. Gide's history, on the other hand—those aspects of himself not governed by nature (in general, Gide's view of human identity is far from essentialist)— becomes uninterpretable to the degree that nature's part in it remains unfathomable. By confronting his reader with the ambiguities which arise from the imponderable fusion of nature and history (cultivating the potential aporia which underlies any polarization of nature and nurture) Gide succeeds in placing his 'moi' outside the frame of the knowable. Ideological legitimation with regard to his homosexual nature serves Gide as a means of withdrawing the self from ideology, and from the market-place of autobiographical representation where the author of *Les Faux-Monnayeurs* had no desire to be exhibited.

BARTHES: *ROLAND BARTHES PAR ROLAND BARTHES*

'Ne sais-je pas que *dans le champ du sujet il n'y a pas de référent?*' (p. 60):[49] of course Barthes 'knows' that the self conceived as essence, 'sujet plein', origin, is an illusion, a superseded ideological mystification, the product of a deluded discourse. But his rhetorical question suggests that the italicized assertion (part of the Lacanian vulgate of the contemporary scene), with its aphoristic aplomb, smacks of ideological discourse—monolithic, irrefutable, arrogant. Must it not, therefore, be resisted or displaced, along with all the other forms of *doxa* which threaten to exclude him, to deny his own

[49] *Roland Barthes par Roland Barthes* was published by Éditions du Seuil in the 'Écrivains de toujours' (or 'par lui-même') series in 1975. References are incorporated in the text. An instant classic, like Sarraute's *Enfance* (1983) and Duras's *L'Amant* (1984), Barthes's autobiography has already been commented on extensively. Most pertinent in our perspective are P. Lejeune, *Moi aussi*, 103–16, G. Brée, *Narcissus Absconditus*; J. Gratton, 'Roland Barthes par Roland Barthes'; A. Jefferson, 'Autobiography as Intertext'.

sense of difference?[50] 'Ce livre', he observes of *Roland Barthes par Roland Barthes*, 'n'est pas le livre de ses idées, il est le livre du Moi, le livre de mes résistances à mes propres idées' (p. 123). Barthes is conscious that there is something regressive about this venture, *vis-à-vis* the avant-garde he has championed, yet it is not a rearguard action by a 'born-again' believer in psychological depth: 'aujourd'hui, le sujet se prend ailleurs, et la "subjectivité" peut revenir à une autre place de la spirale: déconstruite, désunie, déportée, sans ancrage: pourquoi ne parlerais-je pas de "moi" puisque "moi" n'est plus "soi"?' (p. 171).

The notions of exclusion and resistance are important. It is when it is threatened, and in the strategies he adopts to counter what threatens it, that the subjectivity Barthes wishes to disclose signals its existence. The sense of exclusion which makes him aware of his *difference* arises acutely when he listens to the petrifying voice of the *doxa*: 'La Doxa parle, je l'entends, mais je ne suis pas dans son espace . . . je suis sans cesse *à l'écoute de ce dont je suis exclu*' (p. 126). Against the *doxa* there is of course that practice of writing, *l'écriture, le Texte* which displaces and deconstructs. Yet where it matters— in the area of his sexuality for example—such discourse lets Barthes down, imposes its own exclusion: 'l'écriture me soumet à une exclusion sévère . . . Mettant à nu l'inconsistance du sujet, son atopie, dispersant les leurres de l'imaginaire, elle rend intenable tout lyrisme' (p. 89). An ascetic, wholly desubjectified discourse does not merely dispose of the illusory stable self, it obliterates the whole space in which subjectivity operates.

What is this space? What is its topology? Central here is a term borrowed and adapted from the psychoanalytical theory of Jacques Lacan: *l'imagi-naire*. For Lacan, the subject is constituted in a process of splitting, emblematized by the *stade du miroir* when the infant latches on to its clear-cut mirror-image which contrasts with its diffuse, indeterminate sense of existence.[51] The imaginary, associated with looking and being seen, becomes the realm of a coherent and stable self-image, delusive and artificial to the extent that it depends on the suppression of the wider realm in which subjectivity exists—the symbolic order, associated with language. Barthes appropriates Lacan's term (p. 129) but draws it away from a specifically psychoanalytic vision centred on the unconscious (p. 153), and extends it to cover the whole range of factors and contexts through which we credit ourselves with a determinate and stable self. All statements we make about

---

[50] I am indebted here to the excellent analysis of Barthes's phrase in the article by Gratton (see n. 49).

[51] See 'Le Stade du miroir comme formateur de la fonction de je'.

ourselves belong, to a greater or lesser extent, to the imaginary: they involve a certain alienation, the adoption of the perspective of the Other. Yet the imaginary does not have an exclusive monopoly over the territory of subjectivity, and perhaps the central, most vital idea in *Barthes par Barthes* is that, amidst all our transactions—with ourselves, with other people, in speech, in writing, in sexual, political, or economic behaviour—there are different degrees of the imaginary. The space of subjectivity in Barthes, then, is not homogeneous, nor is it simply conflictual; it is theatrical. 'L'effort vital de ce livre est de mettre en scène un imaginaire. "Mettre en scène" veut dire: échelonner des portants, disperser des rôles, établir des niveaux et, à la limite: faire de la rampe une barre incertaine' (p. 109). The last point is crucial. Clearly, as director, stage-manager, impresario, Barthes is involved in an imaginary activity. Yet, he suggests, his *mise en scène* may succeed at times in effacing the borderline between stage and audience, performance and existence. He may, that is, succeed in allowing us to glimpse or to overhear the subjectivity which is dispersed through the performance.

One of the principal devices Barthes employs in his *mise en scène* is to use the second- and third- as well as the first-person pronoun to designate himself. The actors in the play might be envisaged as characters in a novel:

Tout ceci doit être considéré comme dit par un personnage de roman—ou plutôt par plusieurs. Car l'imaginaire, matière fatale du roman et labyrinthe des redans dans lesquels se fourvoie celui qui parle de lui-même, l'imaginaire est pris en charge par plusieurs masques (personae), échelonnés selon la profondeur de la scène (et cependant *personne* derrière) (p. 123).

We must not imagine, however, that the 'real' Barthes is located behind the scenery, or the masks, or at some ideal point of intersection of all the 'eyelines' in the text. What matters about the pronouns is not some imaginary division between aspects of Barthes but the effect of suddenly switching from one to the other, while talking about the same person.[52] The *mise en scène* of the imaginary has the effect of relativizing it, shifting its centre of gravity, catching it off balance and thus denying it its *assise*, or, a term Barthes uses often, its 'consistance': 'il est donc important que l'imaginaire soit traité selon ses degrès (l'imaginaire est une affaire de consistance, et la consistance, une affaire de degrès)' (p. 109). The quality of

---

[52] 'Pronoms dits personnels: tout se joue ici, je suis enfermé à jamais dans la lice pronominale: "je" mobilise l'imaginaire, "vous" et "il", la paranoia. Mais aussi, fugitivement, selon le lecteur, tout, comme les reflets d'une moire, peut se retourner: dans "moi, je" "je" peut n'être pas *moi*, qu'il casse d'une façon carnavalesque . . .' (p. 171).

consistency links the imaginary to ideology, since ideology is 'ce qui se répète et consiste' (p. 108), the denial of difference and subjectivity. To speak about oneself, an activity which pitches one head-first into the imaginary, is to give oneself a consistency, to constitute an image for others ('vous vous constituez', p. 85). In the imaginary we are in the realm of the Other: 'l'imaginaire est ce sur quoi les autres ont barre' (p. 85); we become mass-produced, ideological artefacts. Nothing we say about ourselves is immune from this, but it follows that what we do *in* discourse—the way we take up our position in language—has a bearing on our relationship to the imaginary and to ideology, in short, on our consistency. Hence the considerable attention Barthes gives to his own discourse in *Barthes par Barthes*. As an autobiography the book consists primarily of a fragmented historical retrospect regarding the succession of discourses he has adopted and discarded.

'J'ai une maladie: je *vois* le langage' (p. 164): Barthes sees language, and apprehends his own discourse as something that is exposed to the look of the Other. A high proportion of the fragments in *Barthes par Barthes* centre on the types or features of discourse that he likes or dislikes. This very Stendhalian approach, via pleasure, involves a criterion to which Barthes attaches great importance: that of the body: 'j'aime, je n'aime pas: cela n'a aucune importance pour personne; cela n'a apparemment pas de sens. Et pourtant cela veut dire: *mon corps n'est pas le même que le vôtre*' (p. 121). Barthes identifies in many forms of discourse the tendency to suppress this difference by suppressing the body: 'Le stéréotype, c'est cet emplacement du discours *où le corps manque*' (p. 93). The stereotype is at the heart of the *doxa*, 'l'opinion courante' which is oppressive and deadly by virtue (among other things) of its mechanical repetitiveness, 'une répétition morte, qui ne vient du corps de personne' (p. 75), and of its arrogance (p. 51), its tendency to dominate. Barthes repeatedly points to the hidden violence of forms of discourse (not aggressive *styles* of utterance) which pass themselves off as self-evident, as deriving their legitimacy from an assumed consistency with incontrovertible truth, with what is taken to be 'natural':[53] 'la vraie violence, c'est celle du cela-va-de-soi: ce qui est évident est violent' (p. 88). To call a state of affairs 'natural' is not to refer to an objective or structural property of

---

[53] *Descriptive discourse*, which imposes qualities through the medium of the adjective, is particularly oppressive in the inter-personal domain; to be described is to be confined: 'il supporte mal toute image de lui-même, souffre d'être nommé . . . un rapport qui s'adjective est du côté de l'image, du côté de la domination de la mort' (p. 47). 'L'adjectif est funèbre' (p. 72). *Analogy* denies difference by subjection to the regimen of the *same*: everything resembles something else and is thus deemed to participate in a universal nature (p. 48).

the universe, but to perform a legislative act (p. 134) which always tends to essentialize (in the case of the maxim for example, p. 121), and which invariably implies having the last word, turning the linguistic arena, 'la logosphère', into a conflictual space.

This rather gloomy picture is mitigated, however, by Barthes's enthusiasm for discursive tactics which undermine the tendencies he bemoans. 'Tactics' rather than 'strategies' since, as Barthes explains, the efficacy of his counter-manœuvres springs from their *ad hoc* quality, their lack of finality: 'il s'agit de déplacer, de barrer, comme aux barres, mais non de conquérir' (p. 175). The 'jeu de barres' is used several times as a metaphor for the tactical *déplacement* of the conflictual force of language— partly since the game has spawned the expression 'avoir barre sur', and this jockeying for advantage is what linguistic exchange characteristically involves—but also because the game involves a third role (the one, Barthes assures us, he enjoyed assuming when he played the game as a child (p. 54)!): someone who liberates the prisoners and sets the game going again. However, Barthes's most delightful evocation of this role involves a different image (and self-image): 'il se porte systématiquement là où il y a solidification du langage, consistance, stéréotypie. Telle une cuisinière vigilante, il s'affaire, veille à ce que le langage ne s'épaississe pas, à ce qu'il n'*attache* pas' (p. 166). Given their tactical, formal role, the forms of discourse Barthes likes, and deploys in his role of vigilant 'cuisinière', are often reversals or opposites of those he guards against. Paradox counters *doxa*; homology—comparison based on structural relations—is preferred to analogy, connotation to denotation. He does not prize the polysemic multiplicity of meaning but rather what he calls its *duplicity*, 'le fantasme n'est pas d'entendre tout (n'importe quoi), c'est d'entendre *autre chose*' (p. 77). Pairs of related words appeal to him, in which one denotes something he does not care for, and its cognate a value he cherishes: thus *structuration* is preferred to *structure*, *érotisation* to *érotique* (pp. 66, 131). But it is not what is inherent in the second term that matters so much as the semantic energy produced by the friction of differential meaning. Where opposed values are concerned, what counts is not so much the sense that the binary opposition encompasses and structures the field of meaning, but that a third term is produced, 'qui n'est pas de synthèse mais de déport' (p. 73).[54] 'Déport', which occurs a number of times (e.g. p. 166), is one of a plethora of

[54] In the heyday of structuralism Barthes was passionate about binary oppositions (p. 56) and he celebrated the central insight that all meaning was differential. Subsequently he recognized that, just as structure could be mistakenly seen as stable (p. 66) and inert, so binary contrasts could take on the quality of fixity (he refers to 'la prison binaire', p. 137).

words and phrases Barthes uses to render the operations in language which characterize the ever-changing panoply of terms, figures, and oppositions he keeps generating: *décomposer, échelonner, dévier, déjouer, faire trembler le langage, la secousse, la feinte, l'ellipse.* To some degree, but always for a limited period, it is the term itself which is the locus of pleasure, and Barthes is reluctant to offer precise definitions of the terms he uses: 'on ne peut en même temps approfondir et désirer un mot: chez lui, le désir du mot l'emporte' (p. 78). A sequence of fragments (pp. 131–4) traces Barthes's amorous relationship to his personal lexicon and culminates in the suggestion that words serve him as transitional objects, cherished playthings which provide security but have an uncertain status (p. 134).

One could pursue Barthes's eudemonistic quest for good forms of discourse through some of the wider, more familiar, categories he considers—fiction, aesthetic discourse, fragmentation—but it is time to specify some of the major tendencies which emerge. First, the predilection for what he calls the 'second degré', a tendency for the objects of discourse to be subjected, through the activity of *énonciation*, to a process of potentially infinite qualification which twists them out of the grip of any stable apprehension and re-presents them at another level, where another scale of values obtains. This 'jeu de degrés', based on a corrosive awareness of language, Barthes labels 'bathmologie'—the science of '[les] échelonne-ments du langage' (p. 71). A second general tendency is to identify what he calls 'l'exemption de sens' (p. 90)—the movement outside the realm of determinate meaning into a space of infinite difference—as the most cherished property of his preferred modes of discourse. In this mood Barthes is an avowed Utopian (Utopian discourse itself has his approval) and he acknowledges in this context more than elsewhere (but it is always implied) the element of fantasy in his 'desiring' relationship to language. A third tendency is to identify, as the product of certain favoured operations, the return of an apparently superseded or discredited value 'à une autre place' (p. 70) or at another level of 'le trajet de la spirale' (p. 92). This applies to love (p. 70), friendship (p. 69), and most importantly to the notion of subjectivity itself, which returns by a number of paths in *Barthes par Barthes*, but particularly under the auspices of the notion of 'le corps'.

Absent from the book's index, not susceptible of definition, the body is omnipresent in Barthes's autobiography: 'le corps, c'est la différence irréductible et en même temps c'est le principe de toute structuration' (p. 178). The body's difference is rooted in desire, in the realm of affect, and in its barometric sensitivity to the unconscious and to the troubled life of the psyche. The body is *par excellence* spatial, but its topology favours dispersal—much of what pertains to the somatic area is unlocatable and involves displacement. The body is what we are but cannot see: the relation to one's body-image passes through the relay of the Other: others can see us better than we see ourselves, 'Même et surtout pour votre corps vous êtes condamné à l'imaginaire' (p. 40). These words belong to one of the captions Barthes provides for the family-album-cum-personal-iconography with which his book begins (pp. 5–46). But on the next page we read: 'mon corps n'est libre de tout imaginaire que lorsqu'il retrouve son espace de travail . . .'. In the process of writing, the body is freed of its own *imaginaire* and becomes an agency which attenuates and relativizes the place of the imaginary in the production of discourse, creating clearings or vacancies where something other than the imaginary is *incorporated*. It leads to words as transitional objects: 'Comment le mot devient-il valeur? Au niveau du corps' (p. 131); and to themes: 'le thème, ce lieu du discours'. Ultimately, 'le corps' is itself no more that a 'mot-valeur', a 'mot-mana' which connotes (it does not denote anything) the manifestation in discourse of something other than a self yet which is of the order of subjectivity: 'mon corps n'est pas le même que le vôtre. Ainsi dans cette écume anarchique des goûts et des dégoûts, sorte de hachurage distrait, se dessine peu à peu la figure d'une énigme corporelle . . .' (p. 121). The 'moi' advocated here is like a kind of doodle, a design which can be discerned in the undirected cross-hatching of our desires.

In Barthes's self-writing, the body has another kind of pertinence relating to the question of exclusion. His homosexuality is never addressed (or disclosed) directly, but implied (e.g. p. 134). To confess to or to proclaim his homosexuality would be to invoke the funereal power of the adjective and the image (p. 136), to categorize himself in the terms of others, and to invoke a series of stereotyped oppositions (p. 137). Barthes's tactic is, rather, to use homosexuality as an example of the taboos which weigh on sexuality generally, and to identify in his work a desire to dissolve sexual paradigms, including 'la dualité sexuelle' (p. 73), so that 'Le sexe ne sera pris dans aucune typologie (il n'y aura par exemple que *des* homosexualités, dont le pluriel déjouera tout discours constitué, centré au point qu'il lui apparaît presque inutile d'en parler)' (p. 73). In the Utopian future envisaged here there would *only* be differences and thus no possibility of exclusion.[55]

'Le second degré est aussi une façon de vivre' (p. 70). Barthes treats language (the discourses he likes and does not like), subjectivity, and the

---

[55] References to Gide play an important role in this context: see D. Knight, 'Roland Barthes', 95.

socio-political and affective domains as the sites of discursive operations. He is constantly concerned with values, in particular with the adumbration of a potential transformation of inter-personal relationships. In connection with friendship he writes, 'Dans cet espace des affects *cultivés*, il trouve la pratique de ce nouveau sujet dont la théorie se cherche aujourd'hui' (p. 68). What lies, however, in an imponderable future is not the 'nouveau sujet' itself but its recognition. The new paradigm of a *dispersed* rather than a divided subject, 'un éparpillement dans le jeté duquel il ne reste plus ni noyau principal ni structure de sens' (p. 146), requires, if it is to be the basis of a new 'socialité' (p. 101), the complicity of the Other. The relationship to the reader in *Barthes par Barthes* rehearses the conditions of such a complicity. Barthes's perspicacity about his own *imaginaire* cannot include a secure sense of its relationship to the real or, especially, to the realm of 'le symbolique': 'De celui-là, je n'ai nulle responsabilité (j'ai bien assez à faire avec mon imaginaire): à l'Autre, au transfert, et donc *au lecteur*' (p. 156). Barthes does not simply put his *imaginaire* on display, he sets up a *mise en scène* designed to manifest its degrees and to undo its hold over him. In this aspect of his project the imaginary reader becomes his accomplice; well versed in 'bathmologies', such a reader would gauge the degrees—of irony, conviction, distance—to be credited to each utterance, immediately identifying the invisible 'guillemets' round many of them: 'vision utopique en ce qu'elle suppose un lecteur mobile, qui met et enlève les guillemets d'une façon preste; qui se met à écrire avec moi' (p. 164).

If the notion of *l'imaginaire*, and of course much else in Barthes's intellectual stance, deconstructs the distinction between truth and fiction in the area of self-scrutiny, there is no explicit recourse to fictional fabrication in the book. Barthes is concerned throughout with his *imaginaire*, with what happens when one tries to write the self. His devices—fragmentation, switches of pronoun, theatricality—are not agents of fictionalization, a priori demonstrations of the impossibility of autobiography; they are the prospective, exploratory instruments of a 'nouveau sujet qui se cherche'. The book as a whole has a performative quality, that of a working-model of the new paradigm of subjectivity which it investigates. If it is pervaded by an interrogative note, by questions addressed to the institutions of self-writing, it is, as it were, from the inside: 'Quel droit mon présent a-t-il de parler de mon passé? Mon présent a-t-il barre sur mon passé? Quelle "grâce" m'aurait éclairé? Seulement celle du temps qui passe, ou d'une bonne cause, rencontrée sur mon chemin?' (p. 124). Questions of power and ideology—ethical issues—are involved when we confidently claim to reconstruct the past and thereby endow the passage of time and the detection of causality with a distinct legitimacy ('une bonne cause') and with legislative rights. This is to claim the right to the last word, and to deny the fact that 'who I am' is inextricably bound up with my relation to the Other. To accentuate the temporal dimension of the subject is to attenuate the link to otherness; to maintain that relation, in the temporality of writing itself, is not to erase the pertinence of the past (Barthes's own past figures prominently in his book) but to make it a function of the present act of writing, conceived not as imitation ('je ne cherche pas à mettre mon expression présente au service de ma vérité antérieure', p. 60) but as nomination, the addition of a new layer, 'une autre énonciation, sans que je sache jamais si c'est de mon passé ou de mon présent que je parle . . . Loin d'approfondir, je reste à la surface, parce qu'il s'agit cette fois de "moi" (du Moi) et que la profondeur appartient aux autres' (p. 145).

The relation to the past, to the Other, to memory, incidents, narrative, confession, 'amour-propre', to a pre-existent autobiographical practice: all these features of *Barthes par Barthes* place it within the field of autobiography. But it is in its staging of the relationship between subjectivity and ideology, and in Barthes's concern for the viability of subjectivity, that the book's participation in the genre it treats with a combination of irony and goodwill is most marked. Barthes knows perfectly well that the impulses which make him want to elude the dead hand of *doxa* and dogma (including that of the *end* of subjectivity to which he had himself contributed) is in continuity with the project of autobiography. And he also knows that if the 'sujet qui se cherche' is defined against ideology, it is also ideological. The book's melancholy and its infinite irony (in the end everything asserted in one place is denied or queried somewhere else) are symptoms of that recognition. It would therefore be futile to claim the last word and criticize the book for handing victory to either ideology or subjectivity. Just as it would be idle to deny that Barthes's elaborate *mise en scène* and the concerted elegance of his writing make it hard to hear the 'voix du sujet', or to feel that we are allowed a glimpse of anything Barthes does not want us to see. This is a problem he had of course foreseen, and expressed in terms which seem to reveal his aims (and those of past autobiography) as well as his fears that they are unrealizable and Utopian: 'Comment faire résonner l'affect, sinon à travers des relais si compliqués, qu'il en perdra toute publicité, et donc toute joie?' (p. 89).

7

Existentialist Autobiography

Une vie se déroule en spirales; elle repasse toujours par les mêmes
points mais à des niveaux différents d'intégration et de complexité.

(Sartre: *Questions de méthode*)[1]

Stimulating constant innovation, autobiography's susceptibility to ideological colonization has been a source of strength rather than weakness.
Doctrines, dogmas, and directives of every sort, stemming from all the main
ideological powerhouses of the last two centuries, have left their imprint on a
genre no less absorbent than the novel in this respect. Often more than ready
to take the Other's word for it, and to borrow from the culture's repertoire of
life-models, autobiographers have also in certain cases responded with
admirable inventiveness and flexibility to the challenges ideologies have
(from Romanticism to deconstruction via positivism and surrealism)
consistently posed to the institutions and practices of self-writing. In this
regard Sartrean existentialism presents an especially interesting case. Here
we have a body of ideas with radical implications not only for the way we
conduct our lives but also for our picture of what a life *is*. Moreover, here,
within the ambit of the same movement of ideas, we encounter not just one
attempt to use autobiography as its testing-ground, but several. Parisian
existentialism offers in fact the remarkable spectacle of a colony or family of
texts written under the aegis of the same ideology, but from very different
positions in the ideological field which it constitutes. To examine the family
likenesses between these texts is the principal aim of this chapter.

Between 1946, when an early number featured extracts from Genet's
Journal du voleur,[2] and 1963, when it printed Sartre's *Les Mots* in its
entirety,[3] *Les Temps modernes*, the journal founded after the war by Sartre
and his colleagues, devoted considerable attention to autobiography.
Extracts from Leiris's ongoing cycle *La Règle du jeu* were featured

---

[1] *Questions de méthode* (*QM*), 149.
[2] '*Journal du Voleur* (extraits)', *Les Temps modernes* (*TM*), 10 (Jan.–Feb. 1946), 33–56.
[3] *TM* 209 (Oct. 1963), 577–649, and 210 (Nov. 1963), 769–834.

regularly;[4] 1957 saw the publication of a substantial part of André Gorz's *Le Traître*,[5] and 1963 large sections of Violette Leduc's *La Bâtarde*,[6] shortly after extracts from Simone de Beauvoir's *La Force des choses*.[7] This prompts one to ask whether there is such a thing as existentialist autobiography in the same way that there is existentialist fiction and drama. Certainly there was nothing fortuitous or superficial about the interest in this genre displayed by a group of writers with a shared intellectual background. It could easily be demonstrated that in the context of *Les Temps modernes*, a journal dedicated to a pluri-disciplinary investigation of human affairs, actively concerned with new currents in anthropology, psychoanalysis, and sociology, as well as literature and politics, always with an emphasis on the concrete individual, autobiography had much to offer as a testing-ground for theoretical explorations.[8] But is it possible to discern a common approach or style adopted by writers linked to the existentialist circle when they wrote autobiography? As we shall see, it is not easy to establish a clear set of guidelines, aims, or stylistic practices among these autobiographers. They do not form a school or adhere to a party line; at times their works seem strikingly dissimilar. Despite this, if we set Leiris aside as a special case, the autobiographies on which this chapter will be based—Genet's *Journal du voleur*, Gorz's *Le Traître*, Beauvoir's *Mémoires d'une jeune fille rangée*, Leduc's *La Bâtarde*, and Sartre's *Les Mots*—do seem to have more in common with each other than with other autobiographies.

The network of personal influences and relationships which binds these writers together is obviously important, although this factor probably inhibited as well as encouraged uniformity. Genet, for example, is clearly indebted to Sartre, but this debt is also a burden, and in *Journal du voleur* existentialist features are transmogrified and ironized as they are pulled into the world of the author's obsessions and designs.[9] Nevertheless, Genet's style of autobiography, in its treatment of existential choice and self-enactment, provided a potential model which was to some degree emulated,

---

[4] e.g. extracts from *Biffures* in 1946, from *Fourbis* (including the whole of 'Vois! déjà l'ange') in 1954–5, etc.

[5] *TM* 140 (Oct. 1957), 573–618, and 145 (Mar. 1958), 1537–64.

[6] *TM* 186 (Nov. 1961), 437–74; 207–8 (Sept. 1963), 466–97.

[7] *TM* 203, 204, and 205 (1962–3). Substantial extracts from *Mémoires d'une jeune fille rangée* had earlier been published in nos. 147–8 (May–June 1958), and 149 (July 1958).

[8] On this see the extremely informative study by Howard Davies, *Sartre and 'Les Temps modernes'*, which also contains illuminating remarks on some of the autobiographies dealt with in this chapter.

[9] The precise timing, nature, and extent of Sartre's influence on Genet is difficult to establish with any precision.

and in other respects discarded, by his successors. In addition, Sartre's massive existentialist biography of Genet, *Saint Genet: Comédien et martyr*, published in 1954, which drew extensively on *Journal du voleur*, added a further dimension to the relationship between the two writers and to the context in which Sartre and the others wrote their autobiographies. Writing in roughly the same period, Gorz and Beauvoir, both intimates of Sartre and members of the editorial board of *Les Temps modernes*, adopted very different strategies in their autobiographies. Beauvoir's is by far the most sober and conventional of the works we shall consider, notably restrained in its use of explicitly existentialist themes or categories. *Le Traître*, on the other hand, the most openly theoretical of these texts, is in large part constituted as a debate with existentialism, and Gorz's relationship with Sartre is a prominent theme in the book. Where Leduc is concerned, her relationship to Beauvoir in some respects matches Gorz's with Sartre, while in other respects it resembles Genet's with Sartre. Conscious of her affinity with Genet as a marginal figure, and as an outsider in intellectual circles, Leduc, who had already written a fictionalized account of her infatuation with Beauvoir (*L'Affamée*, 1948), was encouraged to write her autobiography by the author of *Le Deuxième Sexe* who provided a prefatory essay just as Sartre had done for *Le Traître*.[10]

Before leaving these kinship structures, a word should be said about Michel Leiris. Although he was a long-standing friend and comrade of Sartre and Beauvoir, and a member of the *Temps modernes* team from the beginning, Leiris's autobiography does not belong in this network. The impact of existentialist ideas can certainly be registered in *La Règle du jeu*, but the foundations of Leiris's autobiographical project were laid much earlier on. Conversely, Leiris's influence on existentialist autobiography, considerable at a general level—in making autobiography seem interesting and intellectually challenging (Sartre greatly admired *L'Age d'homme*)— seems to have been minimal in practical terms, a fact which is hardly surprising in view of the highly personal and idiosyncratic nature of his enterprise.

Viewed in the light of existentialist fiction and drama, the agenda for the existentialist autobiographer might plausibly be expected to comprise such headings as situation, contingency, freedom, the existence of others, 'mauvaise foi', commitment, and so on. And we might expect the first-person perspective, bearing on the specific complexion and dynamic of the

---

[10] On the Leduc–de Beauvoir relationship see I. de Courtivron, *Violette Leduc*, and Leduc's 'Lettres à Simone de Beauvoir'.

subject's relationship to self and others, to yield insights and foster descriptions similar in kind to those encountered in, say, Sartre's *Le Mur* or Beauvoir's *L'Invitée*. These expectations are certainly fulfilled, to a certain degree, by the autobiographies which concern us, particularly those of Beauvoir and Leduc. But a crucial dimension would be lacking if we did not also take into account a body of concepts, descriptions, and analytical procedures developed outside the context we have so far mentioned. These arise in connection with what Sartre initially called 'la psychanalyse existentielle'. Setting out the principles of this form of investigation in *L'Être et le néant*, he declared that its aim would be to provide an account of concrete individuals which could supplant the inert, atomistic categories of traditional psychology by the lights of which the individual was a mere aggregate of discrete character traits.[11] The individual was, rather, to be conceived as an irreducibly particular synthesis. Some acknowledgement was due to psychoanalysis in this regard, since Freud had shown how any instance of behaviour might be regarded as a manifestation of the complex totality of the individual subject. But, along with the massive predominance of sexuality, Sartre rejected in psychoanalysis both the theory of the unconscious and the potentially reductive idea of the complex, supplanting them with the form of consciousness ('conscience non-thétique') displayed in 'mauvaise foi'—where the subject knows and at the same time denies that it is deceiving itself—and with the vital concept of the *choix originel*.

A person's *choix originel* is the 'secret individuel de son être au monde', the watermark which can be discerned in every aspect of his or her behaviour: 'en chaque inclination, elle s'exprime tout entière, quoique sous un angle différent . . . nous devons découvrir, en chaque conduite du sujet, une signification qui la transcende'.[12] In our early years, in the context of our initial situation, we choose who we are going to be; our project—the dynamic process through which consciousness, always primordially a lack ('manque d'être'), seeks definition—acquires an irreducible colouring or shape. This is not *determined* by inner or outer factors, hence the notion of choice; nor, however, is the *choix originel* to be thought of as being characteristically an act occurring at a particular moment. It is, rather, the mark of a particular way of exercising, or denying, our freedom, and its formation occurs in the context of our response to all the phenomena which surround us. Therefore, to identify the *choix originel* of a given individual, as Sartre set out to do in the case of Baudelaire, and then Genet, may require

---

[11] 'La Psychanalyse existentielle', *L'Être et le néant* (*EN*), part 4, ch. 2, § 1, 643–63.
[12] *EN* 650–2.

minute attention to the most varied aspects of behaviour, to the whole panoply of the subject's 'conduites'. And this is likely to reveal that the *choix* itself (which is in any case inseparable from the 'conduites' which manifest it) has a complex, paradoxical structure, all the more so since every *choix* expresses to some degree the desire to square the circle—to possess being and definition as well as freedom. Thus, in the 1946 essay on Baudelaire (dedicated to Genet, and prefaced by Michel Leiris), the delineation of Baudelaire's *choix originel* occupies half the text, since, like a very elaborate signature, it is shown to have a number of loops, twists, and turns. Then, in the second half, Sartre demonstrates how the structure of Baudelaire's *choix* is discernible in all his well-attested traits and activities—his relation to nature, his dandyism, his attitude to the past, and, finally (and most controversially), his poetic universe.[13] In more complex and elaborate form, Sartre's biography of Genet displays similar features. The nucleus of the *choix originel* is identified on the strength of Genet's own account of an incident in his childhood, but its delineation through analysis of his 'conduites' involves Sartre in an extensive exploration of the phenomenology of poetic writing.[14] This underlines a significant aspect of Sartre's existentialist biographies:[15] by choosing writers as his subjects, he tends to focus more or less exclusively on a particular variety of *choix originel* where the activity of writing is predominant among the subject's 'conduites'.

Sartre's theory of the *choix originel* and his ways of applying it, particularly as regards its relationship to the *projet*, underwent significant modification in the course of the 1950s and this had a marked impact on existentialist autobiography. But before we consider this, it is useful to take stock of the potential orientations this concept, in its original form, might have provided. First and foremost, the autobiographer's aim would be to identify his or her own *choix originel*, a 'rapport originel à soi, au monde et à l'Autre'.[16] What or who have I chosen to be? How is that choice manifested in my way of being in the world? Nothing could more clearly indicate the grip of this way of envisaging the question of selfhood than the predominance of roles in the titles of existentialist autobiographies: 'le

---

[13] In conclusion Sartre writes: 'chaque événement nous renvoie le reflet de cette totalité indécomposable qu'il fut du premier jour jusqu'au dernier. Le choix libre que l'homme fait de soi-même s'identifie absolument avec ce qu'on appelle sa destinée', *Baudelaire*, 245.

[14] *Saint Genet, passim*, esp. pp. 473–644.

[15] For more extensive discussion the following may usefully be consulted: J. Halpern, *Critical Fictions*; D. Collins, *Sartre as Biographer*; M. Scriven, *Sartre's Existentialist Biographies*; C. Howells, *Sartre's Theory of Literature*.

[16] *EN* 650.

Voleur', 'le Traître', 'la Bâtarde', 'la Jeune Fille rangée'. The idea of the *choix* encourages the subject to see itself as a unity, a totality grounded not in the events of a life-history but in the way it engages with experience. Thus a second *desideratum* for the existentialist autobiographer would be to investigate and externalize the climate of his or her consciousness, the habitual motions and strategies of a specific 'rapport originel à soi, au monde et à l'Autre'. Though manifested in the motions of consciousness, rather than housed in the unconscious, the *choix* is constituted as much by what we shut our eyes to as what we choose to see. This poses existentialist autobiographers a challenge: over and above analytical speculation they must find a way of rendering, by stylistic means, the characteristic mental atmosphere, the inner discourse through which, at an imaginary level, they construct themselves and their worlds. Accordingly, from Genet to Sartre, existentialist autobiography will be characterized by a stylistic inventiveness tuned to the specificity of the *choix*, and by the attempt to reproduce through writing its flavour as well as its structure. This is all the more appropriate given that writing itself features in most cases as an important facet of the *choix originel*. The exploration through writing of a choice to construct one's identity through a particular relationship to language accounts for the markedly self-reflexive character of most of the texts we shall consider.

The concept of the *choix originel*, with the concomitants we have outlined, provides an indispensable background to any reading of existentialist autobiography. However, Sartre's ideas in this domain did not remain static; indeed, from the 1950s onwards, biography became one of the principal arenas of his philosophical activity, the crucible in which he experimented with the methodologies through which he sought to answer the fundamental question that inaugurates his great study of Flaubert: 'Que peut-on savoir d'un homme, aujourd'hui?'[17] For our purposes we need to follow Sartre as least as far as the 1957 essay, eventually entitled *Questions de méthode*, whose impact may be felt in the autobiographies written in the years immediately following it. Which is the body of ideas, Sartre asks, which can best help us understand the concrete, singular individual? The encounter with Marxism has led him by this stage to accord far greater power to the milieu in defining the individual's initial situation and the scope of his choice of being. But he finds Marxist theory too abstract and deterministic to deal with the particularity of individual existence. Psychoanalysis, with its concern for the vicissitudes of the child's

---

[17] *L'Idiot de la famille*, 7.

negotiations with the adult world, provides an invaluable redress: 'Seule, aujourd'hui, la psychanalyse permet d'étudier à fond la démarche par laquelle un enfant, dans le noir, à tâtons, va tenter de jouer sans le comprendre le personnage social que les adultes lui imposent.'[18] The aim of Sartre's essay, however, is to advance the claims of a specifically existentialist mode of analysis nourished by Marxism and psychoanalysis. And here we can detect an important reorientation. In the first place, the notion of the 'enfance indépassable'—a structure constituted by the way the child internalizes and accommodates the pressures of its original socio-economic, ideological, and psychological circumstances, mediated by the family group (*QM* 93)—tends to replace the *choix originel* (the word 'choix' is scarcely used). And in the second place, far more emphasis comes to rest on the concept of the *projet* which is now conceived as a perpetual 'dépassement' of the childhood we preserve within us and also transcend in the business of living:

Le donné que nous dépassons à chaque instant, par le simple fait de vivre, ne se réduit pas aux conditions matérielles de notre existence, il faut y faire entrer, je l'ai dit, votre propre enfance. Celle-ci, qui fut à la fois une appréhension obscure de notre classe, de notre conditionnement social à travers le groupe familial et un dépassement aveugle, un effort maladroit pour nous en arracher, finit par s'inscrire en nous sous forme de *caractère* . . . Dépasser tout cela, c'est aussi le conserver: nous penserons *avec* ces déviations originelles, nous agirons *avec* ces gestes appris et que nous voulons refuser (*QM* 141).

On this model, the task of the biographer or autobiographer will be to establish the lineaments of a certain character, shaped in childhood amidst the pressures of the milieu. But thereafter, rather than simply locating the ways in which a stubborn structure is perpetuated in the 'conduites' which are characteristic of the subject in later life, the aim will be to understand the particular ways in which this structure is both preserved and transformed in the historical evolution of the *projet*. In focusing on the *projet*, the task of 'la méthode existentialiste' will be to identify in the individual the dynamic principle—neutral in itself ('le projet n'a jamais de contenu', *QM* 148)— which drives him or her from one kind of self-manifestation to another:

découvrir la loi d'épanouissement qui dépasse une signification *par* la suivante et qui maintient celle-ci dans celle-là. En vérité, il s'agit d'inventer un mouvement, de

---

[18] *QM* 85. Subsequent references (which are to the Gallimard 'Idées' edn.) will be incorporated in the text. *QM* was initially serialized in *Les Temps modernes*: 139 (Sept. 1957), 338–417; 140 (Oct. 1957), 658–98 (the first part of Gorz's *Le Traître* featured in the same issue).

le recréer: mais l'hypothèse est immédiatement vérifiable: seule peut être valable celle qui réalisera dans un mouvement créateur l'unité transversale de *toutes* les structures hétérogènes (*QM* 205).

As before, the goal is to identify the unity of the individual behind apparent heterogeneity. But that unity now resides less in an invariant, a knot or pattern discernible in the variety of 'conduites'; it now appears as the factor which destabilizes identity, which tends towards a different state of affairs: 'cette perpétuelle production de soi-même par le travail et la praxis, c'est notre structure propre . . . pas une substance stable qui se repose en elle-même mais un déséquilibre perpétuel, un arrachement à soi de tout le corps' (*QM* 209).[19]

With the exception of Genet's, the autobiographies to which we shall now turn belong to the period immediately following the publication of Sartre's revised blueprint for an existentialist biography. The influence of Sartre's revisions, with regard to the treatment of the *milieu* and the *projet*, is clearly perceptible in *Le Traître* and in *Les Mots* (and perhaps in Beauvoir's *Mémoires*). An important issue here is the question of change or conversion. Although in theory, as a choice rather than the product of determinism, the *choix originel* could be revoked, in practice the concept is associated with permanence and perpetuation and does not favour a historical account of identity (by his account, Sartre's biographical subjects, especially Baude-laire, chose in any case to deny the possibility of change). In shifting the emphasis from *choix* to *projet* Sartre both allowed for a greater degree of effective determinism, limiting the subject's scope for choice, and also put the stress on the need to remain in perpetual motion even when striving (as most of us do) to stay still, clinging to an identity which is regarded as preordained. In this perspective the subject's history is the story of constant adjustments and renegotiations, a progression through short-lived phases; a constant relative self-transformation which may, as *Le Traître* and *Les Mots* record, lead to something like an authentic conversion. In that eventuality the original mould, the *choix* in its original form, is not completely broken but maintained within a new order.

If it makes sense to talk of existentialist autobiography it is not because a certain range of texts exemplify Sartrean doctrines but because the family resemblances they display make them mutually illuminating when

---

[19] An earlier passage captures vividly the restless dynamism of the life as *projet*: 'Il s'agit de retrouver le mouvement d'enrichissement totalisateur qui engendre chaque moment à partir du moment antérieur, l'élan qui part des obscurités vécues pour parvenir à l'objectivation finale, en un mot le *projet* . . .', *QM* 204.

considered as a group. The traits one could label and enumerate—*choix* and *projet*, roles and 'conduites', true and false situations, conversion and self-transformation, styles of self-consciousness, words and other people—are not combined in the same way in any two of them. Nevertheless most of these, and other links less easy to classify, feature in all of them, and in ways we shall not find elsewhere. It is also important to remember that the five works we shall consider are of exceptional merit and interest in the context of French autobiography generally. That they were produced within a relatively brief period indicates that for a time existentialist ideas and autobiographical motivations formed an exceptionally productive alliance. It may also be the case that, in providing the ideological stratum which inevitably underlies autobiography, existentialist theories may be responsible not only for the strengths but also for the limitations of the writings they stimulated. That, however, is an issue which must be left until after we have looked at the texts in more detail.

GENET AND LEDUC

In an earlier chapter it was suggested that the relationship with the reader is central to *Journal du voleur* and *La Bâtarde*. Genet and Leduc see themselves as victims of social classification who have to some extent succeeded in turning the tables by constructing their own identities, adapting to their own ends the reflections of themselves they perceive in the eyes of others. For both writers the principal arena of the struggle in which they engage is the inner stage on which roles and personae are essayed and generated by perpetual mental creativity before imaginary audiences. In each case writing is an extension of this process and, at least potentially, the activity—the role—through which victory is sought is that of the writer.

The *choix originel* at the heart of *Journal du voleur* is Genet's childhood decision to assume the identity foisted on him by others. Raised as an orphan at public expense, branded a thief, he chooses to become a thief, to follow a path of abjection and sexual deviancy, to make himself an incarnation of otherness.[20] But at the same time, having provided these decoys, he secretly decamps: he is always elsewhere, unfixed, inviolable, free. *Journal du voleur* abounds in scenes where Genet employs this tactic.

---

[20] 'Ainsi refusais-je décidément un monde qui m'avait refusé' (*Journal*, 97). Sartre takes this 'moment' as the starting-point of his biography of Genet: 'son aventure, c'est d'avoir été *nommé*: il en est résulté une métamorphose radicale de sa personne et de son langage', *Saint Genet: Comédien et martyr*, 57. See, more widely, pp. 63–88, and *passim*.

Caught in the act, taken to a police station, he is forced to empty his pockets: the contents spread on the table objectify him in the eyes of the police but Genet exults in his inner freedom to be other than they suppose (pp. 20–5).[21]

Genet's early works, such as his *Notre-dame-des-fleurs* (1942), were written for the most part in captivity, and were autobiographical in the loose sense: verbally luxuriant embroiderings on his experiences in orphanages, reformatories, and prisons, which earned the admiration of Gide, Cocteau, and Sartre. *Journal du voleur* comes much closer to autobiography by virtue of an evident concern with real events but also because, although he does not try to present an overall retrospect of his life, Genet's concern throughout is with the potential meaning—the potential for meaning—of his past experiences. The book is in large part a meditation not on events themselves but on the context, origins, and modalities of Genet's attempts to transform them imaginatively, to turn them into legend. Where his novels had given us the results of this process, *Journal du voleur* is concerned with its mechanisms. Centred principally on episodes from a period in his twenties spent in Barcelona, part of 'cette contrée de moi que j'ai nommée l'Espagne' (p. 306), *Journal du voleur* often takes us abruptly into other periods, earlier and later, but also insistently confronts the reader with the narrator's present. As we move from past to present, from reality to fantasy, and from description to lyrical flights or abstract meditation, no consistent relationship is established between remembered incidents, anecdotes, portrayals of character (Stilitano, Armand, Roger) and the narrator's discourse through which they are filtered.

In fact it is the quest for such a relationship—for a clear sense of how a past, which can only be apprehended through the distortions of the present, might relate to a present which can only be understood in terms of the past that produced it—which seems to generate the narration and to engender its vertiginous, lurching progress. Genet's 'Barcelona days' are important because they can be seen as both a reaffirmation of his childhood choice and an anticipation of the further transformation into a writer. By wilfully making himself abject (materially, sexually, sociologically, morally) he transformed his relative social alienation into an absolute condition. By becoming the Thief or the Prostitute, and by conferring a metaphysical aura on the sordid activities of his fellow pimps and hoodlums, Genet rekindled the imaginative energies of his childhood:

[21] References are to the Folio edn. of *Journal* and will be cited in the text.

c'est l'imagination amoureuse des fastes royaux, du gamin abandonné, qui me permit de dorer ma honte, de la ciseler, d'en faire un travail d'orfévrerie dans le sens habituel de ce mot, jusqu'à ce que, par l'usage peut-être et l'usure des mots la voilant, s'en dégageât l'humilité. Mon amour pour Stilitano me remettait au fait d'une si exceptionnelle disposition (p. 100).

Writing in prison was to be an extension of this process, and writing *Journal du voleur* is now a *prise de conscience*, a recognition of the transformative power of writing—of writing as an avatar of the original choice—and also a search for a new direction. 'Je veux réhabiliter cette époque en l'écrivant avec les noms des choses les plus nobles. Ma victoire est verbale et je la dois à la somptuosité des termes' (p. 65); 'ordonnant ce que ma vie passée me propose, à mesure que je m'obstine dans les rigueurs de la composition . . . je me sens m'affermir dans la volonté d'utiliser, à des fins de vertus, mes misères d'autrefois' (p. 69).This will be the aim of what Genet calls the quest for 'La Sainteté': the verbal transfiguration of abject experience, and Genet's own transformation into a legendary version of himself. Increasingly, as he writes, Genet comes to conceive the *Journal du voleur* as the instrument of this ambition:

Le but de ce récit, c'est d'embellir mes aventures révolues, c'est à dire obtenir d'elles la beauté, découvrir en elles ce qui aujourd'hui suscitera le chant, seule preuve de cette beauté (p. 230).

Non les anecdotes mais l'œuvre d'art. Non ma vie mais son interprétation. C'est ce que m'offre le langage pour l'évoquer, pour parler d'elle, la traduire. Réussir ma légende (pp. 234–5).

Writing becomes a form of spiritual exercise: 'Ce livre, "journal du voleur"': poursuite de l'Impossible Nullité' (p. 106). To achieve 'Nullité' would be to carry things a stage further and become clearly imaginary, or rather become simply the point of convergence for the images fashioned in the imaginative transmutation of experience:

Prétextes à mon irisation—puis à ma transparence—à mon absence enfin,—ces garçons dont je parle s'évaporent. Il ne demeure d'eux que ce qui de moi demeure: je ne suis que par eux qui ne sont rien, n'étant que par moi. Ils m'éclairent, mais je suis la zone d'interférence. Les garçons: ma Garde crépusculaire (p. 106).

But as he analyses and lays bare the desires which have come to inform his writing, Genet reveals the problems which beset their realization. Granted a pardon through the offices of his literary friends, Genet is no longer an outlaw but a celebrity who writes *Journal du voleur* in 'un palace d'une des

villes les plus luxueuses du monde' (p. 100). Though he remains sexually
marginal and socially unclassifiable, he has to some degree reneged on the
choice made in the face of the Other. Hence, in the sphere of writing, his
dependence on the reader as the Other's incarnation. But this is a puppet
reader, and Genet pulls all the strings. The more writing becomes its
exclusive terrain, the more Genet's project risks becoming no more than a
sterile, artificial aestheticism, an empty hall of mirrors, a flirtation with the
impossible. Well aware of this, Genet allows another note to be heard amidst
the repeated variations on the impossible aspiration to 'sainteté' and 'nullité'
to be achieved through writing. He announces that this book will be his last
(p. 232),[22] suggests that he wants to extricate himself from the hall of
mirrors, resists as well as encourages the idea of a wholesale 'engloutissement' in his imaginary world. In doing so he reaffirms his freedom to be
elsewhere, to remain ungraspable. The *Journal du voleur* becomes another
decoy planted in the accuser's path.

Although Genet makes little use of Sartrean terminology, *Journal du
voleur* has an unmistakably existentialist ring. It was Sartre himself who was
to write the full existentialist version of Genet's life, but in its anti-
essentialism, its concern with roles and self-creation, with the look of the
Other, with the derealizing power of the imagination, *Journal du voleur*
paves the way to *Saint Genet: Comédien et martyr*. Another factor is the role
played by style: 'j'utiliserai les mots non afin qu'ils dépeignent mieux un
événement ou son héros mais qu'ils vous instruisent sur moi-même' (p. 17).
In constantly drawing attention to style Genet makes his bizarre syntax, his
discordant lexis, his inimitable *débit*, the embodiment not of his character
but of the mechanisms of his inner drama and its designs on others—the
embodiment, in short, of his *projet* in its ceaseless dynamism and plasticity.
A feature which should also be mentioned is the construction, using past
events as raw material, of scenes and textual sequences which embody the
complexities of the subject's 'rapport à soi, au monde et à l'Autre'. Among
many examples one could cite the elaborate treatment of Genet's first
meeting with Stilitano (pp. 36–44), or the remarkable scene constructed
around a memory of seeing Stilitano unable to find the exit from a
fairground 'Palais des Miroirs' (p. 302). Perhaps the most dizzying and
haunting instances occur when Genet's anxieties about a current (at the time
of writing) obsessive relationship, with Lucien, infiltrate his meditations on

---

[22] Characteristically, Genet contradicts this statement at the end when, like Sartre in *Les
Mots*, he announces an unlikely and, in the event, unrealized sequel (p. 306).

the past. Writing about Lucien may bring Genet the deliverance he wants: 'Mon amour finira par sortir peut-être, me dis-je, de moi, emporté par ces mots, comme un toxique l'est du corps par le lait ou la purge' (p. 165). But Genet also recognizes that, like Stilitano or Armand, Lucien has become an imaginary creation as well as a creature of flesh and blood, and that to end the relationship is impossible. At one point Genet announces that he intends to recount one of the most humiliating experiences which had ever befallen him as if it had happened to Lucien. The incident turns out to involve images, and the experience of being looked at. Genet-Lucien accepts to be photographed by wealthy foreign tourists whose visit to Barcelona would be incomplete without a look at the famous beggars' quarter. For the tourists in their gaberdene raincoats the beggars and pimps in their picturesque rags are no more than local colour, living bits of Goya: 'L'accord est parfait', says one tourist, 'entre la tonalité des ciels et les teintes un peu verdâtres des loques' (p. 185). In consenting to be photographed, Genet had accepted to become no more than an image, a 'reflet', an extra in somebody else's fantasy of Spain. In the text, he subjects Lucien to a comparable manipulation and, at the same time, by making Lucien the narratee of this part of the *Journal*, he changes the role of his readers, placing them in the position of the voyeuristic tourists with their cameras.

Such manipulations are entirely characteristic of *Journal du voleur*: Genet constantly plunges the reader into the unstable milieu of his mental world, involving us in the play of images and desires, the perverse and paradoxical mechanisms of what is conceived very much as a *projet*. In this respect his approach to autobiography foreshadows that of later writers, particularly Leduc, but also Gorz and Sartre. Yet although the climate is unmistakably existentialist, betraying evidence of exchanges with Sartre and perhaps an acquaintance with his study of Baudelaire, Genet remains a free agent untrammelled by doctrinal allegiances and theoretical preoccupations (though he is by no means indifferent to methodological issues and constantly questions his own aims). Moreover, in terms of genre, *Journal du voleur* is more of a hybrid than the works of his successors, who will on the whole adopt the general trappings of autobiography from which Genet retains a parodic distance, not only refusing chronology and any sense of comprehensive coverage, but also blurring the divide between past and present, and pursuing the imaginative ends of his fictional writings. Nevertheless, in the emphasis it places on choice and roles, on the relationship with others, and on the specificity of writing in its relation to self-construction, *Journal du voleur* constitutes an indispensable prelude to existentialist autobiography.

Je suis née brisée. Je suis le malheur d'une autre. Une bâtarde, quoi! (p. 456).[23]

A 'fils de famille' gets a housemaid pregnant, then successfully entreats her to sacrifice her livelihood to his good name. Violette Leduc, the fruit of this union, is brought up amid denunciations of men (but also has to face her mother's remarriage, p. 104); vigorous brushing gives her the glossiest hair of the class, in vain mitigation of her taint. 'J'ai été élevée dans la terreur de l'insécurité' (p. 394). Ultimately *La Bâtarde* will testify that writing provided Leduc with at least partial deliverance from the shackles of the past. But first Leduc's autobiography will show how she chose to perpetuate the chronic insecurities of her childhood condition in the structure of her personal relationships, consistently engendering triangular patterns where desire is fuelled and frustrated by privation, sacrifice, betrayal, tyranny, and enslavement. 'Je me voulais à la proie de mes complexes' (p. 227): yet instead of simply being their prey Leduc, as she now recognizes, actively strove to externalize her inner divisions, creating those 'situations fausses', so prominent in existentialist fictions, where the character, incapable of performing an act which would transcend and transform his or her situation, prefers to regard it as inescapable and to remain in a shadowy, gestural world of false consciousness.

The discovery of erotic intensity in a homosexual affair with Isabelle at boarding-school links sexuality with escape and transgression (p. 112) but also with control and self-absorption. The 'box' (cubicle) where Isabelle and Violette make love is represented as the prototype for those enclosed spaces ('chambres meublées', couturier's changing-rooms, *maisons de passe*, hair-stylists' chairs) where Leduc will seek to control the interplay of self-image and desire, and where the Other will be subject, or subjected, to her terms. Isabelle will be sacrificed to Hermine, but also 'encrypted' by Leduc as a disruptive force within this and subsequent relationships, just as Hermine in her turn will be preserved after she too is left behind: 'Isabelle, Hermine mes candélabres lorsque je pars dans la crypte de ma folie' (p. 157)—the formulaic, talismanic coupling of this and other pairs of names throughout *La Bâtarde* emphasizes the way the protagonists in Leduc's emotional life are absorbed into the polarized structures of her inner world.

Hermine's first sacrifice is her post as 'surveillante-musicienne' which she loses because of her liaison with Violette, who is herself expelled: 'j'exigeais d'elle l'impossible . . . Hermine, déjà mon vertige, déjà ma dureté' (p. 156). By the time their affair resumes, when Hermine finds work near Paris,

---

[23] *La Bâtarde* was first published in 1964. References, incorporated in the text, are to the Folio edn.

Leduc has begun a relationship (initially platonic) with Gabriel. The resulting triangle is dominated by voyeurism, sexual ambiguity, and sacrifice. Accepting to be exploited by Leduc, for whom she provides a certain economic and emotional stability, the older Hermine becomes 'une droguée de sacrifices' (p. 211), addicted to the satisfaction of Violette's imperious needs. Gabriel at this point ensures that the situation remains open and unstable. When he first learns that Leduc has a girl-friend he accepts the sacrifice and anonymously follows the two women in the street (p. 175). In lieu of Hermine's music Gabriel introduces Leduc to modern literature, 'notre contrebande à l'ombre d'Hermine' (p. 399). 'J'étais prise dans l'engrenage de leurs sacrifices' (p. 216): having created a radically indefinite situation—'c'était là le paradis de mon avarice, ma mauvaise foi'—Leduc used it as a springboard for her narcissistic 'aventurisme'; on the fringes of the literary world where, through a series of 'petits emplois', she becomes an avid hanger-on: 'Je me brûlais les ailes au feu des anecdotes' (p. 316); and on the sexual market-place of the fashionable boulevards where Leduc parades herself in thrall to the Other's look: 'Je suis dans le sein de ma famille les passants' (p. 278). A number of episodes—the purchase of a 'tailleur anguille' from Schiaparelli, the overheard remark about her fateful flaw (a big nose), the seduction of male admirers, the imaginary dialogue with a woman at the hairdresser's—vividly re-enact the dynamics of Leduc's world: Hermine's vicarious participation in the desires her lover provokes, the fluctuations in Leduc's self-esteem, and her voracious appetite for material possessions. The relationship with Hermine will terminate in the aftermath of an episode where, in order to obtain the money to buy a lacquered table she covets, Leduc persuades her lover to take part in a sordid 'partie fine' to be witnessed by a 'voyeur'. Ultimately, as Leduc realizes, she is driven to precipitate her own rejection, to make herself the victim of her impossible desires.

The pattern repeats itself when Leduc takes up with the homosexual writer Maurice Sachs: 'Un homosexuel: mon passeport pour l'impossible' (p. 363), while resuming her relationship with Gabriel. Leduc becomes Gabriel's lover at this point, marrying him for security—and out of nostalgia—at the outbreak of war. But with Sachs, an established writer who will play an important part in Leduc's literary formation, 'le trio se reformait' (p. 407): 'Nous étions trois, chacun rôdait entre les deux autres' (p. 408). Sexual ambiguity dominates the triangle—having been a false lesbian, then a false wife, Leduc also becomes a false male homosexual, adopting this role in her love-making with Gabriel (p. 543) and thus subverting their short-lived 'normalization' since, through Gabriel's 'baisers abstraits', she enjoys the 'égarement luxueux' of her impossible desire for Sachs. The 'paradis de l'amour impossible' (p. 546) is the repetition of a situation where desire is a sterile, self-enclosed impasse: 'je ne désire pas Maurice. Je désire l'enfer de notre organisation' (p. 548). While Gabriel will withhold sexual gratification (taking on something of Leduc's role *vis-à-vis* Hermine in the earlier triangle, p. 448), Leduc will betray Gabriel by retaining her name, hiding her ring, sleeping with an almond-vendor (p. 476), and eventually by cannibalizing their relationship to feed her literary ambitions. She will also feel betrayed by, and in turn betray, Sachs in the context of the Occupation where he, as a Jew, was trying to save his life (he does not survive), while she was, she acknowledges, exclusively concerned with herself: 'je trahissais toujours sans envergure . . . Ce n'est pas ma faute. On m'a fermé le bec alors que j'étais pas née' (p. 455). In fact the Occupation offers Leduc the opportunity for another kind of betrayal and another role in a 'situation fausse'—that of 'trafiquante' on the black market—which she plays to perfection, carting joints of beef around the countryside, giving free rein to her self-centred 'rapacité' and also her desire for vengeance against society (p. 462).

As Simone de Beauvoir has suggested, the repeated patterns of Leduc's emotional life, reconstructed in *La Bâtarde*, represent a response to the guilt and betrayals of her childhood: 'Elle s'est blottie en elle-même. Par angoisse, par déception, par rancœur, elle a choisi le narcissisme, l'égocentrisme, la solitude.'[24] But, Beauvoir continues, there is another side to the story, a conversion through which Leduc transforms her choice: 'Dans ses relations avec autrui, elle n'avait fait qu'assumer son destin. Elle lui invente un sens imprévu quand elle s'oriente vers la littérature.'[25] The preliminary stages of this act of self-transformation are narrated in *La Bâtarde*: the child's responsiveness to music and the sensory world, the glamorous appeal of modern literature and the fascination with literary 'stars', the apprenticeship in literary hack-work and minor journalism, Sachs's insistence that she should put her 'malheurs d'enfance' down on paper rather than plaguing him with them (p. 548) which leads her to begin her first book *L'Asphyxie*, the glimpse of Simone de Beauvoir's name on the cover of *L'Invitée* which confirmed that a woman could be a writer (p. 600), the discovery that writing could be a mode in which self-sufficiency became self-affirmation rather than self-obsession: 'Écrire c'était lutter . . .

---

[24] Préface to *La Bâtarde*, 9.
[25] Ibid. 14. Further on, Beauvoir notes: 'Un lecteur inattentif ne verra dans son histoire qu'une suite de hasards. Il s'agit en vérité d'un choix.'

inoubliable après-midi avec mon papier à noircir, avec ma volonté de femme seule qui se suffit et ne veut pas tomber' (p. 486). But the reorientation of Leduc's *projet* ('rien ne change, tout se transforme', p. 324) which occurs essentially in the years after the war (with which the book ends) figures most significantly in *La Bâtarde* at the level of narration.

In Chapter 5 I suggested that Leduc uses the narrator's relation to the reader as a channel through which writing—and particularly writing about herself—is shown to serve as a medium of self-conversion, a 'transferential space', to use Peter Brooks's term, where Leduc evolves in symbolic form a new relation with the Other. Initially claustrophobic, redolent of the manipulative, push-me pull-you dynamics of Leduc's past relationships, the relation with the reader progressively opens up as it becomes tinged with the desire to celebrate the natural world. Moreover, the emergence out of asphyxia into clear air, engendered by writing, and figured in the adoption via the imaginary reader of a new stance towards the Other, is associated with the rediscovery of an acceptable dimension of her childhood—the relationship, rooted in the pastoral, with Fidéline, her adoring and adored grandmother.[26] Other aspects of Leduc's style indicate how the re-enactment of the past in *La Bâtarde* is an act of partial liquidation and transcendence; a victory over what had been disabling; a flight from the mirror of a destiny like her mother's: 'Mon miroir, manman [*sic*], mon miroir. Non, je ne veux pas de toi, hérédité. Mon Dieu, faites que j'écrive une belle phrase, une seule' (p. 32). But in Leduc's case the role of writing is by no means dominated, as in Genet, by the fantasy of an impossible transubstantiation (though there is something of this): its aims and means are more concrete and down to earth. Writing is often represented as a task and a discipline, the response to a summons issued by a fleeting detail or a passing moment resurrected in the process of memory (a striking example is the brilliant passage devoted to the spangled floor of a Paris metro station, pp. 426–8). Writing is a function of the willed rather than the passively accepted self. There is of course always the risk that writing will simply constitute, as Genet too feared it might, an 'engloutissement', a renewed fixation on the dynamics of past desires, and that stylistic invention will amount to no more than a mannerism: 'Jongler avec le vocabulaire pour être remarquée' (p. 432). But it is the stylistic reappropriation of the past and its legacy, the achievement of control, which predominates. By repeatedly recording the passage of time, dating and placing the activity of writing,

---

[26] On 'l'ange Fidéline' (p. 38) see e.g. pp. 28 ff.

Leduc emphasizes the ability to switch the past on and off, to break the circuit of negative desires, or subdue them with the orderly music to which she listens (e.g. p. 85). At one point Leduc interrupts a stylistically exuberant passage in order to pinpoint the origin of an image she had found herself using (p. 292): writing is both a surrender to the drives of the inner world and a lucid, self-conscious activity.[27]

Style in Leduc can thus be seen as the instrument of a certain realism. But it is important to observe that her ability to turn writing into a therapeutic engagement with her past is not the product of abstract analysis and synthesis, the imposition of the kind of order which dominates Beauvoir's *Mémoires*. It derives, rather, from the constant inventiveness and mobility of her writing, the appearance it gives of being mobilized by disparate psychic and physiological energies. If in de Beauvoir existentialist autobiography might be held to serve the ends of feminist critique, in Leduc it leads towards, indeed exemplifies, what was to become known as 'écriture féminine', a writing attuned to the body and to the irrational.[28] Yet if, like Genet, Leduc eschews theorization, *La Bâtarde* belongs to the family of existentialist autobiography by the particular quality of its coherence. A final manifestation of its allegiance may be found in the insistent use of a device we shall note again in Sartre: that of self-designation. The path constructed in *La Bâtarde* is that of a woman who understands the roles in which she has cast herself: 'Bâtarde', 'forgeron de ma douleur' (p. 152), 'femme plaquée' (when Hermine leaves her, p. 372), 'Gros-Nez' (p. 307), 'bas bleu à repriser de tous les côtés' (p. 522), 'malheureuse défroquée de Maurice absent' (p. 599), 'représentante en récits, contes et nouvelles' (p. 425), 'avare' (p. 605), 'trafiquante' (p. 601), 'tricheuse', and ultimately, of course, 'tragédienne de mes ovaires' (p. 451)—in other words, and first and foremost, writer.[29]

---

[27] Two aspects of Leduc's style should be noted. First, her 'petites phrases haletantes' (p. 426), associated at one point with a reaction to the memory of her mother telling her as a schoolgirl that her style was too heavy. Second, her use of the expanded sequence or set-piece which recreates the inner climate of past feelings, sometimes through a 'stream of consciousness' technique (e.g. the remarkable unpunctuated sequence on pp. 239–43); through imaginary dialogue, a device Sartre also uses in *Les Mots*; through fantasy (as in the case of the remark about her nose discussed in an earlier chapter); or through self-parody, as in the brilliant scene based on the long-delayed decision to have plastic surgery on her nose (pp. 617–22).

[28] See I. de Courtivron, *Leduc*.

[29] To this list one might add the author's repeated talismanic use of her own name, e.g. p. 424.

SIMONE DE BEAUVOIR: *MÉMOIRES D'UNE JEUNE FILLE RANGÉE*

Although *La Bâtarde* was published last, I chose to treat it before the autobiographies of Beauvoir, Sartre, and Gorz, because of certain affinities with Genet's *Journal du voleur*. These do not need to be restated but a possible misunderstanding should be dispelled. The autobiographies of Genet and Leduc may have in common (among other things) a more obviously literary quality, a greater kinship with the novel as opposed to, say, the essay, than is the case with Sartre and his fellow philosophers. Yet, as I have sought to show, these works are permeated by the conceptual framework and climate of existentialism. And, indeed, if one were to gauge the existentialist credentials of the five works we are considering, with regard to the various criteria discussed at the beginning of this chapter, it is not in Genet or Leduc that their presence might be found least perceptible but arguably in Beauvoir. That *Mémoires d'une jeune fille rangée* belongs firmly in the framework of existentialist autobiography is not in doubt, but the relatively weak or unobtrusive role played here by existentialist concepts must be examined.

Beauvoir's style in the *Mémoires* is sober, uniform, and rather literary in a conventional way. Existentialist jargon (so abundant in Gorz) figures scarcely at all, although there are traces, such as the repeated use of the word 'condition' in phrases like 'ma condition d'enfant' (p. 59) or 'enfantine' (p. 22), 'sa condition de cadette' (p. 137, of her sister Poupette), or 'sa condition de matronne' (p. 159, applied to Zaza's mother).[30] The narrative is consistently linear and chronological; flashbacks and proleptic anticipation are rare; phases and transitions are identified, and summarized in lapidary formulae—'j'avais une petite sœur: ce poupon ne m'avait pas' (p. 9); 'Enfin le Mal s'etait incarné' (p. 39); 'Je sentis sur mes épaules le joug rassurant de la nécessité' (p. 44)—but the sense of a complex, dialectical structure, which dominates *Les Mots*, is lacking. Methodological discussion and 'in flight' commentary on the problems or the process of writing autobiography are also absent. This is true in Sartre's case, but then *Les Mots* is dominated by the problematic status of a choice of being which involved words and writing, whereas in Beauvoir becoming a writer is portrayed as the logical outcome of a particular process of development. Further, the issues of change, conversion, or self-transformation, which featured to some degree in all the other texts, do not arise in the *Mémoires*: a

---

[30] *Mémoires d'une jeune fille rangée* (hereafter *Mémoires*) was first published in 1958. References, cited in the text, are to the Folio edn.

continuous thread links writer and protagonist, and this affords little scope for their interaction or confrontation to become a prominent feature.

Where the *Mémoires* do seem to bear the existentialist stamp is in the sustained, closely focused attention to the protagonist's *vécu*: from start to finish we are presented with a subtle, dense, and detailed reconstruction of an individual developing through interaction with her social, physical, and intellectual environment. In view of our initial remarks, we must ask whether the notions of the *choix* or *projet* inform Beauvoir's account of her development, or whether a less specific form of rationality is at work. 'La principale fonction de Louise et de maman était de me nourrir; leur tâche n'était pas toujours facile. Par ma bouche, le monde entrait en moi plus intimement que par mes yeux et mes mains. Je ne l'acceptais pas toute entière . . .' (p. 11). Thus begins an early passage where Beauvoir epitomizes an especially revealing 'conduite'. Eating is double: it is associated, for the child, with the security of the maternal lap, with being looked after, 'dorlotée', 'choyée', with being safe and sound; but it is also associated with growth and change: 'Si tu ne manges pas, tu ne grandiras pas . . . Soudain l'avenir existe: il me changerait en une autre qui dirait moi et ne serait pas moi. J'ai pressenti tous les sevrages, les reniements, les abandons et la succession de mes morts' (p. 13). Plunging the reader into the world of her childhood feelings, Beauvoir portrays a secure and stable child, more than willing to go along with parental demands but who is at the same time characterized by a voracious appetite for experience, knowledge, and hence change. Recollections of childhood experience serve to identify a nucleus in which the desire to remain within an established order is combined with the desire to eradicate obstacles threatening the progressive realization of goals which seem to flow naturally from what is initially given. The early parts of the book do, then, seem to delineate an originary structure embodying potential contradictions, but there is little to suggest a choice made in the face of a specific situation. Further on Beauvoir will attribute some significance to the divergent personalities of her parents, but this bears on a later phase of her development and she seems unconcerned or unwilling to give the reader any secure grounds for seeing this as a factor in her early childhood. Her main concern is apparently to describe as accurately as possible the texture and atmosphere of her early years, rather than fit them into any sort of schema: the nucleus of her personality seems more of the order of something given than of something made. Moreover, the description of successive phases does not suggest a dialectical interplay of 'choix' and 'situation' but a linear unfolding. From infancy to academic triumph at the threshold of womanhood Beauvoir presents an unbroken line of experiences. The juxtaposition of different periods is almost non-existent. What predominates is the sense of a coherent and seemingly irresistible evolution. When we reach the last page we feel as if the voracious little girl on her mother's knee could only have turned into the left-bank intellectual. Other possible outcomes are by no means neglected—domesticity if she had married her cousin Jacques, self-destruction if she had emulated his empty 'inquiétude' or if she had allowed herself to become a martyr to bourgeois and Catholic proprieties like her friend Zaza, tedium if she had become a librarian, debauchery if her weakness for cocktails had not been kept in check. Indeed, much of the book is concerned with the threats, impediments, blind alleys, and snares which at every turn threaten to divert her from her path and abort her *projet* at an early stage. Yet Beauvoir never seems anxious to convince us that this was at all likely. She tends to assess her past experience month by month, and year by year, with reference to criteria which presuppose the eventual achievement of her ultimate status and identity as intellectual. It could be suggested that the failure of the adventitious and contingent to alter Beauvoir's course is testimony to the presence of a *choix originel* in which the subject is cocooned, and which shapes her encounters with experience. We shall return to this hypothesis, but at this point it should be noted that Beauvoir's account might equally be seen as confirming the more traditional axiom that 'nature will out', that Beauvoir lived out the life programmed for her by her given psychological make-up.

A constant feature of Beauvoir's appraisal of her development is the sense of individual sovereignty and destiny. In her early childhood this is perfectly consistent with the conformism, the willing endorsement of the framework of parental values, the self-image of a 'jeune fille rangée', which she excavates from her past. The young girl likes to create order: playing the teacher with Poupette, writing stories, imagining herself to be entrusted with a mission. The changes wrought by adolescence lead to a division between the inner world, which loses consistency, and the outer, which loses its authority. The young girl maintains an acute sense of her own self, but the links to the future and to the world of others become problematic. She is not always confident that outer circumstances will provide the conditions for self-realization, and by no means certain about the precise area in which it should be sought. The problem areas of growing-up—sexual ignorance, nature mysticism, friendships and rivalries, the conflict of generations—recur at different levels of a continuous spiral and are often brilliantly handled. Yet if they are clearly germane to a descriptive account of her life, these evocations do not have to carry a heavy interpretative burden. We may, if we wish, incorporate Beauvoir's account of sexual inhibition, shyness, and gaucherie into our theory of how she became who she is, but she herself, on the whole, refrains from doing so. Among the tracks which lead towards her apotheosis as writer and intellectual there is really only one 'live' rail: the constant desire to maintain her independence, to be responsible for her own destiny. Of course this places her in conflict with her parents, who disapprove of her bookishness on different grounds, but if their reactions and pressures do prompt some of the girl's oscillations they do not really deflect her.

At one point Beauvoir affirms that the combination of her mother's hidebound social and religious outlook and her father's contrasting sceptical disposition played a central role in her existence: 'le déséquilibre qui me vouait à la contestation explique en grande partie que je sois devenue une intellectuelle' (p. 58). Yet there is little in the text to support this assertion, if taken at face value. The ingredients are certainly there—diverse parental characters, disequilibrium, contestation, becoming an intellectual, but the verbs *vouer* and *expliquer* seem inappropriate to the ways Beauvoir's complex mode of analysis in fact links them together; indeed, Beauvoir does herself an injustice by suggesting that the multitude of factors which come into play in the course of her development could be reduced to so straightforward a pattern.

The second half of the *Mémoires* (parts 3 and 4) relates to a fairly short period between the ages of 17 and 21. Beauvoir has lost her religious faith and is in conflict with her parents: she yearns to make something of her life, realizes that she will have to break with her background, but feels empty. At this point she looks for succour to a number of sources, most of which will prove arid. Her cousin Jacques provides a link with her childhood security and family background but he also initiates her into the enticing world of modern literature: 'La littérature prit dans mon existence la place qu'y avait occupée la religion' (p. 259). Beauvoir falls in love with Jacques, who responds evasively, dropping hints that his affection is no more than brotherly, but allowing sufficient scope for the girl's inexperience to delude her as to the future of their relationship. In fact the on–off relationship with Jacques (whom she often does not see for long periods) seems to have the effect of preserving her from any sense that she ought to look elsewhere for a male relationship, and offers the chance to explore her own subjective life of which she becomes strongly aware at this stage. She begins to keep a diary (quoted frequently in the text) to document this inner life: 'Je me réfugiai dans "mon moi profond" et décidai que toute mon existence devait lui être subordonnée' (p. 271). The relationship with Jacques becomes a largely inward affair, a surrogate for the active engagement with the external world for which she increasingly hankers: 'La principale raison de mon acharnement, c'est que, en dehors de cet amour, ma vie me semblait désespérément vide et vaine. Jacques n'était que lui; mais à distance il devenait tout: tout ce que je ne possédais pas' (p. 305). Various figures: Robert Garric, the socialist teacher, Pradelle, a friendly *normalien*, serve as stepping-stones on the path towards the synthesis of inner and outer, literature and society, which the *école normale* circle (Sartre, Nizan, Herbaud), and ultimately Sartre himself, eventually provide. As in the case of Jacques, the profusion of circumstantial detail disguises the degree to which particular individuals take on an essentially symbolic role in the narrative.

This is clearest, of course, in the case of Zaza who is eventually cast in the role of sacrificial victim, destroyed in the attempt to placate and reconcile the sectional interests, social and religious, which thwart and distort her existence. In the last pages of the book, exclusively focused on her fate and eventual death, Zaza becomes a botched avatar of Beauvoir herself, a partial *alter ego* who succumbs to the 'destin fangeux' the intellectual will evade. There is a cautionary tale, too, in Jacques's life-history. He comes to represent the false path taken by those young people who settle their scores with their bourgeois backgrounds by recourse to the treble intoxicants of avant-garde literature, alcohol, and 'dépaysement', and whose 'inquiétude' (p. 302) may be sufficient to warrant the label 'nouveau mal du siècle' affixed by Marcel Arland, but does not provide an alternative set of values. A chilling passage (pp. 484–8) charts Jacques's failed life: disastrous marriage, financial ruin, alcoholism, social degradation, and early death. 'Liquidation' is the key to the matter.[31] Jacques, Zaza, Pradelle, even Herbaud with his wife in the provinces, fail entirely to liquidate the ghosts of their upbringing. Beauvoir is more successful because her desire for clarity makes her willing to relinquish an old faith when a new one dawns. Of religious faith she writes: 'Je devais fatalement en arriver à cette liquidation. J'étais trop extrémiste pour vivre sous l'œil de Dieu en disant au siècle à la fois oui et non' (p. 191). The extremism she refers to here can be seen as a wild card dealt her in the cradle, for it reminds us of the furious rages she would fly into as a young child which seemed inconsistent with her otherwise sunny and conformist disposition: 'Je me suis souvent interrogée sur la raison et le sens de mes rages. Je crois qu'elles s'expliquent en partie par une vitalité fougueuse et par un extrémisme auquel je n'ai jamais tout à fait renoncé'

---

[31] The word recurs frequently, e.g. pp. 261, 485, etc.

(p. 18); but 'le scepticisme paternel' also served her in this instance. The liquidation of potentially disabling obstacles to freedom and authenticity does not, in Beauvoir's case, depend on the revision or transformation of an original dispensation but on its successful passage towards final fruition.

The theme of liquidation (which we will find in Gorz) can bring us back to the question of existentialist autobiography. Leiris's *L'Age d'homme*, where the notion has a central place, showed how autobiography could be envisaged as an act of liquidation. But there the activity of composition (and of publication) was given an instrumental role. Genet, Gorz, Leduc, and in some respects Sartre himself, use autobiography as a way of working on the resurrected past, following Leiris's example in making the act of writing (often underlined) central to the aims of the text. But this is not the case with Beauvoir. If the theme of writing is present, since this is after all the story of how she became a writer, the process of writing the autobiographical text gives rise to no comment. This is perhaps not surprising since the literary vocation whose origins and genesis are traced is essentially that of an *écrivant* rather than an *écrivain* (to use Roland Barthes's famous distinction), that of someone who believes writing is an instrumental medium, consistent with a desire to clarify and order. Unlike Sartre, Beauvoir does not question the validity of her choice of writing; she is content to retrace past liquidations rather than engage in a present one.

It is interesting in this connection to consider Francis Jeanson's attempt, in his *Simone de Beauvoir ou l'entreprise de vivre* (1966), to write an existentialist *biography* of Beauvoir on the basis of her autobiography. In two dense discussions of Beauvoir's methodology in the *Mémoires*[32] (much of Jeanson's book is based on this text) he finds it hard to decide whether to criticize her account for being 'assez platement chronologique' and to censure its 'objectivisme naïf qui s'acharne à mentionner tout ce qui eut lieu, comme si le souci de relater l'emportait sur celui de comprendre, comme si la vérité pouvait n'être qu'un attribut des faits et procédait directement de leur simple accumulation';[33] or whether to commend Beauvoir for her telescopic method: 'un mouvement de totalisation dont chaque moment se donne pour absolument décisif, aux dépens de ceux qui l'ont précédé: un peu comme si nous assistions à la reconstitution magique d'une poupée-gigogne à partir de son plus petit élément, chacun des éléments successifs disparaissant à son tour sous un élément qui l'englobe'.[34] On the whole,

---

[32] *Simone de Beauvoir ou l'entreprise de vivre*, 108–11, 195–206.
[33] Ibid. 196.
[34] Ibid. 108.

Jeanson proceeds as if Beauvoir had given all the facts but had failed (or deliberately refused) to submit them to the dialectical reading he himself provides. But he also implies from time to time that her approach may be the outcome of lucidity, while his own formalizations may be arbitrary.

Interestingly, Jeanson's analysis lends some support to the view that the identification of a *choix originel* does underlie the *Mémoires*, but that its particular nature made linearity, chronology, etc., a fitting vehicle for its delineation. Beauvoir sees herself precisely as someone who chose order, coherence, understanding, expression; who pledged herself to the construction of a sovereign identity which would come to self-realization along a straight path. If her autobiography displays, as a text, comparable characteristics this would not be a sign of her failure to make it reflect her life but of her success. Beauvoir chose to be someone who would achieve her ends and have the destiny she wanted, and she succeeded; she chose, in other words, to warrant an autobiography of the kind she wrote for herself. A later volume, *Tout compte fait*, corroborates this view. Here, Beauvoir reappraises her life (particularly the period covered in the *Mémoires*) and, in the light of her sense of being 'satisfaite de ma destinée', she chooses to take as 'fil conducteur' the notion of good luck. Repeatedly she stresses that, after a 'bon départ' secured by loving parents and favourable circumstances, her evolution took the form of satisfying a fundamental desire for knowledge, which she refers to as a 'donnée originelle'. 'Ma liberté a consisté à assumer avec bonne volonté et même zèle le destin qui m'était assigné.'[35] Beauvoir turned everything to good account: Zaza's friendship, the 'divergences morales de mes parents [qui m'ont] acculée à la contestation', and thus made her resolve to be utterly self-reliant; and so on. Here, while offering an extremely simplified account of her life, Beauvoir does not in fact shrink from existentialist vocabulary: 'Ainsi pendant toutes ces années d'enfance, d'adolescence et de jeunesse, ma liberté n'a jamais pris la forme d'un *décret*; ç'a été la poursuite d'un projet originel, incessamment repris et fortifié: savoir et exprimer' (p. 22).[36] Irresistible forward progress and continuity never yield. Referring back to the *Mémoires*, Beauvoir claims that this accounts for their 'unité romanesque', a feature she admits is missing in her subsequent volumes of autobiography. The implication might be that, if many of the ingredients of existentialist autobiography are lacking in the *Mémoires*, this should be attributed to Beauvoir's good fortune in having

---

[35] *Tout compte fait*, 17.

[36] Ibid. 22. A thought-provoking discussion of Beauvoir's 'second version' of her life will be found in T. Keefe, 'Simone de Beauvoir's Second Look at her Life'.

had a life—and made a choice—which rendered such ingredients redundant in her case.

ANDRÉ GORZ: *LE TRAÎTRE*

Published in the same year, André Gorz's autobiography offers a striking contrast to Beauvoir's *Mémoires*. *Le Traître* (1958) is teeming with existentialist terms and makes continual reference to Sartre. The concepts of *L'Être et le néant*, *Saint Genet*, and *Questions de méthode* are omnipresent. It is a strongly self-reflexive work, concerned with problems of method— the comparative evaluation of psychoanalytical, Marxist, and existentialist theories—and with the possibility of self-transformation. Consistently analytical, *Le Traître* features a range of intrusive stylistic devices: alternations between 'Je' and 'Il' to designate the subject; elaborate digressions (often marked by massive parenthetical constructions); a non-linear structure, involving frequent cross-cutting between different periods, and so on. The work's overall shape is particularly complex and I shall begin by examining in turn its four principal sections: 'Nous', 'Eux', 'Toi', and 'Je'.

Nous

Like Leiris, in *L'Âge d'homme*, Gorz begins with an acute sense of self-dissatisfaction and a desire for change. Surveying the characteristics he dislikes in himself he quickly identifies what he calls a 'choix de nullité' (the influence of Genet, via Sartre, will become evident later). His early experience of exclusion and exile as a Jew suggests the possibility of historical determinants (a Marxist approach), but the sudden return of a childhood memory makes him aware that his 'choix' predated any possible awareness of his social conditioning. If the conjunction of subjective and objective 'nullité' is fortuitous, the best approach, he surmises, might be to follow the path of psychoanalysis and seek to extirpate what was instilled in the circumstances of infancy. But Gorz quickly senses that the links are not fortuitous, that his 'choix' did not determine his 'condition' any more than the reverse: they are inseparable, bonded in a process of interaction which produces, like sedimentary deposits, the 'thèmes, tics, motifs dominants de ma vie' (p. 60).[37] Adopting the view that the *choix originel* is like a

---

[37] References, cited in the text, are to the Collection Points edn, Éditions du Seuil, 1978.

watermark, latent in all his behavioural patterns, Gorz proceeds to review his 'conduites'—obsession with writing, reluctance to listen to others, avarice, mania for order—noting the themes they suggest, and then diagnosing a 'conduite globale de fuite'. But what, he asks, was he trying to escape from? Again the temptation is to go back to childhood, and particularly the child's relationship with others. Yet while this convinces him that 'on ne se débarrasse jamais complètement de son enfance' (p. 92) Gorz finds himself acutely conscious that the pressure of the past on the present is matched by the power of the present to remodel the significance of the past. We carry our childhood around inside us, but it does not remain a 'déterminant brut' (p. 94). The degree to which we are determined by the past is attenuated by the 'remaniement perpétuel' to which, through living, we subject it. If the 'choix', to the extent that it does tie us partly to an infantile complex, is a 'facteur de désadaptation' (p. 96), narrowing the range of our engagement with new experience, we cannot simply go back to its most archaic form. The desired aim of liquidation must reckon with the current embodiment of the *choix* in our 'conduites' and with the specific openings our present situation offers. The methodological ruminations of 'Nous', a series of false starts and doublings-back, culminate in a 'programme de travail' which closely resembles the theses of *Questions de méthode* in the course it steers between Marxism and psychoanalysis, and in the modifications it brings to Sartre's original formulation of the concept of the *choix*. Gorz now recognizes that if he is to achieve the self-conversion which is his aim he must understand the interactions which have made him what he is. But where should the historical continuum of past experiences be broached?

Eux

In choosing to start with the moment in 1938 when his exclusion as a Viennese Jew was borne in on him in the Nazi legislation, Gorz opts for an event where historical factors seemingly prompted a 'choix originel de nullité' to resurface. Yet as he analyses his memories of this period, Gorz comes to realize that the integration which the *Anschluss* brought to an end was illusory. Far from exiling him, his explicit exclusion in 1938 offered him the opportunity to lay claim to and reinforce a deep-seated sense of inferiority and guilt. Armed with this recognition Gorz scrutinizes his childhood for further signs of a desire to 'make himself Other', and identifies a 'complexe de trahison'—which he judges to be the best label so far for his original choice. Memories of masochistic activities and of childhood mysticism are interpreted in this light, and are linked to the later role of writing:

N'être pas là; n'être qu'une présence transparente, insaisissable et donc invulnérable, un regard venant de l'au-delà, qui glisse sur les événements sans s'y prendre, que les reproches ne peuvent atteindre, qui est dégagé de tous engagements envers les autres parce qu'absolument engagé envers l'absolument Autre. C'est ainsi qu'il a commencé à être vers sa douzième année, c'est ainsi qu'il est encore aujourd'hui (pp. 161–2).

Increasingly Gorz recognizes that our 'conduites' always mean more than we think and that they take on different meanings as they adapt themselves to new circumstances. For example, his decision when exiled in Switzerland to valorize all things French was, he is certain, a new way of rubbing in his inferiority. Decreeing the French race and language, which were new to him, to be absolutely superior was a form of masochism and a form of mysticism (p. 177), a way of reaffirming the racial inferiority which exile from Nazi rule had seemed to protect him from. Yet France's defeat in 1940, which made her a victim, changed the meaning of Gorz's choice. To identify with France was now an imaginary exercise, a form of negativity (since 'France' did not exist), but of a potentially positive kind.

This analysis not only confirms Gorz's sense of the dialectical play of 'choix' and 'événement' but also makes him recognize that positive and negative are reversible. The application of this idea modifies the analysis of his compulsion to write. Initially, the discussion of the negativity of writing threatens to abort his project since it seems to suggest that, in composing his autobiography, he is engaged in regressive repetition. The more he unveils the links between writing and mysticism, or its purely negative aspects, the more his current activity strikes him as the worst kind of recidivism (p. 195). Yet if Gorz perseveres it is partly because he senses that writing can be the instrument of its own demystification (p. 198), and in some of the densest, most confusing pages of *Le Traître*, heavily indebted to Sartre's *Saint Genet*, he steers his argument towards a positive evaluation of the negativity of writing. If it is at one level the perfect instrument of nullification, by virtue of its derealizing, nocturnal, abstract character, writing is also constructive in that it brings into being something concrete and ordered (pp. 217–18). It turns the relative and contingent into the absolute, but in doing so it becomes potentially a weapon, a way of acting on one's circumstances. Writing for Gorz was initially a kind of prayer, a wholly unreal activity, a striving for what Genet called 'L'impossible Nullité' (pp. 229–30). But at the same time this negative activity amounted to a positive repudiation of the world and an authentic instrument of self-determination. Gorz perceives that if it was fired by a desire to annihilate any possibilities offered by the world, the very comprehensiveness of his rejection led him to engage with every facet of human reality: to reject the world he still had to immerse himself in it (p. 234), to retain an active (if negative) relation to it. On the basis of this Gorz proceeds to identify areas in which he had in fact opted for the concrete, positive, and human over their opposites.

Toi

The first of these, which he discusses in this short third section, is his encounter with Jean-Paul Sartre in Lausanne in 1946, when the man in the flesh, 'drôlement *concret*' (p. 244), not only belied the abstract rigour of his thought, but urged Gorz not to 'mépriser le concret'. The second concerns the breakdown of Gorz's relationship with a woman he calls L. which is contrasted, by a brilliant use of cross-cutting, with a crisis point in his relationship with another woman, Kay, who is still his companion at the time of writing. In the first case, Gorz dwells obsessively on the point when L., who passionately loved and admired him but was frustrated and hurt by his elusiveness, asked him what he would feel if she slept with another man, and some time later told him she had in fact done so. Rather than attempting to understand her underlying feelings or making a serious attempt to liquidate the false elements in their relationship, Gorz had treated the issue in abstract, philosophical, and literary terms (the echoes of a similar scene between Kyo and May in Malraux's *La Condition humaine* had delighted him), failing to treat L. as a human being. When, some years later, Kay forced him to make a choice about the future of their relationship, he had reacted differently, accepting the reality of his situation and his feelings, and committing himself to Kay even though this contradicted his abstract principles regarding relationships in bourgeois society and the responsibilities of intellectuals. The material in 'Toi' is significant to Gorz because it shows that he had been capable at times of recognizing the shortcomings of his habitual stance. But a few swallows do not make a summer: these instances also confirm the potency of a 'choix originel' which severs Gorz from the world. However, as he advances in his 'prise de conscience' Gorz finds that his analysis now provides him with a new way of looking at his choice and a new sense of how it might be modified.

Je

Gorz begins the last section with a further redefinition of his 'choix', now identifying it as a 'terreur de l'identification' inspired by the way his sense of identity was originally formed. If the path of identity-formation usually involves a compromise between our inner sense of being and the image others project on to us, it depends on there being some convergence between the two sources. Gorz claims, however, that in his case the image foisted on him by his mother, with overwhelming verbal and emotional force, bore little relation to his own possibilities. Thus the ceaseless 'sommation à l'identification'—'Be this', 'Be that'—articulated in maternal discourse, made the adoption of a 'moi' a matter of total alienation, a 'chute dans le discours des autres' (p. 285) rather than accession to 'l'univers intersubjectif de la parole'. Gorz now interprets many of his 'conduites'—his tendency to mutter, his taste for slang and foreign languages, for abstraction, for opposition, for convention, his sense of kinship with the oppressed, and of course his mania for the nocturnal realm of writing—as ways of resisting maternal discourse, of denying the right of others to determine his identity: 'car écrire, c'est parler seul, en l'absence de l'Autre, et lui retirer la parole' (p. 290).

Refigured in this way, Gorz's 'choix originel' centred on 'le choix fondamental d'écrire par terreur de l'identification' is no longer consistent with the idea of an identity whose constitution could be revoked: 'Il faut donc réviser le but de ce travail. Au lieu d'écrire pour me désidentifier, pour liquider ce que je suis . . . il s'agirait d'écrire pour définir ce que je puis être' (p. 291). Gorz now realizes that the ploy of using the third person in *Le Traître* did not stem from the desire to distance himself from and potentially disown an identity he wanted to change, but was symptomatic of his inability to say 'I', his inability to find a voice amongst the chorus of Others. But if this confirms his earlier sense that to write an autobiography is necessarily to perpetuate rather than to liquidate, he has now learnt that liquidation is not the point. The 'choix' is not an infantile fixation to be extirpated root and branch: in the course of his self-analysis Gorz has come to appreciate what he now calls the 'devenir dialectique du complexe en choix', the way it evolves in relation to circumstances, acting as an 'instrument de dévoilement'. Rather than remaining fixed, the meaning of the 'choix' has itself evolved and Gorz is now inclined to see its positive aspects, stressing that an infantile attitude has become a coherent if often sterile vision of the world (pp. 292–3). In a striking image, Gorz likens the 'choix' to the sentence which provides the central core of Mallarmé's *Un coup de dés jamais n'abolira le hasard*, whose meaning is expanded, modified, and modulated by the multiple verbal accretions which develop around it. Events, he argues, have interpolated themselves into the 'choix': 'l'événe-ment glisse [les mots] dans sa phrase rudimentaire pour élargir la signification et la portée de cette phrase' (p. 293). Both the positive aspect, the 'fécondité', of Gorz's 'choix' and its drawbacks lie in its role as a 'facteur permanent de désadaptation' (p. 294). On the one hand, it insures him against any 'adaptation complaisante à l'état des choses empirique' (p. 295): it keeps him oppositional, unreconciled, critical; on the other hand, it tends to prevent him from positive commitment and effective action.

In the face of this, liquidation is neither possible nor desirable; but the notions of 'remaniement', 'reconduite', and so on, which tempt Gorz, seem implausible, given that it is hard to see how one could partly revise a 'choix' of the kind he has identified. Gorz settles instead for the view (which he defends against accusations of complacency) that, rather than liquidation or 'remaniement', his aim should be to focus on his empirical situation and to see what scope it offers for the positive dimension of his 'choix' to be marshalled: 'apprendre à se "servir" de ce qu'on est pour se dépasser' (p. 301). In this regard Gorz is heartened by the fact that the plight of the modern French intellectual is to be as objectively 'nul' as Gorz is subjectively. As in the case of his Jewishness and his espousal of French culture in the context of French defeat, there is seemingly a coincidence between Gorz's subjective predicament and his objective social and political one. In the last stages of *Le Traître* Gorz suggests that, far from being unique, he belongs to the category of the modern intellectual and writer, those who are 'incapables d'ignorer qu'ils portent en eux une fêlure définitive . . . tous des traîtres en puissance' (308). Gorz may be right about this but there is something unsatisfactory about the way *Le Traître* tends at the end to dissolve into commonplaces. The Gorz who feels he can say 'Je' at the end anticipates the Sartre of the last stages of *Les Mots*: he has seen through his past delusions but knows that he is incurable; he will carry on writing but now he knows he is just another intellectual, a man among men. Yet Gorz would probably like us to see the tone of his concluding pages as a sign of what the writing of *Le Traître* has accomplished. The tortuous complexities, the horrendous abstractions of the earlier sections were a kind of purgation and a protection against the reader. They now belong to the past, even if his complex remains in force, and Gorz places himself on the same footing as his readership, accepting that 'Ma réalité n'est pas en mon seul pouvoir; elle est aussi ce que vous me ferez' (p. 313). The elaborate stratagems by which he had sought to evade entrapment by the Other are superseded by a fraternal stance of reciprocity.

In the enthusiastic preface he wrote for *Le Traître*[38] Sartre particularly

---

[38] 'Des rats et des hommes', reprinted in the Seuil edn., 9–45.

commended the way Gorz's text acts as a 'machine à feedback' which progressively creates its author: from the 'anonyme chuchotement' of the early pages, to the fraternal 'Je' who addresses us at the end, we listen to a 'voix qui mue' (Préface, p. 15). We hear, Sartre argues, of a man who sets out to track down the vampires and parasites which seem to feed on his every action, consigning him to the fate of being totally other to himself. His victory will lie not in asserting his particularity against such falsification but in understanding how the multiple facets of his identity are dialectically related (Préface, p. 41). Through his critical self-consciousness Gorz accepts the self-dispersion entailed by the constant dialectic of particular and universal: ' moi, je suis ce va-et-vient incessant' (Préface, p. 41). But rather than simply lamenting a further loss of self Gorz succeeds, for Sartre, in the radical project of constructing, through writing, a new stance towards the question of his identity, a new subject position in his discourse: 'Longtemps nous avons écouté "La voix de son maître". A présent c'est Gorz qui parle' (Préface, p. 40).

Yet while he is clearly justified in maintaining that Gorz forges a highly original mode of analysis Sartre fails to mention existentialist concepts in the account of the methodologies (Marxist, psychological, psychoanalytical) that *Le Traître* addresses critically, and this calls for some comment since it raises the issue of Gorz's relation to Sartre himself, and, more widely, the question of existentialist autobiography. Sartre is, after all, one of Gorz's vampires, and his presence is felt throughout *Le Traître*, although when mentioned directly he is nicknamed Morel. Gorz explains this usage rather vaguely at one point in terms of the false image the public has come to attach to the philosopher's name, but it is not unreasonable to interpret it as a symptom of Gorz's desire to distance himself from the father figure (accepting that Sartre should preface the work was of course regressive in this respect). Gorz tells us that he began writing *Le Traître* in anticipation of Morel's negative judgement on the *Fondements pour une morale*, a work in which he had used his mentor's ideas but failed (or so he felt) to give them any concreteness. In its massive reliance on Sartrean concepts *Le Traître* reads as if Gorz had decided to perform a ritual—and masochistic—act of self-criticism, using the instrument Sartre had forged to unveil the false consciousness at work in the conduct of individual lives. Yet, as Sartre asserted, something does happen to Gorz through writing *Le Traître*. As he pursues and exahusts various lines of investigation, testing one method against another, discovering new aspects of his life, and adopting successive versions of his 'choix', Gorz clearly moves from self-incrimination towards self-liberation. Much of the methodological critique and revision repeats

Sartre's own revisionary work in *Questions de méthode*, and therefore remains within the enclosure of existentialist orthodoxy. Sartre had preceded Gorz in the comparative evaluation of Marxist, psychoanalytical and existentialist concepts; and *Le Traître* is indisputably the existentialist autobiography which most closely reproduces the dynamics of Sartrean biography. Yet in consistently applying the analysis to his own concrete case Gorz ultimately adapts 'Morel''s concepts to his own ends. If Gorz can say 'Je' at the end it is partly because he has moved from being the passive guinea-pig of an abstract vocabulary to being the active exponent of a critical discourse.

Even more important is the fact that Gorz's movement towards self-understanding has been achieved through the *process* of writing. As in the case of Leduc, the written 'Je'—bound to the past—progressively recedes as the writing 'Je', the autobiographical subject, moves into its place. One of the strengths of *Le Traître* is its ideological knowingness, the constant sense that the autobiographical act is a passage through ideological constructions of the self. At its weakest *Le Traître* is rebarbative, abstract, self-conscious, directionless (Gorz stresses that it is the opposite of an 'œuvre d'art'). Yet, in Gorz, abstract analysis—diagnosed as part of his 'choix', a live issue in the drama of his identity—is a passion, a 'conduite'; and writing is not only its passive vehicle but its active embodiment. By pursuing the construction and deconstruction of his identity in writing Gorz progressively comes to inhabit his own discourse, to wean himself off abstraction and distance, to remedy his fear of identification by actively *identifying himself*. In *Les Mots* Sartre will write about himself in the light of a conversion which has already taken place. If there is a conversion in *Le Traître*, it takes place, as Sartre suggested, before the reader's eyes. By keeping the painful, frustrating search for an adequate methodology constantly in view Gorz commits himself to relative abstraction but at the same time makes it impossible for past events to determine the course of the narration. Yet the effect is to produce the sense of a genuine dialectic where at each twist the analytical endeavour summons up new incidents and factors—his mother's speech for example—which have to be reckoned with. The need constantly to adjust to what is spawned in and through the act of writing leads to great stylistic energy and inventiveness on Gorz's part. The progressive movement from third to first person, from 'Il' to 'Je', is never just a mannerism, or a matter of routine, but a valid index of the movement from subordination to authority over his discourse. Switches of register (like Sartre, Gorz combines philosophical jargon with demotic idioms and even a certain raciness of tone), the extensive use of parenthetical constructions, and parentheses within parentheses (a trait he shares with Genet), allied to the consistent pace and urgency of the writing, contrive to make *Le Traître* a lively and enlivening text which admirably conveys the conjunction of two quests— the quest for a method and the quest for a self—carried out before the omnipresent gaze of the Other.

SARTRE: *LES MOTS*

Incomparably witty, ironic, and fast-moving (if monotonous at times), *Les Mots* seems to cock a snook not only at our pieties concerning families and children but at the idea that existentialist autobiography must be ponderous, self-indulgent, or top-heavy with theory. Yet Sartre's autobiography is as theoretical as his *Baudelaire* or his *Saint Genet*, though its structure and style disguise this to some degree. Philippe Lejeune has analysed the ways in which the apparent chronological ordering of *Les Mots* masks a rigorously dialectical construction.[39] Here I wish to suggest how closely the book (originally drafted in 1953 but rewritten a decade later) reflects the intellectual reorientations of *Questions de méthode* (written in the period separating the two drafts of *Les Mots*), particularly with regard to the treatment of the *milieu*, the presentation, or enactment, of the 'projet', and the perspective of conversion.[40]

As we saw earlier, *Questions de méthode* declares childhood to be 'indépassable': childhood experience furnishes the indestructible framework which will subsist in later transformations; by pegging his account to the first eleven years of his life, while writing from the standpoint of a mid-life conversion, Sartre amply confirms this view. According to *Questions de méthode*, the *milieu* does not straightforwardly determine individual existence, but provides it with an inescapable shaping context: 'l'enfant devient tel ou tel parce qu'il vit l'universel comme particulier.'[41] This perspective is borne out by the three main avatars of the milieu in *Les Mots*: the family group; the ideological conjuncture in which culture takes over the

[39] 'L'Ordre du récit dans *Les Mots* de Sartre', *Le Pacte autobiographique*, 197–244. See also Lejeune's later essay 'Les Enfances de Sartre' in *Moi aussi*, 117–63. Among the many analyses of *Les Mots* I have found the following especially useful: J. Mehlman, *A Structural Study of Autobiography*; P. J. Eakin, *Fictions in Autobiography*; B. Vercier, 'Les Mots de Sartre'; G. Idt, 'L'Autoparodie dans *Les Mots* de Sartre'; F. Gordon, 'A Parodic Strategy'.

[40] Howard Davies discusses the relationship between the two works from a different point of view in *Sartre and 'Les Temps modernes'*, 156–62, and '*Les Mots* as *Essai sur le don*'.

[41] *QM* 83.

functions of religion; the general socio-historical complexion of the period during which Sartre grew up. He will seek to show how a career ostensibly dedicated to values diametrically opposed to those of his upbringing actually reproduced those values in distorted form. But he will also demonstrate throughout that the child was not the inert plaything of impersonal forces operating from the outside; rather, the child's interaction with the milieu took the form of a dynamic process of interiorization and transformation (the *projet*) whose outcome was always hazardous and—witness the perspective from which he writes—to some degree provisional. Sartre does sometimes appear to make unequivocal assertions regarding, for example, the effects of being fatherless (pp. 18, 97), or his grandfather's off-puttingly insipid account of a literary career (p. 138), or the 'revanchiste' attitudes inspired by the loss of Alsace-Lorraine (p. 101). But in each case the stress falls less on what these *données* did *to* the child, than on what *he* did with *them*. One of the strengths of *Les Mots* is to show how individual existence is utterly permeated and inhabited by collective agencies ('une grande puissance collective m'avait pénétré', p. 210), while at the same time it is in no way wholly assimilable to them. By sticking closely and uninterruptedly to the child's perspective, to the dynamics of the *projet*, Sartre contrives to give an active role to a wide range of socio-cultural and political factors without making them simple determinants or purely background elements. This applies to the mores of an early twentieth-century bourgeois family (the subject of dozens of lightning disquisitions, quips, and asides), to the para-religious ideology of salvation through culture epitomized by Sartre's grandfather, Charles Schweitzer, and, in more localized fashion, to such topics as the impact of the cinema (pp. 102–8), and the progressive programme of the *parti radical* (pp. 197–9).

In re-setting the agenda for the existentialist biographer, *Questions de méthode* transferred the emphasis from the *choix* to the interaction between the *projet*, a contentless 'fuite et bond en avant',[42] and the *données* which it constantly transcends. Correspondingly, the emphasis in *Les Mots* falls less on the layerings or shadings of a particular 'rapport à soi' (though this is important) than on the dynamism of a *projet* which is always on the move— adjusting its line and revising its goals in the face of the inevitable deflections and upheavals engendered by changing conditions and by the inherently limited durability of any given set of existential arrangements. In his autobiography Sartre excels at conveying the 'feel' or atmosphere of the *projet* as a dynamic fusion of interiority and alterity, singular and universal.

---

[42] *QM* 129.

If learning is worn lightly—existentialist vocabulary is used sparingly, and methodological discussion is totally absent—*style* has become the principal agent of analysis.

The dominant stylistic and structural features of *Les Mots* can conveniently be linked to two important aspects of the *projet*, the first of which is its essentially mobile, dynamic, and empty character. The *projet* is always at once a reaction against and a movement towards. The remarkable speed of Sartre's delivery, the relentless analytical drive, the lack of any marked fluctuations of tempo or changes of distance and perspective, effectively convey this, as does the emphasis on phases and transitions. Lejeune's analysis helps us to see how Sartre has artificially segmented the account of his life between 6 and 11 into phases, each of which in fact draws on events that occurred at various points in the overall time-span.[43] Yet the impression of chronological unfolding and forward movement is vital, as is the sense that particular events or activities recur at various stages with renewed or altered significance. Sartre is manifestly less concerned with the factual veracity of his account, the quality of particular moments, than with its effectiveness in communicating the vectors at work within a continuum, the paradoxical mixture of constant change and virtual stasis. Each successive phase is presented as a precarious balancing-act between two disruptions. Thus the 'comédie familiale' which dominates the child's early years is shown to be a function of his initial situation as a fatherless child brought up by a young mother in her parents' household. Instead of being burdened with a monolithic paternal discourse, internalized as the voice of authority, the weightless child floats in the currents created by an unorthodox family structure. A pure reflector of adult vision, he is a 'caniche' ever willing to perform the tricks expected by its adult audience: 'il se trouve que mes gestes et paroles ont une qualité qui m'échappe et qui saute aux yeux des grandes personnes' (p. 29). But the 'comédie' can only last as long as the child remains oblivious to the fact that he is playing a part. Recognition of this precipitates a sense of vacancy and the need to find a new *raison d'être*.

Les Mots is punctuated by such transitional moments and *passages à vide*. When reading provides the child with a source of identity, regalvanizing him with a renewed sense of purpose, the effect is initially (or partially) to give a new lease of life to the 'comédie familiale'. As an 'avid little reader' the boy can resume his play-acting in the context of a 'comédie de la culture' (p. 63), nestling 'inside the whale' of established cultural space: 'jusque dans

---

[43] See the table in *Le Pacte autobiographique*, 210.

la solitude j'étais en représentation' (p. 62). But once again the child's consciousness of its imposture spoils the show with the result that, in order to provide shelter against the invasion of contingency in various forms (pp. 72–95), reading has to undergo a sea-change. Instead of being a public performance, serving to confirm the way the adults see the child, reading comes to provide the raw material for scenarios played out in the child's imagination. Drawing first on the stories of Maurice Bouchor, then on the stoic heroism of Verne's *Michel Strogoff* who places himself at the service of the Tsar, before moving on to find sustenance from a less subservient, more voluntarist model, Zévaco's republican hero Pardaillan, the child tries out different forms of imaginary succour: 'tout se passa dans ma tête; enfant imaginaire, je me défendis par l'imagination' (p. 97). These 'exercices spirituels' (the phrase had been used in a similar context by Genet) received a further stimulus from the jerky excitement of early cinema whose live musical accompaniment could be reproduced at home by his mother's renditions of the overture to *Fingal's Cave* at the piano (p. 107). In imaginary deeds of derring-do the child created an alternative role to the one he had been allocated in the 'comédie familiale'.

Two observations can be made here in passing. First, the imaginary heroics Sartre is dealing with at this juncture no doubt feature in the development of most children. By giving this unexceptional trait (and others like it) such a specific place in the account of his past Sartre amplifies his general case that nothing a child does is innocent (though the relative absence of sexuality makes his attack on childhood far milder than Freud's) and underlines the consistent theoretical 'emplotment' which characterizes *Les Mots*. Second, though globally an attack on his childhood and on the 'inauthenticity' of his vocation as a writer, *Les Mots* is notably charitable towards the child's anxious quest for solutions (though, as we shall see later, this may be hard to distinguish from Sartre's tendency to identify with the mobility of the *projet* itself). This is particularly noticeable where the child adopts a private activity. For example, when Sartre has exhausted the vein of imaginary heroics he had discovered in reading (when, that is, it ceases to offer him a remedy against the sense of vacancy), he finds another activity which subsumes and extends it, namely writing. Initially, this is a private activity—a clandestine solution that the child adopts for itself (p. 131). By 'going public', however, egged on by the plaudits of his mother and her friends (p. 131), the child makes writing 'une singerie de plus'. And from this point we can follow the tortuous path by which writing emerges, through a series of phases and transitions, as the principal arena of Sartre's *projet*. His grandfather's oversubtle attempt to put him off a writer's career, by commending it as a life of noble obscurity and drudgery, backfires both because the fatherless child at this stage heeds the voice of quasi-paternal authority, and because the drab, but cosy and pedestrian, future appeals to the child's timidity. Then there is the phase when the figure of the writer is credited with the heroic status of a Strogoff or a Pardaillan, followed by the alternative image, generated dialectically by logical inconsistencies in the heroic model, of the 'écrivain-martyr'. This last image will owe its power, the all-but-definitive grip it will take on Sartre's self-imaginings, to its complicity with the whole package of ideological assumptions personified by Charles Schweitzer. But if Sartre's writerly vocation ends up freighted with the ideological baggage of his grandfather's generation, it is none the less also something he makes for himself, incorporating other elements of his formation: for example, the idealist preference for words over things fostered by the prominence of books among his early surroundings; or the child's histrionic proclivities (posterity takes over the role of the audience in the 'comédie familiale', p. 173). As a function of the *projet*, writing is a provisional, mobile solution to existential problems: the need to 'be someone', the fear of the openness of existence. By associating it with such terms as 'folie' and 'délire', Sartre confers a Romantic authenticity on the elaborate mythology the child builds around his feverish scribbling. Paradoxically, it is when the child stops writing, undergoes belated socialization at school, and forgets about its problems (p. 193), that writing hardens into a role, an habitual source of self-definition. The inherent mobility of the *projet* itself, evinced in phases, transitions, reactivations of earlier phases, and ultimately in the conversion which provides Sartre's narrative vantage-point, is always maintained.

The second aspect of the *projet* which must be considered is the level of consciousness at which it is operative. Are we to think of the child consciously making choices, adopting roles, trying out new manœuvres? Clearly not. The *projet* belongs to the twilight world of 'non-thetic' consciousness, epitomized especially in 'mauvaise foi' where the subject seeks to be oblivious to its own machinations, but always retains at least vestigial awareness of what he or she is up to. Sartre quite often draws attention to the issue by asking at various points to what extent he was aware of himself, or deluding himself: 'Mais jusqu'à quel point croyais-je à mon délire? C'est la question fondamentale et pourtant je n'en décide pas' (p. 61). In the 'comédie familiale' phase he describes how on entering his grandfather's study he would make straight for the bookshelves. Was he sincere?, Sartre asks. 'Sincèrement? Qu'est-ce que cela veut dire? Comment pourrais-je fixer—après tant d'années, surtout—l'insaisissable et mouvante

frontière qui sépare la possession du cabotinage?' (p. 61, see also p. 174).
Whatever the answer to such questions, there is no doubt that the process
Sartre seeks to reconstruct took place outside the realm of conscious verbal
articulation. As a result, Sartre employs a range of stylistic devices designed
to render a state of semi-awareness, on the borderline between consciousness of self and consciousness of others, to reconstruct the movements
rather than the depths of the child's mental world. The method is
consistently metaphorical and thus quite blatantly artificial; the impression
is not that of being made privy to the child's thoughts but of being presented
with the, necessarily conjectural, translation of states of being into words.
Three characteristic tendencies may be identified. First, Sartre consistently
tends to concretize, dramatize, and narrativize:

[Les adultes] laissaient derrière eux leur regard, mêlé à la lumière; je courais, je
sautais à travers ce regard qui me conservait ma nature de petit-fils modèle, qui
continuait à m'offrir mes jouets et l'univers. Dans mon joli bocal, dans mon âme,
mes pensées tournaient, chacun pouvait suivre leur manège: pas un coin d'ombre.
Pourtant, sans mots, sans forme ni consistance, diluée dans cette innocente
transparence, une transparente certitude gâchait tout: j'étais un imposteur (p. 72).

Throughout *Les Mots* we find passages such as this: often vivid, sometimes
too rapid, elusive, or abstract to make an initial impact, they generally tax
the reader with the task of retranslating concrete and visual movements into
psychological ones. Second, Sartre makes extensive use of leitmotifs and
extended metaphors. Examples of the former would be the recurrent
comparison of the child with a pet dog, 'à défaut d'enfant qu'on prenne un
caniche' (p. 28), 'Je suis un chien: je bâille, les larmes roulent, je les sens
rouler' (p. 81); the motif of weightlessness, familiar to readers of Sartre's
plays; the motifs of flight and 'tournoiement': 'Je fuyais, des forces
extérieures ont modelé ma fuite et m'ont fait' (p. 208); and that of the
mandat. The most prominent extended metaphors are probably those
involving M. Simmonot; the notion of being a 'voyageur clandestin' on the
train to Dijon; and the town of Aurillac as a figure of provincial obscurity.
Each of these, whether or not it originated in a real event, is represented as
having been forged, at least fleetingly, in the child's self-imagining. This
then licenses its metaphorical extension in the text to convey less conscious
moves and counter-moves. While M. Simmonot and the catch-phrase 'il y a
quelqu'un qui manque ici, c'est . . .' (p. 79 and *passim*) come to figure the
desirable condition of being necessary rather than contingent, the 'train'
scenario, together with the 'mandat' motif which recurs a dozen times or so,
conveys the sense of an imperative need to justify one's existence, to imagine

that an urgent mission depends on us for its successful execution. The third device is the restaging of fantasies through the construction of imaginary sketches and dialogues. Sartre seldom dramatizes directly a particular remembered moment (the thematics of memory play scarcely any part in *Les Mots*); the mode is largely iterative rather than singulative: we are not in real time but in the imaginary time of the *projet*. Yet, this distancing serves to legitimate the stylization of states of consciousness, and in achieving this Sartre draws heavily on the repertoire of modern fiction and, naturally, on his own practices as a novelist and playwright. Examples are numerous, particularly in 'Lire' (the second half of *Les Mots*), where each of the successive versions of a literary vocation entertained by the child generates its particular fantasies—for example, the imaginary encounter between Pardaillan and Cervantes (p. 147), the hilarious dialogue with the Holy Spirit (p. 157), or the touching curriculum vitae of the modest 'chantre d'Aurillac' with its alternative endings. In all these cases the focus is on the child's attempt to deal, at a fantasy level, with contradictions in its imaginary future.

All the devices I have outlined in the last few paragraphs serve to render the atmosphere of the *projet*. A further aspect must now be considered. If childhood according to *Questions de méthode* is 'indépassable', it is because we can never quite straighten out the 'déviations originelles' instituted by our initial dealings with the world of things and of others: these deviations become our character. But at the same time the *projet*, a constant dynamic orientation towards changing goals, is always potentially 'dépassement': we are not only our character, we can think and act against 'ourselves'; we can change even if we cannot liquidate. *Les Mots* clearly reflects this way of seeing things:

De là vint cet idéalisme dont j'ai mis trente ans à me défaire (p. 46)

cet aveuglement lucide dont j'ai souffert trente ans (p. 210)

depuis dix ans à peu près je suis un homme qui s'éveille (p. 212)

j'ai désinvesti mais je n'ai pas défroqué (p. 212)

ce vieux bâtiment ruineux, mon imposture, c'est aussi mon caractère: on se défait d'une névrose, on ne se guérit pas de soi (p. 213)

The last pages portray a Sartre who has seen through the ruses of his past self, who has achieved self-understanding, who has eventually reached the end of the long path to atheism, who has unmasked 'l'illusion rétrospective' (p. 212), who now knows who he is because he can see who he had taken himself for. This is, of course, the Sartre who has been writing all along, who has dropped hints that the man whose formation he reconstructs is no longer quite himself, who has adopted the consistently unsentimental, ironic tone which makes *Les Mots* so amusing to read. This, moreover, is the Sartre who, by employing a string of colourful phrases to qualify the child's machinations, consistently appears to underline the division between past and present identities. The insistent strategies of self-designation in *Les Mots* call for inspection.

'La petite merveille' (p. 65), 'l'imposteur' (p. 73), 'Moi, l'enfant prophétique, la jeune Pythonisse, l'Éliacin des Belles-Lettres' (p. 67), 'le petit comédien hagard' (p. 81), 'enfant gâté, don providentiel' (p. 84), 'voyageur clandestin' (p. 95), 'fils de personne' (p. 97), 'enfant imaginaire' (p. 97). Repeatedly labelling himself in this quick-fire and provisional way, Sartre points in the first place to the roles the child plays in the dramaturgy of its self-fashioning. The 'je' is subordinated to these epithets, as the syntax often underlines: 'Idolâtré par tous, débouté de chacun, j'étais un laissé-pour-compte' (p. 95), 'vermine stupéfaite, sans foi, sans loi, sans raison ni fin, je m'évadais dans la comédie familiale' (p. 80). The role comes first, 'je' simply designates a stage, a place of passage, the locus of a process: 'J'étais une ribaude' (p. 147), 'Je devins une dictature militaire' (p. 148). Sartre enjoys denying himself any privileges, treating himself as a 'Labadens', demystifying and exorcising the past in the accents of an unsparing 'règlement de comptes', directed, through the child, at the deluded champion of 'littérature engagée' who reigned for thirty years. Yet the moral of the tale is not that Sartre has at last acceded in mid-life to a true identity by sloughing off the coils adopted in childhood. The revelation which enables the perspective adopted in *Les Mots* is not of this kind but involves, rather, the recognition that one is 'tout un homme', worth no more nor less than 'n'importe qui' (pp. 60, 214). More important, perhaps, than the democratic, anti-élitist flavour of this self-appraisal, is the way it can help us see Sartre's labelling as a strategy which serves to present the child as 'n'importe qui'. The recurrent self-designations in *Les Mots* are not really derogatory, nor do they simply represent the child as a victim. In fact, Sartre's insistent use of the device tends to underline the child's resourcefulness. 'Héros, je luttais contre les tyrannies; démiurge, je me fis tyran moi-même' (p. 126), 'Parsifal tragique' (p. 152), 'le petit prétendant calamiteux' (p. 207): these are the cast-offs of the quick-change artist ('je ne cessai de faire peau neuve', p. 203), the provisional garb of an incorrigible traitor. Ultimately, of course, one of the labels sticks and the child will adhere to the ethos of the generous writer, dedicated to the progress of humanity; he will cast himself, for thirty years, in the role of 'Jean-Paul

Sartre', a man whose pen is his sword, just as his grandfather had taken himself for Victor Hugo. But underneath the labels, even this last one, there is actually nothing, or only a human being like any other—'Je n'étais presque rien, tout au plus une activité sans contenu' (p. 130), 'n'importe qui'; underneath there is only the pure, treacherous dynamics of a *projet*. Across the thirty-year gap of his adult career, the author of *Les Mots* does not simply denounce his childhood inauthenticity but in fact identifies with the child, at least in the extent to which he finds, in the dynamics of his childhood, the dynamism and mobility of the *projet* itself.

Another way of putting this would be to say that, in so far as *Les Mots* reconstructs a *projet*, a 'fuite et bond en avant',[44] a constant 'dépassement'— 'Faute de m'aimer assez, j'ai fui en avant' (p. 200)—it constitutes a portrait of Sartre as he likes to see himself: a perennial traitor ('Je devins traître et je le suis resté', p. 199), willing to think against himself, and who never bears grudges because he is always ready to repudiate his past; a man without a super-ego, addicted to height (p. 54) and velocity—that of speedboats, which scarcely touch water (p. 194)[45]—and that of words. *Les Mots* presents an insistent parallel between three things: the central concept Sartre uses to understand his past (the *projet*); the dynamics of his childhood; and the essential abiding characteristics common to child and adult alike. In this light the belief in the writer's mission is an aberration, a long detour. Sartre can liken himself to 'Swann guéri de son amour' (p. 139), victim of a misunderstanding, an 'aveuglement lucide' (p. 210), which in his case lasted for thirty years. The compelling need to write every day—as if it mattered— may be a relic of the fossilized 'caractère' he can now see through though not cast off; but the disposition to place words above things, to see the world through a verbal screen, which, Sartre realizes, helped to place him in thrall to the idealism he thought he had always combated, also owes its survival to the fact that it predates and transcends the ends it was made to serve in the provisional construction of a 'justified' identity. If the addiction to words can be seen as part of the inauthentic 'baggage' of idealism, the mobility of language, the forward motion and constant 'dérapage' of writing can be associated with the pure momentum of the *projet*.

As I have implied, this raises an awkward question. How can we tell the dancer from the dance? Sartre ends up portraying himself rather as if he were the personification of the *projet* itself: a mobile dynamism, a pure

---

[44] 'Fuite et bond en avant, refus et réalisation tout ensemble, le projet retient et dévoile la réalité dépassée, refusée par le mouvement même qui le dépasse', *QM* 129.

[45] Referring to a well-known psychological test, Sartre recalls (p. 194) that when asked to choose an image representing speed he opted for the speedboat.

energy. Any qualities he displays are accidental, except those which attest
the fact that he is, precisely, a 'man without qualities'. It seems almost as if
the neo-existentialist concepts derived from Sartre's biographical works,
and from *Questions de méthode*, which are deployed consistently if tacitly in
Les Mots, have ultimately served less as the speculative instruments of a new
kind of autobiography than as properties in the rather more traditional *mise
en scène* of a preferred self-image. Certainly the close fusion between subject
and method, and between method and style, has the paradoxical effect,
given the ostensibly ironic and critical relation to conventional autobiography which runs through *Les Mots* (in the brilliant critique of the 'illusion
rétrospective' and so on), of offering the reader many of the staple pleasures
of the genre without their usual drawbacks. For example, in his emphasis on
phases and transitions Sartre tends to heighten rather than play down the
logical cohesion and orderliness of his narrative, and in his treatment of
causalities he quite frequently makes, with brio, resonant and unqualified
pronouncements such as: 'Ainsi s'est forgé mon destin, au numéro un de la
rue Le Goff' (p. 138), which would not seem out of place in an
autobiography based on very traditional assumptions. But, in the first place,
it is not the events of a life which are being given satisfying narrative shape;
rather, the cohesiveness and linear logic pertain to the necessarily fictional
reconstruction of the *projet*, which was itself already a swathe cut through
the jungle, a path made by the child in the attempt to make sense—and give
shape—to its experiences. And therefore, in the second place, if Sartre's
obiter dicta (already ironic in their mock-heroic pomposity) refer to an
identity constituted in the passage of time, it is in a context where that
identity (or series of identities) is in fact constantly transcended by the
projet, which produces concretizations of various kinds, mainly for external
consumption. Sartre is always also elsewhere.

Since its publication in 1963, *Les Mots* has been regarded as a masterpiece
of modern autobiography and a cornerstone of Sartre's work. Not the least
of its attractions is the way it both epitomizes and subtly marks itself off
from the group of texts we have classified as existentialist autobiographies.
Despite the dearth of explicitly philosophical reflection, *Les Mots* is unlikely
to prompt readers to wonder, as they may in the case of Simone de Beauvoir,
whether or not the philosopher's theorizations are operational in this
instance; nor are they likely to complain, as with regard to Gorz, that
abstractions have monopolized the relation to the past. To some degree
Sartre is closer to Genet and Leduc, in that he makes us conscious first of his
style, and only secondarily of the intellectual framework which sustains it,
though in Sartre's case we may, as I have suggested, go on to find just as

close a fit between style and ideas as in the other cases. And indeed, the more we look, the more clearly we see that Sartre concedes nothing to Gorz as regards the philosophical character of his text. What Sartre achieved in *Les Mots* is a remarkable fusion of stylistic virtuosity and philosophical or dialectical order.

In this he develops and brings to fruition tendencies well to the fore in the existentialist autobiographies which already bore his stamp, texts where, on the whole, the existentialist traits were closely interwoven with prominent stylistic features. If, on the basis of this, we sought to identify the relation to ideology characteristic of existentialist autobiography, we might conclude that it was a good deal less restrictive than could have been expected. Existentialist concepts and themes—*choix, projet, roles, conversion,* etc.— seem not so much to provide the wherewithal for the legitimation of a fixed view of the subject as to stimulate the enactment, through writing, of the individual's mobile relationship to his or her past and present self-images. The dynamic aspect of existentialism, the commitment to self-transformation rather than self-recapitulation, offsets the potential limitations of a very specific and limited view of human beings and encourages stylistic rather than abstract and analytical energies. At the same time, limitations dictated by ideological constraint *are* clearly perceptible in these autobiographies, not least in a symptomatically claustrophobic, self-enclosed atmosphere which is by no means simply thematic. This simply reflects the predominance, in existentialist autobiography, of a particular kind of coherence, manifested not in narrative 'enchaînement' but in the presentation of the subject's mental world and the kinds of transaction in which he or she engages. The powerful impression of coherence and unity, reflecting a clear sense of what is permanent and what is not, may strike the reader as a weakness—to the extent that it stems from the exclusion of other ways of relating to one's past—or as a strength—to the extent that it gives indisputable 'bite' and intellectual authority not only to individual works such as *Les Mots* but to the group as a whole. A certain narrowness of scope does undoubtedly characterize existentialist autobiography: a further symptom is the fact that, with possible exceptions in Genet and Leduc, incidents tend to be domesticated rather than wild (to use our earlier terminology), serving the local interests of the text as it evolves, rather than as enigmatic and resistant centres of meaning. Yet reservations such as this are scarcely to the point. What we do find, from *Journal du Voleur* to *Les Mots*, is a family of autobiographies, each member of which is strengthened by the nourishment it draws from a consistent ideological source, a shared picture of human reality.

8

Michel Leiris: Styles of Self-Writing in *La Règle du jeu*

Michel Leiris is the consummate autobiographer, the genre's exemplary saint and martyr whose life was inextricably bound up with its written reflection. Autobiography is writing: Leiris brings this truism to life, making his reader constantly aware of the present act of textual construction, the engagement with materials—words, distant memories, current preoccupations, the heteroclite relics and remnants of one's passage through time—in which connections must be established, and out of which something must be made. Autobiography is concerned with otherness: Leiris constantly draws attention to the strange materiality of words, the manifold receptacles in which memories come to lodge, the discrete and unpredictable locales in which traces of selfhood may be identified, the inherent open-endedness of the quest for identity; in so doing he makes autobiography a process that spawns self-estrangement as much as self-retrieval. What is more, autobiographical desire, in Leiris, is diagnosed as a desire to *become* other. For all his cerebral self-consciousness, he does not present himself as a philosopher of autobiography. Always ready to double back, to comment on his every move, to chide himself for his illusions or to announce the adoption of a new protocol, Leiris never generalizes; if he legislates it is only for himself. Nor should he be seen as a writer 'in search of his true identity', if what we have in mind are difficulties of access, self-knowledge, authentic capture, and so on. The attainment of a greater degree of self-awareness is certainly one of his goals but this is always part of a more ambitious project of self-construction, self-confrontation, and self-transformation. Leiris is neither an epistemologist who asks 'how can I know myself?' nor a moralist who asks 'how can I be a better person?' We should see him perhaps as a kind of hybrid who might be said to ask: how can I progress in what I know about myself to a point where this will, *ipso facto*, produce a new praxis? That, however, is only one side of the story, for Leiris is also an expert diagnostician of his less conscious motives, well able to see that if the ceaseless mobility of writing hardly provides a propitious arena for the definitive showdown, the tauromachic moment of truth he seeks with himself, it also might be the case that this imagined scenario of 'once and for all' self-confrontation masks a desire for the void, and for death—a drive against which the ceaseless and frustrating vectors of writing might, precisely, be the life-preserving antidote.

Leiris's hyper-lucidity is well to the fore in the features of his work I have chosen to emphasize in this chapter: the changing frames and devices he invented in response to the bifurcations and fluctuations of autobiographical desire, and the mixture of continuity and change, stasis and mobility, in his practice of autobiography. The continuity is partly congenital—the Leiris who completes *Frêle bruit* in 1976 is in many respects the same Leiris who embarked on *Biffures* in 1940—and hence it is partly thematic. Death, theatre, opera, sex, poetry, the desire for commitment, the tendency to keep the world at a distance: such is the eternal stuff of Leiris's saga. But the presence of change and innovation is real. It is borne out by the differences between Leiris's two principal works of autobiography, *L'Age d'homme* and *La Règle du jeu*, and most tellingly by the deviations and transformations his writing undergoes from chapter to chapter and from volume to volume of his tetralogy.[1]

Of course *La Règle* has much in common with *L'Age d'homme*: once more Leiris resists any temptation to plunge directly into his past and bases his work on a strict *modus operandi* involving exacting ground rules and constraints. Yet *La Règle* seems the more open text. *L'Age d'homme* is dominated by closure, the desire to corral, constrain, and liquidate the material it treats. The voice is laconic, the stance quasi-scientific, the focus narrowed to the realm of sexuality, and the compass restricted to the promptings of a single stimulus, Cranach's *Judith and Lucretia*; demythologization, demystification, liberation from the grip of the past are the principal goals.[2] By contrast, *La Règle*, imagined from the start as a work in more than one volume, and conceived in vague terms as a quest, lacks a fixed agenda. In *Biffures*, which Leiris embarked on in 1940, language ('des "faits de langage"') initially replaces sexuality as the main field of investigation. This can be seen as a further gesture of demystification, since Leiris now addresses the core of his most deep-seated illusions and obsessions. Yet the

---

[1] References to the 4 vols. of *La Règle du jeu* will be incorporated in the text. The following abbreviations are used: *Biffures* (1948): *Bi*; *Fourbis* (1955): *Fo*; *Fibrilles* (1966): *Fi*; *Frêle Bruit* (1976): *FB*.

[2] See Ch. 4 (above) for a discussion of *L'Age d'homme*. For a detailed treatment of the contrast with *La Règle du jeu* see R. Simon, *Orphée médusé*.

move towards language is also one which favours open-endedness. Moreover, in place of catharsis and liquidation, the aim is now to draw up a hypothetical *règle du jeu* which would establish common ground between the author's obsession with writing and his desire to live coherently. But the *règle du jeu* is a distant horizon, something for the long term which makes it necessary to find short-term purposes and stratagems. Thus *La Règle* proceeds in fits and starts as Leiris explores and exhausts different aims and methods, creating a generative dialectic of method and execution quite different from *L'Age d'homme* where the inevitable deviations from avowed aims gave rise to a sense of failure and frustration.

A change of working method is significant here. As he indicates from time to time (see especially *Bi* 274–95), and as Catherine Maubon has demonstrated in *Michel Leiris au travail*, her invaluable study of some of the manuscripts of *Fourbis*, Leiris's basic *instrument de travail* in writing *La Règle* is the card-index or *fichier*. The starting-point for each chapter is a finite series of *fiches* drawn up, with reference to a notional theme or heading, after a trawl through the journal or scrap book he keeps day by day.[3] Although additional material may be added to the *fiches* as he goes along, composition consists essentially in mobilizing the latent associative energies present in static and laconic form on the *fiches*.[4] The *fiche* asserts, drily as it were, a basic connection between a memory (incident, word, anecdote) and a theme; writing for Leiris consists in the construction of a path which not only develops the initial association between *fiche* and theme, but between one *fiche* and others considered to belong to the same constellation. The challenge is to maximize the resonances and ramifications of each notation, to link it to as many other things as possible. This procedure reflects two recognitions: first, that neither the event itself, nor the theme to which it is connected, can be investigated directly or known 'in itself', but only by the indefinite pursuit of associations; secondly, that what is registered in journal or *fichier* is no more than a nucleus whose potential will not be realized if it is allowed to languish there.[5] As recorded on *fiches*, Leiris's experiences have become immobilized: it is for the act of writing to revivify them in an open-ended process of thematic generation. But if the

---

[3] After Leiris's death in Dec. 1990 it was announced that his journal was being prepared for publication by Jean Jamin.

[4] 'La force de la fiche telle que seul le narrateur est en mesure de la mobiliser au présent de l'écriture devient alors proportionnelle à l'extension de son champ d'influences, à la diversité de ses ramifications', Maubon, *Michel Leiris au travail*, 26.

[5] In *Fo* 138 Leiris notes that he has collected materials 'comme on conserve des objets témoins . . . sans trop savoir ce dont elles viendraient témoigner et quelle serait en fait leur face privilégiée'.

method remains broadly the same throughout *La Règle* its mode of
application and therefore its ultimate significance can vary radically.

At first, as Leiris explains in the last chapter of *Biffures*, the exclusive
focus was to be on language and notably on a category of linguistic event
which has a Freudian ring: 'méprises, erreurs . . . quant à la texture même
ou quant au sens d'un vocable . . . accidents de langage' (*Bi* 277). Named
bifurs, on account of their disruptive quality, their tendency to mark mental
disruptions and slippages, these linguistic phenomena, remembered from
childhood, were, notes Leiris (clearly alluding to the first four chapters of
Biffures), at first carefully inventoried and categorized in a relatively static
way. Dissatisfied with this, he decided not only to widen his definition of
bifurs to encompass any kind of event which had a similar quality (i.e.
anecdotes and incidents, not just words), but also to focus less on the '*bifurs*'
themselves than on the interconnections he could establish between them:

Je laissai de plus en plus s'aiguiller . . . mon attention, non point tant sur ces
expériences privilégiées que je me proposais d'analyser, que sur les ramifications
diverses qui pouvaient s'y brancher, voies de parcours dans lesquelles il ne tenait
qu'à moi de me lancer et dont les recoupements multiples devaient finir par les
tresser en une sorte de réseau semblable à ceux qui mettent en communication
toutes les régions distinctes composant un pays. Nœuds de faits, de sentiments, de
notions se groupant autour d'une expérience colorée plus vivement que les autres et
jouant le rôle d'un signe ou d'une illustration assez frappante pour me servir de
repère, tels furent bientôt les 'bifurs', ma démarche tendant d'autre part à
substituer aux exposés statiques, faits après coup, quelque chose de plus mouvant,
de plus abandonné, qui serait en soi-même une suite de bifurcations ou de 'bifurs'
au lieu d'être seulement la description de ce à quoi, pour commencer, j'avais donné
ce nom. Le gros de mon travail finit donc par consister moins en la découverte, en
l'invention, puis en l'examen de ces nœuds qu'en une méditation zigzaguant au fil de
l'écriture et, 'bifur' après 'bifur', cheminant de thème en thème (ces derniers
ordonnés peu à peu en faisceaux plus ou moins séparés mais juxtaposés en chapitres
constituant, dans leur enchaînement, comme autant d'épisodes successifs d'une
capricieuse course au clocher qu'il me faudrait mener à travers haies, ruisseaux,
terres labourées et autres accidents sur un terrain des plus irréguliers) (*Bi* 281–2).

Leiris points here to the fluid, improvisatory quality of his autobiographical
writing in *La Règle*, and to one of its principal constituents, the 'méditation
zigzaguant au fil de l'écriture', the insistent voice of the present narrator in
the act of writing. And this in a passage where, at the end of the first volume,
he reviews a series of shifts of emphasis and tactic in his autobiographical
stance. But he also goes on, in characteristic style, to bemoan the fact that he
has not achieved his goal of finding out more about who he is and what he

wants. His book has taken on substance but conferred little on its author. The 'plaisir d'avare à entasser' (*Bi* 286): the construction of an artefact, a world in miniature, a network of convergent threads, has all but eclipsed the commitment to tap and channel the disruptive, divergent energy to be derived from the crossing of wires; it has jeopardized the discovery of 'bifurcations décisives' which would help Leiris break out of his self-enclosed mental world—for the ultimate meaning of the elusive *règle* is that it should enable him to reconcile writing and living, the inner life of the poet and the outer life of the citizen. Tempted to abandon his project, Leiris goes on to explain why to do so would simply be to capitulate to the sense of isolation, failure, and absence which prompts him to write. Only by persevering in an activity which often seems diametrically opposed to his goal, constantly trying out new tactics designed to circumvent the contradictions to which this gives rise, can he hope to cling to his aspirations: 'je ne puis me résoudre à me taire et j'opte pour une solution qui est l'absolu contre-pied . . . : parler à tort et à travers, ce qui doit me permettre en tout cas de rompre le cercle enchanté dans lequel m'ont enfermé la raison raisonnante, le discours discoureur, l'écriture écrivante . . .' (*Bi* 294).

'Parler à tort et à travers': the phrase hardly does justice to the concerted rigour and stylistic brio of Leiris's writing, but it does convey something of its free-floating adaptability as well as its willingness to transgress established boundaries, its unpredictability, characteristics much in evidence as Leiris continues, by pursuing a chain of associations running right the way through it, to end his chapter—and *Biffures* as a whole—in less sombre tones. The motif of an object intensely desired but impossible to find—a musical instrument that would be half-drum, half-trumpet, a postcard that would also be a gramophone record—comes at the end to figure the impossible desire for plenitude, the search for an antidote to 'le trou de ce qui nous manque', which animates all Leiris's writing. 'Parvenir à obturer ce trou (ou supprimer un vide)', Leiris asks, 'n'est-ce pas, traduit en négatif, ce que j'entends quand je parle de découvrir un objet, c'est-à-dire de trouver un plein, une sorte de pulpe vitale ou de condensé de saveur?' (*Bi* 294–5). Only the elusive 'fureur' of poetic writing, which for the surrealist in Leiris reconciles contradictions in the 'fulgurance' of a 'point suprême', could be an adequate substitute for the object which would fill this primal hole or lack. Yet Leiris also retains from his surrealist past a feeling that poetry ought not to represent the victory of the imaginary over the real, but a fusion in which the real is truly apprehended by the imagination. And so, needing to continue writing, 'aller de l'avant', it is, by virtue of a further substitution, with memories of a real place, London, 'ville au nom trop ombreux, et où convergent trop de contraires pour n'être pas mythologique' (*Bi* 300), and by a contrast with the more transcendental glories of Rome, that Leiris moves towards a provisional terminus for his autobiographical journey. At the end of *Biffures* Leiris's images of London, centred on the convivial but melancholy strains of barrel-organs, are exhumed, as he puts it (*Bi* 300), from the *fichier* to which they were once consigned, at a point where they can serve as emblems of the variegated reality and momentary intensities for which his writing is ever in mourning.

Leiris's mode of autobiographical writing does not readily lend itself to thematic treatment unless one theme is adopted as the key to all the others. One could take a number of themes and motifs as starting-points—death, theatricality, desire—but the substitutions and imbrications to be traced would soon involve all the other terms one might have started with. In any case it is the way Leiris puts his changing philosophies of composition into practice which really counts: the variations in his writing game, the 'méditation zigzaguant au fil de la plume', the changes rung within an overall continuity. Accordingly, it is the evolution of Leiris's writing in *La Règle du jeu* which must now be considered.

L'ÉCRITURE TRESSÉE

Leiris's predilection for small things—miniatures, models, toys, ephemera, stray details, 'choses minimes'—can be identified in every aspect of his work. In his intellectual genealogy we can link it especially to Proust, Freud, and Roussel,[6] and to various aspects of the surrealist movement in which he participated. Ethnology (Leiris's profession) is also relevant here, since its methods involve the accumulation and classification of a multiplicity of discrete and often minimal data.[7] But to understand the link between small things and Leirisian subjectivity we must look initially at the linguistic domain. What attracted Leiris in the surrealist celebration of language was not so much the marvellous vistas opened up by a liberated discourse, or the intoxications of the 'stupéfiante image', but the remarkable prosperity

---

[6] Leiris's writings on Roussel are collected in his *Roussel l'ingénu*. For a thought-provoking meditation on miniaturization and the appeal of small things see S. Stewart, *On Longing*.

[7] In 'Michel Leiris, le ficheur fiché' Catherine Maubon offers a fascinating account of the ways in which Leiris's ethnological training (and, specifically, the method of using *fiches* stipulated by Mauss) is perpetuated and subverted in his autobiographical writings. See also James Clifford, 'On Ethnographic Surrealism' in *The Predicament of Culture*, 117–51.

surrealist practices seemed to bestow on the substance of individual words. The various kinds of word-chemistry for which Leiris became notorious[8] tend to make the word a microcosm within whose folds a larger reality is enclosed: to explore a word is to discover a world. In his earliest autobiographical writing (for example, the 'novel' *Aurora*) and also in the initial chapters of *La Règle*, the word becomes the paradigm of the autobiographer's materials: minor incidents, memories, objects, snippets of information take on the properties of words—to be explored, interrogated, forced to surrender their secrets.

Some ambiguity surrounds, however, the way the singular word (or memory) is regarded: is it an end in itself, or is it part of a wider network of relationships, so that its virtues reside not in itself but in its combinatory power? In practice, particularly after *L'Age d'homme*, Leiris's autobiographical writing consists largely in the construction of networks, and in a constant transit from one small item to the next, along paths opened by the most subtle threads of association, often prompted by language itself. Yet a powerful pull in another direction is often registered, a desire to find a single all-encompassing event, object, or formulation whose discovery would transform his existence. If Leiris will shy away from such a desire, identifying in it the dangerous allure of death, the petrifying stare of Medusa which he discerns in all attempts to arrest time and short-circuit the mobility of meaning, its attraction will none the less act as a criterion by which the alternative path—the creation of networks—is judged to be hopelessly unsatisfactory. Leiris's self-exploration is always in part an extension of his surrealist nominalism, a quest for an intensity experienced within the act of writing itself, within the *fureur* of poetry. Hence his abiding sense that to weave together the remnants of his past, to construct networks of association out of his memories, is to avoid real confrontation with his psychic reality and particularly, notwithstanding the inspiration his methods derive from psychoanalysis, to avoid engaging with the reality of unconscious desire. To write in the way he does, Leiris recognizes in moments of pessimism, may be to pursue an endless lateral quest which manifests and recycles the psychic matter he needs to deal with, without

---

[8] See especially the celebrated 'Glossaire j'y serre mes gloses' in *Mots sans mémoire*. On the relationship between Leiris's surrealist wordplay and his autobiographical project see P. Lejeune, *Lire Leiris*, ch. 4, and *Le Pacte autobiographique*, 245–310 (further page references to these works will be cited in the text). In addition to the works by Lejeune, Maubon, Mehlman, and Hand referred to in these footnotes I have found the following particularly useful on *La Règle du jeu*: J. Sturrock, 'The Autobiographer Astray'; J.-B. Pontalis, 'Michel Leiris ou la psychanalyse sans fin'; M. Blanchot, 'Combat avec l'ange'; M. Nadeau, *Michel Leiris ou la quadrature du cercle*; P. Chappuis, *Michel Leiris*; M. Beaujour, *Miroirs d'encre*.

enabling him to confront it, and it thus keeps him sequestered from the reality he would like to make contact with.

Philippe Lejeune has emphasized the tendency to self-protection, denial, and resistance which, in a psychoanalytical perspective, characterizes Leiris's strategies as an autobiographer. The creation of associative networks, which Lejeune (drawing on one of Leiris's images) labels 'écriture tressée', is seen as '[une] machine de langage . . . capable de susciter son matériau, de moudre ou tresser faits, souvenirs, fantasmes, mais aussi bien raisonnements ou analyses abstraites, toujours selon la même logique de rêve . . .' (*Pacte*, 272). For Lejeune this writing-as-weaving works as follows: starting with a given corpus of materials, assembled on the basis of some initial analogies, Leiris's activity consists in finding (or inventing) as many links as possible between all the other aspects of the entities he starts with. 'Il veut relier par *tous* leurs aspects à la fois deux faits ayant un seul point commun' (*Pacte*, 273). Lejeune is full of admiration for the dazzling inventiveness of Leiris's performances, but he places particular emphasis on 'l'écriture tressée' as a strategy of defence, a safety routine designed to avert, as much as to engender, confrontation with what is in fact pre-given, since death and *manque* are the eternal truths for Leiris: 'La vérité ne peut être qu'aperçue, située, trou vertigineux dont on a *éprouvé* l'existence au cours du mouvement, et dont on doit se protéger en refermant hermétiquement son discours' (*Lire Leiris*, 162). As a result, Lejeune tends to regard Leirisian networks as a unitary phenomenon, 'qui permet de donner un statut mythologique à n'importe quoi'; and he considers that this mode of writing culminates in the 'logomachie diluée et baroque de la fin de *Fibrilles* où l'énonciation finit par devenir le seul sujet de l'énoncé' (*Pacte*, 272). Our approach will be different, tracing first the development of 'l'écriture tressée' in Leiris by examining in turn and comparing two texts: 'Perséphone' in *Biffures*, and 'Mors' in *Fourbis*; then moving on to consider further transformations, perceptible in 'Vois! déjà l'ange' (the last chapter of *Fourbis*), *Fibrilles*, and, briefly, *Frêle Bruit*. In a final section attention will shift to a specific device: that of enumeration.

'Perséphone'

Pressed for a description of 'Perséphone' (*Bi* 77–138)[9] we might say: under the sign of the goddess of the underworld, and of the mysteries of the

---

[9] A dense but rewarding analysis of 'Perséphone' will be found in Jeffrey Mehlman's chapter, 'Reading (with) Leiris' in *A Structural Study of Autobiography*.

growth-cycle, Leiris weaves together a multitude of tiny fragments of past experience, all associated in some respect with his relation to the natural world. Such a description does not, however, suggest the way his writing persistently draws us towards its own mechanisms, to gaps and borders rather than to entities. On the strength of the title we may expect 'Perséphone' to unify disparate memories into a thematically coherent 'complexe de Perséphone' à la Bachelard, pointing to a Sartrean *choix original*.[10] Yet if this will in a sense be the end-product, the complex in question will turn out to be centred on a primal absence or separation, 'manque' rather than plenitude: 'Perséphone' (whom Leiris considers renaming 'La Fée Personne') will come by the end to signify vacancy or plurality, the empty source of proliferating substitutions with no originating centre. The effect of being linked under the aegis of this figure is that a collection of memories initially held to have in common the quality of a 'surprenante autorité' and an 'étonnante fraîcheur', will turn out to be riddled, as it were, with absence. The negative power of the word 'Perséphone' in the text derives partly from its dual status, as both *signifié* and *signifiant*. As *signifié* the goddess's connotations—'à la fois floral et sous-terrain' (*Bi* 85)—both cultural and personal, are already varied enough to engender complex and contradictory paths of association. But these connotations are undermined as well as amplified when Leiris allows the *signifiant* to come into play: as he explores the associations of the phonemes *perce* or *phone*, a disorientating reversal takes place since these arbitrary properties of the unifying term provide thematic leads of their own, greatly expanding the scope for metaphorical generation but at the price of any possibility of finding a centre. The duality of 'Perséphone', the line dividing signifier from signified, becomes the emblem of a sense of separation—from memory, from others, from immediate reality—ultimately rooted in language itself.[11]

The starting-point of 'Perséphone' is in fact the experience of feeling cut off from reality (a feeling fostered partly by the circumstances of moving

[10] Leiris notes elsewhere (*Bi* 219) how thought-provoking he has found a reading of *L'Être et le néant* in connection with his new autobiographical enterprise.

[11] The starting point of *Biffures* (pp. 9–12) had been the child's discovery, through the incomprehension with which his exclamation '. . . reusement!' had been greeted, that language is not simply a means of self-expression but the territory on which we encounter the existence of others: 'le langage articulé, tissu arachnéen de mes rapports avec les autres, me dépasse, poussant de tous côtés ses antennes mystérieuses' (*Bi* 12). Later in *La Règle* Leiris refers to the experience recounted in '. . . reusement!' as 'un peu mon *cogito*' (*Bi* 94): '*on ne parle pas tout seul* (les autres même absents étant impliqués dans l'acte de parler puisque c'est leurs mots qu'on emploie)'.

house during the Occupation), and Leiris's sense that his separation is exacerbated rather than ameliorated by the activity of writing: hence the desire to gather and explore childhood memories characterized by an acute sense of contact with the natural world. But as they become part of a text, elaborated in camera over many months, the memories cross over into the (subterranean) world of writing. And here separation, in one way or another, seems to become their persistent hallmark, while plenitude of various kinds will turn out to be founded on vacancy. A spectacular example lies in the auditory realm, to which Leiris devotes considerable space—at the prompting of the second syllable of 'Perséphone' and its semi-homophone *perce-oreille*. On the one hand, hearing, in Leiris's *imaginaire*, is associated with depth and cavernous space (he refers to the 'pays profond de l'ouïe', *Bi* 87); on the other hand, the organs and instruments of sound—mouth, ears, musical instruments, gramophones—all show aural plenitude to be dependent on the interface between an immaterial hollow space and a strictly localized material surface or point.[12] Leiris's minute descriptions of gramophones, and of the crackling sounds transmitted to the diaphragm by the needle—the plenitude of auditory space fragmented by 'un fracas qui était fulguration intime du fragment de matière ici présent' (*Bi* 101)—obsessively pinpoint a *border* between presence and absence, matter and the immaterial. As resurrected by writing, childhood memories seem not to provide an antidote to the sense of separation which prompted the attempt to revivify them, but rather to echo this separation, or to convert it into a euphoric communion with borders, with the narrow margin where the opposition between absence and presence is abolished. But this is a tribute less to the memories than to the magic of writing itself, as Leiris recognizes when he describes himself as being 'En porte-à-faux entre présent et passé, entre imagination et souvenir, entre poésie et réalité' (*Bi* 126). In writing 'Perséphone' he is employing a tactic ('un moyen') which enables him to explore his past but which makes the past a satellite of the present, and the present an achronological no man's land. The past becomes an accessory in a tautological, narcissistic exercise. That at least is the fear which exercises

[12] The mystery of sound comes to be located in the fantasy of a micro-world (as a child Leiris imagined that tiny singers inhabited the gramophone) which is intensely present, but from which we are absolutely separated. And the same mysterious conjunction of absence and presence which characterizes borders and limits recurs when Leiris turns successively to the world of minerals (mines, caves, industrial processes which manifest man's control over nature, pp. 103–10), to disasters, natural 'marvels', inventions, experiments (pp. 110–29), and, finally, to the animal kingdom (pp. 130–8)—of an ant's nest, he recalls that it existed 'Aux confins de la vie de sous-sol et de la vie de surface. A la limite de la matière brute et de la matière vivante' (p. 131).

Leiris from time to time, for example when he considers describing himself as:

Narcisse courant à travers bois et retournant toujours à ce lac où dorment ses souvenirs d'enfance, au début simples jalons (mirages, peut-être, échelonnés le long de ses promenades?), maintenant ondes pures lui renvoyant l'image un peu brouillée, mais tout humide et tendre, de lui-même. Il reste encore, toutefois, à effectuer le plongeon, le saut libérateur qui doit permettre de s'immerger dans ces ondes enfantines devenues, dès cet instant, réelles . . . (*Bi* 106).

The comparison, he quickly realizes, is invalid: in his case the 'saut libérateur'—freedom from sterile self-contemplation—even if it could be imagined to proceed from plunging into his childhood (and thus perhaps dispelling the fixations which keep him bound to it), would hardly carry the risk of self-destruction. Only the adoption of a completely different form of activity might do that. Yet the passage does seem to convey the idea that another kind of exploration (or exploitation) of his memories, one which would perhaps be less sterile and more risky, might be possible. Before examining whether 'Mors', the first chapter of *Fourbis*, can be said to implement such a reorientation, let us attempt to sum up the mode of writing we find in 'Perséphone'.

In 'Perséphone' Leiris explores and encapsulates his feelings about concrete reality just as, in other chapters of *Biffures*, he attempts to establish where he stands *vis-à-vis* other major categories of experience: language (in the first four chapters), pastness (in 'Il était une fois'), the conventional structure of a career (in 'Dimanche'). In each case, difference and separation are established, a sense that the 'je' remains outside sociality, encrypted in its 'alvéole' (*Bi* 79), its 'monde ouaté'. In the last chapter ('Tambour-trompette') Leiris reports extensively on the feeling that he has taken a false path, that writing has accentuated rather than remedied his desire for '[des] contacts réels' (*Bi* 267) with himself, with others, and with the world outside. Concerned that he may have converted his memories into trinkets rather than catalysts, he identifies himself with an old aunt who spends her time sitting in an antique coach in the garden. Leiris will never entirely allay such doubts, but he will seek to move on from a form of writing that fossilizes the past. In 'Perséphone', the purest expression of Leiris's writing in *Biffures*, language burrows into itself, excavates its own strata and produces the effect of something as solid, compacted, and self-referential as a Mallarmé poem. As the associative path develops more and more relationships, explicit and implicit, between the items it sucks into its orbit, the text becomes increasingly like a solid block, an overdetermined, self-

sufficient miniature world. As such, of course, it conforms to the desire
Leiris had enunciated in *L'Age d'homme*, that of turning his life into a 'bloc
solide', and we should not underestimate the pleasure he derives from what
is not so much the sterile contemplation of a static self-image as the
jouissance of an evanescent selfhood engendered in the turns of language.
Nor, however, should we underestimate Leiris's wish to make self-writing
fulfil other ambitions. As ever in Leiris, it is never too late to start again.

'Mors'

'Mors' (*Fo* 7–74), the first of the three long chapters of *Fourbis*, resembles
'Perséphone' in the intricacy with which small elements are woven into
associative patterns, but a number of differences point to an evolution in
Leiris's writing: less elements are treated, and each tends to receive more
attention; linguistic association and wordplay are far less prominent;
childhood experiences and recent events are given equal status; the
narrator's metadiscourse and the reader's awareness of the 'présent de
l'écriture' have a greater preponderance. Although it is a 'lacune obsédante'
that stimulates Leiris to write, there is never any doubt as to what the gap is:
set in motion by the absence of an original 'prise de conscience de la mort'
(*Fo* 22), the text constructs a path through a stock of memories which seem
to Leiris to offer insights into how he envisages death. The text begins, it is
true, with a long discursive meditation (pp. 7–22) where Leiris discusses his
difficulties in continuing *La Règle du jeu*, given his recognition that its
composition has become an end in itself rather than a viable instrument of
self-transformation, and given his awareness that gaps, errors, and
distortions of various kinds—some of which, relating to *Biffures*, have come
to light since its publication—make his stock of memories a dubious basis
for genuine self-investigation.[13] However, it is the pursuit of what he calls
'lacunes positives': memory-gaps of which he is acutely conscious, which
provides Leiris with a way of confronting a topic—death—which has always
been at the centre of his preoccupations. Leiris links his inability to locate
the origin of his awareness of death with the observation that he has always
thought of it less as a 'coupure décisive' than as 'une sorte d'autre mode

---

[13] The chance find in an attic of a long-forgotten photograph representing Lucy Arbell in
the role of Massenet's Persephone (*Fi* 18–20) is especially troubling because it suggests to
Leiris that the starting point of his 'Perséphone', with its emphasis on sinuous, spiralling
forms, had in fact been dictated by a single arbitrary source—the disc-shaped ear-rings worn
by the singer in the photograph. From this Leiris infers that beneath the 'parcours officiel' of
his writing there winds a more interesting but mostly concealed 'cheminement souterrain'.

d'existence' (*Fo* 23). This recognition, confirmed perhaps by an initial survey of his *fiches*, seems to provide a basic structure for the text which, despite giving the appearance of an undivided continuum, falls into three main parts, the first centred on a childhood memory, the second on the motif of theatricality, the third on that of 'le cadavre'. In each case it is the sense of a border zone between life and death, rather than the act or event of dying, which predominates. What we have, in fact, are three clusters made up of memories which date from different periods but which are linked associatively to the central motif and to each other. Although the three associative clusters are closely interrelated, and despite the fact that numerous overlaps and continuities exist between them (the central motif in one cluster may have a secondary role in another; a single incident may be exploited in different ways in two clusters), the gradual movement from one to the next—which may be imperceptible—creates the sense of an emergent coherence which contrasts with the impression of total self-reflexivity and linguistic coagulation conveyed by 'Perséphone'.

The first and most self-contained cluster centres on a minute incident dating from childhood holidays at Viroflay: walking with his father on a country road at dusk, the child was frightened by a faint sound, 'une sorte de grelottement rapide et continu, sûrement bruissement d'insecte' (*Fo* 24). The relationship between the memory of this sound and Leiris's notion of death is a given which he sets out to explain, conscious that in doing so he inevitably constructs (pp. 26, 28, 29) and thereby distorts the memory. Pursuing first the idea that the sound was made by an insect, and then an alternative hypothesis, stemming from his father's dismissive explanation that It was a distant horse-drawn carriage, Leiris progressively isolates the sound's solitary uniqueness as the essence of its connection with death. The faint sound somehow out there in the dark, outside the scope of our knowledge and control, affirms the immemorial continuity of things, the fact that ultimately, 'quelque chose peut être vivant *sans* nous' (*Fo* 31). Leiris's analysis here does not tend to radiate out towards other memories; rather, the sparse details of the remembered scenario are filled out (Leiris uses the image of the reclamation of the Zuider Zee, *Fo* 26), by two forms of extrapolation: metonymic, for example via an evocative passage encapsulating memories of a carriage returning to the stables (*Fo* 30); and metaphorical, the insistent parallel with hearing a sound while we are in bed, a parallel which associates death with the border zone between sleeping and waking. The centripetal quality of the analysis here underlines the way in which Leiris's concern is not so much to use the memory as part of a larger network of associations, but to understand, in this case, how a specific memory has, in the course of time, accumulated associations which are part of its current significance. Thus, while he concedes that the hypothesis of the sound having been made by a carriage may not belong to the original memory at all, he insists that at some point the image of a carriage has grafted itself on to the memory, as an indispensable component in its association with fear and death.

The second cluster is not centred on a particular incident but on a class or structure of experiences. We may place theatricality at the centre, but theatre itself is only one manifestation of what is essentially a set of relationships between elements whose power to connote death always depends implicitly on their connection with the other elements. Thus, both certain forms of looking or seeing, when vision is focused on the progressive unfolding of an event, *and* phenomena which display miniaturization or reduction in scale, form part of this network. Combined with each other, or with other elements, these connote death for Leiris, theatre itself being an obvious locus of their conjunction. Yet, by virtue of their independence as structural units, these elements come inevitably to connote and presuppose each other, so that for Leiris experiences of looking, without the factor of miniaturization, can become deathly; and ultimately the whole visual field, all experiences where one is *conscious* of looking, are tinged with death. What is remarkable about this section of 'Mors' is the variety of ingredients which link together, and Leiris's success in conjuring up the hidden deathliness of the commonplace.

The transition to this second cluster occurs in the disjointed paragraphs (*Fo* 31–5) where the exploration of the childhood incident peters out. Here a chain of associations leads from carriage-rides, to a *guinguette* where one takes a *consommation*, to the word *consommé* and its cognates, to the word *bouillon* and the expression 'yeux du bouillon' (globules of fat in a stock or *consommé*). At this point, seeing takes over from hearing as the presiding sense in Leiris's meditation; a dense paragraph, with echoes of Sartre, distinguishes eyes (plural) from the single eye which watches us, or with which we look, and then focuses on the specular effect provoked by certain spectacles which seem to mirror or allegorize inner mental space:

l'air d'outre-tombe revêtu par ce qui est diorama, scène artificiellement éclairée et encastrée dans l'espace, comme par tout ce qui semble agencé pour que nous y reconnaissions la projection externe de la vraie chambre du dedans ... soudain illuminée et passée à une espèce de fixité mortuaire de Musée Grévin. Chapelles ardentes donc, que maints spectacles offrent au regard indivis en quoi s'activent nos deux yeux ... quand ces visions sont empreintes ... d'une certaine allure de théâtre ... (*Fo* 34)

Here, a deathly quality is attributed to sights where the outer scene reflects our inner space by virtue of a theatricality residing in its illusory or artificial (scaled-down) quality and/or the uncanny sense that its unfolding carries a symbolic message for us. Deathliness inheres in the compulsive identification with the scene, which seals off the experience from the ordinary train of events, making outer and inner a function of each other, putting the spectator 'on the spot' and immobilizing him in a death-like rigidity. In his initial exploration of this nexus, Leiris focuses on recollections of the 'Gouffre de Padirac' and of the strange quarries of Les Baux and Saint-Rémy. In each case the specular element involves round, dark spaces, and deathliness also derives from association with the underworld, and with the idea of burial. Equally, a theatrical element is present—connected with *mise en scène*, artifice, reduction in scale, and heedless pleasure (which for Leiris connotes death, because it ignores it). The 'Gouffre de Padirac' is a tourist attraction where one crosses an underground lake in small boats, while in the Roman quarries near Saint-Rémy in the Alpilles ('cette étrange chaîne de montagnes en miniature, guère plus hautes que des montagnes russes dans un parc d'attractions', *Fo* 38) Leiris felt like a child in an unreal environment where real fears and dangers are simulated—such as a church, or the wings of a theatre.

Leiris's account of giving a public lecture at the 'Soirée Max Jacob' in 1948 connects the Viroflay incident (because on this occasion, alone on the brightly lit stage, he identified with the solitary sign of life which persists when all else seems dead, *Fo* 39) with the experience at the core of the second cluster: unable to see the audience, Leiris was confronted by 'une vaste grotte où je ne voyais rien' (*Fo* 42), and felt that he was on the other side of a border between two worlds, those of the living and the dead. This sequence then leads into a more discursive presentation of the links between death and theatre, variously referred to as a 'laboratoire de mirages', a 'lieu factice', and a 'lieu de la mort feinte' (*Fo* 44). Central here is a connection between death and the phenomenon of representation itself. Any representation of an action has the character of a 'rêve objectivé':

Un rêve objectivé, un rêve que nous regardons, qui nous touche quoique nous ne soyons pas dedans, qu'est-ce donc que cela peut être sinon un ensemble d'actions qui nous sont proposées et que nous considérons avec un intérêt passionné, comme nous ferions si nous pouvions, extraits de la vie mais demeurés lucides, être détachés de notre propre histoire et la voir se jouer devant nous, transformée par l'optique inhérente à notre nouveau statut? (*Fo* 46)

For Leiris, to be gripped by a represented action is to be positioned outside its realm, as the spectator *at whom* it is aimed; but, at the same time, involvement turns the spectacle into allegory: fascination and detachment combine to give the viewer a different status—that of someone able to become a vicarious spectator of his own life. The subject of representation is located midway between existence and a deathly world where everything has already occurred, where time has stopped and only repetition is possible. For Leiris theatre is representation in its purest form and all aspects of the stage associate it with death: illusion, reduction in scale, the sense of a necessary and irreversible concatenation of events, the constraints of representation (bad acting or poor scenery accentuate deathliness by suggesting pathetic attempts to disguise the abjection and 'dénuement' of the human condition). All these features make theatrical space 'une antichambre de l'autre monde qu'on ne peut s'empêcher de construire dès qu'on essaie de se représenter la mort' (*Fo* 46).

But the features which make theatre deathly are not confined to the theatre itself and, in fact, rather than talk about experiences in the theatre (as he had in other works, such as *L'Age d'homme*, where the link between theatre and death is already established), Leiris moves on to discuss, in some of the most memorable and characteristic pages in his work, three things: a statue commemorating a volcanic eruption which destroyed part of Saint-Pierre de Martinique in 1902; a macabre slot-machine he had seen at Ramsgate in 1913 in which puppet figures mimed a hanging; and a diorama at Luna-Park where a scale-model reproduced in realistic detail a flood engulfing an American township. What is striking about this sequence is both the evocative power of Leiris's description of these phenomena and the way he moves back and forth between them, developing connections and associations. The eruption links with the flood, as a natural disaster, but also with Luna-Park where another attraction was to see the 'Devil' dive into a silver bathtub. One theory about the statue, which officially symbolizes *Saint-Pierre renaissant de ses cendres*, is that it depicts one of the victims who boiled to death when they plunged into cold water to alleviate the intolerable heat. What also intrigued Leiris about the statue was a further ambivalence deriving from its erotic character (the woman's posture suggesting ecstasy), which echoed his consistent sense of connection between carnal pleasure and death, and which also gave the woman the air of a *diablesse* who, in Creole folklore, leads the unwitting victim to his death. The link between the slot-machine and the diorama resides in the fact that these are spectacles in miniature, and that both have, albeit minimally, a theatrical quality, despite the absence of living participants; above all, both convey 'l'impression de destin, de scénario monté depuis toujours et dont le sec déroulement s'effectue de manière mécanique' (*Fo* 52).

This notion of an implacable mechanism, like the ambivalence of the statue, also provides Leiris with a link to the last cluster centred on the *cadavre* and the idea of the return of the dead. The 'deux mécaniques' can be seen as 'deux machineries . . . systèmes doués, apparemment, d'une sorte de vie personnelle et relevant par conséquent du monde inquiétant des automates' (*Fo* 53), whose avatars include the sounds of mechanical vehicles heard at night, the 'scaphandrier' and the 'somnambule' (both figures mentioned earlier in passing), and, finally, 'le cadavre en qui s'opèrent, jusqu'à ce qu'il soit arrivé à l'immobilité définitive du squelette, certains mouvements internes et inconscientes transformations. Effets—eux aussi—de machinerie, le relâchement qui fait que le mort "se vide" . . .' (*Fo* 53).

Rather than trace the structure of the last cluster, I want to examine briefly an important feature of 'Mors', namely, minor motifs which do not receive specific attention but whose recurrence adds to the closely woven character of the text. In addition to the 'somnambule' and the 'scaphandrier' just mentioned, one could cite the many references to a 'rideau', some of them associated with recurrent allusions to *Hamlet*;[14] or the sound of bells which links the 'grelottement' of the 'frêle bruit' at Viroflay to the theme of theatricality, via the poster for the operetta *Les Clochers de Corneville* which was playing at the theatre in Saint-Pierre when it was destroyed by the eruption; and the 'tintement de cloches' which formed part of the diorama of the American town. By taking on, ironically, the character of funeral bells, the 'cloches' in the disaster scenario retrospectively justify Leiris's hearing a 'bruit de glas' in the distant jingling of a horse and carriage.[15] The effect of this use of minor motifs is to add to the overall density and coherence of the text, superimposing, on the links established by Leiris's painstaking progress from one memory to another, a further level of association.

How is it—to return to our earlier question—that, despite the extraordinary degree of 'tressage', the density of associations and cross-

[14] e.g. Leiris's resemblance, in X-rays, to 'Poor Yorick' (*Fo* 12); the comparison between one of the operations of memory and the Shakespearean 'play within a play' (*Fo* 29, 34); the curtain Polonius hides behind (*Fo* 47).

[15] Surprisingly, Leiris makes no reference to the word *mors* (death in Latin, a horse's bit in French) as part of the bridge connecting the sound of the distant carriage and the idea of death. However, a passage in *Biffures* (p. 47) links the *o* sound in *mort* to a 'frappement de cloche tintant d'un bout à l'autre d'une galerie couverte', and compares the vowel's position, in the middle of the word, to 'l'entrée d'un tunnel, la bouche d'un égout ou l'orée de toute espèce de couloir souterrain qui peut se faire canal d'échos répercutés'. Here we find elements of both the first cluster in 'Mors' and the second, and this might suggest that, as in the case of Lucy Arbell's ear-rings, Leiris's text is based on associations generated retroactively (the *word* death summoning up experiences not originally connected with mortality) rather than genuine recollections.

referencing between 'choses minimes', the sense of a fixed corpus being exhaustively 'X-rayed', 'Mors' seems a more open and fluid text than, say, 'Perséphone'? Part of the explanation is that Leiris's running commentary on what he is doing, his metadiscursive interruptions and asides, are not only more frequent than before but bear on a wider range of questions (the processes of memory, for example, receive close attention throughout).[16] The relative shift of emphasis from childhood to more recent memories (even if many are still very distant) has the effect of keeping the focus more securely on Leiris's present concerns, and of forestalling nostalgic regression to the closed world of the past. Important, too, is the impression that, rather than following—wherever they lead—pathways opened by a fundamentally poetic treatment of his material, Leiris is seeking, via the obsessive processing of memories, to come to terms with fundamental areas of experience; 'tressage' here is oriented by therapeutic and heuristic tasks. Watchful now for the detours brought about by 'un certain entraînement de la plume, toujours si prompte au coq-à-l'âne' (*Fo* 28), mindful of the fact that 'se remémorer n'est après tout qu'une façon plus terre à terre d'imaginer' (*Fo* 33), Leiris aims, on the basis of 'des lambeaux de vérité plus lointains' (*Fo* 64), to arrive at some sort of 'vérité générale'. His desire is to forge, 'avec le vécu à la base, et le langage pour outil, des vérités d'approximation' (*Fo* 65). What does he learn about death in writing 'Mors'? To a large extent, no more than he knew at the outset: that it is 'une chose obscure et sans regard', that it is 'souvent par des voies détournées que se faufile jusqu'à nous la crainte de la mort' (*Fo* 58). Yet by exploring through impressions and associations the ways in which death inhabits the most anodyne recollections and situations, by taking stock of the ubiquity of death in his way of seeing the world, Leiris is able to register, if not to remedy, the way his obsession risks reducing him to the status of a non-person, a zombie— like the one pointed out to him in Haiti: 'comme si la peur, effaçant tout ce qui est en moi, me transformait d'ores et déjà en cette charpente sans conscience que je crains tant de devenir' (*Fo* 62). Writing 'Mors' had been an attempt to stare death down, to face out its petrifying look which lurks at the heart of representation—in short, 'apprivoiser la mort' (*Fo* 72). If the attempt ends in relative failure—in the confirmation that what remains 'la chute dans un trou sans forme qu'aucune cartographie réelle ou imaginaire ne permet de délimiter' (*Fo* 72) cannot be tamed—'Mors' nevertheless suggests that the

---

[16] e.g. discussions of the selectivity of memory (*Fo* 20); the links between memory and imagination (*Fo* 37); the way, once a memory has been fully exhumed and analysed, it will have been 'altéré pour toujours et nul trait ravageur supprimant le passage où l'on s'est fourvoyé ne saurait réparer le dommage ainsi causé' (*Fo* 53).

lucidity it has sponsored, and the resting-place it has provided for certain memories whose debilitating power over Leiris will have been diminished by formulation, may enable him to move on to other tasks, in particular that of coming to terms with the conflict between the closed world of private myths and representations and the wider demands of the 'vécu'.

LE MYTHE VÉCU

Dans certains états de l'âme presque surnaturels, la profondeur de la vie se révèle tout entière dans le spectacle, si ordinaire qu'il soit, qu'on a sous les yeux. Il en devient le symbôle.

In this fragment[17] Baudelaire encapsulated the essence of modernist epiphany: exterior spectacle and inner feeling momentarily fuse; thereafter, the mission of writing (in Proust, Joyce, Rilke, Stevens) is to capture the manifold layerings and linkages which provide the transcendent horizons of what is otherwise a strictly immanent experience. Leiris's relationship to secular epiphany, and to the mourning for religious experience with which it is inevitably tinged, was mediated by the participation in surrealism which inspired him to find oracular energies in the substance of words, and to regard the haphazard experiences of daily life as a propitious forum for what André Breton called 'le magique-circonstanciel', a type of experience where *objets trouvés*, chance events, privileged places or individuals, are held to precipitate the revelation of subjective desire and to manifest 'des échanges mystérieux entre le matériel et le mental', signalling 'l'amorce d'un contact, entre tous éblouissant, de l'homme avec le monde des choses'.[18] Such notions left deep traces in Leiris's writing, but they were also modulated by factors which distanced him from surrealism in the 1930s, leading him, with Georges Bataille and others, via ethnology, towards a somewhat different conception of 'le sacré dans la vie quotidienne'.[19] Here the stress falls not on the evidence certain experiences might offer for an occulted dimension of reality, but on the primacy of a certain kind of contact between human beings and their existential environment. The sacred for Leiris is not parousia, the shining through of another light, but the experience of a border. In *Miroir de la tauromachie*, written in 1937, he refers to a 'limite au

---

[17] *Fusées, Œuvres complètes*, i. 659.

[18] *L'Amour fou*, 49.

[19] Title of the famous lecture Leiris delivered to the Collège de Sociologie he founded with Georges Bataille and Roger Caillois in 1938. The lecture is reproduced and discussed in D. Hollier (ed.), *Le Collège de Sociologie*, 60–74. See also J. Jamin, 'Quand le sacré devint gauche'.

regard de laquelle les choses—abandonnant le caractère inorienté, amorphe, de ce qui est profane—se polarisent en gauche et en droite'. And in the same text he talks of 'certains faits . . . sites, événements, objets, circonstances' which constitute the 'lieux où l'on se sent tangent au monde et à soi-même'.[20] Leiris equates fusion, absolute 'tangence', with death, and, like Bataille, suggests that it is glimpsed in erotic experience.[21] But the return which follows the 'petite mort' of orgasm is reflected in all experiences of this kind: there is always a 'minime décalage', a 'hiatus ou mince faille', something 'infiniment petit' which insists on deviation, maintains division, ensures that the experience is one of 'plénitude déchirante', marked by the recognition of a lack: 'l'infime mais tragique fêlure par laquelle se trahit ce qu'il y a d'inachevé (littéralement: d'infini) dans notre condition' (*Miroir*, 56). We always remain on the border.

The asssociation made in the last quotation could serve as a skeleton key to Leiris's writing: all boundaries could be seen as referring us to the sacred, all small things would be figures of the 'mince faille', all notable experiences would involve 'notre communion future avec le monde de la mort' (*Miroir*, 67). Yet in *La Règle du jeu* Leiris uses the idiom and vocabulary of a text like *Miroir de la tauromachie* very sparingly. In *Biffures* (pp. 139–80) he is rather scathing about the tendency to self-mythologization which he diagnoses in experiences where, as he sees it retrospectively, he had succumbed to the illusion—symbolized by the phrase 'Il était une fois'—that lived events had taken on the mythic aura of stories. The 'tangence' experienced at such moments is not interpreted in terms of the sacred, but as betraying the desire for a return to the mythical plenitude and security attributed to childhood. The sense of loss engendered by solitude and nostalgia had inspired a desire to arrest time and to transform actuality into a kind of static *tableau vivant*: 'il me fallait, si je voulais reprendre pied et me sentir moi-même avec intensité, trouver appui dans l'intangibilité des choses, tirer de la *complicité apparente* de cet extérieur immobile l'impression d'une sorte d'identité' (*Bi* 175–6, my italics). Self-loss is replaced by an identity derived from a magical transmutation of reality, by dint of which self becomes figural: 'un dessin . . . une silhouette . . . un diagramme . . . une figure' (*Bi* 149).[22] In retrospect Leiris denounces the wilful poeticization inherent in this operation. Even the entrancing spectacle of a group of fairground

[20] *Miroir de la tauromachie* [1938], 25, 65–6. For Leiris death, theatre, and representation are uniquely conjoined in the *corrida*.

[21] Leiris is the dedicatee of Bataille's *L'Érotisme* (1957).

[22] A stimulating analysis of 'Il était une fois' will be found in James Leigh, 'The Figure of Autobiography'.

performers at Lannion, which had seemed to require 'aucune macération poétique' (*Bi* 157), is now understood to have captivated Leiris not because of an authentic fusion of inner and outer, subject and object, but as the distillation of the expression 'l'ancien temps'—an imaginary refuge from the fear of ageing and death (*Bi* 166).[23]

In *Fourbis* the possible complicity of subject and spectacle, inner meanings and outer events, is again often at issue; but a marked change of attitude and emphasis is perceptible. First, Leiris focuses less on single moments, or on events detached from their temporal context, than on sequences of events, and the way they unfold, originally in real time. Secondly, the question of self-mythologization comes to be connected not only with the original experiences, or their immediate aftermath, but with their afterlife in the processes of memory and language, as evidenced in the transmutation of *fiches* into continuous text. Thirdly, the somewhat dismissive attitude towards the mythologization of experience—the tendency to chide himself for an activity regarded as regressive—which characterizes *Biffures*, is supplanted by a more nuanced and benevolent view. By no means above suspicion, the tendency to construe certain experiences as instances of what Leiris now calls 'le mythe vécu' is embodied more directly in the text and appraised in the light not simply of a single psychological mechanism but of a complex interaction involving experience, memory, and writing.

'Vois! déjà l'ange'

The final chapter of *Fourbis*, 'Vois! déja l'ange' (pp. 181–239), provides the supreme example of 'le mythe vécu'. For the first time in *La Règle du jeu*, a substantial chapter is focused exclusively on a single matter—Leiris's relationship with the prostitute Khadidja during his sojourn as a soldier stationed in the Algerian desert for the duration of the *drôle de guerre*. Towards the end Leiris refers to his encounter with Khadidja as 'une aventure qui, en son temps, m'avait charmé, parce qu'à chaque instant elle semblait prendre indépendamment de moi sa forme' (*Fo* 234), and it is shown to be an instance of 'l'événement offert d'emblée avec l'ordonnance solennelle d'une expérience cruciale' (*Fo* 228). The prestige and significance of the episode is firmly rooted in the 'vécu', in the particular way events were *lived through* by a passive subjet who succumbed to their spell. At the same

---

[23] Cf. Leiris's dissection, later on (*Bi* 258–61), of his addiction to moments when music seems to lend an intensity to humdrum events.

time, this prestige is only fully apprehended, and as it were verified, by an active process of rememoration which explores the ramifications of each link in the chain, each detail, realizing the symbolic potential which confers a mythic quality. 'Le mythe vécu' depends on an equation between 'le *formalisme*, selon lequel j'aimerais voir les choses s'ajuster comme en un cérémonial', and 'la *formulation*, que pour ne plus être étranger j'impose à ce qui se passe en moi' (*Fo* 219). For the *formulation* to be authentic, the *formalisme*—the desire that lived experience should take on the organic character of a ritual—must emanate from events themselves, independently of the subject's volition.[24] But, equally, retelling must take on the character of a ceremony. For the first time in *La Règle du jeu* Leiris presents himself as a narrator: he will tell 'l'histoire de Khadidja ou plutôt *mon* histoire avec Khadidja' (*Fo* 181), and he punctuates his tale with the ritual *baratin* of a Creole story-teller: 'messieurs, et cric! (Et cric! reprend le chœur) Et crac! (le chœur reprend: Et crac!)' (*Fo* 181). In its ritualized aspect, narration underlines self-distance: it is by reinscribing himself as a vicarious witnessing 'double' of his past self that Leiris seeks to inhabit his story (*Fo* 206). Yet if, in so doing, he turns himself into a mythic protagonist, Leiris's presence in the tale as a subject of memory and writing is also insistently marked. Khadidja's shadowy room is associated with the dim space of memory itself (*Fo* 184); it is 'en m'efforçant de reconstituer notre histoire' (*Fo* 214–15) that Leiris seems fully, but only provisionally, to apprehend Khadidja ('la ressaisir'); when his tale ends her shadow will retreat once more, and now perhaps definitively, into shadows.

At one point Leiris describes his encounter with Khadidja as 'une aventure très vulgaire dans laquelle il est entré pas mal d'exotisme de cinéma mais qui—*grâce à la complicité de quelques apparences*—se hausse pour moi jusqu'à la dignité d'un mythe vécu' (*Fo* 182). The phrase I have italicized seems to place 'le mythe vécu' under the sign of delusion. Yet Leiris's *récit* will consistently point to a distinction between myth-mongering and something more authentic. At various points Khadidja is compared to Rebecca, Aïda, Bérénice, Iphigénie, a female Ganymede, a Valkyrie, a 'gardien du seuil', a sorceress, a nereid, an idol, the Queen of Sheba, a servant of Isis. Leiris, in his turn, becomes a Roman centurion, a shipwrecked sailor, a prince in disguise, and of course Radamès to her Aïda.

---

[24] A burlesque example of the phenomenon is provided by the hilarious sequence in 'Les Tablettes sportives' concerning Leiris's vain attempts to show solidarity by celebrating the news of VE day in Dakar with Africans rather than whites (*Fo* 161–75), which is interpreted as an occasion where events, taking on allegorical meaning, had conspired to teach Leiris a lesson (p. 174).

But whatever pleasure Leiris, and his readers, may derive from these sometimes ironic, mock-heroic, identifications, they are qualified intermittently by a note of censure. Leiris regrets his 'dérisoire envie de poétiser' (*Fo* 212), and he bemoans the schoolboy enthusiasm for Ovid's *Metamorphoses* and other classical works which provide the ferment for his allegorizing zeal (*Fo* 202). He also recognizes that when, in compensation, he underlines the sordid reality of Khadidja's estate, he is liable to confer on his experience the spurious glamour of low life: 'Khadidja la traînée' (*Fo* 238), hard-bitten legionaires (*Fo* 199), the sordid North-African cafés of a hundred B-movies (*Fo* 190), are just as 'mythological', in the restricted sense, as the other images. Moreover, for Leiris to belittle his experience, as no more than a soldier's fling with a tart, is as inauthentic as to see her as a goddess (*Fo* 212). In his tendency to construct idols, and then to spurn the idols he has venerated, Leiris recognizes 'un vieux manichéisme venu de mon enfance' (*Fo* 228) which does not do justice to what he actually experienced. What his 'histoire de Khadidja' will suggest, especially through its emphasis on gestures, signs, and images, is that the constant oscillation between mythologization and demythologization is perhaps endemic to the processes of his imagination and memory and, more than this, that it points to a just balance between the claims of poetry and those of the *polis*.

Ever in pursuit of signs and allegories, Leiris's attention in 'Vois! déjà l'ange' focuses especially on *human* signs. Here, gestures (for instance the delicacy with which, at Figuig, a prostitute served mint tea) provide 'ces menus dons qui, venus à point nommé, sont comme la preuve qu'à un instant déterminé le monde éxtérieur nous a répondu' (*Fo* 188); and it is love—the amorous exchanges of men and women—which provides the cardinal space where gestures signify. The metaphysics of sexuality, the interchanges between love and death, had long preoccupied Leiris, but 'Vois! déjà l'ange' privileges the lover's subjectivity, his 'comportement' as a 'sujet désirant' (*Fo* 193), unveiled in a series of situations and gestures—a gift, a kiss, a few words, an orgasm.

The relationship with Khadidja was always at one level that of prostitute and client, but in his account of these 'journées dorées' (*Fo* 202), Leiris stresses the childlike quality, the paradoxical candour and innocence, the sense of ceremony which attended their dealings, for example when Khadidja bathes him in a tub, or serves endless 'cannettes' to his comrades, or when he and she crouch together in the latrines suffering from the effects of the local beer. Rather than a Bérénice or a Valkyrie, Khadidja, in this homely tenderness, resembles a solicitous landlady (*Fo* 212) or an accomplished hostess. In part what appeals to Leiris is the experience of living several roles at once, the release from fixed identity, the delights of ambiguity. In retrospect, however, as is revealed by a number of interpolations in his *récit* (*Fo* 193, 195-7, 206-7), Leiris discerns here abiding features of his sensibility: he prefers desire to possession, nostalgia to passion (*Fo* 193); he is an Aliocha, 'un mou, un rêvasseur' who would like to see love as 'une amitié très simplement poussée au paroxysme' (*Fo* 195).

The passage concerning Khadidja's orgasm on the second night they spend with each other combines a number of strands, fusing circumstantial detail with symbolic meaning in a remarkable way. For Leiris, whose own orgasm will be delayed until a renewal of love-making at dawn, the experience is initially one of prolonged *imminence*, which he compares with the 'tension abstraite' provided by drugs, where one feels on the verge of self-appropriation or of some revelation (*Fo* 208). But just before abandoning his efforts Leiris discovered

que mon obstination n'était pas vaine car Khadidja, en secret, me révélait qu'elle en était émue: quelque chose comme les pulsations ou contractions légères qu'on pourrait percevoir au fond d'une galerie de mine si la terre était vivante et si les hommes qui la travaillent, perdus dans ses replis recevaient une réponse émanée du plus lointain de ce grand animal sensible (*Fo* 209-10).

The sense of initiation into the secrets of the earth is extended by association with the 'mouvement brownien' of molecules, and with a dream in which Leiris had been vouchsafed 'les schémas de la vérité', including that of his own existence. Leiris then turns to classical allusion, linking the sense of imminence to the 'adieux indéfiniment prolongés' between Bérénice and Titus, as expressed in Suetonius' phrase 'dimisit invitus invitam', an association reinforced at the level of the signifier by his faulty recollection of the phrase: doubling the 's' and displacing the verb to the end, he had felt that it embodied the sense of an absolute, ineluctable reality. (The theme of endless farewells will resurface in Leiris's account of his last glimpses of Khadidja.) Another connection with classicism and theatricality arises through the new ear-rings worn by Khadidja, which cause her lobes to bleed: the blood-stained pillow conjures up, for Leiris, the figure of Iphigénie—'pur sang du dieu qui lance le tonnerre' (*Fo* 211).

As the point of intersection for multiple paths of meaning, Khadidja's orgasm becomes the paradigm for a relation to the Other which amalgamates distance and proximity, the cosmic and the *terre à terre*, tenderness and melancholy, life and death, consummation and endless deferral. Khadidja's vagina, a 'caverne' and a 'voie sans issue' (this association is prompted by a road-sign to the army base where Leiris's unit was drafted), offers initiation into one of those border zones to which Leiris's imagination so often seeks recourse. But in the thematics of 'Vois! déjà l'ange' the orgasm—as a sign of Khadidja's consent, as a gift—also belongs to the domain of the fleeting gesture:

> Parmi ces poussières de notre passé qui nous émeuvent d'autant que leur contenu paraît hors de proportion avec son infime contenant (amorces de quelque chose de capital que le sort a laissé en souffrance ou qui, pour être, n'avait pas même besoin de se produire), parmi ces événements si minces qu'on s'étonne presque de les garder en mémoire mais qui fulgurent çà et là dans le fatras de notre vie, figurent . . . certaines caresses tout à fait anodines, parfois réduites à un geste apparemment négligeable quoique donnant l'illusion (mais était-ce bien une illusion?) qu'il vous lie, autant que l'acte amoureux, à une créature dont le nom même n'est pas forcément connu (*Fo* 193).

In the examples he gives of such gestures Leiris is sometimes the recipient, but in the most significant instance (which recurs later in the text) the gesture is his. After the death of his friend Laure, he had placed his hand gently on her forehead as a sign of farewell, realizing later that this was the repetition of an earlier gesture when he had tended her in drunkenness. The borderline between life and death, and the combination of the sublime with the sordid, provide a link with Khadidja. By linking her with Laure, a woman for whose spiritual qualities he had the utmost respect ('Laure', herself a semi-mythical figure, was in fact Colette Peignot, the 'compagne' of Georges Bataille, and a poet)[25] Leiris adds a further dimension to the mythologization of Khadidja.

A gesture is an incomplete action ('amorce de quelque chose de capital . . . qui, pour être, n'avait pas même besoin de se produire', *Fo* 193). Gestures contain, virtually, the possible sequels and narrative developments which do not actually materialize; a gesture constitutes a special kind of event whose meaning, never defined, depends on the open-ended act of interpretation, and the complicity this may require of the Other. The focus of Leiris's writing in 'Vois! déja l'ange' comes increasingly to bear on Khadidja's gestures, and thereby to raise questions—ethical rather than epistemological—about their status as human signs, and about the 'bon usage' of those events whose imprint in our memory constitutes a vital dimension of our reality. This orientation characterizes Leiris's account of his final encounter with Khadidja, the long passage concerning a gift she gave him, and, finally, the explicit concern with the afterlife of Khadidja's image in his memory.

---

[25] See Laure, *Écrits*, ed. by her nephew Jérome Peignot. Leiris dedicated *Miroir de la tauromachie* to the memory of Colette Peignot.

A ceremonial outfit, white robes and green scarf, which give her the fixed appearance of an 'image pieuse ou une figure du Musée Grévin' (*Fo* 218); the presence of an entourage of other prostitutes and their 'maquerelle'; a few words, 'Tu n'as pas peur du soleil . . .'; an affectionate kiss on the cheek: such are the ingredients of the scene laid on by Khadidja when she summons Leiris to a meeting on his last morning at Béni-Ounif. In the serpentine winds and coils of Leiris's reconstruction, three main paths of interpretation may be identified. To follow the first is to see the scene as the apotheosis of Khadidja-as-myth: she is the 'African Queen', her plainest words, 'Tu n'as pas peur du soleil . . .', have oracular meanings which hoist Leiris to the level of myth. A second path involves looking behind the image for the real concerns conveyed by Khadidja's gestures. Rather than bringing her down to earth, this approach tends to confer a certain moral sublimity on Khadidja's feelings, by contrast with those of Leiris which, in his own eyes, emerge as petty and ignominious. Purged of their mythological trappings, her words about the sun allow for a number of more banal interpretations (for example, 'you'll get sunstroke') but, as such, they reveal 'qu'elle était *attentionnée* à mon égard' (*Fo* 220). Not least for being symptoms of her professionalism, this and other touches betray a delicacy, a sense of *à propos*, an authenticity which Leiris finds lacking in himself. In the sphere of ordinary human intercourse (a sphere to some degree inaccessible to Leiris by virtue of his 'incapacité de toujours à briser le cercle du moi', *Fo* 218), the prostitute has much to teach the soldier-poet. The subtlety of Leiris's own psychological analysis at this point, his desire to get things in proportion, clearly represent a belated homage to an authenticity in Khadidja ill-served, he feels, by his compulsion to mythologize her. The third path—the search for a kind of 'justesse' in the oscillation between mythologization and demythologization—remains tacit at this point but it emerges as a central preoccupation of 'Vois! déjà l'ange' when Leiris comes to consider the immediate aftermath of his encounter with Khadidja.

When he left North Africa Leiris bore with him, as a memento of their encounter, the ornamental cross Khadidja had given him one night. This relic, which he, in turn, presents to his wife, and which then disappears during the Occupation, becomes the displaced embodiment of Khadidja herself; and its vicissitudes, as it passes from hand to hand, come to allegorize the vicissitudes of Khadidja's image in the space of Leiris's memory. If we unravel Leiris's 'méditation zigzagante', it is possible to identify four phases.

1. Initially an object of suspicion ('who gave it to *her*?'), the cross, a standard tourist souvenir, becomes an 'objet de vertu', portable testimony to

the transfiguration of lived experience into myth, emblem of Leiris's naïve delusion that the absolute can be grasped in one's hand like a 'pierre philosophale' (*Fo* 228).

2. Not surprisingly, this delusion does not travel, and the cross, 'le jeton d'entrée d'un paradis de mon invention' (*Fo* 228), is soon devalued in the context of the realities which confront Leiris on his return to France in 1940. The gift of the cross to his wife marks a willingness to give up dreams for reality; and for a time Leiris interprets its subsequent theft by agents of the Gestapo as a judgement on his behaviour in North Africa. The discovery that one of his drinking companions from Béni-Ounif had subsequently been a *milicien* and torturer further tarnishes Khadidja's image, leading Leiris to associate her with 'ces atroces catins qui, entre deux séances de torture, tutoyaient avec les gestapistes ou les miliciens' (*Fo* 228).

3. Up to this point Leiris has simply repeated the 'Manichaean' oppositions to which he is prey. But in a third phase, corresponding to the time of writing (the early 1950s), Leiris extricates himself from this binary strait-jacket and rescinds the summary judgements he had passed, in the context of war and liberation, on his sojourn with Khadidja, reappraising both the gift of the cross to his wife and the significance of its association with the horrors of the Occupation. His original rationale for the offering to his wife (a return to the straight and narrow, as it were) is now viewed as a triple betrayal—of his wife, Khadidja, and himself. Reinterpreted in the light of another memory of Laure, the gift, he now sees, was a complex gesture. On her deathbed the atheist Laure had astonished her friends by performing an abbreviated sign of the cross in reverse (*Fo* 229); after her death Leiris had placed in her coffin a set of poker dice which had a particular significance for him, relating to chance and destiny. Like the dice, the cross is a 'concrétion du destin que l'on tient dans sa main' (*Fo* 225); yet, like Laure's gesture, and Leiris's response, its relation to all orthodoxies is fundamentally ironic and ambiguous: the significance of the gestures through which the cross circulates cannot be governed by any single regime of meaning. In the light of Laure, the gift of the cross to his wife is reread as the expression of a desire that she should one day place this talisman of his destiny in his coffin (*Fo* 225). Leiris also questions the legitimacy of seeing his relationship with Khadidja, whatever the links between policing and prostitution, as the sign of a complicity with oppression, given that it might be more appropriate to see her as the victim of an oppressive system, and to view association with her as a solidarity with 'les réalités les plus aiguës de la vie' (*Fo* 231).

4. The associations with oppression, and with Laure, contribute to

Khadidja's final avatar as 'l'ange de la mort'. This was in fact, Leiris recalls, his initial image of her,[26] but in its final manifestation the image of Khadidja as angel of death is not simply one more mythologization but a compound which both embodies the mobile history of her image in Leiris's psyche, and represents an acceptance of Khadidja *as* image—a construct of memory, writing, and desire. If, in recounting his 'histoire de Khadidja', where writing has become '[une] sorte de veillée *in memoriam*' (*Fo* 234), Leiris has brought about a total internalization of Khadidja, he has nevertheless transcended the sterile opposition between credulous fixation and self-punitive iconoclasm. By encrypting her within himself he may have risked denying Khadidja her otherness, but her image is now one of those 'images véridiques dont j'oserai dire qu'elles sont pour moi, bien qu'embuées de mélancolie, plutôt réconfortantes' (*Fo* 239).

In moving towards a conclusion, 'Vois! déjà l'ange' comes to acknowledge the need for images and the legitimacy of aesthetic sublimation and commemoration when these are based not on facile poeticization, but on attentiveness to that handful of sovereign signs and gestures 'qui fulgurent dans le fatras de notre vie' (*Fo* 193). However emblematic she becomes, however many avatars she accumulates, Khadidja remains real for Leiris by virtue of a number of experiences and associations whose inherently plural and plastic meanings can never be finally stabilized or exhausted. Of course the real Khadidja is irretrievably lost:

Quoi que je fasse pour amender mon texte, rien ne rendra sa réalité palpable à tout cela et je suis sans pouvoir sur la douteuse idole qu'arme maintenant de son ergot fantomatique la trace laissée dans mon cerveau par l'aspérité de chair rasée qui surmontait l'humide ravin ouvert dans le brun de ses cuisses (*Fo* 234).

But for Leiris Khadidja is now a series of traces and (literally) impressions, like the intense sexual memory recorded here. And to think of her in this way—in terms of traces, images, erasures, substitutions; and, by extension, to see Béni-Ounif as more than 'un bled où crever d'immobilité et de désolation' (*Fo* 238)—is a way of 'thinking' which has its own validity. If Khadidja, turned into image, joins the band of 'belles aux noms insidieux' such as 'Rebecca, la servante Agar, Noémi, Rachel' (*Fo* 238), her image is none the less 'véridique'. Janus-faced, the 'image véridique' looks towards both the fixities of mythology and the openness and mutability of signs in a world which is bearable

---

[26] Indeed, although he does not mention it here, Leiris had, soon after the events, written a poem about Khadidja entitled 'L'Ange de la mort' which contains many details subsequently developed in 'Vois! déjà l'ange': see *Haut mal*, 172–4.

tant [qu'il] m'apparaît le lieu où ont surgi une quantité même infinitésimale de gestes et de mots en lesquels un accord humain se formulait, si l'on peut dire, à l'état pur et qui (fût-ce dans le seul éclair d'un heureux coup de dés) s'organisaient en cristaux d'un dessin si parfait qu'ils me faisaient crier merveille

> Vedi? . . . di morte l'angelo
> Radiante a noi si appressa

chantaient suavement Radamès et Aïda, presque joyeux quoique à demi morts d'asphyxie dans leur caveau funèbre (*Fo* 239).

By concluding his story of Khadidja with the image of a *radiant* angel of death, and to the strains of *Aïda* (quoting the passage from which, in the version derived from the French libretto, he had derived the title of his chapter) Leiris weaves together the themes of love, death, art, the gesture, and the image. Yet if this concludes the apologia for image-making we have excavated from the text it does not represent the triumph of the image as such. The matter of Khadidja—gestures, exchanges, and interpretations which took place once in real time, and have reverberated ever since—may find its truth in the movement towards images, but these—like her cross as it passes from hand to hand—always link back to the sovereign traces, gestures, and moments out of which they grew, and refer us forwards to the future horizons Leiris's writing constantly strives to keep open.

POETRY AND POLITICS: *FIBRILLES* AND *FRÊLE BRUIT*

The vicissitudes of Khadidja's image extend, however, beyond 'Vois! déjà l'ange'; and the status of 'le mythe vécu' continues to be a central issue in *Fibrilles* (1966), embarked on in 1956 and, since it was supposed to be the last volume of *La Règle du jeu*, written under the constant pressure to reach a conclusion. What becomes clear to Leiris at this point is the urgent need to come to terms with the antagonism between his poetic vocation and his political and social commitment. He will eventually conclude that in his case the fusion of art and politics (if we may use these terms as shorthand) is impossible; yet if this conclusion is forced on him by the recognition that in practice he has always given priority to the poetic pole, Leiris now finds it possible to formulate an ethic grounded in the primacy of the poetic but which includes, as endemic to it, a constant oscillation or 'tiraillement' between self and other, stasis and temporality, nostalgia and history. If it follows from this that one cannot be 'dans le mythe sans tourner le dos au réel' (*Fi* 235), a constant 'va-et-vient' between myth and reality is seen to be a concomitant of the poet's existence. Moreover, the traffic between events—such as a visit to China, or a failed suicide attempt and its reverberations—and private mythology is no less prominent in *Fibrilles* than it was in *Fourbis*; indeed, since the focus is now almost exclusively on the very recent past, the processes (and credentials) of mythologization are constantly at issue.

And it is precisely as process that mythologization will be condoned. If it were possible to arrest the mobility of images, to receive a definitive 'gage d'une pérennité conquise par la projection de soi en un objet (l'œuvre d'art')' (*Fi* 47), then self-mythologization would indeed involve a rejection of the real.[27] But time, our 'assujettissement au temps' (*Fi* 225), makes this impossible, just as it also undermines the stability of political commitments. The passage of time in the process of writing is more strongly marked in *Fibrilles*—a continuum in four parts—than in the earlier volumes of *La Règle du jeu*.[28] The disparate time-scales of existing, writing, and reading constantly disrupt Leiris's attempts to apprehend his life as a totality. Now more than ever before, he places the 'présent de l'écriture' in the foreground, emphasizing how his painfully slow progress constantly creates time-lags between the '*je* raconté'—that 'éternel retardataire'—and the '*je* raconteur, entraîné par le cours des choses aujourd'hui plus vite encore que hier' (*Fi* 220).[29]

Time also has its way with the images into which past experiences have been distilled. If the image of Khadidja was already anachronistic by the time *Fourbis* was published in 1955, the Algerian war has modified its significance for Leiris. Reconsidering 'Vois! déjà l'ange' in 1962 he feels a belated shame at what he now sees as connivance with an essentially colonial mentality; indifferent to the political realities of Algeria, 'n'ai-je pas été seulement sensible au pittoresque pur cristallisé dans cette idylle terriblement *Butterfly* si ce n'est *Petite Tonkinoise*?' (*Fi* 226). But when, by

---

[27] Leiris had earlier diagnosed his quest for the impossible 'tambour-trompette' as the desire for a 'gage d'accord' between self and universe (*Bi* 260).

[28] Writing is now perceived as 'la formulation écrite de cet immense monologue qui en un certain sens m'est donné, puisque toute la matière en est puisée dans ce que j'ai vécu, mais qui en un autre sens m'oblige à un constant effort d'invention, puisqu'il me faut introduire un ordre dans cette matière indéfiniment renouvelée, brasser ses éléments, les ajuster, les affiner jusqu'à ce que je parvienne à saisir tant soit peu leur signification' (*Fi* 77). The passage from experience ('ce que j'ai vécu') to meaning necessarily passes through a process of invention. *Fibrilles* shows again and again that self-mythologization is an inevitable part of the 'découverte et exposition de réalités non chiffrables que leur mise en forme permet seule de dégager' (*Fi* 203).

[29] Leiris bemoans the fact that this time-lag militates against the realization of his desire to be 'saisi au présent—un présent vrai et non de convention' (*Fi* 221), and he concludes that 'je me débats dans un temps qu'on pourrait dire *détraqué* s'il s'agissait de météorologie' (*Fi* 224).

way of atonement, he seeks to confer on Khadidja the dignity of a real historical subject, imagining her as an FLN militant or as a middle-aged woman encouraging young demonstrators in the kasbah, or transplanting her into the Chinese revolution, he merely succeeds in transposing the ready-made image into new contexts, making Khadidja a 'froide figure' rather than an 'image véridique'.[30]

If time wrecks art it does not spare politics. Leiris begins writing *Fibrilles* after a trip in 1957 to Mao's China where he had felt wholehearted enthusiasm for the cultural revolution. But his inability to totalize his experiences, to assemble the 'miettes de Chine' collected in his journal—fragmentary sights and sounds—into a coherent whole, warns him that his response to China was perhaps ultimately aesthetic rather that political; and the sense of fragmentation is exacerbated by historical events, most notably the Russian suppression of the Hungarian uprising in 1956 which prompted Leiris, along with many intellectuals of the period, to wonder if the time had come to abandon all hopes for communism (*Fi* 45). The slow torture to which Leiris's communist sympathies are subjected in the 1950s and 1960s runs right through *Fibrilles*. Furthermore, the doubt and confusion concerning his ability to combine art and politics form part of the background to Leiris's suicide attempt which, with the Chinese journey, is the other main event on which the text focuses. Much circumstantial detail surrounds Leiris's 'saut dans le vide', but he gives most space to the analysis of a series of dreams he had just prior to it, and to a string of interconnected fantasies experienced during the period after the tracheotomy which saved his life. The dreams, particularly one centred on the poet-politician (and thus role-model) Aimé Césaire, betray the conflict between art and politics in Leiris. Then, Leiris's painstaking interpretative reconstructions of his post-operative daydreams and fantasies—which involve the excavation of a number of human figures 'constructed' partly from childhood memories, distant relatives, etc.— manifest a preoccupation with the figure of the artist which ultimately leads to a cautious rehabilitation of art. As resurrected in his fantasies, Leiris's Tante Claire, the opera singer, comes to symbolize the possibility of which he had despaired: that art and existence might be reconciled: 'L'art sans cheveux en quatre. La vie comme un opéra . . .

---

[30] Yet in asserting pessimistically that the word 'Sarrasins' now resurrects Khadidja more effectively than all the pages of 'Vois! déjà l'ange' (*Fi* 226, 229) Leiris in fact pays homage to the 'mythologizing' process, if not to its end-products. The signifier *Sarrasins* and the cascade of associations it brings with it, which range across childhood, nourishment, sexuality, the Crusades, Clorinde (and therefore Tasso and Monteverdi), further extends the process which, via the poem 'L'Ange de la mort' and then 'Vois! déjà l'ange' 'produced' Khadidja in the first place.

Lustre adamantin de l'art et nudité houleuse de la vie, fiction et réalité, *là-bas* et *ici-même* dont la conjugaison—"pour de vrai" et non en allégorie ou le temps d'un éclair—est peut-être mon grand problème' (*Fi* 148). This represents a displacement of the art/politics opposition. Rehabilitated as a 'mode de vie' (*Fi* 150), art—ceding its autonomy—now embodies in itself the contradictions which divide Leiris.

The point is developed in an important sequence where he contrasts his 'côté de Pékin' (or 'Mao Tse Tung') and his 'côté de Kumasi' (*Fi* 212). The former relates to the 'Fête Nationale Chinoise' he attended as part of a French delegation; the second to an Easter mass he had heard some years earlier in a West African township. Both occasions were religious in character: the African mass vividly manifested all the ingredients of Christian mythology, while the Chinese festivities, celebrating the revolution, demonstrated the mystical, millenarian strain in Marxist-Leninism. At the same time, both ceremonies bore witness to the active 'préparation d'un avenir', a practical engagement with reality. But while the Chinese festival implied participation and faith in a collective endeavour, the African mass, for Leiris at least, was exhilarating partly because of the freedom and detachment it allowed. If it remained a spectacle, the mass was perceived by Leiris as a spectacle for *him*, a 'mythe vécu', 'de l'ordre des événements qui donnent après coup l'impression de n'avoir pas valu simplement par eux-mêmes mais de s'être produits parce que nous étions seuls à pouvoir totalement les vivre' (*Fi* 216).[31] In summarizing the contrast between the two 'côtés' emblematized by the Chinese and the African 'fêtes', Leiris presents them, even-handedly at this stage, as two poles between which he drifts—'des semblants d'action' on the one hand, 'le fil de mes songeries' on the other (*Fi* 218). But the reflections on time, already mentioned, and the further extensions of the meditation on art in the last sections of *Fibrilles*, will lead him towards accepting that for him the 'côté de Kumasi' predominates. The recognition, developed through and then beyond the analysis of his post-operative fantasies, that art can be a 'mode de vie' with its own rigours; the analogies between art, love, and death fuelled by the recollections of the work of a Chinese sculptor; the identification between the *fièvre* of intense experience[32] and the *fureur* of poetry; and

---

[31] Leiris's detachment ('me laissant émouvoir mais restant à distance', *Fi* 216) in fact contributed to his intense engagement in an event which brought together numerous strands of his personal mythology—his Utopian view of an Africa pulsating with natural forces, the hypnotic attraction of 'villes marchandes', the story of Jonah on which the sermon is based, the presence of vocal music, the theatricality of the Mass, the paschal symbolism of death and resurrection.

[32] The pre-eminence of the abiding 'fièvre' of poetry is suggested by the fact that *Fibrilles*

finally the revelation that, by virtue of its status as language, poetic *fureur* 'm'oblige à tenir compte d'autrui' (*Fi* 265), are the most salient stages of Leiris's reclamation of his poetic vocation. The last point is crucial since it obviates the need to think of political and aesthetic commitment as necessarily antagonistic: 'Tirée de mots qui ne sont pas les miens et adressée à quiconque l'accueillera, la poésie—fondamentalement, expansion aveugle hors de mes frontières—ne me lie-t-elle pas au partenaire indiscriminé qui est un *autre* par rapport à moi mais mon semblable à l'échelle de l'espèce?' (*Fi* 265). Communication may not (should not) be the aim of poetry, but poetic *fureur* engages with the community.

It would be wrong to suggest that at the end of *Fibrilles* Leiris is fully reconciled to himself, or that he embraces art and poetry—which he equates and celebrates here—in that spirit of *bondieuserie* he is careful to deprecate. He remains divided, 'écartelé'. To some degree Leiris will always be inclined (partly out of masochism) to polarize the demands of politics and the furious enticements of art. But on the whole he comes to see the 'tiraillement', the oscillations to which he is subject, as inherent in art itself. If he will continue to condemn the illusion that art can transfigure the artist's existence into myth,[33] in practice Leiris will reconcile himself to an art which constantly mythologizes (and demythologizes) his existence, an aesthetic process—autobiography—which dynamically explores the interface of experience and language, event and myth, private and public. Summarizing the paths which, in the analysis of his post-suicide fantasies, led to the figure of Tante Claire, Leiris noted: 'C'est un long rêve éveillé qui pendant des mois et des mois a pris la relève de la rêverie première' (*Fi* 149). We are perhaps entitled to apply this to *Fibrilles* as a whole. Here writing—firmly rooted in the present—becomes a kind of lucid dreamwork, a 'mise en forme' of the *vécu* which constantly invests it with ramified but lacunary structures of meaning. 'Le mythe vécu' is perhaps no longer an appropriate label, but the preoccupations and practices of *Fibrilles* do not simply rescind those of *Fourbis*, any more than it would be true to say that Leiris simply does the same thing again. He has kept moving, and by the end of the later text has found a paradoxical resting-place in the convulsive 'vertige' of poetry.

consists entirely of a text in four parts entitled '*La Fière, la fière...*' (the mispronunciation is explained on p. 69).

[33] To the well-meaning critic who praised the author of *Fourbis* for having discovered 'un système qui permet de supprimer toute distance entre une vie personnelle et la mythologie' (*Fi* 90) Leiris's riposte had been that it was only in retrospect and not 'dans le présent où je la vis' that he achieved this, if at all; 'l'artiste ne vit pas en légende ou en bande dessinée' (*Fi* 289), he observes further on.

At the end of *Fibrilles* Leiris announces that he does not now plan to write the projected *Fibules*, yet a decade later, in 1976, *Frêle Bruit* was presented as a fourth volume of *La Règle du jeu*. For all the pleasures it offers this book of fragments is less a continuation than a series of *addenda*.[34] Its fragmentary character reflects the fact that the quest for a *règle* is now over.[35] Approaching old age, Leiris knows that he is less likely to change than ever. Two longer pieces reconsider some of his oldest preoccupations, revealing that the conclusions of *Fibrilles* have not been superseded. In a sixty-page essay on 'le merveilleux' (*FB* 323–80), Leiris enumerates things which have this quality for him, and looks for their common essence. Several of the examples will be familiar to readers of *Fourbis*: the Gouffre de Padirac and the *Soirée Max Jacob*, Laure's sign of the cross, Khadidja's orgasm. The generic term 'merveilleux', associated particularly with surrealism, here encompasses the fields of 'le sacré' and 'le mythe vécu', and embraces the appeal of the momentary, the minimal, the negative, the *presque rien*: 'c'est le moins qui conduit au plus . . . c'est le négatif qui engendre le positif' (*FB* 356).[36] As an intermittent deliverance from 'la misère de notre condition', an 'ivresse' which temporarily dispels 'les ombres accumulées', 'le merveilleux' is unreservedly praised. The problems and doubts which tended to surround these notions and experiences in the past seem to have evaporated with the adoption of this new term. It might be tempting to put this down to old age, to *bondieuserie*. Yet what it shows is the extent to which, by the end of *Fibrilles*, Leiris had come to terms with himself.

The same point can be made with regard to the passage (*FB* 382–94) where Leiris subjects a 'phrase de sommeil' (one of those gnomic utterances, greatly prized by the surrealists, which come into our head on the verge of sleep) to three successive interpretations. He initially assumes that the words *Ici fruit à la tête se dit : là on s'enlise* must represent an encomium for the inner language of the poet, as against *enlisement* in the external world. But on reflection he is drawn to reverse this: to construe *là* as referring back to poetic interiority, and thus to reread the sentence as a condemnation of

---

[34] *Frêle Bruit* was followed in due course by such vols. as *Le Ruban au cou d'Olympia* (1981), *Langage tangage* (1985), and *A cor et à cri* (1988), each made up of short pieces. These works were not, however, declared to be part of *La Règle du jeu*.

[35] Significantly, Leiris now conceives the idea of a *règle* as essentially static, and associates it with the Sartrean 'choix originel' (*Fi* 309). Abandoning the quest to identify and perhaps transform 'le jeu que règlent mes idées, mes goûts et mes aptitudes', his work has become 'moins le manuel que le terrain de ce jeu'. Fragmentariness is linked to the possibility that death may interrupt the game at any moment, and this gives *Frêle Bruit* a darker tonality than previous vols.

[36] On the abiding appeal of the minimal and marginal for Leiris see also *FB* 347 ff.

poetry for its irrelevance to the real world of action. But a third reading then supervenes as Leiris recognizes, in the first two, a resurgence of that undialectical, Manichaean tendency he has often diagnosed in his way of thinking. He now judges that the sentence does not enjoin him to choose between two kinds of activity, but to desist from perceiving them in terms of a sterile opposition. From this he concludes that if he is intellectually prone to oscillate constantly between *pour* and *contre*, his only recourse should be 'de m'accrocher à ce qui est le mouvement même et se présente à la fois comme affirmation et négation: création esthétique incessamment renouvelée, travail pour une révolution sociale toujours à reprendre et à porter plus loin' (*FB* 392). Art is—or can be—'le mouvement même', and it is not by choosing between art and politics, but by the process of writing itself that Leiris can contribute to the social revolution he desires, which is itself after all partly an imaginative construct, a 'fruit dans ma tête comme dans celle de [mes] compagnons' (*FB* 392), a utopia where class inequality, sexism, and racism would have been eliminated. As in *Fibrilles*, commitment to poetry—with all its failings, and its insubstantial arsenal of signs, gestures, and moments—is ultimately the only valid rule in the game.[37]

ENUMERATIONS

> Les joies ineffables de l'énumération . . .
>
> (Georges Perec, *Penser/Classer*)

To make one's way through *La Règle du jeu* is to become accustomed to certain stylistic devices with strong thematic resonances and no account of Leiris's master work would be complete without consideration of at least one of these. 'Dans ma mémoire gisent—comme des objets hétéroclites (ancres, chaînes, chemises, crayons, papier) dans la boutique d'un *shipchandler* où les navigateurs viennent se réapprovisionner—un certain nombre d'événements . . .'. In this passage from *L'Age d'homme* (p. 144) the Augustinian image of memory as a vast storehouse is adapted to emphasize both the disunity of its contents and—in the images of replenishment and journeying—the psychic needs answered by recourse to memory. To enumerate, we could surmise, is to externalize memory in a manner faithful to its phenomenology; enumeration would be a form of data-retrieval which resisted the false order of concatenation. More,

---

[37] For a very interesting discussion of these issues see S. Hand, 'The Sound and the Fury'.

however, seems at stake in Leiris's enumerations than this would imply. Before looking further, some general consideration of enumeration as a literary mode will be helpful. A convenient point of reference is Francis Spufford's introduction to his anthology of lists in literature. 'Language', writes Spufford,

usually puts the signs that represent things into definite relationships with each other. Syntax joins . . . Lists, however, divide, or leave divided, the things they include. They offer only the relationship of accumulation . . . lists are . . . merely dances-on-the-spot, when the reader may expect the interesting forward movement of a narrative or a line of reflection.[32]

The suspension of narrative or meditative sequence is important, as is the paradox which 'stems from the absence of any straightforward authorial presence inside a list': 'When list-makers construe the world in listable fragments, are they fragmenting the world, actively, or collecting it, passively? Sundering or assembling?' Where lists occur in the context of self-representation (as they frequently have from Montaigne onwards), they may point to a unity underlying fragmentation or, on the contrary, they may convey the fragmentation of self.

Leiris's enumerations can be identified equally with three of his personae—the ethnologist who makes an inventory of his findings before proceeding to analyse; the poet who prizes parataxis, discrete images, flashes of textual intensity; the *aficionado* of details, fragments, the 'presque rien'. As regards the first, it is clear that quasi-ethnographic enumeration often provides Leiris with textual macro-structures: most of the chapters of *L'Age d'homme* enumerate instances of a theme (for example, Judith-figures or bullfights); and the same applies in *Biffures* with regard to verbal phenomena, Sundays, or desired objects, or in *Fibrilles*, with regard to Leiris's encounters with things Chinese prior to his visit there (pp. 9–16). In all these cases enumeration is a framing device which makes up for the lack of a specifically narrative organization. But the heart of Leirisian enumeration does not lie at the level of these macro-structures where the individual units will be a paragraph, or even several pages long; rather, it resides in lists such as the following:

A des faits—ou à des phases—d'une moindre ancienneté s'accrochent d'autres airs de danse: *Liebestraum* de Liszt, dont un arrangement syncopé reste le fond sonore d'un tour qu'il y a dix-huit ans je fis à Nantes, prélude à quelques jours d'hivernage

---

[38] *The Chatto Book of Cabbages and Kings: Lists in Literature.* The quoted passages occur on pp. 1 and 5.

dans la presqu'île de Quiberon durant lesquels s'agencèrent en poèmes les relents d'une virée à travers cette ville où divers irréguliers naquirent, après les négriers pour qui furent bâties les si belles maisons de pierre grise; *Love for sale*, qui se rattache à l'époque trouble où je travaillais à la revue 'Documents' . . . ; *Some of these days*, qu'un haut-parleur diffusa sur le 'Cairo City' lors de l'appareillage de ce paquebot qui m'emmenait en Grèce à la veille de la dernière guerre . . . (*Bi* 258–9).

Goût [du baroque], donc, qu'il serait vain de vouloir enfermer dans une définition rigide, mais dont je suis intimement persuadé qu'il a sa cohérence et qu'il est le ressort commun à nombre de mes comportements, disparates à première vue: mener ce livre comme si une part plus ou moins grande de surcharge—un luxe, pourrais-je dire—m'était, quelque irritation que j'en ressente, indispensable pour échapper à une sécheresse qui me répugnerait plus encore que les retards ainsi causés; au lieu de conduire selon les voies classiques celles de mes publications qui relèvent de la science pure, procéder par 'explosions successives de pensée' comme l'observait, voilà près de trente ans, un spécialiste de l'Islam . . . ; au cours de mon voyage en Chine, m'enticher de l'adventice et traiter comme si elles représentaient l'essentiel fleurs dans les gares ou autour des agents de police, modulations ensorcelantes des voix . . . combinaisons architecturales ingénieuses . . . toutes choses qui ne sont que des broutilles rococo dont il n'est pas surprenant qu'elles n'aient pu me fournir de quoi donner un témoignage consistant sur le pays que j'avais parcouru en visiteur émerveillé . . . (*Fi* 231–2).

Although some are much shorter, the quintessential enumeration in Leiris has at least six and perhaps over a dozen items, most commonly separated by semi-colons and linked by anaphora (unabbreviated, the lists quoted above have eight and seven items respectively). Rather than simple phrases, the items tend to be complete sentences with subordinate clauses. The enumerated material is often concrete and specific, and although the common ingredient may be evident the effect is initially to disjoin, to isolate a discrete fragment of time and space so that we see it vividly, but to restrict its exposure time. A response common to many readers is probably, therefore, after an initial 'survol', to want to go back and attend separately to each item. To do so is often to find more than one had expected. To read again is, on the one hand, to enter the micro-world of each fragment and to find it rich in symbolic potential, and on the other hand to discern, in the movement from the apparently impersonal to the intensely personal, an overall narrative movement. Our first sample (above) illustrates the way in which each enumerated item may in itself constitute a micro-narrative: each tune becomes the embodiment of a whole period or event in the author's life. The written fragment re-enacts the nostalgic power of the tune, becoming itself akin to a snatch of music fleetingly heard. In the second example, metonymy provides the underlying link between the symptoms of a 'goût du baroque' which Leiris diagnoses in widely scattered aspects of his behaviour—in love, writing, travel, and so on.

Can we speak generically of what happens when, at a given point, Leiris adopts the mode of enumeration? The quality of suspension—what Spufford calls the 'dancing-on-the spot' side of enumeration—is important. Although they often have a poetic intensity, Leiris's lists convey the relief from the anxiety of self-writing. Switching to the auxiliary engine of enumeration, with its regular, reassuring piston strokes, the writer glides out of the clutches of syntax. Released from articulation, disengaged from the responsibility to carry the text forward, he pursues his own ends rather than the reader's. The *jouissance* of enumeration also has the character of a particular kind of attention to the world. In this mode each entity is conjured up out of nowhere and slips back into oblivion: what is enumerated is briefly *out there* and then it is gone. Although each item can seem like a freeze-frame, enumeration is not static. In fact it has its own, quite strong, momentum which translates itself into the reader's desire to ask, at each moment: 'What else?' Enumeration in Leiris is, so to speak, profoundly superficial. It is a way of staying on the surface, treading water rather than taking the plunge; yet Leiris notes that it tends to bring things to the surface 'comme si cette procédure même incluait déjà la trouvaille vers quoi elle n'est, en principe, qu'un patient acheminement' (*Fi* 145). 'Chose troublante', he writes elsewhere: 'c'est peut-être surtout quand—gêne intime, incapacité d'expliquer ou répugnance à m'engager dans une longue analyse—je note sans prétendre donner la clé que, moi-même aveugle, je me montre vraiment à découvert' (*Fi* 281). 'Moi-même aveugle': to note without explaining is to reveal more than one knows; enumeration is a way of avoiding the issue, a detour, but it may reveal the true agenda. Enumeration is fetishistic, it latches on to this and this, to then and then, fabricating talismans of displaced desire, petrifying moments into those manageable objects in which Leiris hopes to find fusion—a 'gage d'accord'—between inside and outside. During an enumeration (lists have specific, palpable durations) the text's alignment with the reader changes: the enumerator is knowingly self-indulgent—he does it for his own benefit, acknowledging that it may be tedious for us (Beckett's great enumerators do this with superb archness). Enumeration has a therapeutic aspect and the imaginary reader—who follows, who keeps the tally—is essential to it. There can be something regressive, archaic, or child-like about enumerating, hence the complicity it calls for: taking things one by one, insisting on the singular, enumeration invites recognition for a singular subject, at any rate when, as always in Leiris, the basis of the list, the bottom line, is the claim to recognition of the desiring subject enshrined, as Roland Barthes (another *amateur*) would put it, in the words 'j'aime/j'aime pas'.[39]

Enumerations come thick and fast in the closing pages of *Fibrilles* where the device becomes a protagonist in Leiris's most concerted attempt to come to terms with the contradictions between poetry and *polis*, 'côté de Kumasi' and 'côté de Pékin'. Linked initially with the inexpugnable dominance of poetic *fureur*, enumeration becomes, at a second stage, associated with the recognition that the poetic impulse need not necessarily represent a repudiation of the world of others. The sequence begins with one of those crises which punctuate the composition of *La Règle du jeu*: the complex emotions prompted by a particular shade of red recollected from a dream (*Fi* 257) abruptly bring Leiris face to face with himself, and curtail his attempt to arrive, through abstract discourse, at a dialectical resolution of his contradictions. Instead, he feels impelled to discover what the red colour could represent, and his three attempts to do so constitute a sort of allegory or object lesson, summing up different ways of figuring the relationship between writing and the real. Enumeration plays a part at each stage. Leiris's initial impulse is to recapture a 'visionary gleam', not to interpret the dream but to discover the origin of the faded redness which suffused it. Through enumeration he stages an identity parade, drawing up a list of items, drawn from what he calls elsewhere 'les quatre coins de ma vie', which have in common a similar colour: Lambrusco wine, the houses of Bologna, Roman brickwork, Chinese stucco, the reddish tint of nipples, the quivering orangey flame of oil refineries glimpsed from trains (*Fi* 258–60). This approach, based on a desire to counter loss and vacancy by getting back to an original experience, is metonymic: each enumerated item is a displacement of the original, manifesting one of its aspects. In this fashion, however, Leiris not only fails to retrieve what he felt he had lost, but also drains his enumerated memories of their lifeblood, with the result that they come to exist only 'sur le papier où mon écriture se convulse sans parvenir à se faire autre chose qu'écriture' (*Fi* 259).

In the face of this, Leiris's next move is to think of the red glow as a state of being rather than a particular experience, and to reinterpret the urge to enumerate as a desire to locate past experiences which share the emotive tenor of the dream memory: instead of being a poor copy of a lost original, the enumerated item is now conceived as a substitute or equivalent, a metaphor rather than a metonymy. And it is precisely as a set of linguistic items, an arrangement of signifiers, that the enumeration achieves a match

---

[39] See the section on Barthes in Ch. 6 above.

with the state Leiris seeks to engender and thus repeat. On this view, what is depicted in the enumeration, the past occasion to which it relates, is secondary, a 'texte de convention dont la vraie teneur est révélée par la grille aux découpures adéquates, qui en isole quelques fragments' (*Fi* 261). The particular memory is no more than a pretext: it is what it becomes when remodelled by an adequate verbal formulation that counts. Equally, the faded red of the dream—at the origin—is no longer held to be of much account (it even occurs to Leiris at this point that it may have been inspired by the shade of his pyjamas!). What matters is the global state or emotion which sets language in motion, and which language now seeks to repeat. But, as Leiris observes, this state too becomes less definite the more one focuses on it, so that in the end he is forced to recognize that it is no more than the generic state of *fureur*—poetic emotion and intensity: 'Cette fureur que je tenais pour le moteur originel échappe donc à mes prises et je suis devant elle comme le théologien réduit à dresser l'état des mystères divins sans essayer de les percer' (*Fi* 264). Enumeration has become no more than tautological *ressassement*, and the enumerator a hapless theologian unable to penetrate the mysteries in which he deals. From here it is but a step to the view (the third part of Leiris's lesson) that the only thing that matters is an experience of and in language: the acceptance that all his writing is ultimately motivated by the desire which finds its most memorable expression at this point:

me projeter dans la zone *off-limits* où le langage écrit sera ma pensée devenue chose et moi-même arraché aux vicissitudes de la vie par une mort qui m'en donnerait l'intelligence la plus haute, un pont lancé sur le vide qui m'enferme comme dans une île, le lieu aussi où mon temps s'abolit . . . (*Fo* 264).

In the context of this project enumeration becomes one of the privileged instruments of a poetic operation, a verbal performance designed to obliterate the coordinates of mortal existence and, in a momentary spasm or seizure, to propel the subject beyond his customary sphere. The 'moments . . . totaux' (*Fi* 262) to which Leiris aspires through the *fureur* of poetry involve the sacrificial transmutation or decantation of experience into pure event, realized, momentarily, in language.

Leiris has, of course, voiced this aspiration many times before, generally going on to lament its failure to constitute an appropriate answer to his desire that time and art, the real and the imaginary, should be reconciled. But in giving it hyperbolical expression at this point he aims, it transpires, to indicate a new understanding of how this poetic vocation relates to other commitments. Leiris concludes that he must reconcile himself to the fact that he is essentially a poet, and must renounce the quest for an ethic which would make poetic practice and political praxis inseparable. However, at the conclusion of *Fibrilles*, he wishes, as we saw earlier, to suggest that this does not necessarily involve turning his back on commitment to the world of others, but rather the acceptance of his own divided, contradictory identity. Enumeration plays a crucial role in a final allegory which demonstrates Leiris's recognition of this fact.

With much circumstantial detail he recounts a stop-over in Copenhagen on his journey back from China: he remembers calling at various bars, notably one where two middle-aged women played French music of the 1920s, and enjoying a meal in a restaurant overlooking the harbour. Leiris then repeats these details in the form of an enumeration—'un bar à clientèle aussi platement sophistiqué que l'était son décor. Une musique désuète . . . Des magasins . . . Un restaurant . . . Des navires' (etc.)—before revealing the 'point' of what is deemed to have been one of those occasions when reality conspired to become allegory: 'à Copenhague, l'expérience directe m'avait montré que, si j'étais chez moi quelque part, ce ne pouvait être que dans une ville du monde capitaliste et en face de ce que pareilles villes offrent de moins utile aux collectivités' (*Fi* 272–3). Unable fully to commune in the collective spirit of the Chinese revolution, he found that he was at home in the West at its most commercialized and frivolous—'j'avais retouvé mon folklore' (*Fi* 272). Leiris is, he reminds us, intellectually and emotionally sympathetic to the spirit of Chinese communism, and quite out of sympathy with Western capitalism. It is not, then, the Western dream which seduces him in the spectacle of Copenhagen but rather the intense self-awareness induced by the parallel between his own 'malaise d'homme', his sense of futility, and the West's futile, consumerist pleasures. The many Baudelairean echoes in the passage underline the topos of the 'pays qui te ressemble', a narcissistic mirroring in which self and spectacle enjoy an ironic reciprocity. And at one level the enumeration, repeated in a slightly different form in a subsequent paragraph (*Fi* 273), simply builds up a composite, compacted, and unreal image like that constructed earlier out of shades of red. But at the same time, by insisting on the discrete, variegated textures of the world as refracted by the lens of a particular sensibility, enumeration denies closure and insists on multiplicity. As in the case of the redness of *fureur*, enumeration is linked to poetry, though not simply to the magical transmutations which words can perform. Here the poetic, and enumeration as one of its modes, is linked to what Leiris had called 'les ombres, les lumières et les replis baroques du côté de Kumasi que colore un intime rougeoiement et non un rouge à l'emporte-pièce' (i.e. the red of the 'côté de Pékin': unequivocal political commitment; *Fi* 267). The poetic is no longer viewed as a repudiation of the *polis* but as an option attuned to the contrapuntal, oscillatory character of Leiris's make-up, his 'mouvement pendulaire', encapsulated in yet another enumeration (*Fi* 274).

The predominance of enumeration at the close of *Fibrilles*, where Leiris arrives at a kind of 'morale provisoire' (subsequently to become permanent) to stand in for the elusive 'règle' he now renounces, befits its status as a mode which unites conjunction and disjunction, singular and plural, momentary intensity and endless deferral. Always a potent presence in Leiris's writing, enumeration comes into its own at this point in *La Règle du jeu*, revealing its profound affinities with the ethos which prevails here. The moment of enumeration is neither one of a mythic plenitude which inevitably turns out to be in some measure delusory, nor of a tortuous writhing in the margins of the void. If enumeration has its euphoric aspect it is always also laconic and agnostic: it is a figure of lucidity, and in the end Leiris's writing aspires to that quality above all else.

9

The Otherness of Memory

Souvenir, souvenir, que me veux-tu...?
Verlaine, 'Nevermore'[1]

I

'One is always at home in one's past', observes Vladimir Nabokov in *Speak, Memory*[2]. The remark is many-layered: it encompasses the pathos of exile, as well as the author's visceral anti-Freudianism, but it also goes to the heart of the attitude to memory in his autobiography. Nabokov celebrates 'the pathological keenness of the retrospective faculty' with which he is gifted. In the first instance it is the miraculous preservation of minute details which enchants him, but ultimately 'the supreme achievement of memory' lies in 'the masterly use it makes of innate harmonies when gathering to its fold the suspended and wandering tonalities of the past'. If memory holds the key to our personal homeland it is because of its contrapuntal genius, the capacity to gather disparate threads into an organic whole, to manifest the latent thematic designs which underlie our scattered lives. *Speak, Memory* gives striking expression to a theme which pervades (but, as we shall see, does not monopolize) the autobiographical tradition from Augustine, through Rousseau, Wordsworth, and Dilthey, down to the present. Memory, these writers tell us, gathers and redeems, preserves and reintegrates. If lives and identities have unity it is by virtue of an agency which works on our behalf: we may help or hinder, but essentially Mnemosyne has her own mysterious ways, and these are to be marvelled at, as Augustine indicates in book 10 of the *Confessions*. There he evokes 'the great storehouse of the memory, which in some indescribable way secretes [all these sensations] in its folds', and he goes on to enumerate the all-embracing capacities of this 'vast, immeasurable

---

[1] *Œuvres poétiques*, 27.
[2] *Speak, Memory*, 91. Subsequent quotations are from pp. 60, 134, 110, 23.

sanctuary' with its 'wonderful system of compartments' which contain 'the sky, the earth, and the sea, ready at my summons', and where 'I meet myself as well. I remember myself and what I have done, when and where I did it, and the state of my mind at the time.'[3]

The tendency to think spatially is an essential feature of this view of remembering: in saving experience from the ravages of time, and in overcoming the discontinuity of past and present, memory turns anterior into interior, and converts time into (inner) space. Frequently the capacity to achieve this transmutation is reserved for one variety of memory as against another, baser, variety. Plato's *anamnesis*, properly speaking the recollection within this life of eternal forms, can be seen as a prototype for all those versions of memory[4] where this faculty is held to give access to the realm of essences. Moreover, in its contrast with *memoria*, the generally more mundane faculty elucidated by Aristotle,[5] anamnesis is ancestor to the spiritual term in a host of subsequent pairings from Plotinus, through Condillac ('ressouvenir' as against 'mémoire'), Hegel ('Erinnerung' as against 'Gedächtnis'), to Bergson and Proust ('mémoire involontaire' as against 'mémoire volontaire'). Not the least of the virtues attributed to the positive form of memory in such polarizations is the capacity to transcend its negative avatar, associated with workaday, mechanical remembering and ordinary time. 'True' memory offers a conquest or redemption of time, a retroactive mastery over experience, which gives access to continuity, unity, and permanence: 'la mémoire se définit comme le sens de la permanence humaine à travers le temps', writes Georges Gusdorf in *Mémoire et personne*; and also: 'Dans la temporalité de l'existence, la mémoire vient attester notre intemporalité.'[6]

Memory as gathering, 'rassemblement', self-unity: we are dealing here with a secular myth, deeply rooted in the Western tradition. Contemporary psychological investigation has certainly demonstrated that autobiographical memory plays a central role in personal identity,[7] but the myth we are considering involves a sublimation whose most striking feature, in the context of autobiography, is perhaps the way it elides the subject's active participation in the work of memory. The emphasis on restoration, reintegration, and

---

[3] *Confessions*, 215–16.

[4] The phrase is from J. Olney, 'Some Versions of Memory, Some Versions of Bios', which makes a strong case for autobiography as 'rassemblement', as does B. J. Mandel, 'The Autobiographer's Art'.

[5] R. Sorabji compares the two views at length in *Aristotle on Memory*.

[6] *Mémoire et personne*, 50.

[7] See the excellent collection *Autobiographical Memory*, ed. David C. Rubin, esp. the essays by Robinson, Neisser, Baddeley and Wilson.

redemption tends to exclude or attenuate the possibility of conflict, doubt, ambivalence, pain, or definitive loss: in short, the 'otherness', rather than the 'sameness' of memory. More generally, by insisting on the achieved fusion of 'Mémoire et personne', this view tends to deny any sense of division between a person and his or her memories. The notion that selection or distortion are inevitable is not considered problematic as long as memory itself is credited with the editorial prerogative: what has to be maintained is the notion of a bounteous faculty which preserves the past from annihilation at the hands of time. In view of this, it is hardly surprising that we find autobiographers in the front ranks of Mnemosyne's devotees. The idea that memory secretly sifts and decants tends to indemnify the autobiographer not only against the accusation that what was most important may have been forgotten, but also against the suspicion that memories have been hand-picked and meddled with. 'Rien d'indifférent pour lui ne peut rester dans sa mémoire', observes Rousseau in one of the *Dialogues*.[8] What he has forgotten cannot have been important, what he remembers has the authority of Remembrance. Paul Hoffman notes that for Rousseau 'le souvenir est une mise en perspective spirituelle du vécu': always at work, it assimilates and attunes the contingent to the essential.[9] Autobiographical retrospection can therefore be presented not as an active or transactive process but as a transcription of what has previously been laid down. In composing his autobiography Rousseau feels that he is tapping into the channels his memory has already established, drawing on a repository of authentic as against adventitious experience. He has no need to decide what is essential, memory has already done this for him, and if he finds it necessary to fill in gaps by invention or conjecture this bears only, he claims (p. 278), on what is inessential.

For the autobiographer, one of the great advantages of this view is that it parries in advance questions such as: was the past really like that? or, is that really what happened? When Rousseau makes the famous assertion: 'En me livrant à la fois au souvenir de l'impression reçue et au sentiment présent je peindrai doublement l'état de mon âme, savoir au moment où l'événement m'est arrivé et au moment où je l'ai décrit' (p. 1154), one may be prompted to

---

[8] *Œvres complètes*, i, 808. Cf. passages in the *Confessions* on pp. 21, 115, 122, 138, 226, etc.

[9] 'La Mémoire et les valeurs dans les six premiers livres des *Confessions*', 83. Hoffman argues that memory in Rousseau involves a 'travail de l'imagination' (p. 86) which reconciles empirical experience with a desire for meaningful order: 'l'âme qui se souvient s'est rassemblée en elle-même, merveilleusement unifiée, habitée des visages, hantées des voix dont elle perçoit pleinement enfin le message' (p. 88). The *work* of imagination is, however, erased because it has always already taken place at the point when the subject 'remembers'. Also illuminating is P.-P. Clément, 'De la mémoire aux mémoires'.

wonder whether memory has not in fact erased the very distinction he is making. What he felt then is only accessible to him to the degree that it subsists as an organic part of what he is now. But if one way of explaining this is in terms of the beneficial power of memory, another is to see it as witness to the fact that memory is inevitably a function of present consciousness. Whatever it is that we have remembered or forgotten, it is now—when we write if we are autobiographers—that we have to come to terms with it and determine what it means. In practice, it is evident to the reader of the *Confessions* that Rousseau, far from simply unpacking what his memory has stored up for him, is frequently engaged in such a confrontation, and that, far from taking his memories as they come, he is involved in an active and conscious process of shaping and construction.

In the context of modern literary culture, the notion of memory as gathering and unification has found a *locus classicus* in Proust's *A la recherche du temps perdu*. The famous instances of 'mémoire involontaire'—the 'Madeleine', the uneven paving stones which recapture an experience in Venice—are repeatedly cited as evidence of a particular kind of joy and knowledge which memory can bring. No doubt these passages strike a chord in many readers because they render vividly a certain kind of memory-experience we have had or can imagine having. But when they are taken to represent the essence of memory, as in Mary Warnock's recent study of the topic, one may feel entitled to wonder if myth has not triumphed over reality.[10] Warnock's emphasis throughout *Memory* is on 'the pleasures of memory . . . the peculiar satisfaction of recollection'. Drawing extensively on autobiographers and diarists, as well as philosophers and psychologists, she portrays memory as the key to our continuity as human beings. Memory preserves and attests continuity and is thus very much a place where, in Nabokov's terms, we are 'at home'. In philosophical terms the argument for continuity is based, for Warnock, on the postulate that memory involves causal links between past and present, a view which is associated with Proust: 'It is the causal link between what happened *then* and what is happening in memory *now* which makes memory a possession in which, as Proust said, we triumph over time.' Yet when we read Proust's accounts of involuntary memory, and when we situate them in the wider context of *A la recherche*, are

---

[10] Geoffrey Strickland makes the case against Warnock very well in his review-article 'The Analysis of Memory'. Quotations in the next few sentences are from Warnock, *Memory*, 138, 146, 93. A very different view of memory, which places far more emphasis on its 'otherness'—stressing the 'transformative force of memory', its 'unplumbable depths' and 'multiple pathways'—will be found in a work by another philosopher, Edward S. Casey, *Remembering: A Phenomenological Study*.

we really made to feel that we are dealing with what Warnock calls 'direct knowledge of the past'? Even if Proust points to some sort of causal link at the level of sensations, what he stresses repeatedly is the creative effort required if we are to benefit from what memory has to offer. The triumph *over time*, achieved only on the aesthetic plane, can also be seen as a triumph *over memory* which, in the sphere of identity, manifests discontinuity rather than unity. As Hans Robert Jauss observes, the work of memory in Proust is predicated on a 'prior experience of self-absence in which memory has lost its power to establish identity' and on 'the complete renunciation of the latent Platonism of the age-old aesthetic tradition' which held that the transcendental realm of essences could be apprehended 'through direct anamnesis'.[11] Whatever the transfigurations it achieves through art, memory in Proust is by no means a purely joyous affair. Indeed, in displaying a power to disrupt and problematize identity, it suggests an alternative anatomy of memory to which we must now turn.

'J'ai plus de souvenirs que si j'avais mille ans': In Baudelaire, as Proust once observed, memory is at the heart of both aesthetic creation and human reality. Memory's miraculous power to resurrect leads the poet to evoke the 'charme, profond, magique dont nous grise|Le passé dans le présent restauré'. Through memory we retain contact with the 'années profondes'; the 'vert paradis des amours enfantines' remains with us—memory gathers and unites. This, however, is by no means the whole picture. In 'Le Flacon', for example, memory does not bring reintegration but violent disruption. Mobilized by 'le souvenir enivrant qui voltige', the subject's eyes close:

> . . . le vertige
> Saisit l'âme vaincue et la pousse à deux mains
> Vers un gouffre obscurci de miasmes humains;
>
> Il la terrasse au bord d'un gouffre séculaire,
> Où, Lazare odorant déchirant son suaire
> Se meut dans son réveil le cadavre spectral
> D'un vieil amour ranci, charmant et sépulcral[12]

Rather than retrieving a lost domain, the depersonalized subject (an 'âme vaincue') is assailed by memory and swept to the brink of a temporal abyss. It is not the 'presentness' of the past which returns but its irremediable 'pastness': the 'vieil amour ranci' breaks out of its grave-cloth but remains

---

[11] '1912: Threshold to an Epoch', esp. pp. 58–61.

[12] *Œuvres complètes*, i. 47. The other poems quoted are 'Spleen' (p. 73), 'Un fantôme' (p. 39), 'Moesta et Errabunda' (p. 63).

cadaverous and spectral. Here memory's terrain is an uncanny intermediacy between the living and the dead. To succumb to its pull is to be dragged away from our moorings in the present. Memory breaks up the habitual routines of self-awareness and, rather than fostering unity, threatens everyday self-consistency. The unassimilable past lodges in the present like a foreign body, while the familiar past is disrupted by the invasion of a forgotten dimension. In Baudelaire, memory—conceived above all as process and activity—is heterogeneous: we are subject to (and subjects of) a variety of 'mémoires'. In 'Le Cygne' one form of memory, the painful nostalgia occasioned by a rapidly changing environment, is succeeded and partially checked by another, the associative power through which one memory can spawn another in a centrifugal movement which, if it provisionally fuses disparate planes of experience, promises no definitive resting-place. Baudelairian memory deals in the momentary and the fragmentary, and we might, with some justice, link this to the failure of his autobiographical project—'Mon cœur mis à nu'—which remained a collection of fragments. Does it follow that the kinds of memory which concerned him are incompatible with autobiography? Is autobiography necessarily tied to a smoothing over of the disruptive, discontinuous work of memory, to the victory of unity, however mythic?

This is certainly the view taken by Michel Beaujour when he contrasts the *autoportrait* with the *autobiographie*: 'L'anamnèse de l'autoportrait s'oppose à la réminiscence autobiographique, toujours fondée à quelque degré sur la croyance en la permanence d'un moi individuel dont l'intériorité est antériorité.'[13] Even if we accept Beaujour's postulate regarding 'la permanence d'un moi individuel', it is possible to argue that a conflict between forms of memory which favour narrative continuity and forms of memory which do not is as much a feature of autobiography as it is of the self-portrait. For Beaujour the existence of narrative order automatically commits autobiography to a particular, unifying view of memory which erases the 'work' of remembrance: 'l'autobiographie qui se constitue le long d'un fil narratif événementiel raconte des "contenus de mémoire": elle ne met pas en scène le procès de son invention ou de sa remémoration.'[14] Such a view is hardly borne out, however, by the autobiographies of Chateaubriand and Stendhal, both writing before Baudelaire, where in different ways we find a linear narrative which is allied to a *mise en scène* rather than a suppression of the process of memory itself.

[13] *Miroirs d'encre*, 167.
[14] Ibid. 252.

'Mes souvenirs se font écho': for Chateaubriand the act of remembrance triggers parallels between the shifting contexts in which he writes—Paris, London, Berlin, or Dieppe—and the recollected past. Always advancing on two fronts, the linear progress of the narrative is by no means the sole or indeed the principal agency through which Chateaubriand apprehends his past and present personae. The straightforward transcript of events in the order in which they happened, the externalization of 'contenus de mémoire', in Beaujour's phrase, is repeatedly subordinated to the ramifications—personal, but also cultural or 'historical'—which a given memory brings in its train. What counts for Chateaubriand, as later for Nabokov,[15] is the associative network, the soundings in the echo-chamber; if memory discloses being it is not by resurrecting the past or by establishing continuity ('c'était un autre *moi*, un moi de mes premiers jours finis, qui jadis habita ces lieux, et ce moi a succombé, car nos jours meurent avant nous', p. 497),[16] but by providing materials for the construction of a fundamentally anachronistic space. If Chateaubriand comes alive through his reconstruction of the past, it is by regarding himself as already dead ('Ne suis-je pas moi-même quasimort?'), and by imagining that he speaks 'd'outre-tombe'. From this vantagepoint, indissolubly linked to a mode of utterance, his past, increasingly unamenable to anamnesis, takes on—at an imaginary level—the architectonic values of a funerary edifice.

If in Chateaubriand the frequent references to the processes of memory point to a sense of discontinuity, compensation is found in the (ultimately aesthetic) realm of association and analogy. By taking its place in an associative network, the singular memory loses the power to jar or unsettle. With Stendhal it is quite different. 'Mais pourqoi ce monde? à quelle occasion? C'est ce que l'image ne dit pas. Elle n'est qu'image' (p. 72).[17] To remember, for Stendhal, is to stimulate the resurgence of what had been forgotten, and to be confronted with *images*. The extraordinary precision with which certain moments are recaptured, and the thrill of 'seeing again' (conveyed repeatedly by the phrase 'Je me vois') are no guarantee that a coherent picture will emerge or that a sense of continuity between past and present selves will be established. It is one thing to recapture (some of) our memories, another to decide what their purport is: 'Je m'interroge depuis une

---

[15] Nabokov shared Chateaubriand's fondness for superimposition (cf. Ch. 4 above): 'I confess I do not believe in time. I like to fold my magic carpet, after use, in such a way as to superimpose one part of the pattern upon another', *Speak, Memory*, 109.

[16] *Mémoires d'outre-tombe*, 497. The quotation in the next sentence is from the following page.

[17] References to *Vie de Henry Brulard* are cited in the text.

heure pour savoir si cette scène est bien vraie, réelle, ainsi que vingt autres qui, évoquées des ombres, reparaissent un peu, après des années d'oubli' (p. 131). In Stendhal we are dealing with memories, not Memory, fragments of a past, not the Past. He emphasizes the gaps and blanks which are often as palpable as actual memories, noting the connection between such 'blancs' and episodes of powerful emotion: 'Le trouble extrême chez moi détruit la mémoire' (p. 375). Stendhal's commitment to the authenticity of his 'mémoire d'enfant' makes him reluctant to go beyond this correlation and to adulterate his 'oublis' with speculative 'pourquois'. He tends instead to draw attention to the border between the remembered and the forgotten; as a consequence one sometimes feels that the vividly etched details of a scene are *residua* which owe their survival to proximity with emotional material which has vanished. Acknowledgement of the process of repression, and that type of 'screen-memory' where, according to Freud, the vivid memory of seemingly insignificant details is a sign of displacement, seems but a step away.[18]

The point is well illustrated by the recurrent memory of the 'longues promenades aux Granges' on which, after his mother's death, the child was regularly forced to accompany his father and his aunt Séraphie. The memory figures recurrently as a 'pièce à conviction' in mitigation of the child's antipathy towards his father. Forced to trudge across marshy fields in the role of a *tiers incommode*, on what he felt was the spurious pretext that it was for his own pleasure, the child develops a resentment which helps to justify the suspicions he harboured against his father when a pet thrush was killed (p. 188), and the harshness of his response to his father's weeping when the son left home for Paris (p. 346). But Stendhal also indicates that, at the time of writing, the memory of the 'promenades aux Granges' is linked to the suspicion that his father had fallen in love with Séraphie: 'Je suppose que dans la suite mon père fut amoureux d'elle' (p. 47); 'il me semble aujourd'hui que mon père en devint amoureux' (p. 100). At one point this is alluded to shortly after the recollection that Stendhal himself had once been sexually stimulated by the sight of Séraphie's bare legs—'j'étais tellement emporté par le diable que les jambes de ma plus cruelle ennemie me firent impression. Volontiers j'eusse été amoureux de Séraphie' (p. 185)—but here Stendhal is even more

[18] Stendhal's account of 'Petits souvenirs de ma première enfance' (*Vie de Henry Brulard*, ch. 5)—the aggressive impulse to bite a cousin, the hint of the 'acte manqué' surrounding the incident where a dropped knife narrowly missed Mme. Chenavaz, memories of physical desire for mother coupled to visceral hatred for father—strike the post-Freudian reader as remarkably telling. In this regard Stendhal's reluctance to base a fixed portrayal of his character on such evidence is a tribute to the subtlety and open-mindedness of his fascination with memory.

insistent that the hypothesis of his father's 'amours avec Séraphie' is not directly supported by extant childhood memories. If it ever existed, that part of the fresco (the image is developed at this point) has fallen away. What is striking about the 'promenades aux Granges' is the way a memory becomes the point of intersection for a number of possible insights into patterns of feeling at large in the wider field of a now distant childhood. Stendhal is able to suggest a connection between the child's hostility towards the walks with father and aunt and the awareness of emotional currents involving these two, himself, and also his late mother (for whose love he had considered his father a rival). But he shows a remarkable respect for his memories by refusing to confuse the feelings he specifically remembers with the interpretations prompted by the mature understanding of the adult.[19]

Stendhal's celebration of the power and fascination of memory does not derive from its capacity to unify and reintegrate. The point is not that he fails to identify with or rediscover himself in what he remembers—each page of *Vie de Henry Brulard* is peppered with recognitions—but that such flashes are always local and individual.[20] Memory in Stendhal is tied to the singular and to the momentary: memories are monads—each is a world which can briefly be inhabited and from which the surrounding vista can rapidly be glimpsed; memories are *traces*—vestigial marks pointing to prior actions and presences which always require reflection. Stendhal's impulse is to externalize his memories (as in his diagrams), to inscribe, trace, and 'materialize' them. Remembering remains a present activity: we are always with this memory or

---

[19] Throughout *Vie de Henry Brulard*, Stendhal imparts a sense that memories are precious, vulnerable, and must be handled with utmost care: some may be fakes (p. 131); some are secondhand, derived from things heard (p. 418) or read, or pictures we have seen (p. 427). He knows that what matters is often the aura of a remembered event, and yet that this may be ineffable: 'Le sujet surpasse le disant' (pp. 144, 336, 434) becomes shorthand for this recognition. He fears that to recount one's most cherished memories may be to spoil them: the last words of his MS are: 'On gâte des sentiments si tendres à les raconter en détail' (p. 435). He is conscious of the pitfalls of anachronism: when dealing with the events of a given period, how can he gauge what point in a gradual transformation of feelings or attitudes he had then reached (p. 116)?

[20] Cf. the discussion of what psychoanalysts call 'flashbulb memories' in Rubin (ed.), *Autobiographical Memory*, 35–6 and *passim*. R. Coe makes an interesting link with the Stendhalian *petit fait vrai*, *When the Grass was Taller*, 213–14. The kind of memory that concerns us here—essentially fragmentary, discontinuous, and hostile to centred identity— could be investigated in such texts as Malraux's *Lazare*, Perec's *Je me souviens*, with its enumeration of 480 instances of 'un souvenir presque oublié, inessentiel, banal, commun, sinon à tous, du moins à beaucoup' (p. 119), Khatibi's *La Mémoire tatouée* where, as Barthes observes in his 'Postface' (p. 213), memories have the character of images, signs, traces, letters, marks, producing an identity grounded in otherness and difference (cf. the discussion of Barthes later in this chapter).

that, never securely in the space of Memory. Whatever the degrees of identification, there is always a gap here between the autobiographer and his memories. Stendhal's stance is consistently interrogative and the emphasis on the activity of recall, its physical intensity and immediacy, goes hand in hand with an attitude of caution, an awareness of gaps, problems, and possible disturbances. The work of memory offers no definitive purchase on the past, but an opportunity for endless negotiations; it affords a partly therapeutic, partly pathogenic engagement with the past's residues, always explicitly informed by the concerns of the present. In Stendhal individual memories, in their variety and profusion, take on an enigmatic reality, as traces of aggression, pleasure, desire, or disdain, as signposts for potential explorations and estimations of self. We are at some distance from the myth of gathering and unity: in subsequent challenges to that vision of memory we will find much that Stendhal had anticipated.

II

Memory, it may fairly be claimed, is the essential terrain of psychoanalysis. The psychoanalytic method can be depicted as the attempt to restore psychic wholeness by filling gaps in the analysand's memory, thereby substituting knowledge for incapacitating ignorance. To some degree, therefore, remembering in Freud can be associated with reunification, reintegration, and continuity, and thus with the traditional concept or myth of anamnesis. Yet it is also true that psychoanalysis develops and exacerbates certain features of the second picture of autobiographical memory we have outlined. To remember, for Freud, is not to exercise a faculty or to draw on a stable repository of experiences distilled once and for all.[21] Memories are traces formed in the context of a dynamic relationship between the psyche, at all its levels, and the lived environment in all its aspects. Much of what we are conscious of is not preserved in our memories; a good deal of what we 'remember' never in fact entered our consciousness. Like the proprietary writing-pad which so delighted Freud, our psychic

---

[21] The most important sources for an assessment of Freud's changing and often highly speculative ideas on memory are: *The Psychopathology of Everyday Life*, ch. 7; the papers on metapsychology, esp. *Beyond the Pleasure Principle*, *The Ego and the Id*, 'A Note upon the 'Mystic Wrting-Pad', 'Negation', 'A Disturbance of Memory on the Acropolis'; 'Screen Memories', 'Constructions in Analysis', 'Remembering, Repeating and Working-through'; 'From the history of an Infantile Neurosis (the Wolf Man)'. A useful conspectus will be found in *Mémoires*, a special number of the *Nouvelle Revue de psychanalyse*.

apparatus is many-layered: only some of the inscriptions it registers are retained permanently and these owe their preservation as much to the operations of unconscious needs and desires as to the interests and intensities we are consciously aware of. Our memory is thus a palimpsest of discontinuous traces inscribed through the spasmodic operations of the psyche. Furthermore, our memories do not stand still. Just as, by virtue of the intermittent, selective operations of memory, an event may have been retained in what was already a distorted form, so memory traces are subject to revision, retranscription, and realignment under the pressure of other experiences. What we call our memories often belong not to the period they ostensibly refer us to but to one or more of the stages in a process of 'permanent modification' to which they are subject. It follows from this that remembering in Freud is not constative, the 'reading-off' of settled 'contenus de mémoire', but performative: when a memory comes to mind it exposes a desire or impulse, it has designs on us; when we choose to remember, we act on the past's residues, altering their configurations by the kind of pressure we exert. Remembering bears on the present as much as on the past. A memory is not simply a commemorative trophy, but an *objet trouvé* of uncertain provenance and function. Remembering bears on the future: interpreting what we were contributes to what we will be: as Valéry put it: 'La mémoire est l'avenir du passé.' In a sense Freud invites us to distrust our memories. More importantly, he invites us to attend closely to them, to pay particular attention to stray details, oddities of emphasis and atmosphere, and to be aware that what seems most anodyne may be what is most important. The innocuous and trivial, if insistently remembered, is probably a screen-memory concealing something emotionally important, and the clarity of the memory is a sign of its hidden significance.

A more or less perfunctory dialogue with psychoanalysis has become routine in twentieth-century autobiography, but the impact of what Freud had to say on memory has been diffuse rather than doctrinal. Before pursuing further the central notion of screen-memories, it is worth pausing to consider the aura or 'frisson' which may surround the recollection of apparently trivial and fugitive impressions. This is closely linked to what might be called the cult of impressions, or the progressive aestheticization of memory in autobiography.[22] When Rousseau dwells on 'insignificant' memories he presents this as an interruption of his narrative, warranted

---

[22] Any full survey of this topic would need to pay particular attention to Ruskin's *Praeterita* (1885–9) and the line which runs, via James (discussed below), from Ruskin to Virginia Woolf and beyond. With regard to Woolf, see the collection of her autobiographical writings, *Moments of Being*.

primarily by the desire to testify to the pleasures of memory itself, the enchantment of recalling and recounting certain episodes, and the lasting emotional resonance of certain periods. Remembered detail—a fly on his hand during a lesson at Bossey, M. Le Maistre's tattered cassock—is seen as part of a global picture, a 'concours d'objets vivement retracé'[23] attesting the survival not of a fragment but of a totality. Stendhal, on the other hand, in linking his 'oublis' to strong emotions, and in stressing the immediacy of the memory process, explicitly invests fragmentary memories not only with emotional force but with a strong charge of meaning. Here fragmentariness betokens authenticity.

The same applies in a somewhat different way to Henry James's volumes of autobiography.[24] James found that 'to interrogate the past' was to get more than one had bargained for: 'To knock at the door of the past was in a word to see it open to me quite wide' (p. 3). 'Tiny particles of history' (p. 15) begin to *swarm* and *multiply* (both words are recurrent) as past events are recalled, and then infused with later knowledge and experience. 'I feel that at such a rate I remember too much', James observes, noting that memories place him under an obligation to respond to the 'silent stare of an appeal' which seems to emanate from the past, and to acknowledge elements to which he 'somehow feel[s] morally affiliated' (p. 105). James was in fact only too willing to display how much he remembered, and in what detail, since his principal theme was the emergence of his acute receptivity to the minutiae of experience, 'the personal history, as it were, of an imagination' (p. 454). The exactitude of memory is a tribute to the 'tenacity of [his] impressions' (p. 60), the capacity to assimilate all kinds of experience and 'convert' them into 'soluble stuff' as his father had enjoined (p. 122). Yet, as he acknowledges, 'I lose myself . . . under the whole pressure of the spring of memory . . . these things, at the pressure, flush together again, interweave their pattern, and quite thrust it at me' (p. 131). James's narrative constantly risks being blown off course by the agency of memory as it resurrects events in their singularity, as it multiplies particulars, and as it prompts connections which, turning the tables, interrogate *him*: forcing him, for example, to ponder (in the case of Merridew's library at Boulogne) 'the question of what *that* spot represented, or could be encouraged, could be aided and abetted, to represent' (p. 233). To 'aid and abet' a 'spot' (the word designates both the place and the memory—a 'spot of time' in

[23] *Œuvres complètes*, i. 122.
[24] Collected together and edited, under the title *Autobiography*, by F. N. Dupee. References to this work are incorporated in the text.

Wordsworth's phrase) to 'represent something' is made to sound vaguely disreputable. James prefers to think of his memories as being poised between potential registers of significance (poised principally, that is, between the psychological and the aesthetic), as 'moments of being' brimming with virtual meanings but sanctioning none. What counts is the memory's spell, its potency as an impression and as a nucleus of autobiographical sense, rather than its specific reference.

In his *Notebooks* James exhorts himself at one point to 'give a word if possible to *that* mild memory,—yet without going to smash on the rock of autobiography'.[25] The fear is that autobiography will deprive the memory of its aura, dissipating it in the service of narrow interpretation. Clearly the ideas of Freud potentially aggravated this tendency; as a result, increasingly ritualized responses to the feeling of having one's style cramped by psychoanalytical concepts developed rapidly in autobiography: 'I'm not sure what Dr Freud would make of this', 'no doubt psychoanalysts would have a field day'. Yet Freud also gave a considerable boost to the idea, anticipated by autobiographers from Rousseau onwards, that childhood experience and early memories were of fundamental importance. Moreover, Freud on memory chimed with the cult of impressions—the predilection, observable in, say, James for the compelling evanescence of fragmentary recollections. Accordingly, in post-Freudian autobiography, a refusal to go the whole hog with Freud is often accompanied by the selective adoption and adaptation of certain of his ideas and emphases.

In Michel Leiris, for example, remembered objects, incidents, verbal fragments, or actions are endowed with a kind of elusive significance which suggests that important indicators of the psychic and especially the psycho-sexual life are enfolded in the ostensibly unremarkable. Here, the eeriness and pregnancy of resurgent memory-traces is Freudian in its tonalities. Yet, at the same time, the explanatory power, the epistemological framework, of Freud's concepts is resisted. A Freudian poetics of memory, indebted to the concepts of displacement, substitution, verbal bridges, and so on, is accompanied by a different phenomenology where the engagement with the otherness of memory is predominant. In *Biffures*, Leiris notes that 'un souvenir que j'ai dans la tête, prolongé en tous sens par des ramifications affectives, ce n'est pas un corps étranger qu'il s'agit d'extirper' (p. 20). To trace the 'ramifications affectives' of the memory (which is where the Freudian repertoire of displacement, substitution, etc. plays its role) is not to make it less dense and enigmatic but more so; it is to enhance its

---

[25] *The Complete Notebooks of Henry James*, 241.

fascination and its inherent resistance to appropriation. In *Fourbis* Leiris notes the difficulty he has in resisting the allure of memories which simply bolster his personal mythology, and in attending to those which bear 'aucun signe spectaculaire pour diriger à leur profit l'attention'. But with the latter great effort is required if they are to be brought back to life ('en pratiquant sur eux [souvenirs] quelque chose d'équivalent à cette respiration artificielle au moyen de laquelle on essaye de ranimer des noyés', *Fo* 60). To make such memories meaningful Leiris has to shore up memory with reason and conjecture, to perform 'opérations de comblement' like the engineers of the Zuider Zee—and this at a point when, in the process of writing, he may have lost track of his initial intuition as to the ' "sens" qui aurait pu les animer'. Memories risk being reduced to little more than the materials of the *bricoleur*; in any case, once they have been textualized, memories lose their potential: there is no way back to an original memory when writing has done its work (*Fo* 52). We can view the desire to 'work through' what he remembers, to identify disturbances and repetitions as Freudian; but we must acknowledge Leiris's sense that his engagement with memory is by no means solely therapeutic, and that it often serves to reinforce his obsessions. The status of memories in Leiris illustrates in some degree the convergence of a psychoanalytical vision of remembering with what we have called the aestheticization of memory. But we also need to take into account the fact that for Leiris desire (and thus memory) cannot be separated from metaphysics, and principally the fact of death; and also that for him the aesthetic is not so much a way of apprehending the world as of transforming it, whence the tendency to regard memories as materials.

'Screen-memories' play a central part in Freud's thinking and this concept has had important repercussions in autobiography. In the simplest cases, an authentic memory notable for its insistence and its uncanny clarity, but otherwise apparently trivial and innocuous, acts as a screen for a related memory which has been repressed. More complex screen-memories involve two moments (often, but not always, childhood and maturity) and the process of projection—backwards or forwards—from one to the other. In some instances a safe and innocuous recollection from childhood is adapted and remodelled to serve as a screen for a repressed body of feelings arising in later life. A memory purporting to belong to childhood and which takes its place amongst childhood memories is actually a memory formed at a later stage, a construct 'almost like [a work] of fiction'.[26] The process also works in

---

[26] 'Screen Memories' (1899), 315. This early essay is largely devoted to instances where 'false' memories are produced to serve later psychic purposes.

reverse: the repression of an early memory which threatens to resurface leads to the falsification of a recent memory which becomes the disguised embodiment of the repressed one.[27]

Numerous screen-memories of all kinds are discussed in Freud's writings, notably in the case-histories where they are sometimes linked with another important mechanism, that of deferred action (*Nachträglichkeit*) whereby an impression, which made little or no impact when it occurred, is reactivated at a later stage and then produces delayed effects.[28] In the operations of 'deferred action' we are dealing with causes and effects which work backwards and forwards simultaneously, subverting the logic of linearity; and with events which, while firmly rooted in an individual's psychic history, unsettle the distinction between the fictional and the real. It was partly in the light of his progressive awareness of these mechanisms that Freud reformulated the aims and techniques of psychoanalysis. In 'Remembering, Repeating and Working-through' (1914) he suggested that, rather than attempting to 'bring a particular moment or problem into focus' by encouraging the patient to remember, analysis should aim to 'uncover the resistances which are unknown to the patient' by prompting him to *repeat* them in the context of the analysis. The 'compulsion to repeat' is itself regarded as 'a way of remembering': it reproduces in a new framework the structural connections and disconnections which constitute the patient's current way of 'living with' his past. The illumination or restoration of the past may well ensue from the analytical process, but the main emphasis is placed on the forces which impede this—the blockages of

---

[27] Alternatively, the screen-memory will consist in a substitute version of the repressed childhood event which may borrow certain elements from memories contemporaneous with the period when it is produced: 'One is thus forced by various considerations to suspect that in the so-called earliest childhood memories we possess not the genuine memory-trace but a later revision of it, a revision which may have been subject to the influences of a variety of later psychical forces', *Psychopathology*, 47.

[28] The classic instance occurs in the Wolf Man case, 'From the History of an Infantile Neurosis (The Wolf Man)', where analysis of a childhood dream prompts Freud to postulate that his patient must, while still in infancy, have witnessed his parents' copulation (the primal scene). The reactivation of the scene at age 5 is a new event which engenders effects that must in part be referred back to the original impression but which are also bound up with feelings belonging to the reactivating context. Even if it is not the sole cause of the effects which flow from its reactivation, the original event must, Freud insists, have had a basis in reality. However, in a celebrated footnote (*Case Histories*, ii. 291–5), added to the original account, Freud suggested that, in order to have had the effects in question, the 'event' did not actually need to have taken place. It is possible, he speculated, that the child constructed the primal scene out of two other memories, one to do with his parents, the other with animals copulating. In that case it would be an imaginary event, credited with the force of a real one, whose deferred effects made themselves felt at age 5.

memory. The analyst seeks to enlist the patient's aid in identifying and working through these blockages. 'Working through' involves allowing resistance to make itself felt and then continuing the work of analysis 'in defiance of it'.[29] In the face of the subject's desire to cling to a particular version of events, the analyst will characteristically construct a hypothesis which takes into account the elements apparently disguised by repression.[30] In transferring emphasis from interpretation to construction—an ongoing hypothetical process—Freud suggests that it is less important to arrive at some final truth about the past than to lay bare the latent dynamics at work in the patient's own relationship to that past. What counts ultimately is not so much a true narrative as an efficacious one.

III

'Disturbances' of memory; memory as trace and as screen; 'Remembering, Repeating and Working-through': these notions, which together constitute a formidable challenge to the myth of anamnesis, to the idea of memory as a homeland, have come to figure prominently in the repertoire of the modern autobiographer. Yet, even when, as for example in Georges Perec's *W ou le souvenir d'enfance* (which will be examined presently), the link with Freudian methodology remains clearly perceptible, autobiographers have tended to substitute their own kinds of narrative for those of Freud. There are clearly many reasons for this: resistance to Freud, a sense of coming to autobiography with quite different purposes from those of Freud's patients, a recognition that the unconscious is inherently inaccessible. What remains 'Freudian', none the less, in the appropriation of notions such as those listed above by some of the most interesting twentieth-century autobiographers, is the stance adopted towards the field of memory: the sense of dealing with elusive and refractory materials, the sense of confronting the self as potentially alien and unknown, the emphasis on the mechanisms as well as the contents of memory.

In one of its many echoes of Stendhal, Walter Benjamin's remarkable autobiographical fragment 'A Berlin Chronicle' records the desire to draw a diagram of one's life. But Benjamin issues this disclaimer: 'I am not

---

[29] 'Remembering, Repeating and Working-through', 155. Earlier quotations are from pp. 147, 151.

[30] The patient's response to such constructions, necessarily conjectural in character, provides a further opportunity for new material to emerge and for repression to be repeated, and this also opens new vistas for the analyst.

concerned here with what is installed in the chamber at its enigmatic centre, ego or fate.'[31] What does concern him is the status and experience of memory: 'the mysterious work of remembrance—which is really the capacity for endless interpolations into what has been'. For Benjamin autobiographical memory does not lend itself to narrative. 'He who has once begun to open the fan of memory never comes to the end of its segments; no image satisfies him, for he has seen that it can be unfolded and only in its folds does the truth reside.' The 'endless interpolations' of remembrance are flashes of insight into what lies in the folds of our habitual recollections. Much of our past experience has lost its power through being assimilated into the continuous flow of our existence. But certain things—words, places, events: the word *Brauhausberg*, the sound of the auctioneer's gavel of Benjamin's father or of the knife his mother used to spread rolls for his father's lunch—remain sealed off, disconnected from our subsequent mental evolution, and hence perfectly preserved, until memory disinters them. It is these which authentically resurrect the buried past and confront us with foreshadowings of our present selves. Because its playground is visible from the Savignyplatz station, Benjamin's school stands bereft of memory images—like 'one of those Mexican temples that were excavated much too early and inexpertly, their frescoes having been long effaced by rain'.[32] Never having been lost sight of, it has accrued a variety of thoughts and associations. Only a tiny detail, the crenelated cornice of his classroom, to which he had never paid attention ('never more than a shadow of meaning or reason passed across it'), retains authentic power when Benjamin suddenly comes across it on a trawl through his memory and subjects it to scrutiny: 'I pick it up and question it like Hamlet addressing the skull.' To remember authentically is not to be reintegrated into a past chronology but to establish a topography, to create a map or schema which would indicate relationships, contiguities, and distances between discontinuous landmarks.[33]

[31] *One-Way Street*, 319. Subsequent quotations are from pp. 305, 297, 337, 318. Benjamin's reflections on memory in *Illuminations*, where he refers to Baudelaire, Proust, and Freud, are also very germane to our discussion. See especially the remarks on memory 'shocks', 162 ff.

[32] The archaeological metaphor is also found in the passage quoted as epigraph to Ch. 3 above; on its powerful appeal to Freud see M. Bowie, *Proust, Freud, Lacan*, 13–44.

[33] Susan Sontag has many perceptive remarks on this in her introduction to *One-Way Street*. Cf. also Italo Calvino's reflections on 'Cities and Memory' in his *Invisible Cities*: 'The city does not consist of this, but of relationships between the measurements of its space and the events of its past: the height of a lamppost and the distance from the ground of a hanged usurper's swaying feet . . . the height of [a] railing and the leap of the adulterer who climbed over it at dawn' (p. 13).

Benjamin gives special prominence to words and sounds, and in this he is accompanied by other autobiographers who emphasize the operations of memory, Leiris and Sarraute for example. Of the word *Brauhausberg*, which 'has preserved the unfathomable mystery that certain words from the language of adults possess for children', Benjamin observes: 'To approach what it enfolds is almost impossible.' As in the case of Leiris's 'reusement',[34] *Brauhausberg* marks the frontier between 'two linguistic regions', between 'a larger collective and myself' and between 'the poetic and the profane'.[35] In Nathalie Sarraute's *Enfance* portions of discourse rather than single words serve as privileged conduits of memory. Many of the book's fragments centre on snatches of utterance: interdictions, 'Non, tu ne feras pas ça';[36] admonitions, 'Si tu touches à un poteau comme celui-là, tu meurs' (p. 27); wounding apophthegms, 'femme et mari sont un même parti' (p. 74); put-downs, 'avant de se mettre à écrire un *roman*, il faut apprendre l'orthographe' (p. 85). The prominence of such material reflects the fact that Sarraute's reconstruction of her childhood, centred on the emotional fall-out from a broken marriage, gives precedence to intersubjective relations. Yet Sarraute makes it clear that the stuff of memory lies outside language— 'hors des mots . . . comme toujours . . . ces petits bouts de quelque chose d'encore vivant' (p. 11)—and that autobiography involves the attempt to bring the extra-linguistic into language (p. 41), with all the risks (kept well to the fore through dialogue with her *alter ego*)[37] that this entails. Here autobiography aims, as in Stendhal, to stimulate the resurgence of sensations, impulses, and currents of feeling. The work of autobiography— represented emblematically at the outset by scissors which tear into the smooth fabric of a sofa and release the formless grey matter within (p. 13)—seeks to break through the familiar surfaces of memory to the fluid magma they conceal.

While visual recollections often seem suspiciously inert, verbal fragments repeatedly manifest a transgressive power, and seemingly offer a direct line to the extra-linguistic underworld of tropisms. The phrases which resurface as Sarraute pieces together and tunes into her past are always instances of language in action: force rather than form. They involve situations where words were offensive missiles: 'Le mot frappe . . . de plein fouet' (p. 117); 'La volée de mitraille de ces mots' (p. 244); or when words served to confine or to imprison (p. 118). Words in *Enfance* are the often involuntary

[34] *Bi*, 9–12.
[35] *One-Way Street*, 323.
[36] *Enfance*, 10. Subsequent references are cited in the text.
[37] See the discussion of *Enfance* in Ch. 5 above.

emanations or externalizations of psychic energies: 'Il faudrait pour retrouver ce qui a pu faire surgir d'elle ces paroles réentendre au moins leur intonation . . . sentir passer sur soi les fluides qu'elles dégagent' (p. 127). The power unleashed by their resurgence in the present of writing is a tribute not only to the effects these words had on Sarraute when they were uttered but to the fact that their real virulence was generally reserved for their aftermath in memory. Such utterances are likened to parcels whose contents are only fully disclosed when they are slowly unpacked later on (pp. 93, 178). Preserved in memory they have always been liable to further unwrapping, right down to the present when autobiography aims to expose their contents to scrutiny once and for all. ' "Non tu ne feras pas ça". Dans ces mots un flot épais, lourd coule, ce qu'il charrie s'enfonce en moi pour écraser ce qui en moi remue, veut se dresser . . .' (p. 14). The autobiographer's task is to rediscover the force of such utterances, and to understand the dynamics of the child's and then the adult's resistance to them. The adult autobiographer is now prepared to confront directly what the child may have understood imperfectly, or found it expedient not to understand. But there is a danger that the attempt to identify feelings and forces in their original context will be thwarted by the effects of subsequent resistance. A notable feature of *Enfance* is Sarraute's awareness of the difficulties of circumventing a settled vision of the past which is in fact the product of her success in channelling and neutralizing the potentially destructive elements within it. These difficulties are compounded by a more general risk that the lived reality of the individual past will have been eroded, or contaminated by prefabricated elements culled from literary and cultural stereotypes. Sarraute frequently asks herself whether generic 'souvenirs d'enfance' have not infiltrated her memories, or if the reconstruction of past feelings is not commandeered by the 'vraisemblable' of convention and artifice. At one point she dismisses her reconstruction of past feelings as being no more accurate than the cardboard model of a vanished city (p. 165); but, with the support of her imaginary interlocutor, Sarraute then contrives to dispel this doubt: 'Quelque chose s'elève encore, toujours aussi réel, une masse immense . . .' (p. 165). Behind the facade of ratiocination, the resurgence of past emotions—at a visceral or tropistic level—attests the authenticity of memory.

The kinds of suspicion Sarraute succeeds in allaying are voiced in more radical form throughout Michel Beaujour's *Miroirs d'encre*, a study of the literary self-portrait where the status of memory is a constant focus of attention. Beaujour contrasts two forms of memory at work in the field of self-writing. Autobiography, he claims, rests on belief in a coherent self constituted through time, which can be accessed through the contents of personal memory; in this genre, selfhood, memory, and narrative are mutually supportive, natural phenomena. By contrast, practitioners of the 'autoportrait', from Montaigne and Bacon to Leiris, Malraux, and Barthes, lack confidence in a unified self, and therefore construct textual self-representations—non-narrative 'miroirs d'encre'—out of avowedly heterogeneous materials. Sceptical of the demarcation between individual memory and cultural memory, the self-portraitist assembles a thematic 'bricolage' where, as in the age-old tradition of mnemonic systems—'the Art of Memory' as Frances Yates called it—memories are clustered around impersonal 'lieux': 'le sujet ne se dit qu'à travers ce qui le dépasse, le traverse et le nie'.[38] The autoportraitist accepts as inevitable the second-handedness of memories, and views them as impersonal materials out of which to build a present self-image (p. 164). Rather than trying to rejoin his past—or historical—self he seeks, through the act of writing, to apprehend himself in the present: 'l'autoportrait n'est pas une mémoire mais une machine à perpétuer le présent de l'écriture' (p. 105). The autoportrait always involves a 'mise en scène' of its own construction and the subject is held to be a by-product of this textual play or process.

Beaujour's clear-cut distinction between autobiography and 'autoportrait' leads him towards caricature: on one side the naïve essentialist, on the other (even if few of Beaujour's subjects quite match up to this ideal) the ironically detached avant-garde *écrivain*, for whom the 'voie de l'autoportrait' leads outside the familiar myths and parameters of subjectivity towards a radical experience of utopian dispossession. Viewed in a different perspective, however, Beaujour's opposition points to tensions which are perceptible *within* the field of the autobiographer's engagement with memory. If we acknowledge that, in the hands of Rousseau, Stendhal, or Chateaubriand, and notwithstanding the lure of continuity and narrative, autobiography is a more self-conscious and less homogeneous practice than Beaujour suggests, we can identify there many of the features he ascribes exclusively to the autoportrait. One example would be the desire that the act of writing should in itself be the forum for a particular experience of self. For Beaujour's autoportraitist this leads away from memory towards an emphasis on the *now* of writing. Yet autobiographers have frequently resisted the antithesis this implies. What they may desire (or believe in) is neither self-apprehension in the pure event of writing, nor the 'return' of the past as if it were present again, but a kind of fusion between the *now* of

---

[38] *Miroirs d'encre*, 40. Subsequent references are cited in the text.

writing and the dimension of selfhood to which distant memories seem to hold the key. Rousseau's multi-faceted style, Stendhal's diagrams, Chateaubriand's superimposed time-frames, may all be seen as reflections of the desire to create a special tense, a way of exploring and enunciating the infinite interconnectedness of past and present. To apprehend oneself in or via one's memories is to accept that the selfhood, or 'narrative identity' (Ricœur), realized in autobiography, is a compound of past and present, the textual and the historical. The autobiographer may move away from narrative order, towards an emphasis on the 'moment de l'écriture', in recognition not of the inevitable rigor mortis which afflicts disinterred memories, but of the fact that they may come alive when sundered from pre-existent totalities and discovered as for the first time.

Nor is it only the autoportraitist who sees how difficult it is to deal appropriately with memories. It is often the memory just discovered or never previously examined which seems to disclose being, and this may lead the autobiographer to attend to memories in their singularity, to treat them as monads. As Stendhal repeatedly suggests, what is arresting about a new-found memory is often what is unknown in it, not so much its mystery as a resistance which inspires a centripetal movement, a burrowing back as if into its substance. Yet, as Stendhal also repeatedly demonstrates, to unfurl a memory is ultimately to restore it to a wider context: a memory can only really be explored and kept in play through its resonances and connections. A memory is not so much a plenum as a vacuum waiting to be filled, an incitement to remember. To focus intently on a memory is to be caught in an irresistible drift from one moment to another, both within the field of the past and between past and present. In the context of writing, and of memory as a performative act, only one memory at a time may be given privileged treatment, but its privilege is necessarily of brief duration. Moreover, if a particular memory can offer a vantage point from which to survey the self, a way of inhabiting the present, this can only be provisional: the present rapidly infiltrates a past which both illuminates it and is illuminated by it. The singling out of memories, their consecration, always implies a desecration, as their sovereignty is violated and they are assimilated into the pattern of the individual's past.

For Michel Beaujour the autoportraitist's desire for textual incarnation leads to the cession of personal memory, and the wholesale acceptance of the self as a tapestry of disparate images and materials; by this acceptance of death and disunity the subject accedes to a phantom life of dispersion. Forsaking any relation to 'pastness', the writer seeks to invest a succession of textual spaces with the capacity to act as surrogates of self, consigning himself to what Beaujour, in a memorable phrase, calls 'l'infinie métempsycose que son écriture exige de lui' (p. 68). Yet it is just such a transmigration—from memory to memory—which we have located as one of the rhythms of autobiography, a movement often at odds with an overall narrative order—a rhythm of connection and concatenation—that it subverts, even when ostensibly it succumbs to it. A succession or relay of memories may serve as markers for the autobiographer's most intense engagement with subjectivity; but the power to signify self in this way is never securely vested in any one of them. Indeed, the strength of such memories seems closely allied to their inherent vulnerability. The nature of this vulnerability must now be examined.

One of its aspects is vulnerability to Meaning. To seek to ascertain the significance of a memory is, on the whole, to find one all too readily. Yet to assign specific meaning may be to adulterate the memory and thus to deny its authentic quality. Is it possible, then, for a memory to be of vital importance, to mean something to us, so to speak, whilst at the same time remaining immune from a process which seems to denature it, from the virus of meaning itself? A test case, as it were, is provided by Roland Barthes's concept of *anamnèse*: 'J'appelle *anamnèse* l'action—mélange de jouissance et d'effort—que mène le sujet pour retrouver, *sans l'agrandir ni le faire vibrer*, une ténuité du souvenir: c'est le haiku lui-même.'[39] This form of remembering resembles a spiritual exercise, a kind of active passivity which seeks to home in on the particular quality of memories which are recalled in minute detail but which lack evident or dramatic significance. The effort required is that of resisting the lure of meaning, 'le mouvement de la fable qui tire de tout fragment de réel une leçon, un sens' (p. 154); and the 'jouissance' stems from success in preserving the memory in 'un état d'insignifiance'. Shifting into italics Barthes offers a sample of sixteen memories dating mostly from childhood, of which these are two examples:

Assis à califourchon sur une chaise, au coin du chemin des Arènes, le colonel Poymiro, énorme, violacé, veinulé, moustachu at myope, de parole embarrassée, regardait passer et repasser la foule de la corrida. Quel supplice, quelle peur quand il l'embrassait! (p. 112).

Vers 1932, au Studio 28, un jeudi après-midi de mai, seul je vis le Chien andalou; en sortant, à cinq heures, la rue Tholozé sentait le café au lait que les blanchisseuses prenaient entre deux repassages. Souvenir indicible de décentrement par excès de fadeur (p. 113).

[39] *Roland Barthes par Roland Barthes*, 113. Subsequent references are incorporated in the text.

Physical sensations predominate; as in Stendhal, this is a 'mémoire du corps'.[40] The resemblance to haiku (noted by Barthes, p. 113) includes the throw-away endings or punchlines—the sensation of being kissed by the colonel; the 'décentrement par excès de fadeur' associated with 'café au lait' and 'blanchisseuses'—which seem to draw together the previous details, producing compact, self-sufficient units displaying (in principle) strictly immanent meanings in the manner of 'quelque chose comme une dépense pure'. But are these samples of *anamnèse* as 'mat', as resistant to significance, as Barthes suggests? And for whom? As readers of Barthes, we may find them on the contrary highly meaningful and symptomatic. In both the examples cited gender seems important: the description of Colonel Poymiro seems to bring out a range of male connotations which make him redolent of the father, and of the *doxa*'s unseeing stare. In the other memory we can start at any point and turn the piece into a reflection of Barthes's sexuality: the Bunuël–Dalí film, the 'café au lait' (which in another *anamnèse* is associated with a woman and with nausea), the 'blanchisseuses'. Barthes may succeed in fending off secure autobiographical meaning, but that is not the same as preventing meaning from rapidly forming, like a crust or mould, in the first place. Barthes must be aware that, from the point of view of his readers, these memories are by no means successfully immunized from the irresistible drift towards connections and meaningfulness we identified earlier, or from the fact that to attend to these memories at all is to mobilize them in certain ways.

Given the foregoing, we might surmise that the 'act' of *anamnèse* ('action ... que mène le sujet') is aimed not only at the isolation of a particular quality within the memory, but at isolating the memory from its potential ramifications (from the factors which—on a Freudian reading—led it to be retained so intensely and specifically in the first place). It seems as if the effort to locate, '*sans l'agrandir ni le faire vibrer*, une ténuité du souvenir', is really a form of censorship, designed to suppress the memory's potential vibrations, and we might argue that 'Operation Haiku' involves the effort to neutralize, divert, deny, and launder, that it is a way of channelling the affective burden of certain cherished memories along a harmless aesthetic line. The impression of contentless *ténuité* can itself be attributed to the

---

[40] In a review of Jean Daniel's autobiography, *Le Refuge et la source*, Barthes commends the author for having rendered 'le "*c'est ça!*" du souvenir', grounded not in anecdotes but in sensations and inflections: 'j'atteins la figure incomparable de ce qui ne s'est produit qu'une fois, accomplit la différence absolue, et peut dès lors revenir d'une façon voluptueuse et déchirante. Car se souvenir passionnément, ce n'est pas rappeler une succession d'événements, c'est remémorer des inflexions', 'Le Grain d'une enfance', 86.

cordoning off of memories, the refusal to link and analyse, as well as to various stylistic features. Yet, from another perspective, one could argue that it is not the memories themselves which Barthes considers revealing but his designs on them—the form of 'jouissance' he wants to derive from them, the particular 'détournement' he wishes to submit them to—and the effects he imagines this having on the reader. What he conveys is less the fear of being exposed, of revealing too much, than the fear of being pinned down, labelled, defined by adjectives like Colonel Poymiro. Ultimately Barthes's *anamnèse* belongs to a range of Utopian strategies whose common aim is to resist the tyranny of determinate meaning. In the context of autobiography it echoes a more widespread desire to quarantine a sector of memory from the depredations of interpretative zeal; at the same time it confirms that memories can never successfully be immunized against a meaningfulness which may indeed diminish their aura, but is inevitably a significant factor in the aura to be preserved. However, where Barthes wants all but to eliminate meaning, what many autobiographers wish to preserve is a sense of the plasticity and plurality of their memories, the feeling that their meaningfulness lies precisely in their availability to a variety of meanings. If the construction of any autobiographical text, whatever its formal nature, creates structures which tend to constrain and control meaning, the urge to undermine these structures often reflects a sense that what is most significant in a memory—what Barthes would call its *punctum*[41]—is precisely the aspect which makes it resist such appropriation.

This leads on to another sort of vulnerability, which also underlines something of the refractory quality of autobiographical memories, namely the possibility that the very act of remembering might be detrimental to the material with which it deals. We could begin with the sense that to bring memories back to the light of day, into the foreground of consciousness, into language and on to the page, is to expose them—like the cave-paintings of Lascaux—to a potentially destructive glare. Or we could start from the related feeling that the excavation of memory can have the therapeutic character of an exorcism, that to retrieve something from memory is to draw its sting, to be done with it, to allow it to be forgotten.[42] Instead of reintegrating us with part of our being, the act of memory, in this perspective, engenders splitting and expulsion: remembering becomes dismembering—a way of forgetting. These motifs could be pursued in the

---

[41] See the discussion of *La Chambre claire* in the next section of this chapter.

[42] This process is at the heart of Beckett's *That Time* where the protagonist recalls an experience of repetition/return which brought about the definitive annihilation of a troublesome memory.

work of many autobiographers from Rousseau onwards, but at this stage it will be useful to consider a text where the disjunctive work of memory is articulated in even more radical form.

Jacques Derrida's *Mémoires for Paul de Man* is both an elegy for de Man and a meditation on the topic of memory in his work. For de Man, Derrida argues, remembering is usually aimed at interiorization—not necessarily self-unity but the desire to efface distance, to retrieve past experience as inner presence, and to close in on what is recollected. However, this desire is inevitably frustrated since the *activity* of memory—driven by fascination, fetishistic selectivity, fragmentation—never produces closure but in fact constitutes the object of memory as something separate and other.[43] Memory thus manifests an otherness within us; it reveals that what has been preserved is not the living presence of what *was*, but the trace of its finitude, of its death. In his analysis of Hegel's distinction between *Erinnerung* (memory as remembrance, subjective interiorization, living symbol) and *Gedächtnis* (mechanical memory associated with rote learning, mnemonics, dead signs) de Man denies the possibility of a dialectical relationship between these modes of memory, arguing instead that the disjunction between them is essential to memory in general. In fact, the work of memory can be regarded, he claims, as the movement of this disjunction through which, as Hegel put it, 'memory effaces remembrance'.[44] The disjunction, in other words, marks a reciprocity, a mutual implication, and thus an irreducible linkage, between the impossibility of memory as interiorization and the possibility of memory as trace or inscription. For Derrida this reciprocity points to the fact that de Man's view of memory is not purely negative. De Man in fact suggests that, by consolidating the subject's severance from the past, the work of memory paradoxically fosters a profound engagement with the ontological status of the *present*. In manifesting finitude and distance memory leads us to apprehend the present under the aspect of what Baudelaire called 'sa qualité essentielle de présent', that is, as something which can only be apprehended in its difference from the past, yet which has no content except for the pastness with which it does not coincide.[45] Past and present can only be thought of in terms of each other but they can never fuse; in manifesting their disjunction, the act of memory produces an experience in and of the present: 'The power of memory does

---

[43] See, esp., *Mémoires for Paul de Man*, 47–86. The theory of autobiography outlined in de Man's famous essay 'Autobiography as De-facement' involves a similar logic.

[44] 'Sign and Symbol in Hegel's Aesthetics', 773.

[45] For de Man's discussion of Baudelaire, focused especially on 'Le Peintre de la vie moderne' (1863), see *Blindness and Insight*, 156–8.

not reside in its capacity to resurrect a situation or a feeling that actually existed, but as a constitutive act of the mind bound to its own present and oriented towards the future of its own elaboration.'[46]

In de Man, memory is linked to the suppression of anteriority. To remember is not to forge a link, but to consolidate a disconnection between thought and being. But it is Derrida himself who, in the course of *Mémoires for Paul de Man*, develops the motif of memories as *traces*, taking as a central emblem the marks, inscriptions, and tokens which human beings make to commemorate what is no more:

testamentary traces, hypograms, hypomnemata, signatures and epigraphs, autobiographical 'memoirs' (p. 29).

these hypomnemata, memoranda, signs or symbols, images or mnesic representations which are only lacunary fragments, detached and dispersed—only parts of the departed other (p. 37).

all the figures of death with which we people the 'present' which we inscribe . . . in every trace (otherwise called 'survivals'): these figures strained towards the future across a fabled present, figures we inscribe because they can outlast us, beyond the present of their inscription: signs, words, names, letters (p. 59).[47]

A memory is a memento: a memorial to remind us—for the future—of what is no longer; a material substitute in place of what is absent (p. 106). By underlining the funerary aspect of the memory-as-trace, Derrida brings out the exteriority, otherness, and irreducible particularity of memory, its resistance to incorporation. To remember is to engage with what is always other. The act of remembrance merely disjoins our memories from 'us', turning them into foreign bodies, alien inscriptions.

The memory-as-trace displays the characteristics of the mark, scar, sign, token, or inscription, as analysed by Terence Cave in his study of anagnorisis. What Cave calls the 'scandal of recognition' lies in the fact that it bases itself on materials which, 'however skilfully they may be integrated into a deductive sequence . . . are always contingent in some sense'.[48] The link between the mark, sign, or token and the meaning ascribed to it (a link which fosters 'the momentary comforts, the semblance of therapeutic power that anagnorisis affords') depends on paralogism, a dubious leap of inference motivated by the desire for knowledge: 'the relationship between the accidental surface and the secret depths is a paralogical one in the sense that the second cannot certainly be inferred from the first.' Memory-as-trace

---

[46] *Blindness and Insight*, 92–3.
[47] *Mémoires for Paul de Man*, 29, 37, 59.
[48] *Recognitions*, 250. Subsequent quotations are from pp. 497 and 478.

marks a distance within the subject, a gap which can only be filled by the leap of interpretation, and which therefore perpetually calls into question the relationship between 'secret depths' ('inner' memory) and 'accidental surface' (*this* particular, contingent, memory-trace). In this perspective, to be a subject of memory is to be subject to a law which prohibits the confident fusion of 'mémoire' and 'personne'. To take account of this law is, for the autobiographer, to find a way of attending to his or her memories which acknowledges their vulnerability to the process of remembering itself. It is to preserve their status as traces, as open signs which, since they depend on what we make of them, offer clues to the future as much as to the past. It is not necessarily to refrain from interpretation (a temptation clearly felt by many autobiographers at some point) but to make the work of interpretation manifest, provisional, and open-ended, in recognition of the transformations and effacements it inevitably brings about. It could be shown that, in various forms, the notion of the trace, and the attitude to memories just described, has been present in autobiography throughout its history—in the shadow, to be sure, of the opposed tendency to see memory as a horn of plenty and a land of milk and honey. But, as one would expect, it is especially in the twentieth century, in the 'ère du soupçon' when so many factors have cast shadows over memory itself, that we find autobiographies which reflect the kinds of idea we have been considering. The last part of this chapter will, therefore, consider the status of memories in two recent works.

IV

For Roland Barthes the photograph (which proclaims 'Ça a été') has the capacity to affirm irrefutably that what it depicts once existed, but at the same time the photograph underlines the absence of that very being or entity, manifesting the fact that it is not there now, that it is dead. In *La Chambre claire* Barthes investigates the mortifying character of the photographic image, the way it negates presence and reveals loss or absence. Yet through the concept of the *punctum* he also celebrates the affective power of photography, its capacity to sponsor an intense experience of the here and now. The *punctum* is the singular factor which, outside any general laws, principles, codes, or categories of information (the province of its antithesis, the *studium*) touches me in my 'subjectivité absolue'. The *punctum* is what makes an impression, it is what marks me ('me point'):[49]

---

[49] *La Chambre claire*, 49. Subsequent quotations are from pp. 89 and 127.

often a localizable detail, an 'objet partiel', it inspires close attention, not so much objective scrutiny as submission and expansion: 'ne rien dire, fermer les yeux, laisser le détail remonter à la conscience affective'. The *punctum*, we might say, is the photograph's navel—the trace of the umbilical cord which links it, above and beyond loss and absence, to real moments and beings: 'Une sorte de lien ombilical relie le corps de la chose photographiée à mon regard: la lumière, quoique impalpable, est ici un milieu charnel, une peau que je partage avec celui ou celle qui a été photographié'. A photograph is an emanation of the real: the light which was there, then, made an impression whose trace is still present here, now, perhaps years later.

Barthes's phenomenology makes the photograph the perfect embodiment of the mnemonic image as an object of autobiographical attention—the memory as trace of an event which 'must have' happened back then, and as a trace which still marks us now. For a majority of Westerners in our time photographs are the most telling and evocative tokens of the individual past. As Barthes's own practice shows—in the photo-album section of *Roland Barthes par Roland Barthes* (pp. 5–46), and in the meditation on a photograph of his late mother which occupies much of the second half of *La Chambre claire*—photographs have come to play a prominent part in modern autobiography. For example, in Paul Auster's *The Invention of Solitude*, written in the aftermath of his father's death, they play a central role in the work of mourning and memory. One photograph Auster found among his father's possessions is described as follows:

From a bag of loose pictures: a trick photograph taken in an Atlantic City studio sometime during the Forties. There are several of him sitting around a table, each image shot from a different angle, so that at first you think it might be a group of several different men. Because of the gloom that surrounds them, because of the utter stillness of their poses, it looks as if they have gathered there to conduct a seance. And then, as you study the picture, you begin to realise that all these men are the same man. The seance becomes a real seance, and it is as if he has come here only to invoke himself, to bring himself back from the dead, as if, by multiplying himself, he had inadvertently made himself disappear. There are five of him there, and yet the nature of the trick photography denies the possibility of eye contact among the various selves. Each one is condemned to go on staring into space, as if under the gaze of the others, but seeing nothing, never able to see anything. It is a picture of death, a portrait of an invisible man.[50]

Reproduced on the cover of the book, the trick photograph stands as a haunting emanation of the absent father who survives only as a proliferation

---

[50] *The Invention of Solitude*, 31.

of still images. The photograph's *punctum*—the blank unseeing gaze multiplied by a mechanical contrivance—reveals in concentrated form something of the essence of a man who, for his son, is remembered for his way of staying on the edge of his life, for being 'an invisible man'.

Duras: *L'Amant*

'L'histoire de ma vie n'existe pas. Ça n'existe pas. Il n'y a jamais de centre. Pas de chemin, pas de ligne. Il y a de vastes endroits où l'on fait croire qui'il y avait quelqu'un, ce n'est pas vrai il n'y avait personne.'[51] Starting out with the intention of writing a commentary on a series of family photographs, Marguerite Duras came instead to base her first explicit excursion into autobiography on a photograph which might have been taken, an image which could have existed (at one stage the title was to be 'l'Image absolue').[52] Had it been taken, the photograph would have depicted Duras, aged 15, crossing the Mekong on a ferry:

C'est au cours de ce voyage que l'image se serait détachée, qu'elle aurait été enlevée à la somme. Elle aurait pu exister, une photographie aurait pu être prise, comme une autre, ailleurs, dans d'autres circonstances. Mais elle ne l'a pas été. L'objet était trop mince pour la provoquer. Qui aurait pu penser à Ça? Elle n'aurait pu être prise que si on avait pu préjuger de l'importance de cet événement dans ma vie, cette traversée du fleuve. Or, tandis que celle-ci s'opérait, on ignorait encore jusqu'à son existence. Dieu seul la connaissait. C'est pourquoi, cette image, et il ne pouvait pas en être autrement, elle n'existe pas. Elle a été omise. Elle a été oubliée. Elle n'a pas été détachée, enlevée à la somme. C'est à ce manque d'avoir été faite qu'elle doit sa vertu, celle de représenter un absolu, d'en être justement l'auteur (pp. 16–17).

The image becomes absolute by remaining virtual, imaginary, impossible. If it existed it would be tied to the relative circumstances which produced it, to what it denoted; it would be the origin of memory. Instead, the 'idea' of a photograph generates an unlimited mental process, a particular form of attention addressed to the past not as event but as potential image: memory is mediated, refracted—at an imaginary level—through the medium of the image.

The photograph would have depicted the young Duras at what certainly turns out to have been a significant moment in her life. It was on this

---

[51] *L'Amant*, 14. Subsequent references are incorporated in the text. Duras's text has rapidly inspired extensive critical commentary. I have found the following useful: J. Morgan, 'Fiction and Autobiography/Language and Silence: *L'Amant* by Duras'; S. J. Capitano, 'Perspectives sur l'écriture durassienne: *L'Amant*'.

[52] On this see L. Hill, 'Marguerite Duras and the Limits of Fiction', 14.

crossing that she accepted the invitation to ride in the car of a young Chinese and this led on to her sexual initiation and a scandalous affair. If this is the key event or turning point through which Duras structures her autobiographical narrative, we may wonder what difference does it make that the event is approached through the imaginary image? In fact, Duras does not construe her affair as something which changed her life or fashioned her destiny. What interests her is how it could have come about, what network of potentialities it betrays, what it reveals about the girl and her situation, and the nature of the ageing writer's relationship to that past self. These are the features which the image would have revealed and, in being constantly imagined, does reveal. At one level the 'imagined' photo is simply a metaphor for memory conceived in terms of a scrutiny of memory images, the film of one's past, of which we can ask such questions as: where did those clothes come from? who else was there? Yet the non-existence of the photograph, and the conditional tense this imposes, consistently maintain the ingredients of imagination, invention, and fantasy as part of the process through which a person relates to her memories, while it constantly denies the false implication that the moment is being considered as an objective determinant of subsequent events.

Since the photograph does not exist, what it depicts is not objectively circumscribed, and at one point the image is held to embrace the whole of the ferrycrossing, thus taking in the lover, his car, and the dangerous river-currents which link desire to fear and death. However, attention focuses especially on the girl's appearance—her face, her eyes, her undeveloped body, and her incongruous clothes: a faded hand-me-down dress, gold-lamé shoes, and a man's felt hat. The hat receives particular attention: 'l'ambiguité déterminante de l'image, elle est dans ce chapeau' (p. 19). The ambiguity seems to reside in the way the hat is linked simultaneously to two constituencies: on the one hand to mother, family, social circumstances, childhood, on the other hand to desire, fantasy, the world of others, and ultimately to writing. Uncertain how she acquired the hat, Duras assumes her mother must have bought it in a sale at her request, and then imagines a scene clearly modelled on the Lacanian 'stade du miroir'; trying on the hat for fun, she saw herself in the mirror: 'Soudain je me vois comme une autre, comme une autre serait vue, au-dehors, mise à la disposition de tous, mise à la disposition de tous les regards, mise dans la circulation des villes, des routes, du désir' (p. 20). The hat is connected with the girl apprehending herself as an object of desire. Desire becomes linked to being looked at, to self-dissociation, and to identification with the Other's look (factors which will return in the 'affair'); and the core of the image is located in the girl's consciousness of her power as an object of desire: 'L'Image commence bien avant qu'il ait abordé l'enfant blanche près du bastingage, au moment où il est descendu de la limousine noire, quand il a commencé à s'approcher d'elle, et qu'elle, elle le savait, savait qu'il avait peur' (p. 45). It is the girl's capacity to apprehend herself as an object of desire that makes her a subject of desire and *jouissance*. Thus, the experience of *jouissance* which will follow from this meeting is already virtual on the ferry. 'Déjà, sur le bac, avant son heure, l'image aurait participé de cet instant' (p. 50). Everything which pertains to the sexual experiences in the dark room at Cholen is deemed to have been already present in the image.

The hat also incorporates the mother in the space of the image. By acquiescing in her daughter's whim, buying the hat for her, and sending her to school in 'cette tenue d'enfant prostituée' (p. 33), the mother is implicated in the girl's sexual identity, just as she will be complicit in the affair from which she is willing to reap the financial benefits. The mother is also present as an antithetical image—a victim of circumstance (represented by a real photograph, 'la photo du désespoir', p. 41) debarred from the scene of desire: 'La mère n'a pas connu la jouissance' (p. 50). The hat, a 'solde soldé' also symbolizes the family's history: 'Le lien avec la misère est là aussi dans le chapeau d'homme' (p. 33). That 'histoire commune de ruine et de mort' (p. 34), involving the stunted lives of her two elder brothers, which occupies considerable portions of the text, is inscribed in the girl's appearance and also features in the image in so far as the ferry crossing marks the initial fracture between the girl and her family: 'Dès qu'elle a pénétré dans l'auto noire, elle l'a su, elle est à l'écart de cette famille pour la première fois et pour toujours' (p. 46). The family circle cedes to the space of desire figured by the confined interior of the black limousine—'la grande auto funèbre de mes livres' (p. 25)—which heralds the darkened room at Cholen and the space of writing, already visible in the girl's eyes: 'Je vois bien que tout est là. Tout est là et rien n'est encore joué, je le vois dans les yeux, tout est déjà dans les yeux. Je veux écrire' (p. 29). The imaginary image prefigures everything that will come to pass in the sexual arena. The scenes of love-making in the *garçonnière* at Cholen develop what is virtual in the image, produce an 'enlargement', as it were, of the imaginary photograph. The dark room, separated from the bustling street by thin shutters, is both inside and outside; the world of others inhabits the scene of desire: 'On entend comme s'ils traversaient la chambre' (p. 59).

The young white girl making love to a man of another race sees herself, through his eyes, as 'la petite blanche', and through his desire, as a body 'sans formes arrêtées, à tout instant en train de se faire' (p. 121). As

transgressor of racial and social codes, she sees herself, in the eyes of the
man's father, as one of the 'Famille de voyous blancs' (p. 109). As a subject
of desire, she appropriates and internalizes the view of her she attributes to
others, especially her school-friend Hélène Lagonelle (p. 125). Hélène
becomes a pole in the triangular structure of desire which involves the
'capture' of another look through which we become imaginary spectators of
our own desire, lose our fixed position, and experience the 'ravissement' of
desire as a constant negation and displacement of all fixities, a movement
between identities. Thus the prostitution of the 'petite blanche' engenders
the imaginary prostitution of the virginal Hélène as she is incorporated into
the room at Cholen as witness, as object of the desire in which she
participates ('Je suis exténuée du désir d'Hélène Lagonelle', p. 91), and as
stand-in for the girl in an imagined scenario of ultimate desire where the
young Duras becomes spectator as her lover makes love to Hélène (p. 92).

If the image predicts the girl's destiny as a writer, this too is developed in
the erotic scenario which ties writing to desire. The affair creates a space
marked by exclusion and eccentricity, on the border between two families:
the girl's mother and siblings, and her partners in the desire which removes
her from her original place. This will be the double space of writing. On the
one hand it is adjacent to the inextricable mixture of love and hate binding
her to her natural family: 'Je suis encore là, devant ces enfants possédés, à la
même distance du mystère. Je n'ai jamais écrit, croyant le faire, je n'ai jamais
aimé, croyant aimer, je n'ai jamais rien fait qu'attendre devant la porte
fermée' (p. 35). Autobiographical reflection marks the recognition of an
indissoluble link between writing and the intractable ambivalences of family
relations. But a later passage, reiterating this link (p. 93), also ties writing,
on the other hand, to the space of desire. Viewed from the 'garçonnière de
Cholen' the family space appeared in a new light: 'C'est un lieu irrespirable,
il côtoie la mort, un lieu de violence, de douleur, de désespoir, de
déshonneur. Et tel est le lieu de Cholen. De l'autre côté du fleuve' (p. 93).
The space of desire is both a haven from and a reduplication of the familial
space: for Duras, to enter the 'chambre noire' of writing is to dwell
provisionally in a liminary territory on the open boundary between the two.
In *L'Amant* the confluence of memory and desire is engendered by the
potentially infinite retracing of an imaginary trace. The non-existent
photograph becomes the concentrated embodiment of absence and
presence, history and fantasy, the past and its constantly open future.

In *L'Amant* memory is inextricably linked to desire, and hence to the
endless drift of fantasy of which writing is, for Duras, the prime agent. But
Duras also shows that, for her, the trace and its analogue, the quasi-

photographic image, is at the heart of autobiographical memory. Although its durable power is entirely dependent on an activity of invention and fabrication, so that the image–trace is partly a noematic construct, an intangible abstraction, the memory is also originally an *inscription*: it remains materially linked, therefore, via the body, to the lived reality of past desires.

Perec: *W ou le souvenir d'enfance*

In Georges Perec's *W ou le souvenir d'enfance* a sense of the otherness of memory stems from the recognition that remembering is as much an activity of concealment and displacement as of preservation. What Perec investigates and seeks to come to terms with is not so much what his memories mean, and the story they tell, as what they disguise, and the history they partially supplant. 'Je n'ai pas de souvenirs d'enfance':[53] for a long time Perec found this 'absence d'histoire' reassuring—until he came to suspect that it was perhaps protecting him from his 'histoire vécue', his true history. Like Leiris's *L'Age d'homme*, *W* was written partly in the orbit of psychoanalysis (the book's gestation overlaps with Perec's own experience of analysis in the early 1970s), and the mechanisms of what Freud called 'screen memories' are constantly to the fore. The starting point for the book, however, was a story (and accompanying drawings) Perec had written at the age of 13 and subsequently lost. Many years later it occurred to him that the story, which he remembered as consisting largely in the description of an island colony entirely devoted to sport, was in some way connected with his childhood. On the basis of what he recalled, and of some of the drawings, he initially rewrote the story from memory, and it was published as a serial in the *Quinzaine littéraire* in 1969–70.[54] It was only after a four-year gap, during which he underwent analysis with J.-B. Pontalis, that Perec decided to explore the links between the story and his past history. Then, rather than analysing it, he chose to intersperse chapters of the rewritten story with chapters consisting in a commentary on his meagre crop of childhood memories. At the beginning of *W*, published in 1975, Perec suggests that the story, with its minute reconstruction of a childhood fantasy, and the autobiographical memories necessitate and cast light on each other. But the

---

[53] *W ou le souvenir d'enfance*, 13. Subsequent references are incorporated in the text.

[54] The best account of the gestation of *W ou le souvenir d'enfance* is now to be found in Philippe Lejeune's indispensable *La Mémoire et l'oblique*. Also particularly useful with regard to memory is A. Leak, '*W* dans un réseau de lignes entrecroisées' in M. Ribière (ed.), *Parcours Perec*.

two 'récits' remain separate to the end: neither acknowledges the other's existence, and ultimately the gap between them, their failure to coalesce, is as significant as the contents of either. Each version seemed incomplete without the other, but Perec found it impossible to do more than point to the nature of this incompletion by identifying the shifts and displacements he detected in both 'récits'. In the fiction the main symptoms of displacement lie in the development of the story, which shifts abruptly at one point from being about a man sent in quest of a lost child with the same name as him—a fairly patent fable about loss, absence, and identity—to being the minutely detailed and impersonal description of an island named 'W'. The second shift occurs gradually and inexorably, though never explicitly, as the description of the customs, institutions, and statutes of 'W' undergoes a sinister mutation. An adolescent fantasy of sporting prowess, where everything is subordinated to the Olympic ideal, slowly turns into the description of a regime which forces helpless individuals to participate in degrading competitions where they forfeit all dignity and are subjected to an endless cycle of humiliation and violence alleviated only by the occasional, random 'privilege' of tasting briefly the power of the victor over the vanquished. As details accumulate, the reader progressively senses, and then realizes unmistakably, that the hideous world of the Nazi camps has taken over the story. This recognition is not of course made in the story itself but is signalled (without direct reference to the story) by a quotation from David Rousset's *L'Univers concentrationnaire* which figures in the last of the autobiographical chapters. However, the connection between the story and the Holocaust is foreshadowed from the point when we learn that when Perec was 6 his mother was deported to Auschwitz, and was never seen again.

In the autobiographical chapters of *W ou le souvenir d'enfance* Perec inventories and scrutinizes the relatively small collection of memories he has retained of his childhood, drawing on a small stock of photographs and documents and relying on the testimony of relatives to provide a chronological framework. Amongst the traces of his past, photographs have a privileged role. Seven are described in detail: one of his father, a Polish Jew 'mort pour la France' on 16 June 1940, in military uniform; two of Perec and his mother; one of his mother alone; two of Perec alone; one of Perec, his aunt, a peasant woman, and an assortment of farm animals.[55] The description of his father's photograph occurs in a text written fifteen years

---

[55] None of the photographs are reproduced in the book but most are to be found in C. Burgelin, *Georges Perec*, passim.

earlier, which Perec quotes in full and then rectifies by means of twenty-six footnotes which pinpoint imprecisions, inaccuracies, distortions, but which also add further factual details. In the case of the photograph, Perec corrects the description of his father's greatcoat—he had not looked at the photograph properly—and revises his airy hypothesis about where it had been taken. It is clear that in retrospect Perec finds his text full of tendentiousness, surreptitious attitudinizing, and unwarranted speculation, and that he is irritated at the rather literary rhetoric he had employed fifteen years earlier: in *W* his descriptions will be sober, unrhetorical, and meticulous (even comically so, as he acknowledges by the precise inventory of the animals in the last snapshot he examines, pp. 135–6). As surviving traces of a loss which has made Perec the person he is, and whose main symptom is the fact that he writes, the photographs require commentary not rhapsody. Here each plain fact that can be established is important: the *punctum* of the photograph lies in its very survival.

In classifying his memories Perec's starting point is how little he remembers, and how little of what he does remember has manifest significance. What emerges when they are assembled and submitted to scrutiny is that many of his memories have a false or improbable air about them. In some cases a more likely version of events—the true text beneath the false one—readily suggests itself, even if it inevitably remains conjectural. This applies, for example, to the memory of being brutally stripped of a school medal, which Perec thinks may more plausibly correspond to a suppressed memory of having a yellow star pinned on him. His two earliest memories are characterized by an air of phoniness which resides in their excessively symbolic and fabricated quality. Whatever the 'real events' which may or may not underlie them, these have been overlaid and reconstructed; other materials—both later experiences and cultural determinants—have transformed them. The important thing is the fact of distortion itself; what matters is that when he inspects his memories Perec finds that, like secret panels in a seemingly ordinary room, they begin to slide and open on to other vistas.

A broken arm features in two of Perec's early memories, but in both cases independent testimony suggests that this is a product of fantasy. The first instance concerns his only memory of his mother, and involves her seeing off her son, whose arm is in a sling, at the Gare de Lyon and buying him a magazine whose cover depicted Charlie Chaplin dropping with a parachute attached to his braces. According to his aunt there was no broken arm, but Perec was almost certainly wearing a truss for a hernia which had been operated on a few months later. Perec comments: 'Un triple trait parcourt ce souvenir: parachute, bras en écharpe, bandage herniaire: cela tient de la suspension, du soutien, presque de la prothèse. Pour être, besoin d'étai' (p. 77). The second 'broken arm' involves a sledge accident, and again the gap between memory and fact is filled by independent testimony, in this case a school-friend who recalls that the accident had in fact happened to someone else. Here Perec observes:

Comme pour le bras en écharpe de la Gare de Lyon, je vois bien ce que pouvaient remplacer ces fractures éminemment réparables qu'une immobilisation temporaire suffisait à réduire, même si la métaphore, aujourd'hui, me semble inopérante pour décrire ce qui précisément avait été cassé et qu'il était sans doute vain d'espérer enfermer dans le simulacre d'un membre fantôme. Plus simplement, ces thérapeutiques imaginaires, moins contraignantes que tutoriales, ces *points de suspension*, désignaient des douleurs nommables et venaient à point justifier des cajoleries dont les raisons réelles n'étaient données qu'à voix basse. Quoi qu'il en soit, et d'aussi loin que je me souvienne, le mot 'omoplate' et son comparse, le mot 'clavicule', m'ont toujours été familiers (pp. 109–10).

This passage epitomizes the poignant awkwardness of Perec's stance towards his memories. He begins by laconically deprecating the poverty of the psychic defences to which his memories bear witness. A broken arm: how can such a trifling fracture hope to represent 'ce qui précisément avait été cassé'—his mother's life, his bond with her? Memory's euphemistic subterfuges seem grossly impertinent in the face of a truth the child could not accommodate. Yet if there is a sense of frustration its target is just as much the fact that Perec is no more able to talk directly now about his mother's death than he was then. Through periphrasis ('ce qui précisément avait été cassé', 'les raisons réelles') Perec repeats the occultation of death and absence which he diagnoses in the operations of his memory. The second sentence scarcely succeeds in its initial aim of saying things 'plus simplement', while the third sentence points to the process of substitution through which Perec's encyclopaedic mastery of the verbal world has obliterated the unbearable fact of his mother's death. In a passage of central importance (p. 59) Perec casts doubt on his ability to say anything about his parents in view of the main fact about them—the scandal of their absence. But the inevitable failure of his attempt to write about them is itself a *memento mori*, a repetition of absence and annihilation. Regardless of its relative success or failure, the *act* of writing—in its inherent endlessness, its eternal severance from the concrete, its intrinsic incapacity to grasp the real, its basis in absence—is attuned to the reality of loss. Writing is the point at which memory, biography, identity, and loss coincide: 'j'écris parce qu'ils

ont laissé en moi leur marque indélébile et que la trace en est l'écriture: leur
souvenir est mort à l'écriture; l'écriture est le souvenir de leur mort et
l'affirmation de ma vie' (p. 59).

Perec's tendency to draw attention to the fact of distortion, rather than to
engage in full-blown 'interpretation' of his memories, reflects a feeling
which is never expressly articulated but constantly implied: that all his early
memories relate to the disappearance of his parents and invite interpretation
from the standpoint of that primordial context. This, we may imagine, is
what was progressively borne in on Perec as he rewrote the fantasy-story,
underwent analysis, collected his memories, and composed *W*: it is thus a
recognition which belongs to the work of memory rather than a hypothesis
or a conclusion. Moreover, what is at stake here—the mark of the Holocaust
in Perec's past—is all the more indelible for being impossible to localize. As
a child, the source of anxiety was the uncertainty surrounding his parents'
absence: it is the trace of this absence—and particularly the subterfuges by
which it is covered up—that Perec comes to identify in his memories. As an
adult Perec is in possession of certain facts which can help him to perceive
the distortions of his memory, but this does not put him in a position to
determine their ultimate significance. That significance is not simply a
matter of interpretation but of how he comes to terms with the past and its
abiding traces in the present. The power of Perec's treatment of memory in
W derives not from ingenious interpretations but from the way recurrent
details and situations take on a significance which does not have to be
explicitly stated.

What does he remember? At Villard de Lans in 1942–5, Perec is shuffled
between aunts, homes, and schools. One day at school he is told his aunt has
come to see him, but finds a stranger there; it is not the familiar Esther but
Tante Berthe. At the core of the memory is the feeling that henceforth 'il ne
viendra à toi que des étrangères; tu les chercheras et tu les repousseras sans
cesse' (pp. 137–8); the mother's absence is reaffirmed; Perec's future
relationships with women are prefigured. In another memory Perec is (quite
implausibly) alone in the school attic, where he finds some rolls of film and
purloins a sequence showing a desert oasis with palm trees and camels. He
then uses this talisman as proof to his school-fellows that he is to go to
Palestine the following year, hoping to inveigle them, in return for his
promise to send them large quantities of oranges (a 'magical' fruit they have
never seen), to share with him the four o'clock 'goûters' they enjoyed, but of
which he was deprived. Only one pupil falls for this ploy, but he then
denounces Perec to the headmistress who punishes him severely. As Perec
indicates, everything is unlikely in this scenario: why, for example, would he

be the only pupil not to be entitled to a 'goûter'? Perec tells us he learnt later that his grandmother was anxious that he should accompany her to Palestine, but he leaves the reader to fathom the powerful but imponderable current of fantasy at work here which seems to bear on the child's desire for integration, the wish to turn his special condition into a mark of election, together with a sense that there is something culpable in his desires.

A number of Perec's memories involve marks or traces. Unjustly accused of locking a girl in the playroom cupboard, he is isolated and sent to Coventry. Some time later, in the same room, he is stung by a bee, his thigh swells to a vast size, and this quite separate incident is interpreted by the children, but especially, Perec stresses, by himself, as a proof that he had indeed locked the little girl up (p. 172). The bee-sting is a mark of irrational, inalienable guilt. Perec receives another mark (p. 141) when a boy whom he has slightly grazed with a ski flies into a rage and strikes him a blow which results in a permanent scar on the upper lip. The scar, Perec tells us, later became a kind of talisman of his identity, playing a considerable role in his writing from his first novel onwards. These instances of receiving a mark may be linked with Perec's 'gaucherie contrariée' (p. 182): the effects of what he assumes were attempts to correct left-handedness. The main symptom is the inability to remember which is which when confronted with paired concepts such as concave and convex, or Guelph and Ghibelline. This 'deficiency' is illustrated by a childhood memory (Perec is uncertain whether it is true or false) of causing a bobsleigh accident by leaning to the left on a bend when the other occupants correctly leaned right. Running through this memory, and the defect it reveals, one can perhaps identify, once again, notions of difference, and of a mark of difference. Here it is significant that attempts to straighten the child out, to make him 'the same', should have led Perec to have, as one of his 'marques particulières', a malfunction in the area of memory. The centrality of this trait is further underlined by the fact that, as Perec indicates, the defect has actually inspired a fascination with mnemonic techniques. Indeed, Perec's jubilant enumeration of the symptoms of his deficiency provides one of the many signs of his remarkable mnemonic capacities, an extraordinary ability to retain factual and material detail, which at times seems to border on the pathological, and which also seems to serve as a defence mechanism. What is troubling in the sphere of memory is suppressed or displaced not by forgetfulness but by hypermnesia, an excess of remembering which drowns out what one would prefer not to remember. The bee-sting, the facial scar, the memory disorder, have in common the fact that they are marks wrought by external action, but which Perec has appropriated so that they have come to be inextricably bound up with his identity: they are marks of otherness which have come to represent the self.

The mark is a sign which is both objective and visible, but meaningless without a code of interpretation. In its most elementary form it is a pure cipher. Yet Perec observes that for him the letter 'x', the conventional algebraic sign for an unknown quantity, or the spot where something occurred, has a powerful materiality. 'X', he points out, is the only letter of the alphabet which is also a word, and an object—an 'x' is a sawing-horse made up of two crosses (p. 105). Perec remembers such an object, used by an old man to saw logs at Villard, but at the centre of this memory is the word. The word 'x' mediates between the materiality of a physical object and the letter 'x' as sign of absence, erasure, and, as Perec informs us, citing a scholarly article from the *Journal of Applied Physiology*, oblation. A word, an object, a cipher, the 'x' is also a graphic symbol: Perec suggests that it is as 'point de départ d'une géométrie fantasmatique dont le V dédoublé constitue la figure de base', that the 'x' encompasses 'les symboles majeurs de l'histoire de mon enfance' (p. 106). Dismembered and dismantled into two 'v's, the 'x' proliferates, becoming a swastika, the letters SS, the star of David, and of course (though Perec does not mention it here) the ubiquitous 'double V'—W—of his writings. But *W ou le souvenir d'enfance* constantly suggests that, behind these playful substitutions, the 'x', the mark, is linked to the disappearance of his mother, to memory in general, to the act of writing, and to life and death: 'J'écris parce qu'ils ont laissé en moi leur *marque* indélébile et que la *trace* en est l'écriture: leur souvenir est mort à l'écriture; l'écriture est le souvenir de leur mort et l'affirmation de ma vie' (p. 59). By a circular process, writing, the inscription of marks and traces, perpetuates Perec's links to his parents, even as it annihilates them again by marking their absence. Ultimately, each of his childhood memories is a mark, an 'x', something both material and immaterial, burdensome and imponderable, external but also consubstantial with his being. In *W ou le souvenir d'enfance* the writing of memory becomes (to use Perec's own terms, p. 54) an *encrage*, an inking, which provides an *ancrage*, an anchorage—a place of inscription for the traces of a scandalous absence which writing cannot redeem but whose place it can mark forever.

Postscript: The Future of Memory

S'il n'y avait la crainte de l'inévitable affrontement, de la cruelle et décisive confrontation avec *l'autre*, l'autobiographie n'aurait-elle pas vite fait, en dépit des réticences instinctives de l'auteur, de se transformer en une quelconque opération de complaisance envers soi-même?

(Edmond Jabès, 'L'Epée nue')

Autobiography has always been an art of memory. In Perec's *W ou le souvenir d'enfance*, remembering, through its negotiations with material traces (photographs) and with immaterial gaps and fissures, operates at the intersection of personal and collective experience, and involves the interplay of knowledge (the terrain of history) and desire (the domain of psychoanalysis). Approaching and evading potential truths, each according to its own lights, a fictional narrative and a factual investigation interact without ever fusing. Autobiographical truth remains relative, plural, contingent. What is more, the twin *récits* of *W* may be set alongside other branches of a multi-faceted autobiographical enterprise whose full extent has come to light since the author's death.[1] For Perec the process of autobiography could not be conducted within the confines of any one genre or practice, but had to be carried out simultaneously or successively on several fronts. The same could, of course, be said of Rousseau who, from the 'Lettres à Malesherbes' to the *Dialogues*, with the incomplete *Confessions* as a massive centrepiece, struggled for much of his adult life, in different genres, with the demands of self-writing. It is fitting, therefore, at the conclusion of this study of French autobiography, to emphasize both innovation (or diversity) and perpetuation (or canonicity).

Roland Barthes par Roland Barthes, published in the same year as Perec's *W* and comparably bold in its approach, helped to rescue autobiography from the paraliterary doldrums to which the genre had been consigned by some aspects of contemporary theory, and to rehabilitate it as an endeavour worthy of serious intellectual consideration.[2] But if one of the achievements

---

[1] See the collection *Je suis né*, ed. by P. Lejeune, which assembles a fascinating range of articles and documents tracing the diversity of Perec's autobiographical projects.

[2] Lejeune's *Le Pacte autobiographique*, which also did much to place autobiography firmly on the contemporary critical map, was also published in 1975.

of Barthes (and Perec) was to clear autobiography of the slur that it necessarily perpetuated belief in the old stable ego, the 'sujet plein' discredited by Lacanian psychoanalysis, there was ample room for confusion. It could, for example, be maintained that in switching between first- and third-person pronouns, or in juxtaposing different kinds of discourse about the self, Barthes and Perec had not only charted in new ways the treacherous border territory of truth and fiction in autobiography, but had totally obliterated the border between them. This, at any rate, often seems to be the moral of what Serge Doubrovsky has labelled 'autofiction', a species of text where the reader is teased and titillated as the author stages a masquerade in which truth and falsity, authentic recollection and patent fantasy, cease to be distinguishable.[3]

At its best, as in Alain Robbe-Grillet's *Le Miroir qui revient* and *Angélique ou l'enchantement*,[4] autofiction is mesmerizing, if ultimately enervating. To offset what he considers to be the congenital defects of the autobiographical enterprise, 'où l'on prétend rassembler toute une existence vécue (qui, dans l'instant, faisait eau de toute part) en un volume clos, sans manques et sans bavures',[5] Robbe-Grillet introduces a fictional ingredient in the shape of a patently imaginary character, Henri de Corinthe, whose role seems to be to ensure that the currents of fantasy at large in the author's reminiscences are strong enough to prevent the constitution of a consistent self-image. Playing repeated variations on the theme of the double, Robbe-Grillet, in *Angélique* especially, gives a kind of slow-motion view of the process of autobiographical writing as he sees it, allowing the drift of fantasy to take over, and then, like the dreamer who pinches himself to see if he is awake, intervening abruptly so as to investigate, as Perec did in *W*, the credentials of his compulsive mythologizing. The stop–start mechanism is entertaining enough, but the insights into both the autobiographical act and the identity of the actor prove insubstantial. Memories, Robbe-Grillet observes at one point, are no more certain or less evanescent than our present experiences: 'aussi soudainement apparus que vite effacés, nous ne pouvons ni les tenir immobiles, ni en fixer la trace de façon définitive, ni les réunir en une durée continue au sein d'organisations causales à sens unique et sans faille'.[6] This is well said, but the conclusion Robbe-Grillet goes on to draw seems

---

[3] See S. Doubrovsky, *Autobiographiques*. Doubrovsky is himself a leading exponent of 'autofiction', in works such as *Fils* and *Le Récit brisé*. P. Lejeune discusses 'autofictions' by Doubrovsky and J. Lanzmann in *Moi aussi*, 37–72, and by F. Nourissier in *French Autobiography*, ii. 7–19.

[4] Published in 1984 and 1988 respectively.

[5] *Le Miroir qui revient*, 58.

[6] *Angélique ou l'enchantement*, 67.

questionable: 'La patiente écriture des fragments qui demeurent (provisoir-
ement, je le sais) ne peut en aucun cas considérer mon passé comme
producteur de signification (un sens à ma vie), mais au contraire comme
producteur de récit: un devenir à mon projet d'écrivain.'[7] Memories, in
other words, can only be fodder for fiction, while fiction, for its part, is
simply autobiography carried on by other means ('Je n'ai jamais parlé
d'autre chose que de moi' proclaims the opening of *Le Miroir qui revient*,[8]
with reference to Robbe-Grillet's reputedly self-contained novels). Robbe-
Grillet elides any distinction between the excavation and discrimination of
meanings in the territory of pastness ('considérer mon passé comme
producteur de signification') and the act of foisting a monolithic and rigid
meaning on one's life ('un sens à ma vie'). Any sense of a middle way
between the deluded quest for incontrovertible truth and the contention
that all is fiction seems to be missing here. And what this reveals, above all
perhaps, is the lack of a truly compelling motive on Robbe-Grillet's part—
an insufficiency of autobiographical desire—and also the absence of that
climate of otherness which is the sign that autobiography involves a
confrontation with what is unknown.

It is revealing to contrast Robbe-Grillet's autobiographies with another
work written in the same period. Jean Genet's *Un Captif amoureux* (1986) is
the account of a period of some two years spent in the company of
Palestinian *feddayin* in the Occupied Territories in the early 1970s, and of
return visits in 1982 and 1984. Mainly written in the mid-1980s, Genet's
text draws to some extent on fragmentary notes and journals, and on
material published earlier, notably an article written after the Chatilla and
Sabra massacres, but it is above all, and explicitly, an exercise in memory.
Genet constantly seeks to render not only the elusive quality of past
experience but also the vicissitudes of the memory process as they are
manifested in the process of writing. In addition, as in the *Journal du voleur*,
Genet repeatedly scrutinizes and reassesses his motives for writing,
registering the wax and wane of autobiographical desire in response to 'un
certain ébranlement de la mémoire'.[9] A compelling ethical solidarity with
the *feddayin* is important here, but for Genet it does not dictate slavish
adherence to facts, issues, or a party line, but commitment to the detail of
past sensations and emotions. Like the American Black Panthers, with
whom he repeatedly compares them, the Palestinians, without territory or
acknowledged legitimacy, inhabit a world of images and reflections (partly

[7] *Angélique ou l'enchantement*, 68.
[8] *Le Miroir qui revient*, 10.
[9] *Un Captif amoureux*, 320.

those projected by the media coverage on which they thrive), and Genet strives to record his own vicarious participation, at the level of his dreams and fantasies, in the imaginary universe of his captivating 'captors'. Reportage becomes autobiography by virtue of the work of identification. Powerfully drawn to the *feddayin*, in part because of their capacity to live— and live festively—day by day, fuelled by hopes and longings for an imaginary homeland, Genet finds himself repeatedly reappraising the constituents from which he has fashioned his own life. His first-hand experience of incarceration, exile, and repudiation; his images of the Orient nurtured since childhood; his interest in religion and ceremony; the improvised, provisional relationships engendered by his sexuality—all these take on new shades in the light of the Palestinian experience. Genet's narrative is partly structured around a single element, the quest he undertook in 1984 for Hamza and his mother who, in the period since the early 1970s, had come to symbolize for him the Palestinian revolution. The quest for traces of the pair enables Genet to write under the sign of loss. But the fourteen-year gap, together with the shorter time-lag before he starts writing, provide a framework (again it is similar to that of the *Journal du voleur*) where the past is apprehended both as a succession of moments and as a mosaic of interlocking and self-mirroring elements. Only by bringing it into language, but treating each word as a potential traitor before entrusting it with the task in hand, can Genet discover what it is that he lived through. But if nearly every page of *Un Captif amoureux* carries at least one reference to words, the equal predominance of references to memory ensures that it is the interplay of experiencing, remembering, and writing which is constantly to the fore.

There is clearly a certain arbitrariness in contrasting, and indeed adjudicating between, Robbe-Grillet and Genet in the context of innovation in autobiography. The justification for doing so is to suggest, firstly, that when autobiographers do something new it is against the background of existing responses to enduring problems and preoccupations, and secondly that these can provide criteria for assessing the effectiveness of new strategies. In the preceding chapters, otherness, intention, desire, incidents, reading, narrative, ideology, intertextuality, and memory are the principal categories which have enabled us to analyse and compare autobiographies in terms of a set of interrelated issues and parameters. If other categories could certainly be added, the usefulness of those enumerated is borne out, in one respect, by the way they may help us to delineate, however loosely, an autobiographical canon in the wider context of French literature of the last two hundred years. Admirably resourceful and formally inventive as they have been, the autobiographers we have considered participate in an endeavour whose communality is discernible in comparable transactions with consistent obstacles as well as new perplexities. By drawing frequent parallels with non-French writers—Wordsworth, James, Benjamin, Nabokov—I have sought to avoid confining French autobiography within a narrow literary tradition, and to emphasize that the features which help to pinpoint the particular qualities of a given work are in no way specific to the French. English, American, and German autobiographers also engage with incidents, ideologies, readers, and memories. Nevertheless, when they manifest a serious negotiation with these agencies (a criterion vital to the constitution of our canon) French autobiographies have tended to show signs that intertextual affiliations within the French domain have been of paramount importance. It is above all the sense of operating within an intertextual nexus which makes it rewarding to take French autobiography as a specific object of study. I hope, therefore, that the consanguinity as well as the inherent interest of the works studied here has been sufficiently demonstrated for the reader to feel that 'French autobiography', rather than a mere catch-all label, designates a range of itineraries, within the territory of a particular kind of literary discourse, which link Rousseau and his precursors with Barthes, Perec, Genet, and their successors. In years to come, new ground will certainly be broken in the field of autobiography: questions of race, gender, and the development of new media, are already having an impact. It seems safe to predict, however, that change will come about, as before, through the autobiographer's engagement with challenges akin to those which for over two centuries have been at the heart of the autobiographical enterprise.

Bibliography

Unless otherwise specified, place of publication is Paris in the case of French books, London in the case of English books.

Abraham, Nicholas, and Maria Torok, *Cryptonymie: Le Verbier de l'Homme aux Loups* (Aubier-Flammarion, 1976).

Althusser, Louis, *Lénine et la philosophie* (Maspéro, 1972).

Apter, Emily, *Feminizing the Fetish* (New York: Cornell University Press, 1991).

Augustine, *Confessions*, trans. with an introduction by R. S. Pine-Coffin (Harmondsworth: Penguin Books, 1961).

Auster, Paul, *The Invention of Solitude* (Faber & Faber, 1988).

Autobiography: Essays Theoretical and Critical, ed. James Olney (Princeton University Press, 1980).

Badiou, Alain, *L'Être et l'événement* (Éditions du Seuil, 1988).

Bakhtin, Mikhail, 'Discourse in the Novel', in Michael Holquist (ed.), *The Dialogic Imagination* (Austin: Texas University Press, 1981, 259–422).

Barthes, Roland, *Le Bruissement de la langue* (Éditions du Seuil, 1984).

—— *La Chambre claire* (Gallimard and Seuil, 1980).

—— 'Le Grain d'une enfance', *Le Nouvel Observateur* (9 May 1977), 86–7.

—— *Incidents* (Éditions du Seuil, 1987).

—— 'Introduction à l'étude structurale du récit', in *Poétique du récit* (Éditions du Seuil, 1977).

—— *L'Obvie et l'obtus* (Éditions du Seuil, 1982).

—— 'Pour un Chateaubriand de papier', in *Le Grain de la voix: Entretiens, 1962–1980* (Éditions du Seuil, 1981).

—— *Roland Barthes par Roland Barthes* (Éditions du Seuil, 1975).

Bataille, Georges, *La Littérature et le mal* (Collection Idées, Gallimard, 1967).

—— *L'Érotisme* (Éditions de Minuit, 1957).

Baudelaire, Charles, *Œuvres complètes*, ed. Claude Pichois, 2 vols. (Bibliothèque de la Pléiade, Gallimard, 1975).

Beaujour, Michel, *Miroirs d'encre: Rhétorique de l'autoportrait* (Éditions du Seuil, 1980).

Beauvoir, Simone de, *Mémoires d'une jeune fille rangée* (Collection Folio, Gallimard).

—— *Tout compte fait* (Gallimard, 1972).

Beckett, Samuel, *Endgame, That Time*, in *The Complete Dramatic Works* (Faber & Faber, 1986).

Benjamin, Walter, *Illuminations* (Jonathan Cape, 1970).

Benjamin, Walter, *One-Way Street* (New Left Books, 1979).

Bennett, Jonathan, *Events and Their Names* (Oxford University Press, 1988).

Bennington, Geoffrey, *Sententiousness and the Novel* (Cambridge University Press, 1985).

Benveniste, Emile, 'L'Appareil formel de l'énonciation', in *Problèmes de linguistique générale*, ii (Éditions de Minuit), 79 88.

Berlioz, *Mémoires*, 2 vols. (Garnier-Flammarion, 1969).

Bersani, Leo, *A Future for Astyanax: Character and Desire in Literature* (Marion Boyars, 1978).

Berthier, *Stendhal et Chateaubriand* (Geneva: Droz, 1987).

Blanchot, Maurice, 'Combat avec l'ange', in *L'Amitié* (Gallimard, 1971), 150–61.

—— 'Le Demain joueur' in *L'Entretien infini* (Gallimard, 1969), 597–619.

Blin, Georges, *Stendhal et les problèmes de la personnalité* (José Corti, 1958).

Bloom, Harold, *The Anxiety of Influence* (New York: Oxford University Press, 1973).

Bowie, Malcolm, *Proust, Freud, Lacan* (Cambridge University Press, 1987).

Bréchon, Robert, *L'Age d'homme de Michel Leiris* (Hachette, 1973).

Brée, Germaine, *Narcissus Absconditus* (Oxford University Press, 1978).

Breton, André, *L'Amour fou* (Gallimard, 1968).

Brooks, Peter, 'Psychoanalytic Constructions and Narrative Meanings', *Paragraph*, 7 (1986), 53–76.

—— *Reading for the Plot* (Oxford University Press, 1984).

Brunet, E., *Index-Concordance d'Emile ou de l'éducation* (Geneva: Slatkine, 1980).

Bruss, Elizabeth, *Autobiographical Acts: The Changing Situation of a Literary Genre* (Johns Hopkins University Press, 1976).

Bryson, Norman, *Word and Image* (Cambridge University Press, 1981).

Burgelin, Claude, *Georges Perec* (Éditions du Seuil, 1988).

Burt, E. S., 'Developments in Character: Reading and Interpretation in "The Children's Punishment" and "The Broken Comb"', *Yale French Studies*, 69 (1985), 192–210.

Calvino, Italo, *Invisible Cities* (Picador, 1979).

Capitano, Sarah J., 'Perspectives sur l'écriture durassienne: *L'Amant*', *Symposium* (Spring 1987), 15–27.

Casey, Edward S., *Remembering: A Phenomenological Study* (Indiana University Press, 1987).

Cave, Terence, *Recognitions: A Study in Poetics* (Oxford University Press, 1988).

Chappuis, Pierre, *Michel Leiris* (Seghers, 1973).

Charity, A. C., *Events and Their Afterlife* (Cambridge University Press, 1966).

Charlton, D. G., *Positivist Thought in France during the Second Empire 1852–1870* (Oxford University Press, 1959).

Chateaubriand, François-René de, *Mémoires d'outre-tombe*, ed. Maurice Levaillant, 4 vols. (Garnier-Flammarion, 1982).

Cioffi, Frank, 'When Do Empirical Methods Bypass "The Problems Which

Trouble Us"?' in A. Phillips Griffiths (ed.), *Philosophy and Literature* (Cambridge University Press, 1984), 155–72.

Clément, Pierre-Paul, 'De la mémoire aux mémoires: Construction d'un espace autobiographique dans les *Confessions* de J.-J. Rousseau', *Nouvelle Revue de psychanalyse*, 15 (1977), 185–201.

—— *Jean-Jacques Rousseau: De l'éros coupable à l'éros glorieux* (Neuchâtel: La Baconnière, 1976).

Clifford, James, *The Predicament of Culture: Twentieth-Century Ethnography, Literature and Art* (Harvard University Press, 1988).

Cockshut, A. O. J., *The Art of Autobiography* (Yale University Press, 1984).

Coe, Richard N., *When the Grass was Taller: Autobiography and the Experience of Childhood* (Yale University Press, 1984).

Coetzee, J. M., *Truth in Autobiography*, Inaugural Lecture, 3 Oct. 1984 (University of Cape Town, [1984]).

Collins, Douglas, *Sartre as Biographer* (Harvard University Press, 1980).

Compagnon, Antoine, *La Seconde Main ou le travail de la citation* (Éditions du Seuil, 1979).

Condillac, Étienne Bonnot de, *Essai sur l'origine des connaissances humaines*, with an essay by Jacques Derrida (Galilée, 1973).

Coulont-Henderson, Françoise, 'Remarques sur la mémoire et les croquis de la *Vie de Henry Brulard*', *Stendhal-Club*, 102 (1984), 141–51.

Courtivron, Isabelle de, *Violette Leduc* (Twayne, 1985).

Coward, Rosalind, and John Ellis, *Language and Materialism* (Routledge and Kegan Paul, 1977).

Crouzet, Michel, 'Écriture et autobiographie dans la *Vie de Henry Brulard*', in Victor Del Litto (ed.), *Stendhal et les problèmes de l'autobiographie* (Presses Universitaires de Grenoble, 1976), 105–32.

—— *Stendhal et le langage* (José Corti, 1981).

—— *La Vie de Henry Brulard ou l'enfance de la révolte* (José Corti, 1982).

Culler, Jonathan, 'Apostrophe', in *The Pursuit of Signs* (Routledge and Kegan Paul, 1981), 135–54.

Davidson, Donald, *Essays on Actions and Events* (Oxford University Press, 1980).

Davies, Howard, '*Les Mots* as *Essai sur le don*: Contribution to an Origin Myth', *Yale French Studies*, 68 (1985), 57–72.

—— *Sartre and 'Les Temps modernes'* (Cambridge University Press, 1987).

Dejean, Joan, *Literary Fortifications: Rousseau, Laclos, Sade* (Princeton University Press, 1984), 137–61.

De Man, Paul, *Allegories of Reading* (Yale University Press, 1979).

—— 'Autobiography as De-Facement', in *The Rhetoric of Romanticism* (New York: Columbia University Press, 1984), 67–82.

—— *Blindness and Insight* (Oxford University Press, 1971).

—— 'Sign and Symbol in Hegel's Aesthetics', *Critical Inquiry*, 8 (1982), 761–75.

Derrida, Jacques, *De la grammatologie* (Éditions de Minuit, 1967).

Derrida, Jacques, 'La Loi du genre', *Parages* (Galilée, 1986), 249–87.

—— *Limited Inc.*, supplement to *Glyph*, Johns Hopkins Textual Studies, 2 (1977).

—— *L'Oreille de l'autre: Textes et débats* (Montreal: VLB, 1982).

—— *Marges de la philosophie* (Édtions de Minuit, 1972).

—— *Mémoires for Paul de Man* (New York: Columbia University Press, 1986).

—— *Otobiographies: L'Enseignement de Nietzsche et la pratique du nom propre* (Galilée, 1984).

Didier, Béatrice, 'L'Adresse au lecteur dans les textes autobiographiques de Stendhal', in *Colloque de Cerisy-la-Salle: Stendhal* (Aux amateurs des livres, 1986), 119–33.

—— *Stendhal autobiographe* (Presses Universitaires de France, 1982).

Dilthey, Wilhelm, *Selected Writings of Wilhelm Dilthey*, ed. H. P. Rickman (Cambridge University Press, 1976).

Dollimore, Jonathan, 'Different Desires: Subjectivity and Transgression in Wilde and Gide', *Textual Practice*, i. 1 (1987), 48–67.

Doubrovsky, Serge, *Autobiographiques: De Corneille à Sartre* (Presses Universitaires de France, 1988).

Duras, Marguerite, *L'Amant* (Éditions de Minuit, 1984).

Eakin, Paul John, *Fictions in Autobiography: Studies in the Art of Self-Invention* (Princeton, NJ: Princeton University Press, 1985).

Ehrenzweig, Anton, *The Hidden Order of Art* (Paladin, 1970).

Elbaz, Robert, *The Changing Nature of the Self* (Croom Helm, 1988).

Ellis, David, *Wordsworth, Freud and the Spots of Time* (Cambridge University Press, 1985).

Ellrich, R. J., *Rousseau and his Reader* (Durham, NC: North Carolina University Press, 1969).

Evans, M. N., 'La Mythologie de l'écriture dans *La Bâtarde* de Violette Leduc', *Littérature*, 46 (1982), 82–92.

Fleishman, Avrom, *Figures of Autobiography* (Berkeley, Calif., California University Press, 1983).

Fleuret, C., *Rousseau et Montaigne* (Nizet, 1980).

Florence, Penny, *Mallarmé, Manet and Redon: Visual and Aural Signs and the Generation of Meaning* (Cambridge University Press, 1986).

Foster, D., *Confession and Complicity in Narrative* (Cambridge University Press, 1987).

France, Peter, *Rousseau: Confessions* (Cambridge University Press, 1987).

French Autobiography: Texts, Contexts, Poetics, proceedings of a Conference at the University of Kent, Apr. 1985, with a preface by Michael Sheringham, *Romance Studies*, 8 (Summer 1986) and 9 (Winter 1986). (In cross-references these vols. are designated i and ii.)

Freud, Sigmund, 'Childhood Memories and Screen Memories', *The Standard*

Edition of the Complete Psychological Work of Sigmund Freud, Hogarth Press, 1953–74 (hereafter *SE*), vi. 43–52.

Freud, Sigmund, 'Constructions in Analysis', *SE* xxiii. 257–69.

—— 'Remembering, Repeating and Working-through', *SE* xii. 147–56.

—— 'Screen Memories' (1899), *SE* iii. 301–22.

—— *Beyond the Pleasure Principle* (Pelican Freud Library (hereafter PFL), 11; Harmondsworth: Penguin Books, 1984), 269–338.

—— 'A Disturbance of Memory on the Acropolis' (PFL 11; 1984), 443–56.

—— *The Ego and the Id* (PFL, 11; 1984), 350–403.

—— 'Fetishism' (1927) (PFL 7; 1977), 345–58.

—— 'From the History of an Infantile Neurosis (The Wolf Man)' (PFL 9; 1979), 227–366.

—— 'Negation' (PFL 11; 1984), 435–42.

—— 'A Note upon the "Mystic Writing-Pad"' (PFL 11; 1984), 427–34.

—— *The Psychopathology of Everyday Life* (PFL 5; 1975).

—— *Three Essays on the Theory of Sexuality* (1905) (PFL 7; 1977).

Freund, Elizabeth, *The Return of the Reader* (Methuen, 1987).

Fumaroli, Marc, 'Les Mémoires du 17ᵉ siècle au carrefour des genres en prose', *XVIIᵉ Siècle* (1972), 7–37.

Gearhart, Susan, *The Open Boundary of History and Fiction* (Princeton, NJ: Princeton University Press, 1984).

Genet, Jean, *Un Captif amoureux* (Gallimard, 1986).

—— *Journal du voleur* (Collection Folio, Gallimard, 1982).

Genette, Gérard, 'Frontières du récit', in *Figures I* (Éditions du Seuil, 1966).

Gide, André, *Correspondance André Gide—Dorothy Bussy, Cahiers André Gide*, 9 (Gallimard, 1979).

—— *The Correspondence of André Gide and Edmund Gosse*, ed. L. F. Brugmans (Peter Owen, 1960).

—— *Corydon* (Gallimard, 1968).

—— *Entretiens André Gide—Jean Amrouche* [1949], in Eric Marty, *André Gide: Qui êtes-vous?* (Lyons: La Manufacture, 1987).

—— *Journal, 1889–1939* (Bibliothèque de la Pléiade, Gallimard, 1952).

—— *Si le grain ne meurt* (Collection Folio, Gallimard, 1978).

Goethe, Johann Wolfgang von, *The Autobiography of Johann Wolfgang von Goethe* [*Dichtung und Wahrheit*, 1832], trans. by John Oxenford with an introduction by Karl J. Weintraub, 2 vols. (Chicago University Press, 1974).

Gordon, Felicia, 'A Parodic Strategy: Sartre's *Les Mots*', *Nottingham French Studies*, 23 (1984), 51–68.

Gore, Keith, *L'Idée de progrès dans la pensée de Renan* (Nizet, 1970).

Gorz, André, *Le Traître* (Collection Points, Éditions du Seuil, 1978).

Gosse, Edmund, *Father and Son*, ed. by Peter Abbs (Harmondsworth: Penguin Books, 1983).

Gossman, Lionel, 'Time and History in Rousseau', *Studies on Voltaire and the Eighteenth Century*, 30 (1964), 311-50.

Gratton, J., '*Roland Barthes par Roland Barthes*: Autobiography and the Notion of Expression', in *French Autobiography: Texts, Contexts, Poetics* (q.v.), i. 57-66.

Green, Julien, *Partir avant le jour* (1963), *Mille chemins ouverts* (1964), *Terre lointaine* (1966), *Jeunesse* (1974), reissued in revised and expanded form as *Jeunes Années, Autobiographie*, 2 vols. (Éditions du Seuil, 1984).

Greene, Thomas, *The Light from Troy* (Yale University Press, 1982).

Gunn, Janet Varner, *Autobiography: Towards a Poetics of Experience* (Philadelphia: Pennsylvania University Press, 1982).

Gusdorf, Georges, 'Conditions et limites de l'autobiographie', in Philippe Lejeune, *L'Autobiographie en France*, Armand Colin, 1971), 217-36. (Originally publ. in *Formen der Selbstdarstellung*, Festgabe fur Fritz Neubert, Berlin, Duncker und Humblot, 1956, 105-9 and 111-21.)

—— 'De l'autobiographie initiatique à l'autobiographie genre littéraire', *Revue d'histoire littéraire de la France*, 75 (1975), 957-1002.

—— *Mémoire et personne*, 2 vols. (Presses Universitaires de France, 1950).

Halbwachs, Maurice, *La Mémoire collective* [1950] (Presses Universitaires de France, 1968).

Halpern, Joseph, *Critical Fictions: The Literary Criticism of Jean-Paul Sartre* (Yale University Press, 1976).

Hand, Séan, 'The Orchestration of Man: The Structure of *L'Age d'homme*', in *French Autobiography: Texts, Contexts, Poetics* (q.v.), i. 67-80.

—— 'The Sound and the Fury: Language in Leiris', *Paragraph*, 7 (1988), 102-20.

Hart, Francis R., 'Notes for an Anatomy of Modern Autobiography', *New Literary History*, 1 (1970), 485-511.

Hill, Leslie, 'Marguerite Duras and the Limits of Fiction', *Paragraph*, 12 (1989), 1-22.

Hoffman, Paul, 'La Mémoire et les valeurs dans les six premiers livres des *Confessions*', *Annales Jean-Jacques Rousseau*, 39 (1972-7), 79-92.

Hollier, Denis, *Le Collège de Sociologie* (Collection Idées, Gallimard, 1979).

Howells, Christina, *Sartre's Theory of Literature* (Modern Humanities Research Association, 1979).

Idt, Geneviève, 'L'Autoparodie dans *Les Mots* de Sartre', *Cahiers du 20ᵉ siècle*, 6 (1976), 53-86.

Jabès, Edmond, 'L'Épée nue', in *Autour de Michel Leiris: L'Ire des vents*, 3-4 (1981), 160-5.

Jacob, François, *La Statue intérieure* (Collection Folio, Gallimard, 1990).

James, Henry, *Autobiography*, ed. by F. N. Dupee (Princeton, NJ: Princeton University Press, 1983).

—— 'The Turning Point of My Life' [1900], in *The Complete Notebooks of Henry James*, ed. Leon Edel and Lyall H. Powers (New York: Oxford University Press, 1987).

Jamin, Jean, 'Quand le sacré devint gauche', in *Autour de Michel Leiris: L'Ire des vents*, 3–4 (1981), 98–118.

Jauss, Hans-Robert, '1912: Threshold to an Epoch: Apollinaire's "Zone" and "Lundi Rue Christine"', *Yale French Studies*, 74 (1988), 39–66.

Jay, Paul, *Being in the Text: Self-Representation from Wordsworth to Roland Barthes* (New York: Cornell University Press, 1983).

Jeanson, Henri, *Simone de Beauvoir ou l'entreprise de vivre* (Éditions du Seuil, 1966).

Jefferson, Ann, 'Autobiography as Intertext: Barthes, Sarraute, Robbe-Grillet', in Michael Worton and Judith Still (eds.), *Intertextuality* (Manchester University Press, 1990), 108–29.

—— 'Beyond Contract: The Reader of Autobiography and Stendhal's *Vie de Henry Brulard*', in *French Autobiography: Texts, Contexts, Poetics* (q.v.), ii. 53–69.

—— *Reading Realism in Stendhal* (Cambridge University Press, 1988).

Keefe, Terry, 'Simone de Beauvoir's Second Look at her Life', in *French Autobiography: Texts, Contexts, Poetics* (q.v.), i. 41–55.

Khatibi, Abdelkebir, *La Mémoire tatouée* (Denoël, 1971).

Knight, Diana, 'Roland Barthes: An Intertextual Figure', in Michael Worton and Judith Still (eds.), *Intertextuality* (Manchester University Press, 1990), 92–107.

Kristeva, Julia, *Histoires d'amour* (Collection Folio, Gallimard, 1986).

—— *La Révolution du langage poétique* (Éditions du Seuil, 1974).

Lacan, Jacques, 'Le Stade du miroir comme fondateur de la fonction du je', in *Écrits* (Éditions du Seuil, 1966), 93–100.

Lacoue-Labarthe, Philippe, 'L'Écho du sujet', in *Le Sujet de la philosophie: Typographies I* (Flammarion, 1979).

Lalande, André, *Vocabulaire technique et critique de la philosophie* (Presses Universitaires de France, 1947).

Laporte, Roger, *Une vie* (P.O.L. éditeur, 1986).

Laure [Colette Peignot], *Écrits*, ed. by Jérome Peignot (Pauvert, 1979).

Leak, Andy, '*W* dans un réseau de lignes entrecroisées: Souvenir, souvenir-écran et construction dans *W ou le souvenir d'enfance*', in Mireille Ribière (ed.), *Parcours Perec* (Presses Universitaires de Lyon, 1990), 75–90.

Lecercle, J.-L., *Rousseau et l'art du roman* (Armand Colin, 1969).

Leduc, Violette, *La Bâtarde* (Collection Folio, Gallimard, 1980).

—— *La Chasse à l'amour* (Gallimard, 1973).

—— *La Folie en tête* (Gallimard, 1970).

—— 'Lettres à Simone de Beauvoir', *Les Temps modernes*, 495 (Oct. 1987), 1–41.

Leigh, James, 'The Figure of Autobiography', *Modern Language Notes*, 93 (1978), 733–49.

Leiris, Michel, *L'Age d'homme* [1938] (Collection Folio, Gallimard, 1979).

—— *Biffures* (Gallimard, 1948).

—— *A cor et à cri* (Gallimard, 1988).

—— *Fibrilles* (Gallimard, 1966).

—— *Fourbis* (Gallimard, 1955).

Leiris, Michel, *Frêle bruit* (Gallimard, 1976).

—— 'Glossaire j'y serre mes gloses', in *Mots sans mémoire* (Gallimard, 1969).

—— *Haut mal* (Collection Poésie, Gallimard, 1969).

—— *Langage tangage* (Gallimard, 1985).

—— *Miroir de la tauromachie* (Montpellier: Fata Morgana, 1981).

—— *Roussel l'ingénu* (Montpellier: Fata Morgana, 1987).

—— *Le Ruban au cou d'Olympia* (Gallimard, 1981).

—— 'Le Sacré dans la vie quotidienne', in Denis Hollier (ed.), *Le Collège de Sociologie* (Collection Idées, Galliniard, 1979), 60–74.

Lejeune, Philippe, *L'Autobiographie en France* (Armand Colin, 1971).

—— *Exercices d'ambiguïté: Lectures de 'Si le grain ne meurt' d'André Gide* (Minard, 1974).

—— *Je est un autre* (Éditions du Seuil, 1980).

—— *Lire Leiris: Autobiographie et langage* (Klincksieck, 1975).

—— *La Mémoire et l'oblique: Georges Perec autobiographe* (POL, 1991).

—— *Moi aussi* (Éditions du Seuil, 1986).

—— *Le Pacte autobiographique* (Éditions du Seuil, 1975).

—— 'Paroles d'enfance', *Revue des sciences humaines*, 93 (1990), 23–38.

—— 'Stendhal et les problèmes de l'autobiographie', in Victor Del Litto (ed.), *Stendhal et les problèmes de l'autobiographie* (Presses Universitaires de Grenoble, 1976), 21–36.

Lévi-Strauss, Claude, *La Pensée sauvage* (Plon, 1962).

—— *Tristes Tropiques* (1955) (Plon, 1984).

Loesberg, Jonathan, 'Autobiography as Genre, Act of Consciousness, Text', *Prose Studies* (1981), 169–85.

Lovejoy, H., *The Great Chain of Being* (New York: Harper & Row, 1960).

Lyons, John D., *Exemplum: The Rhetoric of Example in Early Modern France and Italy* (Princeton University Press, 1989).

Lyons, William, *The Disappearance of Introspection* (Boston, Mass.: MIT Press, 1986).

Lyotard, Jean-François, *Discours, Figure* (Klincksieck, 1971).

Macleod, Jock, 'Rousseau and the Epistemology of "Sentiment"', *Journal of European Studies*, 17 (1970), 107–28.

Malraux, André, *Antimémoires* (Collection Folio, Gallimard, 1972).

Mandel, Barrett J., 'The Autobiographer's Art', *The Journal of Aesthetics and Art Criticism*, 26 (1968–9), 215–26.

—— 'Full of Life Now' in *Autobiography: Essays Theoretical and Critical* (q.v.), 49–72.

Marcus, Laura, 'How Shall We Live? A Metacritique of Autobiographical Criticism', Ph.D. thesis (University of Kent at Canterbury, 1989).

Marin, Louis, 'Images dans le texte autobiographique: Sur le chapitre XLIV de la *Vie de Henry Brulard*', *Saggi et richerche di letteratura francese*, 23 (1984), 197–231.

—— *La Voix excommuniée* (Galilée, 1981).

Marty, Eric, *L'Écriture du jour: Le 'Journal' d'André Gide* (Éditions du Seuil, 1985).

Maubon, Catherine, *Michel Leiris au travail* (Pisa: Pacini, 1987).

—— 'Michel Leiris, le ficheur fiché', in Béatrice Didier and Jacques Neefs (eds.), *Penser, Classer, Écrire* (Presses Universitaires de Vincennes, 1990), 149–70.

May, Georges, *L'Autobiographie* (Presses Universitaires de France, 1979).

Mehlman, Jeffery, *A Structural Study of Autobiography* (New York: Cornell University Press, 1974).

Meitinger, Serge, 'L'Irréel de jouissance dans le *Journal du voleur* de Genet', *Littérature* (Apr. 1986), 65–74.

Mémoires, Nouvelle Revue de psychanalyse, 15 (1977).

Mercier, Roger, 'Sur le sensualisme de Rousseau: Sensation et sentiment dans la première partie des *Confessions*', *Revue des sciences humaines*, 41 (1976), 19–33.

Mesnard, Jean, 'Pascal et le "moi haïssable"', in George Graig and Margaret McGowan (eds.), *Moy qui me voy: The Writer and the Self from Montaigne to Leiris* (Oxford University Press, 1989), 19–29.

Mill, John Stuart, *Autobiography*, ed. Jack Stillinger (Oxford University Press, 1971).

Miller, J. Hillis, 'Narrative', in Frank Lentricchia and Thomas McLaughlin (eds.), *Critical Terms for Literary Study* (Chicago University Press, 1990).

Minogue, Valerie, 'Fragments of a Childhood: Nathalie Sarraute's *Enfance*', in *French Autobiography: Texts, Contexts, Poetics* (q.v.), ii. 71–83.

—— 'Nathalie Sarraute's *Enfance*: From the Experience of Language to the Language of Experience', in Robert Gibson (ed.), *Studies in Fiction in Honour of Vivienne Mylne* (Grant & Cutler, 1988), 209–24.

—— *Nathalie Sarraute: The War of the Words* (Edinburgh University Press, 1981).

Montaigne, Michel de, *Essais*, 3 vols. (Garnier-Flammarion, 1969).

Morgan, Janice, 'Fiction and Autobiography/Language and Silence: *L'Amant* by Duras', *French Review*, 63 (1969), 271–9.

Morris, John N., *Versions of the Self: Studies in English Autobiography from John Bunyan to John Stuart Mill* (New York: Basic Books, 1966).

Munteano, Basil, *Solitude et contradictions de Jean-Jacques Rousseau* (Nizet, 1975).

Nabokov, Vladimir, *Speak, Memory* (Harmondsworth, Penguin Books, 1969).

Nadeau, Maurice, *Michel Leiris ou la quadrature du cercle* (Julliard, 1963).

Newman, John Henry, *Apologia pro vita sua*, ed. M. J. Svaglic (Oxford University Press, 1967).

Nietzsche, Friedrich, *The Birth of Tragedy and the Genealogy of Morals*, trans. Francis Golfing (New York, Doubleday Anchor Books, 1956).

O'Dea, Michael, 'The Double Narrative of the Stolen Ribbon', *Nottingham French Studies*, 23/2 (1984), 1–8.

Olney, James, *Metaphors of Self: The Meaning of Autobiography* (Princeton University Press, 1972).

—— 'Some Versions of Memory, Some Versions of Bios: The Ontology of

Autobiography', in *Autobiography: Essays Theoretical and Critical* (q.v.), 236–67.

Pascal, Roy, *Design and Truth in Autobiography* (Routledge & Kegan Paul, 1960).

Pauly, Rebecca, N, *Le Berceau et la bibliothèque: le paradoxe de l'écriture autobiographique* (Saratoga: Anma Libri, 1989).

Perec, Georges, *Je me souviens* (Hachette, 1978).

—— *Je suis né* (Éditions du Seuil, 1990).

—— *Penser/Classer* (Hachette, 1985).

—— *W ou le souvenir d'enfance* (Denoël, 1975).

Peterson, Linda H., *Victorian Autobiography: The Tradition of Self-Interpretation* (Yale University Press, 1986).

Petrarch, Francis, *Petrarca, Francesco, Rerum Familiarum Libri I–VIII*, trans. Aldo S. Bernardo (Albany, NY: State University of New York Press, 1975).

Pingaud, Bernard, 'L'Écriture et la cure', *Nouvelle Revue Française*, 18 (1970), 159–63.

Pontalis, J.-B., *Après Freud* (Collection Idées, Gallimard, 1971).

—— 'Lieux et séparation', in *Entre le rêve et la douleur* (Collection Tel, Gallimard, 1983), 139–58.

—— 'Michel Leiris ou la psychanalyse sans fin', in *Après Freud* (Collection Idées, Gallimard, 1971), 313–35.

Poulet, Georges, *Études sur le temps humain*, i (Plon, 1950).

Powys, John Cowper, *Autobiography* [1934], (Picador, 1982).

Prendergast, Christopher, *The Order of Mimesis* (Cambridge University Press, 1986).

Rannaud, Gérard, 'Le Moi et l'histoire chez Chateaubriand et Stendhal', *Revue d'histoire littéraire de la France*, 75 (1975), 1004–17.

Raymond, Marcel, *Jean-Jacques Rousseau: La Quête de soi et la rêverie* (José Corti, 1962).

Reid, Martine, 'Représentation d'Henry Beyle', *Poétique*, 65 (1986), 29–42.

Renan, Ernest, *Souvenirs d'enfance et de jeunesse*, ed. by Jean Pommier (Collection Folio, Gallimard, 1983).

Renza, Louis A., 'The Veto of the Imagination: A Theory of Autobiography', in *Autobiography: Essays Theoretical and Critical* (q.v.), 268–95.

Restif de la Bretonne, Nicholas, *Monsieur Nicholas*, 6 vols. (Éditions Jean-Jacques Pauvert, 1959).

Ribière, Mireille (ed.), *Parcours Perec* (Presses Universitaires de Lyon, 1990).

Richard, Jean-Pierre, *Paysage de Chateaubriand* (Éditions du Seuil, 1967).

Ricoeur, Paul, *Soi-même comme un autre* (Éditions du Seuil, 1990).

—— *Temps et récit*, 3 vols. (Éditions du Seuil, 1983–5).

Riffaterre, Michael, 'Les *Antimémoires* d'André Malraux', in *Essais de stylistique structurale* (Flammarion, 1972), 286–306.

—— 'Chateaubriand et le monument imaginaire', in Richard Switzer (ed.), *Chateaubriand: Actes du congrès de Wisconsin* (Geneva: Droz, 1970), 63–81.

Rinsler, Norma, 'Nerval's *Promenades et Souvenirs*: The Structure of Chance', in *French Autobiography: Texts, Contexts, Poetics* (q.v.), ii. 85–96.

Robbe-Grillet, Alain, *Angélique ou l'enchantement* (Éditions de Minuit, 1988).

—— *Le Miroir qui revient* (Éditions de Minuit, 1984).

Robinson, Philip, 'The "Actor's Talent" and the "Accent of the Passions": Rousseau on his Childhood Reading', in *French Autobiography: Texts, Contexts, Poetics* (q.v.), i. 15–26.

—— *Jean-Jacques Rousseau's Doctrine of the Arts* (Berne: Peter Lang, 1984).

Roey-Roux, Françoise van, '*Enfance* de Nathalie Sarraute ou de la fiction à l'autobiographie', *Études littéraires*, 17 (1985), 273–82.

Rosset, Clément, *L'Objet singulier* (Éditions de Minuit, 1979).

Rousseau, Jean-Jacques, *Les Confessions*, in *Œuvres complètes*, i, ed. Bernard Gagnebin and Marcel Raymond (Bibliothèque de la Pléiade, Gallimard, 1959).

—— *Écrits sur la musique* (Stock, 1979).

—— *Essai sur l'origine des langues*, ed. Angèle Kremer-Marietti (Aubier Montaigne, 1974).

Rubin, David C. (ed.), *Autobiographical Memory* (Cambridge University Press, 1986).

Ruskin, John, *Praeterita* (1899) (Oxford University Press, 1978).

Said, Edward, *Beginnings: Intention and Method* (Johns Hopkins University Press, 1975).

—— *Orientalism* (Routledge & Kegan Paul, 1986).

Saint Jean, Robert de, and Luc Estang, *Julien Green* (Éditions du Seuil, 1990).

Sand, George, *Histoire de ma vie*, in *Œuvres autobiographiques*, i, ed. Georges Lubin (Bibliothèque de la Pléiade, Gallimard, 1970).

Sarraute, Nathalie, *Enfance* (Collection Folio, Gallimard, 1986).

—— *L'Ère du soupçon* (Collection Idées, Gallimard, 1978).

Sartre, Jean-Paul, *Baudelaire* (Collection Idées, Gallimard, 1963).

—— *L'Être et le néant* (Gallimard, 1943).

—— *L'Idiot de la famille*, 3 vols. (Collection Tel, Gallimard, 1983).

—— *Les Mots* (Collection Folio, Gallimard, 1972).

—— *La Nausée* (Livre de Poche, Gallimard, 1966).

—— *Questions de méthode* (Collection Idées, Gallimard, 1967).

—— 'Des rats et des hommes', Preface to André Gorz, *Le Traître* (q.v.), 9–45.

—— *Saint-Genet: Comédien et martyr* (Gallimard, 1952).

Scriven, Michael, *Sartre's Existentialist Biographies* (Macmillan, 1984).

Searle, John, *Speech Acts* (Cambridge University Press, 1969).

Sérodès, Serge, 'Les Blancs dans les manuscrits de la *Vie de Henry Brulard*', in *Colloque de Cerisy-la-Salle: Stendhal* (Aux amateurs des livres, 1986), 135–50.

Simon, Roland, *Orphée médusé* (Lausanne: L'Age d'homme, 1984).

Sorabji, Richard, *Aristotle on Memory* (Duckworth, 1972).

Spengemann, William C., *The Forms of Autobiography* (Yale University Press, 1980).

Spufford, Francis (ed.), *The Chatto Book of Cabbages and Kings: Lists in Literature* (Chatto & Windus, 1989).

Starobinski, Jean, *La Relation critique* (Gallimard, 1970).

—— 'Jean-Jacques Rousseau et le péril de la réflexion', in *L'Œil vivant* (Gallimard, 1961).

——*Jean-Jacques Rousseau: La Transparence et l'obstacle* [1957] (Gallimard, 1971).

—— 'Le Style de l'autobiographe', *Poétique*, 1 (1970), 257–65.

Stendhal, *Vie de Henry Brulard*, ed. by Béatrice Didier (Collection Folio, Gallimard, 1973).

Stewart, Philip, *Imitation and Illusion in the French Memoir-Novel, 1700-1750* (Yale University Press, 1969).

Stewart, Susan, *On Longing: Narratives of the Miniature, the Gigantic, the Souvenir, the Collection* (Baltimore: Johns Hopkins University Press, 1984).

Strickland, Geoffrey, 'The Analysis of Memory', *Cambridge Quarterly*, 17/4 (1989), 386–97.

Sturrock, John, 'The Autobiographer Astray: Leiris and *La Règle du jeu*', in George Craig and Margaret McGowan (eds.), *Moy qui me voy: the Writer and the Self from Montaigne to Leiris* (Oxford University Press, 1989).

—— 'The New Model Autobiographer', *New Literary History*, 9 (1977), 51–63.

Suleiman, Susan R., and Inge Crosman, *The Reader in the Text* (Princeton University Press, 1980).

Szondi, Peter, 'Hope in the Past: On Walter Benjamin', *Critical Inquiry* (1978), 491–506.

Tambling, Jeremy, *Confession: Sexuality, Sin, the Subject* (Manchester University Press, 1990).

Teresa of Avila, *Confessions* (Harmondsworth: Penguin Books, 1962).

Tolton, C. D. E., *André Gide and the Art of Autobiography* (Toronto: Macmillan, 1975).

Tompkins, Jane P. (ed.), *Reader-Response Criticism* (Baltimore: Johns Hopkins University Press, 1980).

Trousson, Raymond, *Stendhal et Rousseau* (Cologne: DME Verlag, 1986).

Vercier, Bruno, '*Les Mots* de Sartre: Un cas limite de l'autobiographie?', *Revue d'Histoire Littéraire de la France*, 75 (1975), 1047–61.

Verlaine, Paul, *Œuvres poétiques*, ed. by Jacques Robichez (Garnier, 1969).

Vial, André, *Chateaubriand et le temps perdu*, new edn. (UGE 10/18, 1971).

Voisine, Jacques, 'Le Dialogue avec le lecteur dans *Les Confessions*', *Jean-Jacques Rousseau et son œuvre* (Actes et Colloques du Collège de France, 1964).

Warnock, Mary, *Memory* (Faber & Faber, 1987).

Weintraub, Karl J., 'Autobiography and Historical Consciousness', *Critical Inquiry*, 1 (1975), 821–48.

—— *The Value of the Individual: Self and Circumstance in Autobiography* (Chicago University Press, 1978).

Went-Daoust, Yvette, '*Enfance* de Nathalie Sarraute ou le pouvoir de la parole', *Les Lettres Romanes*, 41 (1987), 337–50.

Williams, Huntington, *Rousseau and Romantic Autobiography* (Oxford University Press, 1983).

Winnicott, D. W., *Playing and Reality* (Harmondsworth: Penguin Books, 1971).

Wittgenstein, Ludwig, 'Remarks on Frazer's *Golden Bough*', *The Human World*, 3 (1971), 28–41.

Woolf, Virginia, *Moments of Being* (Hogarth Press, 1985).

Wordsworth, William, *The Prelude* (1805), ed. Jonathan Wordsworth *et al.* (New York: W. W. Norton, 1979).

Index

Apollinaire, G. 117
apostrophe 149
Aristotle 289
Augustine, St 8, 10, 97, 144, 168, 169,
    280, 288-9
  and memory 288-9
  'Tolle, lege!' 11
  and turning points 10
Auster, P. 315-16
autobiography:
  as contract 1, 19-20
  fetishistic dimension in 6-7, 19, 126,
    137
  and fiction 18, 124, 138, 328
  heterogeneity of 13, 14, 21, 24, 56
  hybridity of 13, 15, 16, 19 n, 21, 24
  intentions in 1-5, 12, 14, 137
  as process 2, 3, 5, 9, 13, 19, 21, 27, 30,
    164, 246, 278, 328
  subjectivity in 19, 21, 24
  as transaction 20, 29
  will-to-form in 4, 5, 6, 7, 12
  see also body; canon; desire; devices;
    'engagement'; existentialist; genre;
    ideology; incidents; intertextuality;
    liquidation; memory; mise-en-scène;
    narrative; Other; psychoanalysis;
    reader; self; style; therapy; traces;
    turning points
autofiction 328-9
autoportrait 306-7, 308

Bachelard G. 254
Badiou, A. 101 and n.
Barthes, R. 64, 86 n., 72 n., 91 n., 102 n.,
    117 n., 165, 172, 193-201, 225, 284,
    296 n., 307, 309-11, 310 n., 314-15,
    322, 327, 328, 331
  and anamnèse 309-11
  La Chambre claire 311 n., 314-15
  discourses in 196
  doxa 193, 194
  exclusion in 194, 199
  and the imaginary 194

Incidents 102
Roland Barthes par Roland Barthes
    193-201
  'second degré' 198
Bassompierre, F. 98 n., 111
Bataille, G. 147 n., 264, 265 and n., 270
Baudelaire, C. 205, 206, 209, 214, 264,
    286, 292-3, 304 n., 312
Beaujour, M. 293, 294, 306-7, 308, 309
Beauvoir, S. de 15, 16, 153-4, 203, 204,
    209, 217, 220-7
  and 'choix originel' 221, 222, 226
  and existentialist autobiography 220-7
  and Leduc 153-4, 217
  and liquidation 224-5
  Mémoires d'une jeune fille rangée 220-7
  Tout compt fait 226
  and Zaza 224
Beckett, S. 6 n., 283, 311 n.
Benjamin, W. 67, 303-5, 331
Bentham, J. 11
Benveniste, E. 20 n.
Bergson, H. 289
Berlioz, H. 103-4, 116
Bersani, L. 88
Blanchot, M. 101
Blin, G. 86 n., 89
Bloom, H. 15
body, the:
  in Barthes 196, 198-9, 310, 318, 320
  in Green 125
  in Leduc 155
  in Rousseau 60
Breton, A. 15, 117, 154, 264
Brooks, P. 27-30, 96, 218
Bussy, D. 184
Butor, M. 117

Camus, C. 29
Cabanis, P. 171
Calvino, I. 304 n
Cave, T. 313-14
canon 15, 330-1
Césaire, A. 276

Printed in the United Kingdom
by Lightning Source UK Ltd.
119172UK00001BA/24